E.D.E.N. Southworth's Hidden Hand

E.D.E.N. Southworth's Hidden Hand

The Untold Story of America's Famous Forgotten Nineteenth-Century Author

Rose Neal, PhD

LYONS PRESS

Essex, Connecticut

LYONS PRESS

An imprint of The Globe Pequot Publishing Group, Inc.
64 South Main Street
Essex, CT 06426
www.globepequot.com

Distributed by NATIONAL BOOK NETWORK

British Library Cataloguing in Publication Information available

Library of Congress Cataloging-in-Publication Data
Names: Neal, Rose, author.
Title: E.D.E.N. Southworth's hidden hand: the untold story of America's famous forgotten nineteenth-century author / Rose Neal, PhD.
Description: Essex, Connecticut: Lyons Press, 2025. | Includes bibliographical references and index. | Summary: "E.D.E.N. Southworth wrote more novels than Hawthorne, Melville, and Twain combined, and readers adored her feisty heroines. She wrote about taboo topics for the nineteenth century—alcoholism, domestic violence, poverty, and more—and encouraged generations of her readers to challenge the status quo. The story of her fascinating life has gone untold until now"—Provided by publisher.
Identifiers: LCCN 2024039716 (print) | LCCN 2024039717 (ebook) | ISBN 9781493089130 (cloth) | ISBN 9781493089147 (epub)
Subjects: LCSH: Southworth, Emma Dorothy Eliza Nevitte, 1819–1899. | Novelists, American—19th century—Biography. | Women and literature—United States—History—19th century. | LCGFT: Biographies.
Classification: LCC PS2893 .N43 2025 (print) | LCC PS2893 (ebook) | DDC 813/.4 [B]—dc23/eng/20240910
LC record available at https://lccn.loc.gov/2024039716
LC ebook record available at https://lccn.loc.gov/2024039717

∞™ The paper used in this publication meets the minimum requirements of American National Standard for Information Sciences—Permanence of Paper for Printed Library Materials, ANSI/NISO Z39.48-1992.

Dedicated to my dear friend and mentor,

Dr. Pamela T. Washington.

We will forever be Southworth sisters.

Contents

Foreword

Like *E.D.E.N. Southworth's Hidden Hand*'s author, Rose Neal, I first encountered E.D.E.N. Southworth's work in graduate school. This coincidence isn't too surprising, as literature study is still where many readers find her today—a nineteenth-century sentimental or sensational writer, apt for contextualization and examination. But in her day, Southworth was known by a very wide audience. She was a celebrity author, her books read for their thrilling, serpentine plots and dauntless heroines.

The next time I ran into Southworth was in Oak Hill Cemetery in Washington, DC, where I saw her gravestone. It listed to one side and was in some disrepair. I wrote a magazine story about Southworth in 2016 and, in the years since, have understood her as a Washington writer and as a historic one, an artist of a certain place and time. That gravestone was restored in time for the two hundredth anniversary of Southworth's birth. But awareness of her work and contributions has still languished in the twenty-first century. "It's kind of remarkable to me that we don't know more about her," DC novelist Mary Kay Zuravleff told a reporter in 2020.[1]

E.D.E.N. Southworth's Hidden Hand seeks to address that lapse, and Neal's work adds to all of Southworth's identities, including those of best-selling author and Washingtonian. Neal's deep research into primary-source materials—including Southworth's correspondence collection housed at Duke University and letters stored at the Library of Congress—allows Southworth, who told so many stories, to here become the hero of her own. In Neal's telling, Southworth is as important a figure as her characters—something Neal demonstrates through a series of close readings that showcase moments when Southworth's life and her novels dovetailed.

Classified as one of Nathaniel Hawthorne's "damned mob of scribbling women," and criticized in later life for her over-the-top characterizations and tidily-wrapped-up endings, Southworth herself was, as Neal writes here, quite complex. Southworth raised two children, dealt with ceaseless publishing woes, and, like some of her characters, managed her own sometimes-villainous husband, Frederick. By 1868, when she was a bona fide celebrity, a newspaper article listed Southworth's earnings alongside those of other famous Americans. She had her own dramatic flair, having two of her gold pens melted into rings for her children.

Yet, Neal points out, as lively and transgressive as many of Southworth's heroines were, the author herself was often constrained by the laws and customs of her day. She embodied contrasts, as Neal argues, "to advocate positive societal changes." Neal focuses on the tension of key moments in Southworth's life, such as when Southworth confronted an editor who wanted a scene of male aggression toned down or when she praised her ancestors' patriotism without mentioning that they enslaved people. She supported her family through writing, and fought for her rights and for appropriate pay, but simultaneously said that writing her books was more of an economic necessity than a calling.

Her home was complicated, too. By 1852, she was installed in Prospect Cottage, a former hotel that overlooked the Potomac and had a spacious library. During the Civil War, she flew a United States flag over her house and watched the Second Battle of Bull Run from her house alongside neighbors who supported the Confederacy. When I researched Southworth years ago, I was captivated by the idea of her as part of the city's weft, her house a crucial piece of streetscape, engaged through sightlines with the waterways that characterize and enliven Washington. Prospect Cottage was demolished in 1942, but even today the block's relation to the water as well as the city showcases Southworth's vantage point as a Washingtonian, which she experienced so vividly during the Civil War. "Situated in what she viewed as the 'sacred heart of the nation,'" Professor Ann C. Beebe writes, "E.D.E.N. Southworth absorbed the atmosphere of the Civil War capital and the experiences of her close relatives to create multiple narratives that would start the process of national healing for hundreds of thousands of her readers."[2]

With Neal's book, I see more clearly Southworth's presence here in Washington. "As Columbia Historical Society member Sarah M. Huddleson noted in a 1919 address to the organization, Southworth was born here, lived here, wrote here and died here. 'Mrs. Southworth,' she said, 'belongs to our national capital,'" I wrote in my 2016 piece.[3]

"May this be the first of many resurrections," Zuravleff said of the refurbished gravestone in 2020. Here is another. As someone who gave her readers such rich insight into her characters' lives, E.D.E.N. Southworth deserves this biography, in which Neal uses primary and secondary sources to elucidate connections between Southworth's world and her fiction, as well as her world and ours. Through Neal's work, readers now can more fully envision, inhabit, and comprehend the work of Southworth's no-longer-hidden hand.

Eliza McGraw
Author of *Edna Ferber's America*

Introduction

Rejoicing in her freedom, Cap galloped down to the water's edge, and . . . gathering up her riding-skirt and throwing it over the neck of her horse, she plunged boldly into the stream, and with the water splashing and foaming all around her, urged him onward until they crossed the river and climbed up the opposite bank.[1]

I became intrigued with E.D.E.N. Southworth while working on a master's degree in American literature. As part of the required courses, I took the "Nineteenth-Century American Women Writers" class taught by Dr. Pamela Washington in 2009. I wasn't sure I was going to like the class as we slogged our way through Susan Warner's *The Wide Wide World* (1850), in which protagonist Ellen Montgomery cries for five hundred pages until she finds a man who can take care of her. Then I read Southworth's best-selling *The Hidden Hand* (1859). Southworth's protagonist was no histrionic little sissy. The main character was, indeed, a feisty heroine who could ride a horse, shoot a pistol, capture notorious villain Black Donald, and rescue her kidnapped mother. I was enchanted with this pintsized heroine named Capitola Black. In an age in which middle- and upper-class women were expected to behave with gentility and subservience to men, Southworth thumbed her nose at the patriarchy by creating her little tomboy and artfully hid her approval of Capitola when horseback riding without her uncle's approval. "I do not defend, far less approve, poor Cap!" Southworth commented. "I only tell her story and describe her as I have seen her, leaving her to your charitable interpretation."[2] Reading "poor Cap's" adventures, I understood Southworth's tongue-in-cheek joke. She approved of her heroine's actions and wanted her female audience to interpret her favorably.

The Hidden Hand became wildly successful throughout the rest of the nineteenth century and well into the twentieth. The *New York Ledger* republished it serially three times between 1859 and 1883 before G. W. Dillingham published it as a book in 1888, in which form it achieved monumental success, with ten thousand copies sold in the first run. Other publishers from Chicago, New York, and Boston republished it until the 1920s.[3] Mothers named their daughters Capitola after their favorite heroine, and even boats and racehorses bore her name. Wearing Capitola hats became all the rage in the fashion industry, and across the United States and Great Britain, playwrights turned *The Hidden Hand* into a theatrical act with sold-out performances.[4] As I read this delightfully funny and witty novel, many questions came to my mind. I had earned a bachelor's degree in English in 1984 and taught high school English for a number of years before returning to college to work on my master's degree. How was it that I had never heard of *The Hidden Hand*? Through continued research, I discovered that, in addition to *The Hidden Hand*, Southworth had written more than fifty other novels and was considered one of the most famous and well-paid novelists of the nineteenth century. I asked my English colleagues whether they'd were familiar with her. They had never heard of Southworth or any of her novels. How did a novelist as popular as Southworth slip into the dustbin of history?

I learned some answers throughout the course taught by Dr. Washington. She helped students like me discover a world full of nineteenth-century American women writers in addition to Southworth—women like Fanny Fern, Mary Jane Holmes, Caroline Lee Hentz, Elizabeth Stuart Phelps, and Harriet E. Wilson. We also read Harriet Beecher Stowe and Louisa May Alcott. They were the only two I knew, and even they weren't listed in anthologies I used when teaching high school courses. In fact, there were very few women writers in either high school or college texts. I incorrectly believed there weren't many women writers in the nineteenth century. I realized as I read story after story that an entire generation of women writers had been erased from American history. In truth, by the nineteenth century, American women were becoming increasingly literate, and weekly magazines like the *New York Ledger* provided the types of stories that women wanted to read—stories written by women, for women.

By the 1840s, the age of domestic sensational literature began—a genre filled with women writers. The number of female authors was so large that Nathaniel Hawthorne complained to his publisher that the American literary market had been consumed by "a damned mob of scribbling women."[5] Leading this list of successful literary women was E.D.E.N. Southworth. Much like Southworth's readers of a hundred years ago, I hungrily consumed novel after novel—*The Deserted Wife*, *The Three Beauties*, *The Discarded Daughter*, *Britomarte*, *Miriam, the Avenger*—all with heroines like Capitola. In each novel, Southworth's message was clear: girls could do anything they wanted, from riding horses, shooting bows and arrows, climbing trees, and rowing boats to becoming nurses, teachers, soldiers, and even sea captains. Emma Southworth's progressive ideas helped encourage generations of women readers to question and challenge the status quo. Not only did Emma inspire women to be more self-sufficient, but she had other liberal ideas as well—all nicely tucked away within the pages of her domestic fiction. She wrote about unspeakable things—alcoholism, domestic violence, poverty—social issues we still struggle with today. She advocated better physical education for girls and was against the kinds of restrictive but popular clothing that kept girls from growing properly. She believed in the abolition of slavery. She was against capital punishment. She favored improved educational opportunities and living conditions for the poor. The more novels I read, the more fascinated and curious I became about the woman behind the author.

Only partial biographies had been written about her life—and those were ones that she had carefully constructed to portray an appropriate woman of the nineteenth century. When Emma Southworth began writing, she needed the money and had to be careful because she had two young children to support after being abandoned by her husband. She wrote during an age when women were blamed if their husbands left them. Being labeled "a fallen woman" meant destruction of a woman's reputation, leading to certain poverty. No man would marry or hire such a woman to work for him. Therefore, she wrote about her life in a way that was meant hide anything that might have seemed unsavory. She referred to herself as Mrs. Southworth, even though she and her husband Frederick had lived together only a few years before he left. She used the name long after Frederick had died, and she refused to ever marry again. She emphasized that she worked as a writer only to earn a living. Reading biographies written in her lifetime would lead to the conclusion that she was against many of the causes she supported in her novels. Why would she contradict herself?

The short answer is that she did it in order to advocate positive societal changes. On the surface, she was a meek domestic woman just trying to make a living in a man's world out of necessity. Her novels were cute little love stories that young girls liked to read. But hidden underneath was much more. As Southworth became increasingly successful, she gradually became more outspoken. She actively favored emancipation before the American Civil War and was involved in the women's rights movement in the mid-1870s. She also served on the boards of educational institutions that provided learning opportunities for the poor. Readers would learn none of these details in published biographical sketches during her lifetime, which covered only the early part of her life and only the details she wanted to reveal. I learned much more about her life by painstakingly combing through newspapers and magazines from that time period. Southworth also left clues in the letters she left behind, most of which have been preserved in two collections: the Duke collection of correspondence between Southworth and her editor and friend Robert Bonner of the *New York Ledger* and the Library of Congress collection of letters between Southworth and her daughter Lottie. By combining details from Southworth's novels, the partial biographies, newspaper reports, and letters, I pieced together the fascinating life of a woman who was as determined as any of the heroines she created.

Emma Dorothy Eliza Nevitte Southworth (called Emma by her family and friends) led a bold and daring life that spanned almost the entire nineteenth century. She was a woman who made mistakes that caused suffering and hardships for herself and her children, but many of the trials she faced were through no fault of her own. Still, she met each challenge head on, overcoming obstacles time and again. She is one of the most courageous, independent, and self-sufficient women I've ever come to know. Unfortunately, most people today know nothing about who she was, what she wrote, or how she influenced a nation. Despite being one of the most beloved and well-known writers of the nineteenth century, as domestic sensational fiction declined in popularity, Southworth was entirely forgotten, as was an entire generation of women writers. For Southworth, it was partly because she had done so well at hiding her own progressive ideas. Nevertheless, she should be rediscovered and given her rightful place in American history. My hope is that modern readers of this first full biography of her life will enjoy rediscovering this iconic American woman.

Chapter 1

Coming of Age in the Heart of a New Nation

God breathed into her the breath of life, and she became a living soul. A breath of divine life incarnated, a new soul sent upon this planet to live, to struggle . . . and oh! how surely to suffer.[1]

Like the fictional heroines she would later create, Emma D.E.N. Southworth was born into a life of uncertainty. Her life began on December 26, 1819. Although Emma became one of the most published and well-paid authors of the nineteenth century, she did not begin life in a way that granted her luxury or security. She was christened Emma Dorothy Eliza Nevitte, the initials she would use in her life as an author.[2] She joked that when she was born, "my people were too poor to give anything else, so they gave me all those names." Additionally, Emma was frail and sickly from birth. "I was a child of sorrow from the very first year of my life. Thin and dark, I had no beauty except a pair of large, wild eyes—but even this was destined to be tarnished," she wrote. "At twelve months old I was attacked with an inflammation of the eyes, that ended in total, though temporary, blindness; thus my first view of life was through a dim, mysterious 'cathedral light,' in which every object in the world looked larger, vaguer, and more distant and imposing than it really was."[3] These early days of poor health, combined with her parents' poverty, profoundly affected the rest of Emma's life; consequently, much of her familial history appeared in her books.

Her father was Captain Charles Lecompte Nevitte, whose ancestors were among the elite and indentured classes of Maryland's founding fathers. The tie that bound them all was a patriotic duty to serve their new country. Charles became a successful flour merchant in Alexandria, Virginia; however, America's involvement in the French Revolution would reverse his fortunes. The newly formed American government wanted to remain neutral in the war between Britain and France, but both countries repeatedly attacked American merchant ships. Charles was one merchant whose ships were seized by the French, leading to his financial ruin. By 1801, unable to repay creditors, he went to debtors' prison in Washington County. By 1810, he partially recovered and was elected to the Common Council in Alexandria, where he helped revise laws concerning tax collections and served on a committee to build water wells for the town.[4] Charles's dedication to his community despite his financial hardships reflects what he'd learned from earlier generations—a legacy that continued in Emma's storytelling.

At the onset of the war, on December 3, 1812, Emma's parents married. Charles was thirty-five years old while her mother, Susanna George Wailes, was only fifteen.[5] It was an unusual marriage. Not only did Charles no longer have land or money, but he was already married to Martha Baden Nevitte, and they had two children. Although his wife Martha died on August 20, 1813, he was simultaneously married to Martha and Susanna for several months. One explanation for his bigamy lies in understanding the concept of marriage and divorce in early nineteenth-century America. Divorce laws were extremely rigid, so couples often separated and remarried without the formality of a legal divorce. While most states had laws prohibiting bigamy, it was rarely brought to court and even rarer that it made headlines in the newspapers. A publicized case would have been scandalous, but most citizens simply looked the other way when it was a mutual decision. Not until the passage of the Morrill Anti-Bigamy Act of 1862 did bigamy charges increase and become a highly controversial subject.[6] Interestingly, in Emma's novels, she repeatedly warned about the dangers of the "secret marriage" and steered women away from being duped by the male bigamist in order to steal their virtue, their money, or both. Whether Emma knew the circumstances surrounding her parents' union is unknown, but she would not have approved. Nevertheless, the marriage did occur—likely a financial arrangement between Charles and his new wife's mother, Dorothy Wailes.

Like Charles, Dorothy had fallen on hard times. Emma's maternal family—the Covingtons, the Greenfields, and the Waileses—had been prominent wealthy landowners in Maryland. Dorothy Greenfield must have thought she'd made a good match when she married George Wailes on November 28, 1796. Her marriage was short lived, however, as George died shortly after their union, leaving Dorothy to care for their infant daughter Susanna. While she inherited some property upon George's death, this income soon ran out.[7] Her brother George Greenfield eased her financial crisis when he made a sketchy deal with Charles. In 1805, George's business associate Henry Anderson claimed that George owed him "upwards of two thousand dollars" and, instead of paying his debt, George asked Charles, to whom he also owed money, to give that money to his sister Dorothy Wailes.[8] This arrangement allowed Charles to hide money since he was largely in debt to his creditors. Marrying Dorothy's young daughter Susanna allowed him to secure an income for them with the "hidden money"; Charles also earned an income as a soldier.

In order to recruit and keep soldiers, Congress boosted army pay and made it illegal to imprison any soldier who had debts. The earliest record of Charles's militia service was 1807, when he was listed as a commissioned lieutenant in the Second Legion of the Militia of the District of Columbia. His enlistment explains how he worked his way out of his previous debts. Charles served as ensign under Captain James McGuire from November 30, 1812, until March 30, 1813, when the unit was mustered out. On May 8, 1813, however, troops were reorganized to protect Washington from a British invasion. Charles joined the first Regimental District of Columbia Militia as a captain of infantry under Adjutant-General Walter Smith, and on August 24, 1814, this regiment fought the British in the Battle of Bladensburg. By that evening, the British overwhelmed the American regiment and stormed into Washington.[9] American militia suffered heavy losses, and Charles was wounded in the chest, leaving him disabled for the rest of his life. Because he died when Emma was very young, most of what she knew about her father came from stories she heard. These tales of valor led Emma to idolize him and influenced her ideal American hero. His patriotism and bravery were characteristics found in many heroes in her novels, often set during the War of 1812.

Charles continued to receive a pension, which was extended to widows and orphans after the war. Although this money helped provide an income, more funds were needed once Emma was born. To bring in extra revenue, Dorothy took in boarders at "the old Hillman House" on North Capitol Street and New Jersey Avenue. Built in 1800, the townhome was once owned by George Washington and was referred to as "General Washington's house," but he died before he could actually live in it. Emma later wrote that her grandmother ran a boardinghouse after Charles died; however, the 1820 census record shows ten additional people living in the house, so Dorothy rented to boarders while Charles was debilitated from war injuries.[10] Emma's recollection of her grandmother running a boardinghouse was vague, partly because she was so young when she lived there and partly because boardinghouses frequently attracted unsavory people—not the kind of life Emma wanted to portray in biographical sketches.

In 1822, Emma's sister Charlotte LeCompte Nevitte was born. Emma described her in stark contrast to her own thin, dark complexion. Charlotte was a beauty with a "fair, rosy complexion, soft blue eyes, and flaxen hair" and a "happy, social, loving" child the whole family adored. Charles was particularly attached to Charlotte, referring to her as his "Dove-eyed darling." Emma's feelings about her physical inferiority to Charlotte would later become evident in her novel *The Deserted Wife* with the similarity between the sisters Hagar and Rosalie to Emma and Charlotte. Critic Susan Harris has also made this comparison, calling the novel Emma's "spiritual biography."[11]

Despite Charles's preference for Charlotte, Emma became very attached to her father from an early age. Her life seemed marked by sadness when her father was away and happiness when he was home. On one occasion when Charles was in St. Mary's, he caught a severe cold and lung infection, and his health quickly deteriorated. Emma described her state of happiness between when "Father is able to walk about" and when "Father is confined to his bed." On March 28, 1823, Emma vividly remembered a solemn occasion in which she and Charlotte were taken into her father's room to be baptized by Father James Lucas, the priest at St. Peter's Catholic Church. Wearing his "sacred vestments," he administered last rites to Charles before baptizing Emma and Charlotte, while family and friends gathered around her father's bed. Then her father "laid his dying hands upon our heads and blessed us." Five days later, Charles died. Emma painfully recalled the traumatic event with startling clarity: "I felt as if I had received a sudden stunning blow upon the brow. I reeled back from the blow an instant, unable to meet it, and then—with an impulse to fly, to escape from the calamity—turned and fled—fled with my utmost speed, until . . . I fell upon my face exhausted, insensible." Then came the "dark pageantry of the funeral" that seemed to Emma "like a hideous dream."[12]

Afterward, Emma spent much of her time alone with big questions on life and death, heaven and hell, which her family thought was "injurious as it was unnatural to a child so young," so Emma's religious education began. Charles had been Catholic, while Susanna and Dorothy were Episcopalian, but these differences were not problematic in the family, as "there was an absolute toleration and respect for each other's opinions." This tolerance later appeared in Emma's novels such as *The Missing Bride* through characters who have different religious beliefs and yet get along with their fellow neighbors. Emma, therefore, was taught the catechism in the Catholic church as well as "the thirty-nine articles" in the Episcopalian church.[13] Despite the best efforts of religious teachers in both places of worship, five-year-old Emma had more questions for them than they had satisfactory answers.

Offering answers to young Emma was "Uncle Biggs," whom Emma called her "spiritual instructor." In actuality, Biggs was one of the slaves Dorothy had inherited from her late husband.[14] He treated Emma and Charlotte with great care and kindness. Wearing "short breeches and white stockings, shoe-buckles and cocked hat," he considered himself a "gentleman of all avocations." He often took the sisters on his knee and told them ghost stories. He claimed to be a "ghost-seer, holding frequent communion with the visible spirits of the departed." Of utmost interest to Emma was that "he professed frequently to see and speak with the spirit of her father." She also heard stories about "when the old folks (her forefathers) were rich, and saw no end to the company which made them poor at last." Biggs also recalled when Dorothy "was rich and saw lots of grand company."[15] These stories impacted Emma greatly, and she regularly retold them in her novels.

Dorothy strongly influenced Emma as well. After Charles died, Susanna received "half pay pensions for five years," or approximately $1,200 per year—an insufficient income to support such a large household. Dorothy attempted to continue running the boardinghouse on her own; however, she "never could learn to present a bill," and the venture lasted only around a year. Referring to her grandmother as "a lady of the lofty old school," Emma learned the values and behaviors of a traditional woman, which "made the earliest and deepest personal impression" on her.[16] Emma later replicated Dorothy in *The Three Beauties* as Winny Darling's grandmother, who is a passive widow entirely dependent on her son and daughter.[17] Emma concluded that this kind of dependence wasn't one she wanted to emulate.

Although money was tight, Emma fondly remembered the times when Dorothy and Susanna took her and Charlotte on frequent visits to St. Mary's to the "old colonial homesteads," where she heard magical stories of "heroic adventures, family legends, Indian traditions, and tales of courage and of cruelty, of wonder and fear." Still feeling awkward and unlovable, Emma spent much of her time alone, preferring the beauty of the Maryland "grand old forest" and the glorious Potomac River from Blackstone's Island to St. Clement's Bay, and this area became her outdoor playground. It was here that she participated "in country sports and in active exercise, particularly that of horseback riding, to which she was excessively addicted" and where her health improved drastically.[18] The fresh air and outdoor activities that improved her strength led to her advocacy of physical education for young girls.

While Emma physically benefited from her time spent in the Maryland woods, she was soon to encounter a new life event just before her seventh birthday that profoundly affected the rest of her childhood. On November 14, 1826, Susanna married Joshua Laurens Henshaw. Although they continued to live in the same home, her mother's marriage to Henshaw only worsened the isolation Emma felt. "Year after year, from my eighth to my sixteenth year, I grew more lonely, retired more into myself," Emma remembered. "Until, notwithstanding a strong, ardent, demonstrative temperament, I became cold, reserved, and abstracted." This seclusion intensified as Henshaw and Susanna had four children of their own. "What a sad time I and my sister Charlotte had when we were children, how forlorn we were, and how we suffered for everything," Emma opined. "Though our father left us a large and handsomely furnished house, we would be left to play in a freezing garret and driven away from the fire in the parlor, and never allowed to come to the table until everybody else had done and there was little left for us, hardly ever having a kind word given to us." Comforting Emma and Charlotte was Dorothy, who continued to live with the family.[19] Based on the kind of relationship Emma developed early on with Henshaw, Emma learned how much power a man had to reward or punish the members of his household—a patriarchal constraint Emma later sought to upend as she created independent heroines who fought against being controlled.

Even though Henshaw was cold and distant, he ensured that his stepdaughters received a stellar education—rare for women of the early nineteenth century. Henshaw and Susanna opened a private school in their home when Emma was ten, and she and Charlotte were its first students. Emma claimed that she "was indebted" to Henshaw for her education, which continued from 1826 to 1835. While the specific subjects Henshaw taught the girls are unknown, it might be inferred from a curriculum he used in 1837 that Emma's lessons included scripture, arithmetic, geography, the Constitution and government, the history of the United States, and bookkeeping. For his later work in public education, he became known as "the father of the public school system in the District." Henshaw was a good teacher, and his encouragement helped Emma understand her intelligence. "I first discovered that I possessed some mental power—a discovery quite as surprising to myself as it was to others," she wrote. "The hours not devoted to legitimate study were passed in the old garret, or the great old-fashioned, heavily-shaded garden, reading every book of every sort that I could get my hands on."[20] She loved reading the classics, on which she relied heavily as a writer. Emma also gained the skills necessary to do what her mother and grandmother before her could not—work in a job outside the realm of domestic duties. This formal education at her parents' school laid the foundation for her later success.

As Emma grew intellectually, she also blossomed into a young woman who carried herself with beauty and grace. One reporter, who was mesmerized by her clear, blue eyes, remembered that she was "modest and unassuming" and well liked by her friends. Another biographer wrote:

> Her hair was dark brown, or black, or golden according to the light or shadow that fell upon it or the sunshine glinted through it. Her eyes were two living wells of varying thoughtful moods and meaning, and deep-set in the caverns of a noble temple, they conveyed hope, comfort, encouragement, consolation, warning, even contentment or amusement as her good offices seemed to be required.[21]

While this description indicates affectionate admiration from the unnamed biographer, Emma's demeanor and ability to carry herself with intelligence and kindness helped her secure a job after leaving Henshaw's school.

When Emma was fifteen, she helped support her family by copying land warrants, a job she continued even after she began teaching at Miss Talbot's female seminary located on 4½ Street in Washington, DC. While no specific records of Miss Talbot's school remain, many other private schools flourished during that time, and it's possible that Miss Talbot was subcontracted to one of these, such as the Alexandria Female Academy and Boarding School. Included in the $140 tuition for the semester was Latin, English, mathematics, natural and moral philosophy, chemistry, astronomy, and rhetoric. Courses in French, music, drawing, and painting were also available at an additional charge.[22] The kinds of classes being taught in the nation's capital were quite progressive for the time; however, this type of education would have been available only for

Emma D.E.N. Southworth in the frontispiece from *Old Neighbourhoods* (1853). (*Clifton Waller Barrett Collection*)

wealthy girls. Emma viewed this disparity as problematic, and she later wrote about the ways poverty limited opportunities available to women.

Using the educational advantages she'd been given, Emma found a new teaching position in 1837, this time in Upperville, Virginia, around fifty-five miles from DC—a one-day trip by stagecoach. Because the 1830s saw a revival in American education, especially in the creation of academies, it's not surprising that she could have easily found a position there. At that time, Virginia had fifteen female academies and seven coeducational ones, and Virginians showed a tendency to favor educating both sexes. Similar to private schools in DC, the Virginian academies taught the classics, higher mathematics skills, chemistry, physics, and botany. Wealthy Virginians paid good money to educate their children; however, allocating state monies to support public education for all social classes was contentious. Because the academy was so successful in providing good schooling for well-to-do students, it remained the primary source of education in Virginia until after the Civil War.[23] Education aside, Emma valued the beautiful scenery she observed during her time here, later using it as the setting for many of her stories.

Emma's next job took her four hundred miles from home to Springfield, Ohio. Traveling from Upperville to Springfield wouldn't have been an easy journey for nineteen-year-old Emma. In those days, railroad and canal travel was in its infancy, with few passages built to completion. The most common mode of travel into Ohio was still via stagecoach. Most likely, Emma took a stagecoach the eighty-six miles from Upperville to Cumberland, Maryland, a trip that would require one overnight stop. Then travelers took the Cumberland Road, which was the first national road authorized by Congress in 1806; it joined the eastern part of the United States to the West, allowing for increased transportation of people and goods. Stagecoaches traveled an average of sixty to seventy miles per day through towns such as Uniontown, Wheeling, Zanesville, and Columbus, with tavern stops that offered passengers food, drink, and lodging.[24] The journey itself would have been fascinating for Emma, who had loved exploring the forest of Maryland and had found a great interest in learning new things as a child.

Although Emma wrote that she taught in Springfield, Ohio, she never specifically stated to which Springfield she traveled. In the late 1830s, there were three. The one that's most well known today was at the end of the National Road, giving it the title of the "city at the end of the road."[25] Because there weren't many teaching positions available there, this Springfield doesn't seem a probable destination. A second Springfield was in Williams County in the far northwest corner of the state. The distance and remoteness of this second Springfield make it unlikely Emma went there either. A third Springfield was in Hamilton County and close to where Emma had relatives living in Kentucky. Springfield township, seven miles to downtown Cincinnati, was filled with teaching opportunities, making it Emma's expected destination.

Another clue that Emma was in Springfield township near Cincinnati is that this area was more progressive in education, the arts, and technology—definitely an area Emma would have found appealing. Listed in the 1836 city directory of Cincinnati and the surrounding townships were eleven female academies—any one of which could have hired Emma. Also in the Cincinnati area at the time were other women who would later become as famous as Emma, including Catharine Beecher and her sister Harriet Beecher Stowe. They ran the Western Female Institute from 1831 to 1837 but continued to live in Cincinnati after it closed.[26]

In addition to teaching, the Beecher sisters were involved in local cultural endeavors such as the Semi-Colon Club, a literary society that was popular in Cincinnati during the 1830s and 1840s, meeting at community leaders' homes such as Rev. E. B. Hall, Edwin Cranch, and Samuel Foote. Unlike other societies, the Semi-Colon Club welcomed participation from both men and women. Although history has ferreted out some of its members, one of the club's rules was that manuscripts read during the meetings would remain anonymous. This secrecy allowed participants to try new styles and modes of writing and watch how listeners responded, which was freeing to mature and amateur writers alike. Topics varied from "immortality to cranberry sauce, from Adam and Eve to 'old' Dr. Lyman Beecher." Hostesses offered light dinners, and evenings usually ended with dancing.[27] It was a short drive from Springfield township to the homes that hosted the Semi-Colon Club. As she was an adventuresome and intellectual woman, Emma's attendance and participation in at least a few of the meetings seems credible.

Emma never specifically mentioned being involved in the Semi-Colon Club, but she later recalled being invited to the "home of a gentleman," where she met three young women approximately her own age. She told a reporter, "This quartette of girls, fated to become famous, were congenial spirits, and the intimacy then formed has continued unbroken, throughout the changes of nearly half a century."[28] One intimate friend was Harriet Beecher Stowe, who agreed with Emma on the abolition of slavery, which "bound their friendship all the firmer." When Stowe visited student Elizabeth Marshall Key's Kentucky home in 1833, Elizabeth took Stowe to a slave auction, and this event left a distressing and long-lasting impact on her. It seems plausible that Harriet first told Emma about her trip to Kentucky when Emma came to the Cincinnati area in 1838 and that they met at a Semi-Colon Club meeting. Stowe later claimed that her most famous story, *Uncle Tom's Cabin*, began to take shape while living in Ohio. Years later, Harriet visited Emma after she began writing for Gamaliel Bailey, proprietor of the *National Era*; both Emma and Dr. Bailey encouraged Harriet to submit *Uncle Tom's Cabin* to the magazine for publication.[29]

Another acquaintance Emma mentioned meeting in Ohio was Elizabeth Blackwell—the first woman in the United States to earn a medical degree. Elizabeth's father had moved the family from New York to Cincinnati in 1838, but he died soon after, leaving his wife and nine children virtually destitute. In order to provide for the family, Elizabeth and two of her sisters opened a private boarding school in their home. During this time, Elizabeth also became increasingly interested in topics of the day, such as the education of women, abolition, transcendentalism, and politics. "We became acquainted with the very intelligent circle of New England society settled in Cincinnati," Elizabeth recalled. "It was a most exciting time." While never mentioning either Emma or Harriet Beecher Stowe in her diary, Elizabeth made an indirect reference to the Semi-Colon Club, mentioning many of the known members of the group and saying it was "a society which strongly attracted us."[30] Clearly,

Harriet Beecher Stowe (1853). (*National Portrait Gallery, Washington, DC*)

Elizabeth and her sisters attended Semi-Colon Club meetings, likely meeting Harriet Beecher Stowe and Emma Southworth, as the girls were all similar in age and intellectual tastes. It's not hard to imagine that here is where they first formed a long-lasting friendship.

It's a matter of speculation who the third girl was whom Emma mentioned meeting in Ohio, but a strong contender is Alice Cary. She and her younger sister Phoebe became well-known poets. They lived on a rural farm in Mount Healthy, again a short distance to Cincinnati and even closer to Springfield township. Unlike Emma Southworth, Harriet Beecher Stowe, or Elizabeth Blackwell, Alice and Phoebe Cary did not receive a formal education and could only occasionally attend the local common schools. Yet the sisters loved reading and writing and were largely self-taught. By 1838, both had poems published.[31] Considering their interests in literature, they could have attended a Semi-Colon Club meeting. Another clue that links the three girls to an early friendship was that they later wrote for the same publication. Emma and Alice began writing for Gamaliel Bailey's *National Era* in 1847, with Harriet joining the duo in 1851—all having lived at the same time in the Cincinnati area.

In addition to Emma's friendship with these women, she met a young intellectual inventor who had a profound impact on the rest of her life. Full of ideas, twenty-two-year-old Frederick Hamilton Southworth

Alice Cary (1850). (*Cary Cottage, North College Hill, Ohio*)

arrived in Cincinnati in 1838. He was born on May 4, 1816, in Clinton, New York, the second oldest in a family of six brothers and sisters. His mother had died in 1828 when he was twelve, with his father dying soon after in 1831. Frederick was sent to Cortland Academy in Homer, New York, where he proved to be a bright and innovative student. Here, Frederick invented a new type of waterwheel called the "Tide and Current Water Wheel." He tested his idea by building a seven-inch model and placing it in a four-mile-per-hour current. After demonstrating the efficiency of his model, the Mechanics Association of Utica, New York, awarded him a silver medal in June 1838. Because of the proximity to the Ohio River and the Ohio Mechanics Institute, Frederick soon traveled to Cincinnati, where he hoped to build a full-scale waterwheel to be used in an ever-growing industrialized country.[32]

Cincinnati had become known as the "Queen of the West," with the population tripling between 1810 and 1830, resulting in many new manufacturing businesses. Also in Cincinnati was the Ohio Mechanics Institute, which began in 1828 and was the first technical school in the United States. Members had access to lectures, training, and a research library. No doubt, Frederick found the institute ideal for working on inventions, and yet, as a young man, he also likely wanted fun and entertainment. Institute founders John Foote and William Greene were members of the Semi-Colon Club, and since they welcomed visitors and newcomers to participate, Frederick might have joined, especially for the food and dancing that occurred after the literary readings. Emma and Frederick could have met here, but other exciting events also might have brought these ill-fated lovers together.

One was the Mechanics' and Citizens' Ball. In February 1838, the institute organized a fund-raiser dance. Eight hundred tickets were sold, generating a total of $2,400. Its success inspired a second ball given in February 1839 and held at the National Theatre, where the pit was level with the stage to accommodate an even larger dance area. More than two thousand attended this event. For Emma, attending the ball would have seemed magical, made even more so if an intellectually gifted young man such as Frederick had asked her to dance. Even though Emma was well educated and had grown out of the gawky stages of her childhood, she

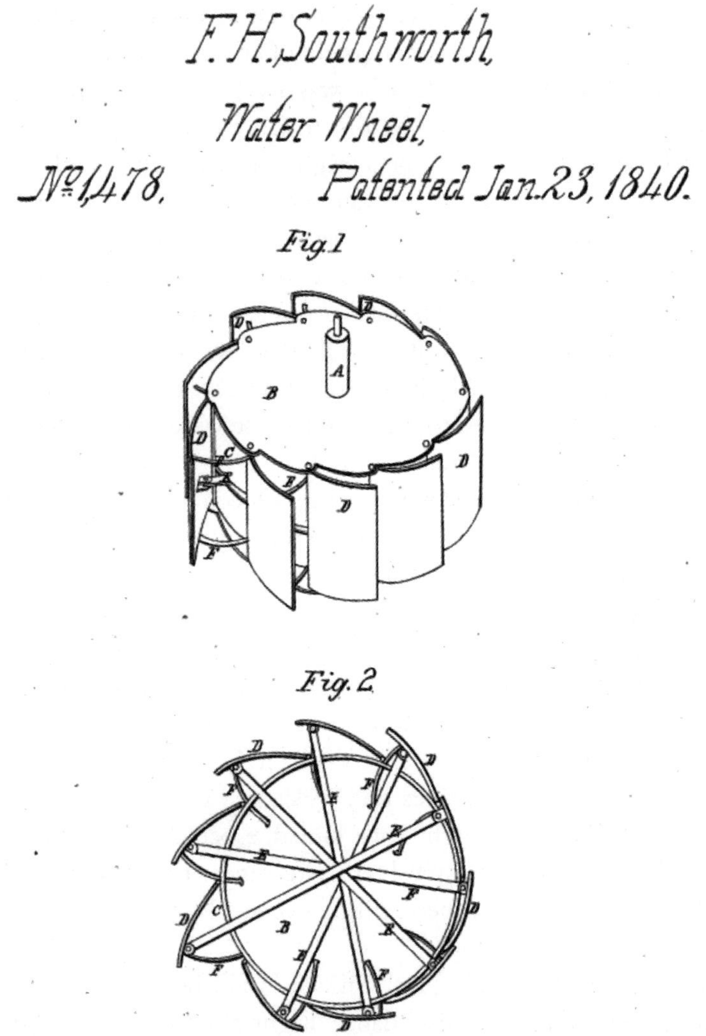

Frederick Southworth Tide and Current Water Wheel, patent no. 1,478 (January 23, 1840). (*United States Patent Office*)

still thought herself unattractive, in stark contrast to Frederick, who stood around five feet nine and had blond hair, hazel eyes, a high forehead, and a straight nose.[33]

Lending more credence to the theory that Emma met Frederick here, she later wrote a strikingly similar account in *The Haunted Homestead*. The female character Mathilde Legare attends a ball that is "quite crowded, leaving but little room for the motion of the dancers." At first, Mathilde considers the event "the very stupidest ball" she ever attended, as she "seemed destined to adorn the sofa as a 'wall flower' all evening," despite her best efforts to look beautiful. Finally, a "Magnus Apollo" notices her from across the room. The hero is Frank Howard, an accomplished mechanic from Boston. Mathilde notices the handsomeness of his head:

> It was a very remarkable, characteristic, individual sort of head—a monarchial head, with a forehead that in its commanding height and breadth seemed the natural throne of intellectual sovereignty, with a strongly and clearly-marked nose and mouth, with eyes full of calm power—that surveyed the multitude below with the quiet interest of a king inspecting his army on some festive parade day.

Frank asks Mathilde to dance, and "he danced as well as he conversed." From that moment, the two are constant companions, and in a matter of several weeks, they fall in love.[34]

Likewise, by the middle of 1839, Emma and Frederick were in love and inexorably fated to be married; however, they had one problem. Not only were they young, but they also had little money. Frederick was a far cry from the kind of man Emma's mother and stepfather wanted her to marry. As of yet, he had a brilliant idea with the waterwheel but no money to build one, so Frederick invented a more practical device—an improved premium feather dresser machine. In the nineteenth century, mattresses were filled with feathers, and Frederick saw a need for an improved way of cleaning them. His new machine cleaned out all impurities, odors, and dust often found in feathers used for bedmaking. Frederick claimed that his machine would solve the problem of beds that contained "carbonic acid . . . which when inhaled by the lungs is most pernicious to health" and that sleepers would "do well to take care that they do not contract disease from the very beds upon which they sleep." By July 1839, he was in Buffalo, New York, where he had an operational machine on display before selling it to a prominent manufacturer.[35] He had money; now he had to convince Emma's parents to bless the marriage.

By the fall of 1839, Frederick and Emma had made their marriage plans known, but, despite the money from the feather dresser, Susanna remained unhappy about Emma's choice for a husband.[36] Considering they were in their early twenties and Frederick had no continued income, Susanna's objections were understandable. Another clue about how upset Emma's own mother and stepfather were appears in *The Haunted Homestead* when Mathilde asks for her parents' marital blessing. Mathilde begins:

> "A very accomplished young machinist, and mathematical instrument maker, sir, who has realized quite a handsome fortune by his patented improvement in—"
>
> "The foul fiend!" exclaimed the old aristocrat, throwing up his hands in consternation, as he trotted off.
>
> His daughter talking, dancing, riding, flirting with a mechanic! Oh! horror, horror, horror!

Mathilde eventually gains her parents' approval, and on New Year's Day the engagement is announced.[37] Similarly, Emma and Frederick were betrothed despite the objections, and while Emma and her mother planned the wedding, Frederick busily marketed his Tide and Current Water Wheel.

Frederick was a talented strategist and salesman, using newspapers to advertise his invention. However, Frederick knew that the waterwheel required substantial funding to build a full-scale model, with one reporter noting, "Mr. Southworth is without the means of making a practical experiment effectually to test the value of his invention. If successful, it must prove of great usefulness." Searching for investors, Frederick took his small-scale model to St. Louis in December 1839, where he demonstrated to investors "that on a large scale it would prove 'a most admirable motive power.'"[38] When he left St. Louis, he believed he had procured the money needed to build it.

Frederick was even more excited about the success of his waterwheel after obtaining a patent on January 23, 1840. He then became one of the mechanics and inventors selected to showcase their new American designs during a grand display at the National Gallery in DC. Inventions were first put on display in the Rotunda of the Capitol. Not one to miss an opportunity at self-promotion, Frederick wrote an article about his invention being on display in the Rotunda, even though his waterwheel was only one of thousands of models displayed. The models were later moved to the National Gallery in the new Patent Office Building, which would allow for even more of America's best and brightest inventors to showcase their talents. "I am happy to say that the mechanics and manufacturers are improving the opportunity to present the choicest contributions," commissioner of patents Henry Ellsworth claimed. "The hall, considered by some so spacious, will, in a short time, be entirely filled; presenting a display of national skill and ingenuity not surpassed by any exhibition in the world." The patented models were preserved in glass cases to prevent them from being destroyed because of a fire that had destroyed the previous patent office along with all patents and models. Most important, the new Patent Office allowed America to tout a message of national pride and showcase the country as an emerging world presence.[39] Being a part of a national display gave Frederick a greater chance to build his waterwheel, and he felt fairly confident in achieving it.

On the same day Frederick had secured his new patent, he and Emma were married by Rev. Dr. Hawley at St. John's Episcopal Church. While no record exists of what Emma wore, many of her female characters became brides, and Emma vividly describes these bridal dresses. In *The Deserted Wife*, the garment worn by Emma's main character Hagar likely mirrored Emma's own dress: "A white Mechlin lace over white satin; pearls on her arms and neck, and a wreath of orange blossom-buds twined irregularly in and out among her glittering blue-black tresses." As was also custom of the time, celebrations continued after the wedding, which was just as well since Frederick wanted to stay until mid-February to see his waterwheel model on display in the Capitol. Again, Emma described what those celebrations were like for her characters Mathilde and Frank in *The Haunted Homestead*: "It was a wedding in the fine old-fashioned country style, with a ball and supper, the same evening; and dinner parties and dancing parties, given successively by the neighbors, in honor of the bride, almost every day and night for the next two weeks."[40] Considering Emma had family in not only DC but also Maryland, she and Frederick encountered similar parties until they were at last ready to leave for their first grand adventure as a newly married couple.

It would be the grandest adventure yet for Emma. Frederick had just returned from St. Louis a few weeks before the wedding, and, believing he had investors in that city, he was intent on building a full-scale working model of the waterwheel. St. Louis—the city where the Illinois, the Missouri, and the mighty Mississippi Rivers merged—had plenty of the one ingredient he needed to build his invention: water. St. Louis was one of the fastest-growing cities in the West. They departed in the middle of February 1840—during the midst of winter—and faced a long and arduous journey. Emma's family waved goodbye, and the married pair stepped excitedly onto the train toward what looked like a bright and promising future.

Chapter 2

From Hopeful Dreams to Dark Days

Let us pass in silence over the disastrous days of Emma's fatal marriage.[1]

In the years that followed, Emma Southworth said virtually nothing about her brief time living with Frederick except that her marriage "stamped upon [her] brow of youth the furrows of fifty years" and left her "a widow in fate but not in fact."[2] The young, inexperienced couple knew none of the tribulations that were ahead of them. Even knowing that a journey from Washington, DC, to St. Louis, Missouri, in the middle of winter would be difficult, they were urged on by their dreams of an idyllic future. Travel in those days was long and arduous, requiring various combinations and modes of transportation from stagecoach to railroad to canal to river passages. The first leg of their journey was aboard the recently opened B&O Washington Line, with its steam locomotives that had only been operational since 1835. The *Native American* advertised two daily trips from DC to Baltimore, Maryland, advising passengers to purchase tickets in advance since "under no circumstances whatever can the train be delayed beyond the hour fixed for starting."[3] Since Emma had spent most of her life in DC, which had the reputation as a dismal and dirty city, this first stop in Baltimore seemed not only a refreshing change from the drudgery of the nation's capital but also a sign of a prosperous life with her new husband.

Baltimore was just the first stop in what would be at least a ten-day journey to St. Louis, and once Frederick and Emma arrived on March 5, 1840, Frederick received horrible news. The country was again suffering an economic crisis. The Panic of 1837 had already taken its toll on many banking institutions because of an inability to pay lenders in gold or silver coin, instead insisting on paper money transactions. Lending practices ceased, and despite a brief recovery, the Panic deepened in 1839 at precisely the time that Frederick hoped to get investors.[4] Sadly, there were none to be found in St. Louis, and Frederick and Emma had to make new plans. Their money was rapidly dwindling. They couldn't go back to DC, as Emma's parents hadn't favored the marriage from the beginning. Frederick's parents had both died when he was a boy, but he had a sister Lydia who lived even farther west in the small but growing village of Platteville, Wisconsin. Lydia had married the wealthiest man in town—perhaps he could help.

Even though Emma never explicitly wrote about her travels with Frederick, she left clues in her novel *Mark Sutherland*, which resonates with similarities between Emma and Frederick and her fictional characters, Mark Sutherland and his new bride Rosalie, who were traveling on a steamboat to the West. Emma described the lovers aboard ship:

> They were standing upon the hurricane deck of the steamer *Indian Queen*, which was puffing and blowing its rapid course down the Ohio river. She was leaning on the arm of her husband; their heads were bare, the better to enjoy the freshness of the morning air; her eyes were sparkling, and her cheeks glowing with animation, and her sunny ringlets, blown back, floated on the breeze.[5]

In real life, Emma and Frederick also rode the *Indian Queen* down the Ohio River, and Emma's passage reveals her excitement before learning there would be no life on arrival in St. Louis. They departed the same day, still aboard the *Indian Queen* but now bound for Galena, Illinois, on the Mississippi River, where they would then take the stagecoach to Platteville. Emma later claimed her stories were always "founded on facts," so it's highly plausible that the tale of Mark and Rosalie Sutherland was Emma's recollection of her own newlywed days.[6]

Despite the bitter disappointment that there were no investors, Emma wasn't ready to give up hope, as evidenced by the romantic vision of the future she created for her characters Mark and Rosalie as they traveled to the West. On board the *Indian Queen*, Mark tells Rosalie what a joy and comfort she is to him before asking her whether she'll be happy in the "wild West." Rosalie answers Mark with "her eyes sparkling with delight":

> Westward the star of empire wends its way. Who can look upon the shores of this great river, and note the many thriving new villages, without joyfully perceiving that? The South is a beautiful, a luxuriant region, where, "lapped in Elysium," you may dream your soul away; but the West is a magnificently vigorous land, whose clarion voice summons you to action. . . . Mark Sutherland—"*Thou art the man*!"

Rosalie admires her new husband as any young newlywed would, so it's not hard to imagine that twenty-year-old Emma felt similarly about Frederick. Emma left more clues about her own journey hidden within Mark and Rosalie's passage. Of their love for each other, Emma wrote that "the two grew into one—with one heart, soul, and spirit—one interest, purpose, and object."[7] Considering how Emma was likely writing about her own feelings, this passage shows how she trusted Frederick. She envisioned herself as an inventor's wife, and together they were going into a newly settled territory, where she believed his ideas would improve the lives of people who lived there.

Wisconsin had been separated from Michigan into its own territory only since 1836. As the stagecoach approached Platteville, Emma observed a newly formed village in a clearing of about forty acres among a thick forest. Around six hundred residents lived in the town, which had five stores, a church, two schools, a well-attended lyceum, and a newspaper with immediate plans to begin a fine hotel. While there were a couple of brick structures, the town primarily consisted of frame and log buildings. Just outside the village, there were three smelting furnaces, a grist mill, and four saw mills.[8] The beating heart of the idyllic village was attributed to its founder, Major John H. Rountree, who had married Frederick's sister Lydia. He had wealth, power, and a renowned reputation as a businessman—the kind of investor Frederick needed for his waterwheel. Rountree was a "radical temperance man" who never smoked or drank alcohol and was "a splendid man to his family."[9] Frederick banked on the fact that he would be welcomed as family when he brought his bride to Platteville in the spring of 1840.

While Emma never spoke of what kind of reception she and Frederick received on their arrival, she left more clues in *Mark Sutherland* when her fictitious newlyweds arrive at a small village in the Northwest. Mark and Rosalie spend their first night in the unnamed village in a crowded hotel, where the landlady questions Rosalie about the validity of her marriage to Mark. "Umph! Humph! Now tell me the truth—I shan't blame you—it's none of my business you know, but ain't you and that young man a runaway match?" the landlady asks. "You somehow looked so young and delicate for such a life as you're come to, that I couldn't help but think that it must o' been a *love-match*." Rosalie reddens and laughs before answering, "Why, no, certainly not. We were married in my uncle's house, and left it with his blessing and good wishes."[10]

Similar to Emma's fictional characters, she and Frederick were very young. The idea that the couple had run away together was an easy conclusion to make considering that Frederick had no fortune, no job, and no prospects. At the time, the idea of romantic love was often low on the list of reasons to marry. Economic security, consolidating landholdings, and familial obligations mattered more to a woman in that era.[11] Lydia's marriage to Rountree was rational and respectable, whereas Emma's marriage to Frederick was rash and foolish.

Initially, Rountree was a welcoming host, inviting Frederick and Emma to stay with him and Lydia, but soon it became apparent the couple had no immediate plans to leave. Even though the Rountree home was spacious for its day, two additional guests made long-term accommodations inconvenient. Not only did Rountree and Lydia already have three children from his previous marriage, but Lydia was pregnant and would soon add another child to the household. Still, Rountree remained

Major John Hawkins Rountree (1856). (*Wisconsin Historical Society*)

hospitable and provided a place for Frederick and Emma to live. "[We] were obliged to move in the spring to a rude log structure, a mile from the settlement, that had been occupied as a church," Emma wrote, "as every house and shanty in the village . . . was occupied."[12]

Emma's recollections were only partly true, however. A Platteville resident from 1840 claimed that one reason to give his village a good recommendation was that travelers "who visit will find excellent accommodations." In fact, Frederick had little to no money by the time he and Emma arrived in Platteville. The money he'd made from his feather-dressing machine as well as any money Emma had from teaching was most certainly depleted from buying passage fares, hotel bills, and food. Of course, Emma might have been completely unaware of their financial situation. According to marital law at that time, she was *feme covert* or dependent on her husband. A woman's property and earnings legally became those of the husband.[13]

Without money, Frederick and Emma were entirely dependent on Rountree. In 1834, Rountree had donated much of his own land and money to build Platteville. The abandoned church that Rountree let Frederick and Emma occupy was one of the earliest buildings in the area. Built north of Court Street, the small, one-story log structure had been used as a school and a church and was roughly a mile from the center of the village. When Emma first saw where she would live, she realized, in addition to the distance from town, other challenges lay ahead. "There was but one room, a clumsy constructed fireplace was on one side," Emma recalled. "If there had ever been any sash and glass to the . . . windows they had been taken away when the place was abandoned as a house of worship."[14]

Once again, Emma's memory of her own arrival at the cottage in the woods closely mirrored the experiences of her fictional characters. "There is one building on the spot—a large log cabin, that was put up for a meeting-house, but has fallen into disuse since the rise of this village," Mark explains to Rosalie. "The cabin is in good repair, and I have already engaged it."[15] While Emma's cabin was by no means as large as the one in her fictional novel, its location and description was so blatantly parallel to her own life that there's little doubt Emma romanticized her and Frederick's little log cabin in the woods.

In the novel, Emma named the woods "Wolf's Grove," a description that matched the landscape from Platteville to the log cabin:

> When breakfast was over, "the Colonel" geared up the carryall to take his young guests across the prairie to Wolf's Grove. It was a fresh, bright, blithe morning, scarcely seven o'clock, when they set out, and

> the prairie still glistened with dew. There was no road to Wolf's Grove; but the driver took a beeline over the level ground, and the wheels of the carryall tracked deep through the sedgy grass and gorgeous wildflowers.

Interestingly, John Rountree's last appointment prior to Emma and Frederick's arrival in Platteville was that of aide to the governor in which he was promoted to the rank of colonel. Similarly, in *Mark Sutherland*, it is the landlord of the hotel in which Mark and Rosalie had stayed who takes them to the cabin. Everyone in the fictional village calls the landlord "the Colonel," even though it was really only an honorary title. Emma's use of quotes around "the Colonel" in this passage seems a likely nod to Rountree. In actuality, Rountree refused to go by "Colonel," as he felt the appointment was primarily a social and advisory one, and he preferred the title of major instead of carrying pretentious airs.[16]

Another similarity between the arrival of the fictional Mark and Rosalie and that of Frederick and Emma was Emma's description in the novel of the nearby stream. In real life, the water source had been a primary reason for the location of the log school and church. Emma also made the stream a feature in her novel. "If you'd like a drink, there's one of the finest springs in the whole country down there," the Colonel explained. Then Mark and Rosalie went to the spring and "found the water cold and clear as crystal" and counted it a "great blessing" before going back to the cabin to bid the Colonel farewell.[17]

Much like the Colonel in Emma's novel, in real life, Rountree helped Frederick and Emma unload the goods for their new house. At once, Emma began setting up the old, abandoned log cabin, using all the resources she had to turn it into the couple's first home. Since there was no glass in the windows, she "nailed some unbleached cotton" and arranged the furniture. When it came time to make supper, Emma and Frederick realized that they had neither matches to start the fire nor salt to cure the "large quarter of beef that their brother-in-law had given them on leaving his house in the morning." Even though the sun was preparing to set, Frederick and Rountree decided that Frederick would go back with Rountree to the village to get the items they needed for the night and then walk back to the cabin. Emma remembered that, after the men had gone, she brought a chair outside the cabin to enjoy the evening, but it turned out to be anything but peaceful. "All at once a sense of the appalling stillness abroad startled [me]," Emma recalled, "when a long, low murmur like the winds in the tree tops, so filled [me] with dread, that [I] rushed into the house and barred the door."[18] Considering that Emma was a young, inexperienced city girl who had been left alone on her first night in an isolated cabin, her sudden fright was understandable.

Coming to the Northwest Territory, Emma encountered not only a new and strange landscape but also previously unknown peoples, foods, and animals. One 1840s resident, John Evans, recalled that there were many old Indian trails; one he remembered in detail passed "through the ravine northwest of the village, and down the waters of the Platte towards the Mississippi." This trail was in the same direction as the cabin Frederick and Emma occupied. Evans described seeing the Potawatomi and Winnebago in the area; however, they were peaceable tribes. What Emma heard and saw that night were not Native Americans. Once locked inside the cabin, Emma slowly and carefully pulled aside the cotton that was hanging at the pane-less windows. "[I] looked out and saw the scintillating hungry eyes of a pack of wolves." She realized they were probably enticed to the cabin by the scent of the fresh meat that was hanging between the door and front window, so she dragged it away from the front of her house to the farthest corner. The "wolf-beleaguered lady" then waited until she heard "the welcome sound of men's voices, and the report of guns." In the novel, Rosalie is also frightened by wolves at the door; she faints moments before Mark rushes in to save her.[19]

While the fierce timber wolf existed in the southern region of Wisconsin Territory, much more common was what people in that area referred to as the prairie wolf. Wisconsinites generally thought they were more of a nuisance than a threat to people because they often raided their livestock for food. Newcomers to the region often mistook them for their more ferocious cousin, the timber wolf. What Emma encountered that night was a prairie wolf—a mistake she clarified in her novel. "They were prairie wolves—a small, cowardly race—who go in packs, and who are generally very easily driven off," Mark explained to Rosalie. "I have heard a pioneer say, that he would as [likely] as not tumble himself, unarmed, down into a dingle full of them, and trust to his muscular strength and courage to conquer."[20] Nevertheless, Emma had probably never encountered any type of wolf that close, and the experience would have been terrifying—one that she would have remembered vividly for years to come. She had learned on that night that being a pioneer woman wasn't just an exciting adventure; it also came with dangers, both real and imagined.

Despite the dangers, Emma remembered her time as a new bride in the log cabin in Wisconsin as "some of the happiest hours of [her] life." Similarly, Rosalie is neither bored nor lonely, and she has "bright hopes for the future" as she does her daily household work, forages for wild plums and raspberries, and waits for Mark to return, at which time they "partook of an early supper, rested, and then took a pleasant woodland walk, or occupied the evening hours with a book."[21] Given the comparisons, Emma was likely recalling her own early days with Frederick. Unfortunately, this idyllic life in the woods was short lived, and in just two months, Frederick and Emma were asked to leave Platteville.

By the end of May 1840, Rountree's generosity was growing thin. Frederick had no job, even though Platteville was booming. Frederick's uncle, Sylvester Gridley, was a merchant in one of the stores, and Rountree owned almost everything else. He had farms and mines and smelting furnaces, and there were at least two hundred miners employed around the village. A job should have been easy enough for Frederick to obtain if he had wanted one. Clearly, he did not. Frederick never intended to start a new life in the wilderness as a miner, farmer, or merchant. He had the same goal in mind—to procure funding to build his Tide and Current Water Wheel—but he was unable to convince either Rountree or Uncle Sylvester to invest. Instead, his family gave him money and asked him "to return from whence he came."[22]

More evidence of Frederick's impending eviction and what it meant for both him and Emma is found in his sister Lydia's friendship album, which was a way of keeping personal messages written by family and friends; friendship albums were popular in America from the 1820s to the 1880s, particularly among women who were educated and had money. Even though the poems, letters, and kind words were sentimental, these messages went deeper than mere frivolities on paper. The practice of writing in the friendship album became a "ritual of linguistic play in which young women and young men exchanged verses and emblematic images . . . to memorialize the present as a stay against the future."[23] Within the pages of Lydia's album, this "linguistic play" can be seen in the messages left by Frederick and Emma. When analyzing the different styles and messages they sent to each other and to Lydia, the problems in their early life are revealed.

The poem penned by Frederick, dated May 26, 1840, conveys a rather passionate farewell message that clearly indicates he didn't want to leave Platteville:

I go, sweet sister! yet think of me
  When spring's low voice awakes the flowers
For we have wandered far and free
  In those bright hours—the violet's hours!

I go—but when you pause to hear
  From distant hills, the sabbath bell
On summer's wind float silvery clear
  Think of me then—I loved it well!

Forget me not around your hearth,
  When clearly shines the ruddy blaze;
For dear has been its hour of mirth
  To me, sweet friends! in other days.

And oh! When music's voice is heard
  To melt in strains of parting wo [*sic*];
When hearts to tender thought are stirr'd
  Think on me then! I go, I go!

Farewell
F.H.S.[24]

Frederick Southworth's sister, Lydia Southworth Rountree. (*University of Wisconsin, Platteville*)

The poem is not an original verse by Frederick but one he copied from Felicia Hemans, originally titled "A Farewell Song," published in 1836. Plagiarism was not uncommon in friendship albums, however, and "was a natural part of its circulation."[25] Frederick was motivated by more than just showing off his poetry acumen. Even though the poem is signed with initials, the name of the writer is easily proved. In the first line, the original poem reads, "I go, sweet friends," but Frederick changed it to "sweet sister." The initials *F. H. S.* could belong only to the brother who bore them: Frederick Hamilton Southworth. The poem he chose is filled with a sense of regret in his parting, repeatedly asking Lydia to "think of me" and "forget me not" and lamenting that leaving fills Frederick with "strains of parting woe." Frederick was clearly trying to cajole his sister into convincing Rountree to let him stay.

Written on the previous page is Emma's original short tale, and in it she left a message that starkly contrasted with Frederick's. While no date marked her entry, she likely wrote the short story in Lydia's album close to the same time. Though riddled with missing words and obvious grammatical mistakes, the passage bears several key characteristics of Emma's later published works.

The Death Bed

> A young and beautiful Countess lay upon her death bed. Her face was lighted up with Heavenly inspiration. Was it not hard for her to die, so young, so beautiful. We will hear her own words. A fair girl was bending over her. "Listen Charlotte" said she "and I will tell you what has made this dying bed more soft and soothing than a mother's bosom and why death comes welcome and pleasant as rest after weariness. I have been a dreamer. Youth are always dreamers. My dream was of home & Happiness, I seldom thought of God or Heaven. My young Husband seemed a God, my home seemed Heaven. Beautiful ones bloomed around me and called me Mother, but Death breathed on them and they withered. I nerved my soul to endurance for his sake who was now my all, but Death stern and relentless, despite my tears, despite my agony, despite my frantic cries bore him away, and when the grave closed over him, my husband, my idol, I was alone! I was frantic! What then to me was my high rank, my boundless wealth, my princely halls, What were even the sympathy of friends and kindred? Oh they were all less than vanity. The beautiful world seemed changed. The glorious sunlight mocked my anguish. I fled from all, and concealed myself in the darkness of my chamber. At length one came—a disciple of our Lord. He penetrated

> to the dark abode of my grief. He spoke of God, of Jesus, of Heaven; of the all-sufficiency of religion to fill the aching void of my heart. I[t] was long before I could turn from my grief to look upon my sins, and then how far, how infinite—beyond the utmost stretch of imagination was my distance from the Holiest. I could not pray, I could not lift my thought to Heaven. The wings of my spirit, laden with sin, could not bear me to the foot of the Throne. I was in despair until the pitying Jesus whispered to my heart. 'Come unto me all ye that labour and are heavy laden and I will give ye rest.' The still small voice gave peace to my soul for I obeyed it. I laid my sins at the foot of the cross, and my spirit no long[er] borne down by the burden of guilt, rose in communion with God, the living fount of love and joy. My dream has been realized. I returned to life and its duties cheerfully, and now that my masters work is almost done, I wait joyfully Oh how joyfully for his coming. I wish that I had breath and strength to tell how great is the peace and joy of believing. But I am weary now, and must sleep." These were the last words of the young countess. She fell asleep—and woke we hope in Heaven.[26]

While the story did not contain a signature, another person signed below it on her behalf: "Mrs. E.D.E.N. Southworth—written before her name appeared in print." This story predates by seven years her first known published work. Lydia's album was the one place Emma felt confident enough to express her own growing concerns of her marriage. When considering that Emma and Frederick had just been summarily asked to leave, the fact that Emma didn't sign her story might indicate that she didn't want anyone, either at that time or in the future, to know that she was ever there. Being asked by Frederick's family to leave must have been shockingly embarrassing for her.

Where Emma and Frederick went after they were asked to leave Platteville remains something of a mystery, but there are a couple of valid possibilities. One is that at the beginning of June 1840, Frederick used the money his family gave him to travel with Emma to Natchez, Mississippi, where Emma's uncle, J. B. Nevitte, lived and owned a profitable cotton plantation called Clermont. Perhaps Frederick hoped that Nevitte might see value in his waterwheel and would fund building it there. It's also plausible that Uncle Nevitte gave them some money to help the struggling pair at least return to Platteville. Considering that a letter for an F. H. Southworth remained unclaimed at the post office on August 1, 1840, the time line supports the theory that the couple briefly visited Emma's uncle during that summer.[27]

Frederick and Emma might have also spent some time in Potosi, Wisconsin, which was another small, newly developed village that was about fifteen miles southwest of Platteville. In addition to his sister Lydia, Frederick had two brothers—Philip Southworth, who had a thriving mercantile business in San Francisco, and Alden Benjamin (A. B.) Southworth, who had a stove and tin business in Potosi. While Rountree later claimed that Frederick and Emma never lived in Potosi, they could have at least visited A. B. after leaving Platteville.[28] Considering that Uncle Sylvester Gridley was a successful business owner in Platteville, it seems reasonable to believe that Sylvester helped A. B. start his business in nearby Potosi. Perhaps after spending time with his brother, Frederick also reassessed his next move.

Despite being given money to leave, Frederick was "indisposed to do so" and was soon settled again in Platteville. With the money he gained from his local family and "some further assistance from other sources," he opened his own copper, tin, sheet metal, and stove business. The earliest evidence of when Frederick returned exists in a newspaper advertisement that he originally posted on September 11, 1840. Much like A. B.'s business in Potosi, Frederick announced to "the inhabitants of Platteville" that he was "ready to execute any work in his line at short notice." He sold "stovepipe and stove trimmings of all kinds or made to order" as well as "cheap sheet-iron stoves suitable for Miners, and small Families, with or without Trimmings." Frederick set up his "small shop in the front part of his residence." The Southworths' new home and business was "one of the old school houses . . . standing on the west side of Second Street on the corner south of Furnace Street."[29]

In *Mark Sutherland*, the fictional couple also moves from the cabin in the woods into town. Emma described the change in Rosalie:

> A return to the society of her fellow-beings produced a very happy change in the spirit of Rosalie. Patient, cheerful, and hopeful, she had been before; but now, the sight of people about her—all active, lively, energetic, each engaged in the pursuit of some calling, whose object was at once the benefit of his individual self and the community—this gave strong impetus to her enterprise, and suggested many plans of usefulness and improvement.

For Rosalie, one of these plans of improvement was to start a girls' school in the village, for "the want of one was greatly felt . . . and it grew and prospered."[30]

Similarly, Emma did not remain a passive wife waiting to see whether Frederick would succeed in his new business. If the past eight months had taught her anything, it was that her dream of being a famous inventor's wife or a pioneer's wife was not as glorious as she had imagined. Additionally, by September 1840, Emma was pregnant with their first child, and she realized that depending on Frederick to provide an income for them was risky. So she took action, and in part of the schoolhouse in which they lived, she also taught the village children. One advertisement for the Platteville School ran in the local newspaper, the *Northern Badger*, on the same page as Frederick's tin shop advertisement. The Winter Session cost $9 for a twenty-two-week session for students studying primary branches of English and $12 for "higher branches of English, the use of the Apparatus and the Original Languages." Patrons were required not only to pay Emma a quarterly salary but also to "furnish the house, and keep it in repair."[31] Emma's teaching job provided for most of the couple's necessary living expenses.

Even though tensions were probably high between Rountree and Frederick, Emma was still a welcome guest. One story of Emma at the Rountree home came from "Aunt Rachel," a former slave who continued to live with the family after she was freed in 1841 until her death in 1854.[32] Aunt Rachel recalled:

> Early or late I want to tell somewhat about that first newspaper, myself and the first author in Platteville. Plain and common as could be the first author lived on second street, Mrs. E.D.E.N. Southworth, lived

> here in 1840; and clar-to-goodness she did play a joke on the Major's family! She came over to the house one day, opened the *Northern Badger*, and read a story that made us more scared than the "ghoses" (ghosts). . . . Later in the day the Major went to read the paper and said, "Where is that story? I can't find that story?" Nobody could find it! Just a plain every day woman living on Second street had made up that there story as she went along![33]

Laura Rountree Smith, a daughter of Rountree and Lydia, included Aunt Rachel's recollection in an article she wrote on Platteville's history; this story was clearly one that had been retold many times in the family and says much about who Emma was. Not only did she have a wonderful sense of humor, but she was also creating stories and carefully observing how they would be received long before she became a published author.

While Emma tried to become a valuable member of Platteville, she couldn't do enough to support both herself and Frederick. One newspaper later reported that he "did not seem to be very successful in his business."[34] One key reason seems evident in the way he advertised his establishment. In his quest to sell cheap, below competing prices, he marketed himself right out of business. Furthermore, his brother A. B. was just fifteen miles away and was not only selling but also manufacturing copper, tin, and sheet iron ware. Even though Frederick might have bought his supply from A. B. to reduce transportation costs, he also overestimated the market for his products. Mining families needed to buy items like stoves, pots, and pans only once, unlike dry goods, hardware, or groceries that continually needed to be resupplied. Frederick's business was unsustainable.

Emma's description of Mark Sutherland's success in business is entirely different from Frederick's experience and reveals how Emma wished real life would have turned out. Like Frederick's advertisement for his tin business, Mark hangs out a shingle to practice law. At first, Mark's business "was not profitable," but Rosalie suppressed "all complaint and concealing all her personal privations, continued to cheer and strengthen the struggler. She alone had invincible faith in his future—his future of greatness and wide usefulness." After four years of labor, Mark's "success was wonderful," and he became "the most able lawyer in the West." Not only was Mark's business profitable, but he also "had been elected to the State Senate; he had been named as a candidate for Governor."[35]

In her fictional work, Emma created the kind of husband she wished Frederick would have become, but, in reality, her support of Frederick's dreams didn't pan out. By April 1841, Frederick's stove business utterly failed. Not only that, but Emma also had to quit teaching. She replicated her own feelings about leaving her students through the lens of Rosalie, who was similarly forced to quit the job she loved:

> But the day came at last when her school had to be closed, and the labourer was obliged to rest from her labour. It was during the afternoon session of a certain Friday—a day never to be forgotten by the young girls, who loved their gentle teacher with enthusiastic devotion—in the midst of one of the class-exercises—a little extempore lecture on their history lesson—that sudden failure of strength drew all colour from her face, her head dropped forward on her desk, and she swooned. And after this she did not teach.[36]

While Emma was not fragile and suffering from a heart condition like Rosalie, she did have a condition—she was pregnant. In the nineteenth century, women were expected to quit teaching by the time they married, but because teachers were in short supply in the more remote villages, the townspeople were grateful to have a teacher who was willing to work and take care of her husband. Baby, husband, and household duties made continuing a career virtually impossible, however. On April 23, 1841, Emma and Frederick became parents to their firstborn son, Richmond Joseph Southworth, named after Frederick's father.[37] What should have been a happy occasion, though, was marred by financial hardship.

Later that year, the family of three boarded a steamer back "from whence they came," returning to Washington. Emma must have felt quite different than she had two years earlier when they departed for the West with such dreams. While Emma didn't die from her disappointment, Rosalie's failing health finally leads to her tragic death as Mark "sat gazing upon the dead face, holding the cold hand."[38] Perhaps Rosalie became a symbolic representation of what Emma felt as she saw her hope of being married to a successful businessman sink, forever disappearing into the deep, dark churning waters of the Mississippi. As Platteville slipped farther away, the life she had created as a pioneer wife ended as much as Rosalie herself had died. Emma wondered what was to come. As it turned out, Frederick had already moved on to what he would do next. And it involved being in the East. More specifically, he needed to return to DC, where he would work out the details for his next great invention.

Chapter 3

Darker Days to Renewed Hope

Mrs. Southworth found herself broken in health, spirits and fortune, a widow in fate though not in fact. . . . It was in the darkest days of the woman's life, that the author's life commenced.[1]

By 1841, Frederick and Emma had returned to Washington.[2] Even after selling his inventory once the tin business had closed, Frederick had little money left, having spent it on passage to return. Since Richmond was only five or six months old when they returned, Emma had little hope that she could secure employment. Nor did Emma have hope that Susanna and Joshua Henshaw would help them. They had advised Emma against marrying a man like Frederick, who had no sustainable income. Additionally, the Henshaws had moved out of Dorothy's house on New Jersey Avenue to a house closer to the Western Academy where Joshua was the principal and Susanna taught in the girls' department. Along with working full-time jobs, Joshua and Susanna had added to their own family with five-year-old Frances, three-year-old Edith, and newborn Henry Clay.[3] They wouldn't be able to take in Emma, Frederick, and baby Richmond even if they wanted.

Emma had one hope left—her grandmother, "whose unvarying kindness was the greatest earthly blessing" Emma had ever known. Of course Dorothy would help.[4] Adding three more mouths to feed could not have been easy for the seventy-five-year-old matriarch. Living with Dorothy was one of the slaves she had inherited forty years earlier,

Leonard Taylor Sr.; his wife Cassy; Amanda (Mandy), who was around eight years old; and Leonard Jr., who was seven. Cassy and Leonard Sr. also had another daughter, Caroline, who was sent to live with Susanna and Joshua Henshaw. Uncle Biggs, the father figure in Emma's childhood, had died.[5] Even though Leonard and Cassy worked at jobs outside the home to bring in a source of income, there would have been precious little to spare. Nevertheless, Frederick, Emma, and Richmond moved in with Dorothy and the Taylor family.

Whether Frederick was employed is unknown, but he was busily working on his new invention—an improved lard lamp. In the nineteenth century, people used their fireplace, candles, and oil lamps to light their homes after dark, but fireplaces offered a limited light source; the wax in candles burned quickly; and whale and vegetable oils were expensive, smelly, and smoky. Frederick experimented with lard and other types of oils to use in his improved lamp, which he patented on July 2, 1842. His lamp was an immediate success, and more than thirty newspapers in Philadelphia, New York, Hartford, Baltimore, and Boston advertised where customers could buy it. By December 1842, the Annual Fair of the American Institute awarded Frederick a diploma for the best lamp for burning lard or common oils.[6] Frederick had achieved a stunning success with his new invention. For a while at least, he could provide for the family and revel in his accomplishments as an inventor.

Frederick's success was short lived, as other lamp makers used his idea to market lamps of their own. By 1843, only around ten newspapers were still running advertisements for Frederick's original lamp, mostly in Washington, DC. Several stores noted that customers should "be careful to call for Southworth Pat. as the market is filled with imitations." Because of the competitive market, by 1846, stores were no longer advertising it. Seeing profits dwindle, Frederick worked on his next invention. A seasoned traveler aboard steamboats along the Ohio and Mississippi Rivers, Frederick noticed that the major obstacles for the steamers were tree limbs and other debris that snagged paddles and stern wheels, causing catastrophic accidents and delays. In December 1843, Frederick petitioned Congress to look at his plans to construct new snag boats that could come up alongside and free the large paddle wheels of obstructions.

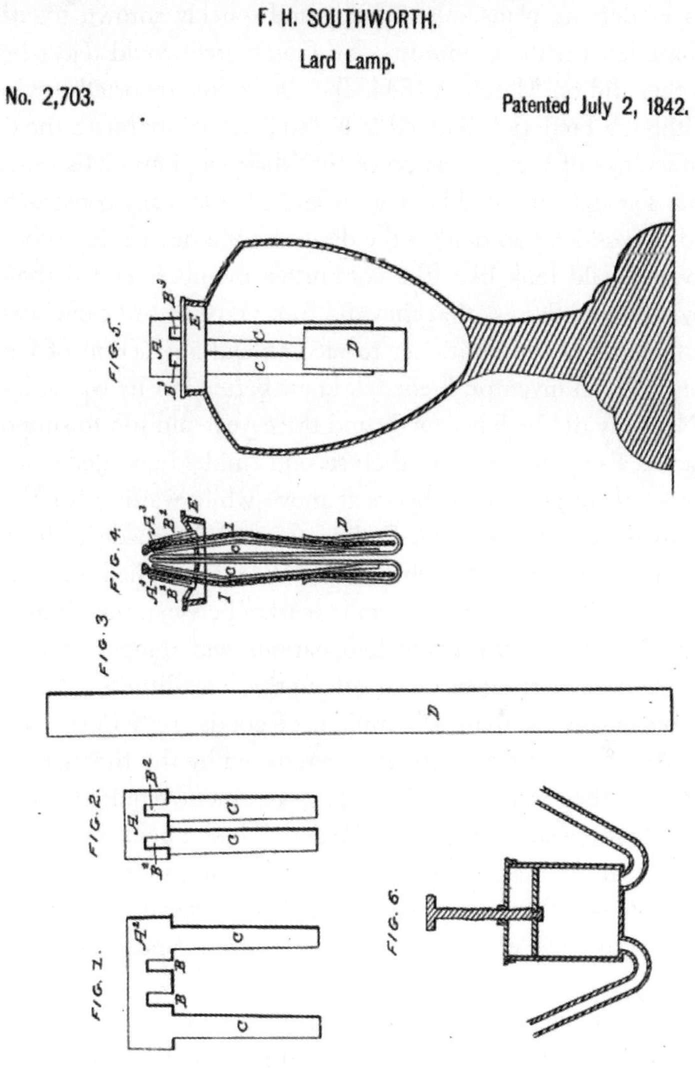

Frederick Southworth Lard Lamp, patent no. 2,703 (July 2, 1842). (*United States Patent Office*)

He used St. Louis as his hometown, possibly thinking it lent credibility to his expertise at building such boats, since the city lay at the crossroads of two major river thoroughfares.[7]

As Frederick's plans were shoddy and quickly thrown together, he must have known the Committee on Commerce would reject his plan, which they did on March 7, 1844. The committee reported to Congress that, although Frederick claimed to be "well acquainted with the dangers and difficulties of the navigation of the Mississippi and Missouri rivers" and that a snag boat could be "readily and economically constructed and applied," Frederick had neither the designs nor a description of what the snag boat would look like. The committee members ended their findings by telling Congress that they did "not perceive sufficient reasons in the statements of the petitioner to recommend any action of Congress thereon."[8] As an inventor, Frederick knew better, but he was a desperate man. Not only did he have a wife and three-year-old son to support, but Emma was also pregnant with their second child. He needed a new plan.

Frederick implemented his next move while waiting for the committee to release its decision. Feeling trapped, he made a drastic and life-changing decision. On February 26, 1844, he applied for a passport. Frederick had learned about the trade market between the United States and Brazil. Trade between the two nations had ramped up, with the United States exporting products amounting to a little over $5 million and importing more than $11 million of goods from Brazil, and even though the United States' products were taxed by the Brazilian government before they were sold, the U.S. government required no taxation of products received from Brazil.[9] Frederick had a bent toward building machines that increased production and efficiency, so it stands to reason that he believed Brazil might be a place to discover a new source of energy that could be economically imported from Brazil into the United States.

As he formulated this plan, he and Emma were forced to leave Dorothy's house. "Mr. Henshaw had broken up the only home I had left—my dear grandmother's home and I with my babies was thrown out," Emma later recalled. "It was *then* that Mr. S. finally abandoned us and went to Brazil. *Grandmother had supported us until* her home was broken up and S. had no mind for supporting wife or children." While written in a hyperbolic style, as Emma often did, she revealed several important facts. They were living with Dorothy until sometime in 1844. Considering that

Frederick and Emma had lived with her since their return from Wisconsin and that Dorothy was seventy-eight years old and in failing health, Henshaw's request for them to move out seems reasonable. Emma also emphasized the word *then*, indicating that Frederick was living with them until this point. Before departing, Frederick moved Emma (now eight months pregnant) and Richmond to a rented room at 13th and C Streets SW, still in relatively close proximity to Emma's parents and Dorothy.[10]

Frederick soon left for Portsmouth, Virginia, where he awaited passage aboard the USS *Pioneer*. Frederick had obviously been given some type of assistance from Emma's stepfather Joshua Henshaw, whose relative David Henshaw was secretary of the navy. Additionally, Joshua had at one time been the personal secretary of Daniel Webster, who had just left his post as secretary of state. On March 26, 1844, Frederick sent a letter to Commander T. D. Shaw of the *Pioneer*, informing Shaw that the secretary of state had granted Frederick passage aboard the navy ship to Rio de Janeiro. He further petitioned Captain Shaw for help with a problem he had encountered with the director of the mess, a Mr. Semour, to whom Frederick had paid $20 for his share of the food during the passage. Apparently, Semour had pocketed the money; Frederick explained that he had no more money for food and asked Shaw to draw that sum out of Semour's salary. The matter was settled, and Frederick departed aboard the *Pioneer* on April 8, 1844.[11] No more was heard from Mr. Southworth for a very long time.

Despite Frederick leaving a very pregnant Emma alone with their three-year-old son Richmond, the parting seems to have been agreed on, as she expected communication from him about his success and possibly joining him in Brazil.[12] Hoping for a letter, she walked to the post office every day for weeks and came home sadly disappointed. Then, on May 7, Emma gave birth to a daughter, Charlotte Emma, nicknamed Lottie, and her birth was a bright spot in an otherwise dismal and depressing time. Emma described Lottie as

> [a] little angel from the heart of the Heavenly Father to heal and comfort my own broken heart! In those sad days . . . I would hear Mandy

> say so tenderly to you, "Here's Ayah!," and as I dropped into a chair she would put you in my arms and I would press you close to my breast, close to my aching heart and you seemed like a balm that drew out all the pain.[13]

Emma's servant Mandy became a crucial caregiver for Emma and her children. Even though Dorothy could no longer care for herself, she supported Emma by sending Mandy to help. "Mandy" was Amanda Taylor, one of the slave children born in Dorothy's home. Emma and her sister Charlotte had known Mandy from an infant and did not think of her as a slave. Emma's letters and biographical accounts indicate a tender (if not familial) relationship with Mandy, who lived with Emma for many years.

After Lottie's birth, Emma became desperate to find work, and she depended on Mandy to help her with the children as she searched. "I had only little baby fingers wandering over my bosom and I so starved that I had not milk enough," Emma bleakly wrote. "There was my dear Mandy—my little 12 year old colored nurse who used to go into the woods at night and gather trash to make me a poor fire . . . I had not a shoe at my foot except an old pair of India rubbers . . . no cradle for my baby, no rocking chair to rock her."[14] Emma spent months looking for a job and was grateful when Rev. William Matthews, a member of the school board, helped her secure a teaching position in the newly formed public schools.[15] In September 1844, she worked as an assistant teacher in the Fourth District of Washington under Principal Henry Hardy, who would become one of Emma's most intimate friends. Located on Sixth Street South near Virginia Avenue, the school "was a large, airy, and commodious building" that taught both male and female students.[16]

Despite helpful friends, Emma felt abandoned and alone. Sometime before 1840, her sister Charlotte had moved to Natchez, Mississippi, to live with their uncle J. B. Nevitte on his plantation, Clermont Hall. Then, on February 10, 1845, Dorothy died. "I—alas—in my trouble had no one. My own dear, dear, dear friend—my grandmother had been ruthlessly taken away from me," wrote Emma. Susanna and Henshaw "were sufficiently occupied in the care of their school, and of their young and growing family."[17] Emma later wrote about her loneliness and grief in *The Lady of the Isle; or, The Island Princess*:

> The heart thus cut off from the love which is its life, does not find the peace of death but the dull anguish of the living tomb—it cannot die, but continues to throb, to yearn and to suffer. Thus the TEST is not in the fierce struggle with temptation and the keen pangs of sacrifice, but in the terrible reaction; in the dull gnawing pain of all the after-time; in the aching sense of bereavement, loneliness and utter desolation; in the long succession of dreary, weary days that dawn without hope, and decline without comfort—each an added link to the heavy chain of hapless years, that drag the spirit to the dust; years of slow heart-wasting; years of death in life![18]

The grief deepened as the days and weeks of waiting for word from Frederick turned into years. She knew not whether he had abandoned her or died.

The thought of being abandoned invoked a sense of shame in Emma—a shame heightened by none other than her cherished dead father. She had kept his letter close. In her youth, she challenged his and Henshaw's advice, but now, with two children to support alone, her father's words stung bitterly. "Let me entreat you to cherish and preserve the affection of your husband as the greatest gift of heaven and always hold in mind that to lose his love will be the greatest loss you can sustain on earth," Charles warned from beyond the grave. "Look around you at those who have lost the affection of their husbands. Are they happy? Are they respected? No! No! They are lost to themselves—they are lost to society."[19] She had returned to reread his message time and again, even later transcribing the handwritten letter into type.

Not only was her personal shame of being abandoned a great load for Emma to carry, but her father was not wrong. Society would also judge her. Her fear of being labeled an "abandoned woman" remained for the rest of her life. When her granddaughter Rose's husband left her in 1895, Emma warned Lottie, "Do not mention this separation in any of your letters to your other correspondence in Washington! Write of it to none outside of this house . . . best that the matter should not be spoken of or written about." The common assumption was that if the husband abandoned the wife, she must have mistreated him. A woman had much better prospects economically and for remarriage if she were widowed. Because Emma didn't know whether Frederick was dead or alive, she constructed an image of herself as "a widow in fate though not in fact."[20] Emma used the possibility that she was a widow to her advantage to get a teaching job.

Working as a teacher helped secure her position as a respectable woman, but the job was fraught with difficulties. As more students took advantage of public schools, spacious rooms that were designed for up to eighty pupils became overcrowded with twice that many. Student seats were crude and simple, composed of three planed boards for the desk with a narrower, slanted board for the seat. The slanted seat created an uncomfortable problem for students, who were forced downward into the desk, which caused them to either slump forward or lean backward onto the desk behind them. Teachers had to constantly tell students to sit up straight in order to reduce physical ailments with their spines and lungs. In this overcrowded environment, mischievous boys often played practical jokes despite frequent recesses. The rat-infested stable next door added to the problems since the rodents frequently made their way into the schoolrooms and ran across pupils' feet.[21]

Despite difficult circumstances, Emma poured into her work the same kind of courage and enthusiasm she had displayed when she'd ventured into the wild West. She loved her students and gained a reputation as an excellent teacher. Emma used these experiences later in her writing career to demonstrate the importance of having quality teachers. In *The Missing Bride*, the town of St. Mary's begins "an academy for young ladies" to provide a curriculum similar to the one they have for young men. Community leaders recommend Marian, who's well respected for her good deeds. She is successful, and the school grows so fast that she has to hire assistants and, like Emma herself, is promoted to principal. Marian explains the importance of providing a good education in that "the children of this generation will be the law-givers of the next."[22] Even though Emma's female characters are limited to a profession that restricts the amount of financial freedom they can attain, Emma showed how they could contribute in creating a better future.

Still, earning a living and taking care of domestic duties regularly overwhelmed Emma. When Lottie contracted whooping cough, Emma continued to work. "I had to get money to buy our food and clothes and fuel and to pay our rent. And so I had to leave my poor sick child every day," she lamented. "I used to cry . . . when I had to leave her and she would hold out her little arms and beg me not to go." Emma's salary in those early days was also abysmal. Since there were no dedicated funds set aside for assistant teachers, her salary was often negligible—if she received payment at all. Compounding the problem, female teachers were paid anywhere from one-half to three-fourths less than their male counterparts. Emma later addressed the inequality in teacher pay in *Fair Play* when Emma's heroine Britomarte explains how the wage disparity existed even when the woman had to provide for a family and the man did not.[23]

After two and a half years working as an assistant teacher, Emma decided something had to change. Christmas Eve in 1846 was a depressing and discouraging time. Her children had been put to bed, and Mandy had gone to a prayer meeting at church. As Emma sat by her fireplace, she thought about one of the old stories she had heard as a child and wondered whether she could write a story that she could sell. "It was in the darkest days of my *woman's life*, that my *author's life* commenced," Emma wrote, adding that "up to this time the latent powers as a writer had not begun to be developed."[24] Emma reexamined lessons she had learned from her parents and grandmother and reimagined a life in which she would not be subservient to men. Emma vowed to become something more than an underpaid and overworked school mistress. She would become a writer.

The story that came out of Emma's pen that night was called "August Vacations, or Flittings to the Country: A Tale of Real Life," with themes of forbidden love, social class disparity, and hope born out of a tragic ending. Emma sent it to the Baltimore *Saturday Visiter*, which had published several works by Edgar Allan Poe. The editor and proprietor of the *Visiter*, Dr. Joseph Evans Snodgrass, was an outspoken abolitionist who was raised, much like Emma, in a slave-owning family. Considering the public position Snodgrass had taken on abolition, Emma knew she was taking a side when she chose the *Visiter*. Submitting her story to an abolitionist paper was a courageous act on Emma's part, even though she used the pseudonym "A Lady of Washington." It ran in the *Visiter* from March 13 to April 3, 1847. Emma followed with other stories, making one stipulation—Snodgrass could not publish the story using her name; instead, she preferred to use the initial *E* or at most "Emma."[25] Anonymity was Emma's safest option to publish in the *Visiter* since she could support the abolitionist cause while minimizing familial alienation. At the heart of the danger was Mandy, who was still a slave on loan to Emma. Emma's sister Charlotte had inherited Mandy on Dorothy's death, so if Charlotte had wanted or if Susanna insisted, Mandy could have been taken from Emma's home, and she would have been powerless to stop it. Emma was desperately poor and completely dependent on Mandy to care for Lottie and Richmond when she was teaching.

Since Emma received no payment for her story, her writing career might have ended there. Snodgrass observed that Emma "had a painful lack of confidence in her own ability." He sent her an encouraging note to keep writing. "This little note was an epoch in my life," Emma wrote. "Under Divine Providence it decided my vocation. By inspiring hope, it gave me courage." She said if her first story had been rejected, she "should never have had the heart to write another one—so broken in spirit, so despairing of life was she at this time." As a reminder of this important event, Emma published a short story every Christmas season, even after she had made the transition to serialized novels later in her career.[26]

After the final installment of "August Vacations," Dr. Gamaliel Bailey bought the *Visiter*, changing its name to the *National Era* and its location to DC. Bailey pledged to keep the focus of the paper on the slavery question. Pro-slavery leaders in nearby Georgetown considered taking legislative action against the periodical, arguing that it would "arouse the worst feelings" and "lead to a breach of the peace." The famous poet John Greenleaf Whittier joined Bailey as coeditor, and the two were described as "bold men" for leading the abolitionist movement through the *Era*. Although it was a controversial publication, its location was convenient for Emma. Rather than sending her submissions all the way to Baltimore, the new office was less than a mile from both her home and her school in a two-story brick house on 7th Street NW. Over the main door was a sixteen-inch square sign in gold letters that read *NATIONAL ERA*. The publishing agent's office was on the first floor, where the editorial staff entered subscribers' names and wrapped and mailed out issues. In the rear of the building was the press, where the Blanchard brothers, two free colored men, cranked out the pages of the newspaper.[27]

Emma had already written her second short story, "The Better Way; or, The Wife's Victory," before the paper changed ownership, but, after reviewing her story, Snodgrass passed it onto Bailey and strongly recommended that he publish it. Bailey agreed, and it appeared in the *Era* between August 19 and August 26, 1847. Unfortunately for Emma, communication about her strong desire to publish anonymously was either lost in the shuffle or completely ignored by Bailey, and the story appeared with her full name: Mrs. Emma D.E.N. Southworth. Her worst fears were realized, and she "fell out of favor with friends and neighbors" for writing in an abolitionist newspaper.[28] Although this second story also avoided the issue of slavery, Emma tackled another controversial subject known as the Woman Question, which addressed a wide variety of issues surrounding women's moral, religious, and social obligations. In "The Better Way," Emma questioned the extent to which a wife should submit to her husband's will, especially when he was unjust, cruel, and unfair.

The unexpected revelation of Emma's identity might explain why this story was quickly followed by a sequel called "The Wife's Mistake," published from September 16 to September 23, 1847. The central figures are two sisters, Mary and Kate, who argue about a wife's role in marriage. Mary holds a traditional view that a woman should obey her husband even when he wants to send her daughter Sylvia away to be raised by a grandmother. She doesn't speak up for what she wants, and if not for Kate stepping in, she would have lost her daughter. Meanwhile, Kate has a strong will and always expects to get her way. She doesn't see that her husband has become so unhappy, he begins drinking excessively. Kate even puts her own well-being over that of her son, which leads to his illness. The husband sails away and is gone for three years; left alone,

Kate finally realizes her selfishness and asks for his forgiveness when he returns.[29] The shift in Emma's perspective about a wife's duty to her husband seemed to be spurred by a desire to soothe her loved ones' ruffled feathers as she challenged marital norms and the status quo.

The timing of these two stories also coincided with a seemingly unrelated event: the return of Henry A. Wise, the U.S. minister to Brazil. Wise and his family had left New York just a month after Frederick had sailed for Rio de Janeiro. Three years had passed, which was interestingly the same amount of time that Kate's husband in Emma's story had been gone. Emma told Wise that she hadn't heard from Frederick "since your return from Rio de Janeiro."[30] The implication seems obvious—she had heard either from or about Frederick in those years before Wise returned in 1847. If Emma had been expecting Frederick to come home, the stories she wrote about women's role in marriage seem to mirror her own feelings. She did not favor Mary's decision to be wholly submissive to her husband, but neither did she support Kate's wild and neglectful ways. Instead, when examining these two stories together, Emma favored and may have hoped for an egalitarian reunion with Frederick—one in which they would mutually decide the best interests of their marriage and family. Frederick didn't return, however, and several more years would pass before Emma heard about him again.

Emma kept teaching and writing. Her third short story, "The Thunderbolt to the Hearth," was published in the *Era* from October 14 to October 21, 1847, with a rather benign theme: sometimes bad things happen to good people. Her avoidance of any controversial subject suggests that she had no intention of alienating more family and friends. Additionally, though Emma was flattered that her work was being published, she was still not being paid for it. "Writing for 'glory' alone was much too rich and costly for so poor a young mother to indulge in," Emma pondered.[31] So she stopped writing, spent her evenings repairing her children's clothing, and desperately questioned what was to become of herself and her family. She was exhausted from teaching, writing, and taking care of her home; her teacher's salary had not been paid. Wintertime was upon them—it was another dark and depressing time for Emma.

Two months had passed since she had stopped submitting stories to the *Era*. Then, one day after school ended, Emma waited for Mandy to bring her an umbrella as snow and sleet poured from the darkened skies. Suddenly a carriage appeared at the school doors, and in walked the editor and proprietor of the *Era* himself—Gamaliel Bailey. He explained that his coeditor John Greenleaf Whittier, noticing the absence of Emma's stories, had asked whether she was being paid for her work. He told Emma that readers had missed her stories, and he asked whether she would continue writing for the paper, but not before putting money in her hands for all her stories he had previously published. Emma later told her daughter, "Oh Lottie, if the Lord had not given me the gift of writing what would have become of me or you? Worse than widowed as I was—worse than fatherless as you were?"[32] Relieved that she could now buy clothing that her children desperately needed, she immediately began writing her next story, "The Temptation."

What Emma thought would be a single run in the *Era* turned into a much longer story published in seven installments from December 30, 1847, to February 10, 1848, for which she was paid $10 per column. The overarching theme in this story is how social class and wealth intertwine to dictate who a woman should marry. The main character Sybil becomes a pawn between her once-wealthy grandmother and her husband, a poor painter named Middleton. Middleton incorrectly assumes Sybil is rich and abandons her when he learns she's poor. Later, believing Middleton has died, she falls in love with Reverend Livingston. When hearing Middleton isn't dead, Livingston asks Sybil to divorce him. Sybil searches the Bible to see what it says about divorce, but, finding no satisfactory answer, she turns down Livingston's marriage proposal and chooses to live out her days alone.[33] The similarities between this story and Emma's own life cannot be overlooked. Through the fictitious Sybil, Emma worked through her own issues of poverty, abandonment, and betrayal. Treading lightly into the subject of divorce, Emma might have been testing how readers would respond—ever fearful of being labeled an abandoned or fallen woman.

Emma next wrote "Neighbors' Prescriptions," which was published in the *Era* on March 2–9, 1848, but this would be her last story for the

Gamaliel Bailey (1857), in *Cosmopolitan* 3 (November 1889–April 1890): 438.

next nine months. The cause for her hiatus was not the return of Frederick but an event that ignited a much greater cause for alarm. On April 15, the schooner *Pearl* left Washington City with seventy-seven slaves on board who were hoping to escape to New Jersey, a free state. Two days later, however, the schooner was captured, the slaves returned to their owners, and three white men arrested—captains Daniel Drayton and Edward Sayres and a cook, Chester English. The attempted escape was the largest slave uprising in the nation, and pro-slavery advocates were alarmed. In an effort to send a message to other slaves in Washington and Maryland, the owners quickly sold all escapees to various traders who took these slaves to the Deep South, thereby separating them from family and friends. Still, fear of future uprisings grew among the anti-abolitionists, and riots broke out in the city.[34]

The primary target for the mob was Gamaliel Bailey and the *Era*, as the paper was funded in part by Lewis Tappan's group, the American and Foreign Anti-Slavery Society. Even though Drayton, Sayres, and English were jailed, fear escalated when abolition supporter Joshua R. Giddings, a member of the U.S. House of Representatives from Ohio, proposed a resolution to "give aid and comfort" to the accused men. A mob gathered in front of the *Era* office building on Tuesday, April 18, and an estimated one thousand rioters threatened to lynch Bailey and hurled rocks and brickbats, knocking out several windows. Before dispersing for the evening, they told Bailey that he had until 10:00 a.m. the next day to remove his printing press from the city or they would destroy it.[35] Because Emma lived such a short distance from the *Era* office, she must have been terrified for herself and her children. It was no secret that she was a writer for the paper, and if protestors knew where the *Era* was, they likely could find out where she lived, too.

Bailey was concerned for his children's safety as well, and as tensions escalated on Wednesday, he sent family out of the city. Guards and police placed themselves between the gathering crowd and the *Era* building. Leading citizens of Washington urged Bailey to "restore peace to the city and secure his own safety" by a promise to discontinue the *Era* and hand over his press to the rioters. Bailey denied knowing about the escape plan aboard the *Pearl* until after its capture, and he insisted he had a right as a law-abiding citizen to print his paper. The deadline for him to remove his press passed, and the crowds once again dispersed for the day. They returned on Thursday, and concerned officials told President James K. Polk that they feared rioters would do harm to Bailey and the building. At least one hundred guards were sent to protect the *Era*, and by that evening, the crowd dispersed for the final time.[36]

Even though the mob had been quelled for the time being, tensions continued on the streets and in Congress. In June, a grand jury indicted Drayton, Sayres, and English on thirty-six counts for stealing slaves and seventy-four counts for transporting them for a total of 330 indictments. The trial concluded at the end of August. English was acquitted of all charges. Drayton was convicted of stealing and transporting slaves, fined $150 for each slave, and sentenced to twenty years' imprisonment. Sayres was acquitted of stealing any slaves but was convicted of transporting seventy-four slaves and fined $150.[37] The *Era* covered the proceedings, but by the time the trial concluded, tensions over the *Pearl* incident had subsided. Yet, given the mob mentality toward the *Era* that had existed just months earlier, Emma would have been understandably wary about writing for Bailey's paper.

Emma's teaching career had become more stable in terms of position and salary. As the public school system grew, more schools, principals, and teachers were needed. On November 1, 1848, Congress passed the Primary School Act, which increased the number of schools from four to fourteen in Washington. In January 1849, Emma became the principal of one of these new schools. Because there were not enough schools built to accommodate the increase in student population, principals frequently gave up part of their homes. Similarly, Emma used the two larger rooms on the first floor of her home at the southeast corner of Thirteenth and C Streets SW, where she opened Primary School No. 10 in the Seventh Ward. She was both principal and teacher to eighty boys and girls. Although the location was more convenient and her salary more consistent, she was still paid only $250 a year.[38] This income kept her family from starvation, but it was barely enough to pay essential bills. The increased responsibility of her new position combined with a substandard wage helped Emma decide to continue writing, but these facts do not explain why she resumed writing for the *Era*. She had received praise for her stories, not only from Snodgrass, Bailey, and Whittier but also from the reading public. She could have chosen to write for other, less controversial publications.

It's easy to stand on principles when you have nothing to lose. Emma stood on principles when she had *everything* to lose. She risked having

Mandy taken away from her—Mandy, who had become so crucial in caring for her children and her home. She risked losing the teaching position she had just been given—the one constant source of money that kept her family from homelessness and starvation. Nevertheless, when Bailey made another trip to see her about writing a story for the new year "as a special feature," Emma heartily agreed. They discussed a variety of possible topics, from the psychological and philosophical to the practical, finally settling on the subject of moral retribution. She centered the tale on the trials and suffering of her own life. "I commenced, and somehow or other, my head and heart were teeming with thought and emotion, and the idea that had at first but glimmered faintly upon my perceptions, blazed into a perfect glory of light," Emma wrote.[39] In this new story, she broached the topic of freeing slaves through her character Hester Grey and bravely stepped into an entirely new world for herself. Most assuredly while writing her next work, *Retribution*, she continued to alienate those closest to her—family, friends, and school patrons.

As Emma firmly sided with abolition, she made new friendships through her work at the *Era*. Bailey and his wife Margaret hosted parties at their home on E Street, near Sixth Street, and later in their more spacious house on C Street. Here, Emma met abolition supporters from the Senate and House as well as other contributors to the paper. Emma reconnected with friends from her days in Cincinnati, such as Harriet Beecher Stowe and Alice and Phoebe Cary. She also developed friendships with other female writers, including Grace Greenwood and Gail Hamilton. During one of these parties in 1849, Emma met the "illustrious poet" and the *Era*'s corresponding editor, John Greenleaf Whittier. Emma remembered him as "a tall, muscular, dark-complexioned man with short black hair and whiskers framing a strong, fine face." Whittier made a profound impression on the new and obscure young writer. He "received me with distinction as if I had been somebody," Emma recalled. There were many at Bailey's house who would one day be leaders of the nation and who supported the cause of ending slavery. "But we thought it would take a long time," Emma wrote, "that the abolition of slavery would be gradually and peacefully effected by moral persuasion, not suddenly and violently by war and revolution!"[40]

John Greenleaf Whittier (1842), in *Cosmopolitan* 3 (November 1889–April 1890): 441.

A few weeks later, Emma saw Whittier again in DC, on his way back to his home in the North. He told Emma his perceptions of the slave owners he encountered:

> He had seen slavery at its home, and he saw two sides of it—not the dark and fair sides, for there could be no fair side to so black an institution—but the dark and the less dark; instances where the slaves were treated as affectionately as children; instances where they were treated more cruelly than brutes. He found that even in the Slave States where a man was a good son, brother, husband, father, and neighbor, he was also a good master, even beloved by his slaves as he was by his family. And that a man who was a bad son, brother, husband, father, and neighbor, was also a very bad master, hated and feared by his slaves. And between these extremes there was every grade of character. But the very best and most tender and considerate master with the most faithful and devoted servants was no apology for the hideous moral monstrosity of the slave system.[41]

With the influences of Whittier and Bailey at the *Era* combined with her own personal life experiences, Emma plunged headlong into what would become her first full-length serialized book, *Retribution*. She still had trials ahead. The year 1849 was turning out much better than the previous five years, in which starvation was constantly at her door, but she had her name firmly associated with an abolitionist newspaper, alienating the friends and family she still loved. She was also both writing and teaching full time, all while taking care of her children and home. Something would have to give.

Chapter 4

After the Storm Comes a Sun Burst

Friends crowded around me—offers for contributions poured in upon me. And I, who six months before had been poor, ill, forsaken, slandered, killed by sorrow, privation, toil, and friendliness, found myself born as it were into a new life; found independence, sympathy, friendship, and honour, and an occupation in which I could delight. All this came very suddenly, as after a terrible storm, a sun burst.[1]

Emma intended for *Retribution* to run in three installments for the *Era*, but she kept envisioning new characters and story lines. "My story grew into a volume. Every week I would supply a portion to the paper, until weeks grew into months, and months into quarters, before it was finished." Emma wrote to John Greenleaf Whittier for direction: "I can stop the story at once, but I cannot finish it, and, as you know, there is a vast difference between stopping a story and finishing it." Whittier responded, "Go on with it, by all means. My Quaker constituents complain that there is too much carnal affection in it, but I observe that they continue to buy the papers." Being paid $10 per column doubled Emma's teaching salary, and she submitted new chapters each week, writing under the most trying circumstances. She wrote at her desk during the schoolchildren's recess—held indoors, as there was no yard in which they could play. As she wrote, the rowdy scholars played, inevitably knocking over chairs and leaping over desks. After school and household duties, Emma continued writing, often late into the night. She wrote even during those hours devoted to church. "The best scene in 'Retribution,'" Emma recalled, "was composed at a Baptist revival in the midst of a shouting congregation."[2] Emma was determined to finish *Retribution*, but working long hours came at a huge cost.

Emma's son, Richmond, was seven years old and one of the eighty children she taught. Early in 1849, he "fell dangerously ill" and was confined to bed. "He would suffer no one to move him but myself," Emma lamented. "In fact no one else *could* do so without putting him in pain." Richmond's illness was quite serious. Common childhood diseases of the time were diphtheria, pneumonia, and scarlet fever, and as vaccines were still another century away, these illnesses were life threatening. Given Richmond's symptoms, the most likely culprit was scarlet fever, which was highly contagious, affected children between the ages of four to eight, and was the leading cause of death among infectious childhood diseases. Caused by bacteria, scarlet fever sufferers developed a red rash over their bodies and tongues and were prone to severe sore throat, high fever, chills, vomiting, and headache. One Washington editor noted there had been a "prevalence and virulence of this fever in our neighborhood during the past few months." He suggested following the advice of the popular Pittsburgh editor Jane Swisshelm, who owned the *Saturday Visiter*. "Its cure depends so much on constant care and attention to the little things—keeping the mind easy and the body clean," Swisshelm advised. "We feel quite certain that more than half of the children who die of this disease, fall victims to want of skill or energy in nursing."[3] Under Emma's constant care, Richmond would not become one of these victims.

Taking care of Richmond increased Emma's already heavy load, eventually leading to her own health failing. "It was too much for me. It was too much for any human being," she admitted. "My health broke down. I was attacked with frequent hemorrhage of the lungs." The cause of Emma's illness was tuberculosis, a common disease for the urban poor between the ages of fifteen and forty-four. The bacterial infection affected the lungs with a recurring chronic cough, resulting in a bloody mucus, fever, night sweats, and weight loss. Because of the weight loss, tuberculosis was commonly called consumption. While not particularly contagious, it spread in overcrowded cities in which living conditions were often unclean. Some who contracted the bacteria showed no symptoms, sometimes for years, but once symptoms developed, around half of those with the disease died. For those who recovered, symptoms frequently developed again. Like scarlet fever, without antibiotics to treat the disease, doctors recommended fresh air, exercise, and rest. According to a health report from July 1849, there were more consumption cases listed than any other illness. Emma's sister Charlotte also suffered from tuberculosis for most of her adult life. "Every member of my family," Emma wrote, "has died of lung trouble, and it has only been by taking constant care that I have warded off consumption."[4] Taking care of herself, however, had to wait until she finished the story.

Retribution ran through fifteen installments before Emma completed it on April 12, 1849. It was the most challenging period of her life. Whittier regularly rejected entire pages of a submission. Little did he know they had been written "amid grief, and pain, and toil." Emma felt that, during those six months, everyone suffered. Richmond was in constant pain and crying out for her. The parents of her schoolchildren grew dissatisfied with her work and often hurled insults at her. Her submissions to the *Era* constantly needed revisions. By June, she finally rested. Richmond recovered. Her own health improved.[5] Yet she could not stop for long, as she was the family's breadwinner.

Whittier encouraged her to submit *Retribution* to Harper & Brothers, a leading book publisher in America that influenced the growth of the popular market. Even though Emma was a first-time author, she sent her novel to them. Harper liked it enough to hand it off to Henry J. Raymond, who had established himself as a knowledgeable journalist and editor. He liked Emma's book but advised her to revise one of the chapters. Emma, however, believed the scene was crucial to the overall message about morality and refused to change it.[6]

The chapter in question was "The Grasp of the Destroyer," in which the main character and femme fatale Juliette Summers has overplayed her hand in an attempt to win the affections of Colonel Dent, a rich senator who's married to her best friend Hester Gray. Juliette plans to marry Dent after her friend Hester, who unknowingly suffers from consumption, dies from her disease, but her flirtatious ways rile Dent up into uncontrolled lust. In the questionable scene, the two are alone, and Dent tells Juliette, "If I were about to die this moment, Juliette, I should kill you, lest anyone else should have you." In an effort to escape his untowardly advancements, Juliette bites his hand "to the bone," but rather than having the desired effect, Dent responds, "Bite it again, Juliette. I like it!" Fearing that Dent is actually going to have his way with her, Juliette succumbs to tears, and her weeping finally breaks the spell she has put on Dent.[7]

When Raymond read this passage, he remarked that he "never was in a passion in his life" and that he couldn't understand "how a beautiful and fascinating woman could be moved to *bite*—even in self-defence."[8] But Emma understood that if a woman were put in such a precarious position in which rape (an unmentionable word at the time) was eminent, she would bite or fight in order to escape. Emma saw the scene as one that was imperative to her overall message about moral retribution—women were responsible for their behavior, and Juliette's betrayal and seduction led to her own demise. Emma determinedly refused to omit the passage, demonstrating the courage and tenacity she had previously exhibited. The passage remained.

Betrayal and appropriate moral behavior weren't the only themes in *Retribution*. In one subplot, Emma finally addressed the moral and legal issues surrounding slavery. When Dent becomes guardian to the wealthy and gullible orphan Hester Gray, he convinces her to buy a farm that uses slave labor. Knowing Hester's strong objections to slavery, Dent lies, promising to free and then pay wages to the farm laborers. He delays freeing them by telling Hester that she must wait to take action until she turns twenty-one and a legal adult. Before she reaches that age, she marries Dent and discovers she's dying from consumption. In a desperate attempt to free the slaves, she signs the necessary paperwork just moments before she turns twenty-one and dies. After the funeral, Dent convinces her lawyer that the papers are invalid, insisting that they be destroyed. All along, Dent had married Hester in order to legally control her property, which he uses to increase his own wealth through slave labor. Through Dent's power and authority over Hester, Emma showed the problems within the current laws that kept even well-intentioned slave owners from manumitting slaves.

Emma further demonstrated ugly truths about a patriarchally controlled slave labor system in the ways it affected female slaves. After Hester and Dent marry, she's dismayed when he buys Minny Dozier. Even more horrifying, Dent's purpose for buying the young and beautiful Minny is to have sex with her. Further details of Minny's life reveal that she's of mixed race. Her father was a white sugar planter and her mother a slave. When her mother died, she was raised in her father's house, never realizing that she was his slave. Because of slave laws, a child born from a slave mother was also considered a slave. When her father dies and his estate matters settled, Minny discovers that she and her daughter are both slaves. In order to pay her father's debts, Minny and her daughter are separated and sold to different owners.[9] In this way, Emma highlighted the powerlessness of female slaves over not only their own bodies but also the bodies of their children. Through Minny's character, Emma showed the horrors slave women faced as white men raped them and sold their own children.

This problem is one that Emma experienced firsthand within her own slave-holding family, as the Taylor family were described as "copper-colored mulattos," meaning white owners had likely taken advantage of their female slaves. Oddly, Emma dedicated this novel to her mother "as an expression of respect and affection."[10] Coming from a slave-owning family, Emma had to wonder how Susanna would respond to the immorality of slavery she highlighted in the novel. As a slave owner in 1849, Susanna objected to Emma's abolitionist beliefs. Perhaps, through the maternal bond, Emma hoped to persuade Susanna that she needed to free the Taylor family—including Mandy. Even though Emma never referred to Mandy as a slave, she was one—a fact that troubled Emma greatly.

The extent to which Emma influenced Susanna is unknown, but readers and critics alike heartily approved of the novel, which was an instant success. By September 1849, as many as three bookshops advertised it in one newspaper alone. Also endorsing *Retribution*, Whittier claimed, "Mrs. Southworth writes with a good deal of power. Some of her delineations are equal to those of 'Jane Eyre' or Miss Bremer. . . . The production is one of unusual vigor; and no one can overlook the moral lesson conveyed by it." Editors of the *Daily Union* remarked that, while they had not yet read it, their readers of "some taste" stated that "this tale is among the most interesting they have ever read." Actress turned poet Harriet Marion Stephens wrote, "The time is not far distant when the name of Emma D.N. Southworth will rank among the first, as she is already the best of American novelists." Stephens also accurately predicted, "Mrs. Southworth is not always beyond the reach of criticism, as some of our censure-loving critics have already discovered."[11]

As Stephens predicted, the harshest critics found Emma's book. One unnamed critic dubbed the novel "unpromising" and "weakly mysterious." Equally troubling to him was the author's name "a *nom de plume*, of course—enough to alarm anybody but a romantic school girl. Who could have imagined that a person capable of selecting such a name as 'Emma D.E. Nevitte Southworth,' could write a page worth reading?" He finally gets to a praise of sorts, noting the book as an American work, and even though he felt it was "disfigured by many defects in style" and "by the ungraceful manner" in which Emma handled her plots, "we are clear in the opinion that it is the best work of fiction written in this country for several years, and quite equal to Jane Eyre."[12] The comparison to *Jane Eyre* was an obvious sign that he already knew Emma had received top praise by the well-respected Whittier.

Despite the negative critic, most reviewers gave Emma's first novel praise, and sales were robust enough that she could quit teaching to focus on her writing. Other literary journals approached her to write for them, but she chose the well-known and popular *Saturday Evening Post* located in Philadelphia with Henry Peterson as the editor. The *Post* had been in operation for thirty years, so by submitting to this publication, Emma's stories would reach a larger audience. Her next novel, *The Deserted Wife*, began on August 4, 1849, in the *Post* and ran for seventeen installments.[13] Similar to her earlier stories, she addressed themes such as betrayal and loyalty, but she also tackled the importance of women's physical education as well as taboo societal problems such as domestic violence and mental illness, especially highlighing the impact these issues have on women's well-being. The main plot revolves around two young women who question and search for their appropriate societal roles. Similar to her earlier works, Emma's female characters reflect the ways in which Emma herself struggled to find a balance between submissiveness and independence.

Many similarities exist between Emma's real life and *The Deserted Wife*. In addition to the character Hagar Withers mirroring Emma's own looks and behavior, Hagar's husband Raymond Withers is much like Emma's husband Frederick. Although Emma never accused Frederick of physical or emotional abuse, Raymond abuses Hagar, breaking her once-robust and vital spirit as well as her health. Then, exactly like Frederick, Raymond abandons Hagar and their two young children, which forces Hagar to earn her own living. Once free from the abuse and financial destitution that Raymond has imposed on her, Hagar thrives, becoming both famous and wealthy as an international singer.[14] As Emma worked through these issues in her own life, her message became clear to her female readers. Emma argued that a woman's submissiveness, even in marriage, could lead to abuse. She instead advocated that a wife should maintain her own sense of identity and independence. *Post* subscriptions soared as female readers craved more chapters of *The Deserted Wife*. Naturally, Henry Peterson approved, as it increased the *Post*'s profits—until Emma submitted the chapter called "Magnetism."

Peterson wrote to Emma on September 10, 1849, about the latest chapter, outlining his objections regarding two subplot characters in the story. When Rev. John Withers becomes sexually attracted to the very young Sophie Churchill, he uses his pastoral privileges to visit her alone each evening. Sophie increasingly becomes uncomfortable with Withers and his nightly visitations, but as she tries to thwart his advances, he tells her a story about when he was a child. He had preferred to play with kittens that would "kick, scratch, and bite," and if the kitten became docile and weak, he would "throw it heavily upon the ground, and thereby kill it." Sophie becomes increasingly fearful, and she turns down his marriage proposal, saying, "I cannot give myself to you." He returns with the words "Then I can take you, that's all, Sophie." After Withers forces her into the marriage, he plunges further into complete madness. Peterson considered

THE SATURDAY EVENING POST.

Deacon & Peterson, Publishers. | Two Dollars Per Annum, In Advance.

A FAMILY NEWSPAPER: NEUTRAL IN POLITICS.

DEVOTED TO MORALITY, PURE LITERATURE, FOREIGN AND DOMESTIC NEWS, AGRICULTURE, THE COMMERCIAL INTEREST, SCIENCE, ART AND AMUSEMENT.

VOLUME XXVIII. | PHILADELPHIA, SATURDAY, AUGUST 4, 1849. | WHOLE NO. 1462.

Original Poetry.

Pictures of Life.

A Thrilling Scene.

THE DESERTED WIFE.

AN ORIGINAL NOVELETTE.

In our next number we shall commence a novelette of deep interest, with the above title, by a lady who we think is destined to take a high place among the female authors of America—Mrs. Emma D. E. Southworth, author of a tale called "Retribution," now in process of publication by the Harpers.

Judging from what we have already received of "The Deserted Wife," we shall be surprised if it does not make a sensation equal, to say the least, to that produced by any original story ever published in an American paper.

As the demand for this story, before it has run many weeks, will probably be very great, we would advise all wishing to procure it, to send on their subscriptions as soon as possible—*as there has not been a single instance yet, in which we have been able to supply all the demands for back numbers of our continued stories.*

We shall endeavor, in this case, to print a sufficient extra number of Mrs. Southworth's story, to supply all new subscribers. But we would advise those who wish it, to apply as early as possible, for our rule always is, "first come, first served."

We embrace this opportunity to return thanks to our numerous friends in all sections of the country, and to assure them that we are rapidly approaching, *if we have not already attained*, that position, when we can claim that the Post has, without a single exception, a larger circulation than any other paper, daily or weekly, in the Union.

Saturday Evening Post advertises *The Deserted Wife* (August 4, 1849). (*Internet Archive*)

this plotline something he could not "place on the parlour table of a family," and he felt it "completely spoiled the story up to that point" and asked Emma to omit it.[15] Because no issues of that particular edition have survived, it's uncertain whether Emma took out the offensive chapter for the *Post*, but when Harper & Brothers published *The Deserted Wife* as a book in 1849, the offensive chapter was included.

By the end of Peterson's letter, he must have thought better about what he had asked Emma to do because he closed by stating that he feared he had "spoken in places too earnestly, and with greater freedom than my acquaintance with you warrants." Even though Peterson began the letter by telling Emma he would help her find other houses that would publish her work, he was obviously bluffing. When her stories appeared in the *Post*, subscriptions increased from twelve hundred to an estimated thirty thousand.[16] Peterson might have been offended by her portrayal of the reverend, but her female readers obviously were not, and they were making him a lot of money.

Even though Emma wrote for the *Post*, she had not forgotten about the kind support first shown to her by Gamaliel Bailey and Whittier, and on November 22, she began a new novel called the *Mother-in-Law* for the *National Era* while still finishing *The Deserted Wife* for the *Post*. As if she wasn't busy enough simultaneously keeping plots and subplots going in two novels for two different publications, she wrote a third short story published in November and December called "The Fine Figure" for *Friend of Youth*, a monthly magazine published by Bailey's wife Margaret. Soon bookshops not only were selling *Retribution*, which had been published in book form, but also were carrying copies of the *Post* and the *Era* to sell the serialized chapters of *The Deserted Wife* and *Mother-in-Law* as soon as they came out.[17]

As if she were not busy enough, Emma was already planning to publish *The Deserted Wife* as a book once it finished its serial run in the *Post*. Peterson sent Emma another letter in October with an attached clipping about the print quality of *Retribution* that Harper had published. The book reviewer from *Graham's Magazine* felt *Retribution* was so good that it should have been printed using higher-quality material. Harper, he claimed, printed books in an "uncouth shape in order to reduce their price to twenty-five cents" and that "no man of taste, who has regard for his eyesight, is likely to read pamphlet novels." The critic ended with a plea that *Retribution* be printed "in a form which will enable it to take its

Henry Peterson, *Saturday Evening Post* editor. (*The Literary History of Philadelphia*, 1906, 368)

appropriate place in American literature." Even though Henry's cousin T. B. Peterson owned a publishing company that competed with Harper, Henry promised Emma that he "had no hand" in what the reviewer had written.[18] Obviously, though, Henry was planting a suggestion in Emma's mind that she should carefully consider who her next book publisher should be.

Emma cared about the quality and durability of her published books and realized there was more to consider about book publication than how many copies could be cheaply sold. She considered the well-respected D. Appleton & Company to publish *The Deserted Wife*. Because Emma was an avid reader, she knew about the publisher's reputation. Appleton advertised books that were not only "beautifully printed" and "elegantly bound" but also "illustrated with fine steel engravings . . . in various styles of binding." Showcasing the quality they had to offer, Appleton sent Emma a copy of the newly printed *The Prelude; or, Growth of a Poet's Mind: An Autobiographical Poem* by William Wordsworth with "respects of the publishers" inscribed on the flyleaf. In 1850, Emma chose Appleton to print *The Deserted Wife*, which sold in bookstores for thirty-seven cents, reflecting not only an increased price but also superior printing.[19]

As the profitable year of 1849 came to a close, Emma continued to meet new writers and editors who shared her political and personal views, such as Jane Grey Swisshelm, who owned and edited the *Pittsburgh Saturday Visiter*. Founded in 1847, the weekly newspaper focused on abolition, women's rights, and temperance. In December, Emma was on a trip to Philadelphia, where she might have first met Swisshelm, who asked Emma to write a series of letters about Washington for the *Visiter*. When Swisshelm received her first letter from Emma, however, it wasn't about Washington City at all. Instead, because Emma had just returned from a four-week tour of Philadelphia, her first rather lengthy letter was about her time spent in that city. She wrote about the numerous omnibuses, the city's clean pavements, and their dedication to physical education.

The last half of her letter had one focus—to describe the Pennsylvania Institution for the Education of the Blind. Perhaps because of her own brief childhood illness that had left her temporarily blind, she wrote in great depth about the history of the institution, its blind residents, and teachers. She was fascinated by how well students learned using "raised or embossed letters." Created in 1824 by Frenchman Louis Braille and revised for use in 1837, these raised letters used for instruction of the blind was relatively new. She ended by encouraging readers to support the blind institution by buying goods that were made there, emphasizing that, if supported by citizens and government aid, the blind could become productive members of their cities.[20]

Emma's next letter for the *Visiter* finally addressed what Swisshelm wanted to know: what was happening in the nation's capital during the congressional session of 1850—particularly regarding the slavery question. Emma noted the main topic was "the free-soil question," which centered on whether new states being added to the Union should be free or slave, and, because of this controversy, the "dissolution of the Union" was frequently at the center of citizens' conversations. "Perhaps you at a distance do not participate in the intense excitement felt here in the very whirl of the conflict," Emma wrote. "Many people openly express a wish that the President should 'hang up' a few of the most turbulent leaders on *both sides*, and wonder whether the crime of TREASON is recognized, or what it really *meant*."

Perhaps as a way to quell Pennsylvanians' fears of dissolution, Emma shifted to a detailed description of what it was like to visit President Zachary Taylor. Emma explained that the White House was open to all who wanted to attend Taylor's weekly Friday evening parties. She vividly portrayed what it was like to arrive and wait to be admitted to the reception room where guests could meet the president. Emma described him as a man who greeted his guests "as though he stood at the door of his own country house receiving a neighbor—as though he were not surrounded by all the pride, pomp and circumstance of place, honor and power." Emma let *Visiter* readers know they had a president of whom they could be proud—a president who was much like any "plain old farmer from the western part of Pennsylvania."

After greeting the president, visitors were led into a fourth and final room for the evening—the celebrated "East Room," a "magnificent saloon" that extended the entire depth of the mansion. The East Room was grand indeed with "gorgeous carpet," "costly mirrors reaching from the lofty ceiling to the floor," and "three immense chandeliers lighted with gas." Emma emphasized that this place was the people's house, where visitors could "see the elite of the aristocracy, and the plainest of the industrious classes." She carefully avoided endorsing any particular political party, instead quipping, "I have nothing to do with any parties, except tea-parties."[21] Emma's complimentary portrayal of the way Taylor steered the United States into a more egalitarian society aligned with the novels she wrote in which she condemned snobbery of an elitist wealthy class and the evils that arose from social class disparity.

Even though Swisshelm believed Emma would write more letters for the *Visiter*, her first letter describing Washington was also the last. In the February 23 issue, Swisshelm told readers that Emma's letter had not arrived in time to be printed in that edition. She put an advertisement in the *Era* assuring subscribers that she had secured Mrs. Southworth as a regular contributor. On March 9, however, Swisshelm conceded there would be no more letters, citing Southworth's illness as a cause. "We are uneasy about her," Swisshelm wrote. "She has already lost one lobe of the lungs, and her present sickness is a severe cold settled on the lungs." Perhaps hoping to receive more letters once Emma recovered, Swisshelm exaggerated their friendship. "It appears as if she were *ours*—a dear, kind

Presidential reception in the East Room of the White House (1853). (*White House Historical Association*)

friend—a sister, of whom delicacy should forbid our speaking in terms of praise such as are suitable from an admirer."[22]

Swisshelm's description of Emma's illness indicated another flare-up of tuberculosis, brought on not only by Emma's vigorous writing schedule but also by the possible reappearance of her long-lost husband Frederick. Financially, Emma was achieving success, making money from both serial and book publications. She had not heard from Frederick for several years, but by March she discovered that he'd returned to the United States, and she knew he could cause trouble. Marriage laws at the time considered a wife and children under the "cover" of the husband, who had total rights to all property and earnings a wife might gain during the marriage.[23] He could take everything.

The frightful stress of Frederick's return prompted Emma to take immediate action to protect herself. Divorce laws in DC before 1860 were quite limited; a divorce was very difficult to obtain and usually favored the husband. The best Emma could really hope for was a partial divorce, meaning that while she and Frederick would still be legally married, her assets would be protected. In order to achieve what was called a "bed and board divorce," she had to prove either cruelty or desertion.[24] She was intent on proving desertion, and in March 1850, she wrote a heartfelt letter to Henry Wise, the former ambassador to Brazil:

> Dear Sir:
>
> I have not received one line, word, message from F. H. Southworth since your return from Rio-de-Janeiro. I am about to petition Congress for a divorce and need all the proof of my husband's desertion that I can procure. I shall be eternally obliged to you if you will do the following favor—namely—to certify in a few lines all you know of this desertion—if it be merely the fact of Southworth's residence in Rio-de-Janeiro and his expressed determination to remain there, without sending for his family, or any thing else bearing upon the question that you may be so kind as to remember.
>
> Mr. Wise if you will do this for me I shall never never cease to pray for you. If you would also write a line upon the subject to one or two of the leading members of the Virginia delegation you

could through them carry the votes of the whole delegation for my petition.

Already I can carry the votes of the Mississippi delegation through the influence of my uncle who is a leading publican in his own state. I can carry the favor of the delegation from the Western states through other friends. So sir if you will lend me the aid of your powerful word with the Virginia delegation you may secure the lasting happiness of my life.

Yours Respectfully

Emma D.E.N. Southworth

P.S. Will you honour me by accepting the accompanying copy of my first novel?[25]

The hurried and frenzied tone of Emma's letter highlights the desperation she felt, and her sudden rush to procure a divorce after Frederick's prolonged absence indicates that she was worried about her finances. Based on Frederick's previous quests to obtain investment money for his latest invention, Emma's fears were justified. She could have little doubt that because of her popularity in the newspapers, he had learned of her writing success.

Oddly, the divorce petition never made it to Congress. While the reasons are unknown, when looking through the bills that were passed during the thirty-first session, none of them were about either men or women petitioning for divorce. Considering what Emma herself had written to Swisshelm just a month earlier, Congress had serious, contentious, and pressing matters regarding the question of slavery and the preservation of the Union. Radicals for the North demanded immediate abolition of slavery while Southern plantation owners were apprehensive that such an act would destroy their economy built on slave labor. A compromise was needed.

This controversial issue interested Jane Swisshelm, and she traveled to DC to get a front-row seat to the debates. She wrote to Horace Greeley, editor of the *New York Tribune*, offering to write a series of letters for his newspaper about the congressional proceedings. Greeley agreed to pay her $5 a week for her contributions. She petitioned Congress to allow her into the Senate gallery, and, on April 17, she became the first woman of the press to be admitted. Influenced by her overzealous beliefs on abolition, women's rights, temperance, and anti-Catholicism, Jane resorted to rumor-mongering to gain support for her causes. When disagreeing with a speech given by Daniel Webster, instead of criticizing the speech, Swisshelm went after his character, writing, "His mistresses are said to be . . . as ugly and vulgar as himself." Even though Swisshelm apologized for spreading the rumor, her Washington visit became uncomfortable for her.[26]

Swisshelm felt she could no longer remain where she was boarding, so she asked her "good friend" Emma whether she could stay with her. Swisshelm met Richmond and Lottie as well as Mandy, and she was outraged to learn that Mandy was still enslaved. Swisshelm concluded her visit by the end of July, and as soon as she returned to Pittsburgh, she wrote a paragraph about Emma's household, highly insinuating that Emma was a hypocrite, saying, "She was born, raised, and now is, a slaveholder, as completely dependent upon servants for her domestic comforts as any other Southern lady." Swisshelm soft-shoed the insult by describing the freedom and household responsibility given to Mandy: "She is evidently a most indulgent mistress. Amanda looks after Miss Emma, makes purchases and settles accounts—dresses the children and scolds them too, very much as if she were special guardian of the household."[27] Swisshelm acknowledged that Emma didn't own Mandy and, as such, had no legal power to free her, but the attack stung Emma, who felt a close bond with Mandy.

As Swisshelm returned home, Emma finished another novel and was ready to escape the troubles that now plagued the city. One trouble was the sudden death of sixty-five-year-old President Taylor, reportedly from a stomach ailment. Vice President Millard Fillmore was sworn in as president. This disruption further delayed the passage of the five bills of the Compromise of 1850, which finally happened in September. However, other than the congressmen who had to stay until the bills were passed, most citizens who could escape the inexorable heat of the DC summers left the city. As congressmen's families returned home, shops and boardinghouses closed for the season. Wealthy families fled to "fashionable water places" while middle-class citizens remained, looking "languid and listless."[28] No longer one of the poorer citizens of the city, Emma became eager to find a watering place to visit.

For the moment, Frederick was far from Washington, living in San Francisco, where his brothers Philip and A. B. Southworth now owned a successful mercantile and lumber business. During his stay, two gamblers got into a pistol fight at the City Hotel, with one grazing the other with a gunshot wound to the head. Even though Frederick was supposedly only a passerby, he made sure the reporter emphasized his innocent role in the incident:

> Mr. F. H. Southworth and another gentleman, were passing, and the former expressed a casual remark, reflecting upon gambling and its consequences. This was overheard by one of the fraternity, who furiously assaulted, and threw bottles and other missiles at him, some of which took effect, but happily without any serious injury. Mr. Southworth is one of our most respectful citizens, and holds a responsible office under the city government.[29]

Always in need of money, it seems more plausible that Frederick was trying his own hand at gambling and was in the midst of the fracas. Either way, with Frederick in California, he was less of a threat for Emma, at least for the time being.

Still, leaving Washington would ensure that Frederick couldn't easily find her. And Emma needed a break. After completing serialization of *Mother-in-Law*, Emma retreated to Shannondale Springs, a day's journey by railroad and stagecoach.[30] Rest and relaxation was exactly what Emma needed, and by the end of July, she packed up Richmond, Lottie, and Mandy and headed for the resort. Although Emma had more to say about slavery, women's rights, and social class disparity, she had the peaceful and beautiful surroundings of the Blue Ridge Mountains and the Shenandoah River in which to do it. Indeed, Shannondale Springs would prove to be a place that would further propel her into stardom.

Chapter 5
The Magical Realm of Shannondale Springs

Behind these trees the western sun was sinking like a world in flames, lighting up the whole western sky and all the river with intense and blinding effulgence of a conflagration!—And every gigantic oak with its great azure and its mazes of heavy green foliage, and every golden cloud melting in that sea of fire, was reflected and invested in the crystal water below! We were all silent, subdued—awed by the over-powering sense of the glory and grandeur around us![1]

Such was the scene Emma described upon arriving at Shannondale Springs at the end of July 1850. Their first stop was Harpers Ferry, where they had lunch before catching the Winchester and Potomac Railroad to Charlestown. Finally, they took a five-mile stagecoach ride to the ferry, where they crossed the beautiful Shenandoah River to the resort and caught the first glimpse of the healing waters of the hot springs. "A few yards from the path, you see the health-giving fountain," newspaperman John S. Gallaher reported, "whose waters incessantly bubble up from the waters beneath and are surrounded by a circular block of sandstone." Invalids as well as artists and the social and political elite came to the resort to take in these healing waters. Vacationers at Shannondale Springs were "unassuming people," Gallaher claimed, none of those "codfish aristocracy and those sets of would-be exclusives" of the watering places in the North.[2]

Emma decided Shannondale Springs suited her and her family well. The resort boasted not only the famous hot springs, the beautiful Shenandoah River, and the Blue Ridge Mountains but also stellar accommodations. Guests arrived at a two-story hotel, its red roof and white limestone structure a stark contrast among the green and lush foliage next to the river. The expansive twenty-five-room hotel also boasted a large dining and ballroom as well as a wide veranda that spanned the length of the hotel. Proprietor Joseph F. Abells offered rooms for $9 per week or $30 per month, which included daily stagecoach services to Charlestown. Additionally, the resort had ten single-story guest cottages that formed a semicircle around the hotel. Emma rented one of the cottages for herself and her family. "It is the most enchanting spot on earth—it has filled my whole soul with beauty," Emma wrote to Henry Peterson. "I occupy a most lovely cottage, with the Blue Ridge rising behind, and the Shenandoah flowing before."[3]

Emma might have found what she called the "most delightful place of retreat," but she did anything but rest. By the time Emma had unpacked, she already had a plan for her next book and wrote to Henry Peterson about submitting the first chapter by the second week of August. Her new novel was called *Shannondale; or, The Nun of Mount Carmel.* Peterson immediately told *Post* readers of her upcoming chapter, suggesting they renew subscriptions so they wouldn't miss out on the new story. When the *Post* had released Emma's last serialized novel, *The Deserted Wife*, there weren't enough copies printed to meet the demand.[4] As with previous novels, *Shannondale* addressed how an elitist patriarchal system limits a woman's ability to make her own choices. Particularly in harm's way are her female characters born into a wealthy class in which their choices about marriage and social duties have been made for them by their ruling fathers.

Emma also portrayed the Catholic Church's role in helping to instill these patriarchal beliefs. Emma's anti-Catholic sentiments seem surprising considering that her father was Catholic and that she was baptized into the Catholic faith. However, considering the letter Charles had

Shannondale Springs along the banks of the Shenandoah River. (*Historical Collections of Virginia*, 1845, 341)

written before he died, her attitude toward the church becomes more understandable. His advice that her duty in life was to obey and please her husband was an attitude supported by the church. Emma showed her objection that wives must blindly submit to their husbands through her female characters in *Shannondale*, who each fall in love with unsuitable partners. Even though Emma's own biographical accounts and later novels suggest her desire for societal acceptance for differing religious views, *Shannondale* questions several Catholic beliefs, most notably women's complete submission to husband and church.

Emma was well aware of anti-Catholic sentiment during the nineteenth century. Prior to the publication of *Shannondale*, a massive riot broke out in Philadelphia in 1844 between Protestants and Catholics. One of the arguments that sparked the turmoil was over what role churches should play in public education. As a nation born out of colonial

Protestant development, the riot reflected the growing fear Protestants held as thousands of Irish Catholic immigrants settled in America.[5] Considering that the *Post* was published in Philadelphia, Emma's religious views in this novel suggest that she understood the contentious religious climate of that city and wanted to separate herself from Catholicism.

While most of the controversial themes have little to do with it being set in Shannondale, one story line put the resort on the map. In the fourth installment in the *Post*, Emma created the "Legend of Lover's Leap." The tale revolves around a beautiful Shenandoah Indian queen named Lulu, the highly respected matriarch of her people. She meets Reginald Clinton, an English officer who comes to Shannondale at the request of Bushrod Summerfield, one of the first English gentlemen to settle in the region. Her warriors had rescued Clinton after a near-fatal fall from a cliff that hung over the Shenandoah River, and as Lulu nurses him to health, they fall in love. Despite protestations from her braves, she lives with Clinton in a remote cabin until he tires of her and returns to his English friends. Clinton then proposes marriage to Bushrod's sister Rose, and during the wedding celebration, they hear the wailing death cries of Lulu, who has gone to the cliff where her men had saved Clinton's life. Clinton runs to the cliff to save Lulu, but she jumps and plunges to her death. Within this subplot, Emma remained consistent with her theme about women's loss of independence living within patriarchy. Lulu lived in a matriarchal society, but when she stepped outside of it, Clinton assumed power over her. Perhaps this point became lost as readers flocked to Lover's Leap, which helped promote Shannondale Springs as a tourist destination.[6]

In addition to *Shannondale*, Emma wrote a short story called "The Little Slave" for Margaret Bailey's *Friend of Youth*, and yet she still found time to enjoy playing backgammon, checkers, puzzle boards, and bowling. One vacationer remembered that at the resort's bowling saloon, he "had the pleasure of rolling with the distinguished authoress, Mrs. Southworth." The holiday spot also boasted recreational activities that included walking, hiking, fishing, boating, and rock hunting. Vacationers could use the floating bathhouses with stairs leading down into the river, where bathers could either swim or stroll along the sandy bottom. "After tea, a

Lover's Leap at Shannondale Springs. (*New York Public Library*)

party of us walked down the rolling green hill," Emma described for the *Post*. "We got into a boat for a short excursion. I told you that the mountain and the river curved around the vale in the shape of a horse-shoe—well, we embarked near the center." Her boating expedition was one of many activities she chose. "One event succeeds another, and one amusement follows another with such a dizzy rapidity here," she wrote. "It is impossible to seize and describe one before a successor, new and more brilliant, put it out of our head." The festivities eventually concluded in the last week of August with a tournament, grand ball, and fireworks. "Oh me," Emma lamented. "I wish it were as endless as the long sessions of Congress."[7]

Returning that fall to Washington, Emma finished the serialization of *Shannondale* by the end of November before Appleton quickly published it in book form, advertising its near-release in December. *The Deserted Wife* continued to sell, with advertisers promoting the book as one that would "suit the ladies" and noting it was "published in a better style than usual." Although Emma still received good reviews, she had to contend with competition between the *Post* and the *Era*. On October

31, 1850, Peterson claimed that Emma wrote exclusively for the *Post*. On November 15, however, Gamaliel Bailey added that even though Emma wrote for the *Post*, she also wrote for the *Era*. Bailey ended his *Era* advertisement saying, "We like to see our literary women liberally paid for their contributions to American Literature."[8] Emma was already writing her next serial, *Hickory Hall*, for the *Era* in November while simultaneously finishing *Shannondale* for the *Post*, showing that she wasn't exclusive with either publication.

With Emma's continued popularity, it was only a matter of time before the male critics came after her again. One such critical response was from a reader known only as H. C. H. in a letter to the editor of the *Era*. Although the review offers high praise of Emma's female characters, he's upset about the way she portrays men. "I would like to read a story from Mrs. Southworth's pen," he wrote, "of a truly Christian hero—suffering, striving, conquering, *never* 'overcome of evil,' but overcoming evil with good." Other reviewers were considerably harsher. Editor and proprietor for the *Southern Literary Messenger* John R. Thompson admitted that Emma's first novel *Retribution* had escaped his watchful eye, but he'd read *The Deserted Wife*, "a work of the very worst description of the loose-tunic and guilty-passion school." He further condemned Appleton for publishing it, noting that though the company usually produced works of "discretion and good taste," by printing *The Deserted Wife*, "they have committed a *faux pas*." He concluded that the novel was so disrespectable that "no pure and right-thinking family" would ever allow it to "find its way to the hearth-stone."[9] As troubling as poor critical reviews were, they weren't Emma's only problems as 1850 drew to a close.

While concluding *Hickory Hall* for the *Era*, Emma's health worsened again. On December 26, instead of the expected installment, Bailey wrote, "Much to our regret, Mrs. Southworth, after the issue of our last number, was seized with a sudden and painful affliction of the eyes, which has totally disqualified her for completing in this number the last chapter of her story." This was hardly the way Emma would have wanted to celebrate her thirty-first birthday, but her vigorous writing schedule was bound to catch up with her sooner or later. "Ordinarily, I labor four days each week," Emma wrote. "Constantly, devotedly, scarcely taking time to eat, and I work from noon to midnight." Not only did she maintain a twelve-hour work day, but she also wrote under difficult circumstances. In the days before typewriters, Emma either wrote her stories with a dip pen, which required continuously rewetting the tip of the pen from an inkwell, or a fountain pen, a relatively new type of pen that contained a reservoir inside, eliminating the need for the inkwell. She also wrote at two small desks. One was eighteen inches square with a small drawer in front. The other was a folding portable desk that had once belonged to her father, one of her most beloved possessions.[10] Further complicating her writing process was that, for several hours a day, she wrote after the sun had set, which meant working by dimly lit oil lamps. No wonder she suffered from painful eye strain.

Despite the inconvenience Emma caused Bailey, he remained loyal. During her eye illness, he told readers that if their subscriptions were soon to expire, he would provide them with a free paper so that they could read the conclusion of *Hickory Hall.* The next month, he advertised his literary stars for the upcoming 1851 publication of the *Era*: John Greenleaf Whittier, Grace Greenwood, Alice and Phoebe Cary, and Mrs. H. B. Stowe, along with Mrs. Emma D.E.N. Southworth, who had already been "engaged to furnish a story for our new volume." Emma finished *Hickory Hall* on January 9, but she would not write another story for the *Era* for two years. The only work she produced for the Baileys in 1851 was "Across the Street" for Margaret's *Friend of Youth* in the January and February editions.[11]

Not only was Emma's health problematic, but critics had also turned up the heat with their negative and even hateful commentary, as Henry Peterson had predicted the previous year. By January 1851, a critic for the *Southern Quarterly Review* said *The Deserted Wife* was "too frequently questionable in its moral tendency." The same critic claimed *Shannondale* was "careless" and that Emma was "now at a perilous moment in her career." The *International Monthly Magazine* editor wrote that, even though Mrs. Southworth was "the most popular of our female novelists," he questioned the "doubtful morality of her works." Perhaps the most venomous attacks came again from John R. Thompson, who called *Shannondale* "flat, stupid, and absurd," suggesting that it was "high time that respectable publishers should unite in suppressing this demoralizing sort of literature." In a thinly veiled attempt to review *The Mother-in-Law*, he attacked all of her novels in one fell swoop, claiming, "It is rather in the tone, the coloring, the general moulding of character and feeling that this lady's strong, unfeminine, thoroughly *French* organization betrays itself." He strongly warned families to stay away from her novels, of which he claimed "there could be few greater evils."[12]

Wholly aware of the critical reviews, Emma needed to do something about them; however, she had no intention of leaving the controversial subjects of domestic abuse, betrayal, and abandonment buried in dark corners. When she began serialization of *Virginia and Magdalene; or, The Foster Sisters* on January 4, 1851, for the *Post*, Emma had to find a way to seem less threatening to critics. Emma had suffered at the hands of emotionally abusive men, and she knew she was not the only one. She was going to tell these stories, not only so that her female readers knew that they weren't alone but also to give them hope. In March, hoping to hide the controversial themes in the novel, Emma created a somewhat fictionalized version of herself:

> A widow in fate, though not a widow in fact—a helpless woman, with two children, thrown upon her own exertions for a livelihood—who can wonder that her mind became somewhat morbid and unhealthy in its tone? And who can wonder that in the unavoidable haste of writing for daily bread, many things have crept into her productions which a cool revision would have erased.[13]

Emma's biography wasn't exactly a lie, but it was carefully constructed, emphasizing her helplessness and her desperate need to provide an income for her family. Emma, however, was anything but helpless. She had already proven that she was a courageous survivor, unafraid to tackle tough social issues. This creation allowed her to hide in plain sight. Over time, she became better at forming this nonthreatening persona—in essence branding herself as the authoress Mrs. E.D.E.N. Southworth—all the while spreading encouraging messages to those who struggled through desperate circumstances.

As Emma planned her next moves, she finally took a proper rest. The last installment of *Virginia and Magdalene* appeared in the *Post* on May 3, followed by nothing for the next ten weeks—her longest break since she began writing. Then, on June 23, Emma again headed to Shannondale Springs. This time she took a longer route, favoring a change of scenery—or so she claimed. Emma promised to write a series of letters for the *Post* during her vacation, but the intent of her first installment was really about cleaning up her image. Although Emma portrayed the beauty of the South, her real focus was to describe the "heroes of Virginia," praising former president James Monroe, Edward Braddock, George Washington, and General Daniel Morgan.[14] Her emphasis on these heroes leaves little doubt that she had read the harsh critical reviews that questioned the moral quality of her male characters, so she gave a list of honorable men, thereby showing she didn't believe all men were bad.

At the end of Emma's three-day journey to Shannondale, she ended her first letter to the *Post* with a detailed description of her cottage. The resort was at a horseshoe bend along the Shenandoah River on the opposite side from Charlestown, which meant crossing a ferry to reach the resort. Emma's cabin was farthest from the hotel but closest to the river. It sat at the top of a hill. As Emma described it, "The front view, from the window at which I am writing, commands a fine prospect of the descending dale, the waving trees, the rushing river, and the still and awful mountains, rising on from the other side."[15] When looking at a map of the estate, this view also gave her a clear shot at the ledge that hung out over the river, the one she had written about in *Shannondale* and named Lover's Leap, the place that tourists came to see at the Springs.

One visitor was an "occasional correspondent" known only as "F." for Washington's *Daily Union*. He had been to Charlestown on business and had a day off, so he decided to see for himself whether Shannondale Springs lived up to Southworth's description. He had been to several other springs and tasted their waters. He was desperate to escape the insufferable summer heat he'd encountered in Washington, Baltimore, Harpers Ferry, and Charlestown. "I have come to this most delightful spot that I have ever visited . . . the beautiful Shenandoah winding its way along almost at my feet, with . . . 'the Lover's Leap' towering on the opposite bank," F. observed. He heartily recommended the resort. If Emma had questioned her writing as a result of the critics, she had nothing to worry about from F., who described her as "a lady who had written some of the best novels in the United States, and among them 'Shannondale,' the scene of which, abounding in beauties, is laid here."[16]

Also spending the summer of 1851 at Shannondale Springs were Emma's friends from the *Era*, Gamaliel Bailey, Margaret, and their family. Bailey had just spent some months traveling around the country and, like Emma, desperately needed to rest. Always the consummate abolitionist, Bailey found great comfort the fact that he did not observe any "visible tokens" of slavery at the resort. He also took special notice of the spring water, which, according to Dr. De Butts's analysis, largely contained sulfates, lime, and magnesia. "People here take copious draughts morning, noon, and night, and profess to derive great benefit," Bailey postulated. "One thing is certain, it does not affect their appetite injuriously." Emma herself wrote about the grand meals at the Springs: "Epicures and gourmands here, are quite as enthusiastic upon the subject of the dinners as amateur poets and artists are upon the theme of scenery." Meals often consisted of "fragrant mocha, the green or black souchong, the rich cream, snowy light, hot rolls, rice cakes, mutton and beefsteaks, ham, fish, and above all, poultry, which always graces the morning board." Lunches and dinners contained similar fare.[17]

Another guest who observed the popular pastime of drinking the spring water was Mary Jane Windle, who, like Emma, wrote a series of letters that summer—Emma for Philadelphia's *Saturday Evening Post*, Windle for DC's *Southern Press*. As a gossip columnist, Windle keenly observed Emma: "We hardly dare tread on this section of Virginia, which Mrs. Southworth has made classical ground by her more powerful pen." At the same time, Windle was not above copying Emma as she coincidentally signed off her letter with "But our leaves are filled, and we must abruptly close."[18] Emma's letters were titled "Leaves from Shannondale."

With tensions growing between Northern and Southern states, Emma took the opportunity to emphasize the need for the country's unity by describing the Fourth of July activities at Shannondale Springs. The celebration drew a great crowd, and Dr. L. M. Smith read the

Declaration of Independence. "Poor old George Third," Emma quipped, "how his bones must rattle in his grave once a year!" After speeches were made, the crowd enjoyed dinner, drinking, music, and dancing long into the evening.[19] Emma strongly supported the Union and didn't want states to secede. Considering her descriptions of Virginia's heroes and how they fought to gain freedom from European countries, Emma used her letters not only to get away from those negative critical reviews of her works but also to advocate preserving the Union.

In addition to the unity of the resort residents, Emma again wrote about the games and activities she enjoyed, listing "bathing, gymnastics, walking, riding over the mountains, driving along the deeply shaded banks of the beautiful river . . . playing at various games; music, singing, dancing in the evening air." One particular outing she recalled was a walk she took with friends along the Shenandoah River to Raven's Rock, which involved a three-hundred-foot climb. The breathtaking view at the top made the entire effort worthwhile. Later that day, her party took a boat across the river and climbed to the "celebrated Lover's Leap."[20] This excursion must have pleased Emma tremendously, knowing she had invented the so-called legend in the first place.

Emma frequently wrote that summer about her numerous outings with friends. One particularly rugged hike she described was with Dr. and Mrs. Bailey, a Miss E_____, and a Mr. H_____. Also in tow were ten-year-old Richmond and seven-year-old Lottie. They packed a lunch and put on "stout shoes" before beginning the day with a five-mile hilly walk to the base of Mount Shannon. Using walking staffs, they climbed "one mile of steep precipice!" After a brief rest, they hiked up another cliff to look down on the Valley of the Upper Potomac. As if that weren't enough, Emma and "a gentleman" climbed a third summit to view both the Shenandoah and the Upper Potomac simultaneously. By the time their group returned, they had hiked an astonishing thirteen miles, and while the rest of Emma's group complained about their sore muscles, she had a bath, ate dinner, and took a walk before going to the dance that evening.[21] No doubt the fresh air, sunshine, and waters had worked their magic on Emma's health, and she seemed to no longer be suffering from eye ailments or lung issues.

By August, Emma's letters in the *Post* had done their own magic; the resort swelled from 50 guests only a few weeks earlier to a whopping 150 vacationers from all across the country. One particular sensation was the arrival of President Millard Fillmore, who traveled with his family along with members of his cabinet. When they arrived, not only were the guests ready to meet the president, but residents also came from the surrounding counties. The hotel ballroom overflowed that evening as dinner and dancing commenced. The next day, before the president departed, the host prepared an elegant dinner in which the "table actually groaned . . . with luxuries of every kind."[22]

As exciting as the presidential visit was, another event soon overshadowed even such a monumental occasion—the wedding of Appolonia Jagiello and Gaspar Tochman. Although incorrectly noted by the press as Hungarian, Appolonia was actually born in Lithuania and educated in Krakow. She became a part of a Polish uprising that fought for independence by dressing as a man and joining the fight. The uprising was crushed, but Appolonia escaped, making her way to Hungary, where she joined the Hungarian Revolution of 1848 against the Austrian Empire. When this revolution also failed, she immigrated to the United States. Correspondent for the *New York Herald* Dr. Wallis remarked, "Really, we must have Mrs. Southworth write a novel about [her]; it would be so interesting." Although Emma never wrote that novel, Appolonia's story impressed her, and, in future novels, she often had female characters dress as men in order to accomplish some heroic deed. Appolonia's groom was Major Gaspar Tochman, who also fought in the Polish uprisings against the Russian Empire before immigrating to the United States. As newspapers learned of their stories, they gained celebrity status while at Shannondale Springs, leading to a large attendance at their wedding on August 9, 1851.[23]

Shannondale Springs ended the season in September with a mock tournament and Fancy Ball. Dr. Wallis predicted that the novelty of the medieval mock tournament had worn off and, other than the money to be made by the resort owners, the event would draw few people. Wallis was wrong, and on the day of the tournament, partygoers arose to a beautiful fall morning. To the west of the hotel, a large open field had been set up as the jousting arena, where two poles had been installed that were twenty feet high and twenty-five feet apart, and between the poles a cord stretched between them. Hanging from the center of the cord was an iron ring covered with blue ribbon. Nine men had signed up to play the part of the knights, each taking turns galloping on their trusted steeds toward the iron ring with the purpose of using their lance to bend down and pluck the ring from the hook.

The festivities began around eleven in the morning with guests filling up seats upon an elevated platform. Hundreds of onlookers filled the stands with the overflow standing under shade trees. As heralders trumpeted the beginning of the games, the costumed knights rode their horses and lined up in front of the crowd. Henry Bedinger, former U.S. House representative for Virginia and president of the day, rose to speak, explaining in "serio-comic eloquence" the honors and privileges that the victor had in "crowning the Queen of his Affection, Queen of Love, of Beauty, and of Chivalry." More trumpets sounded as the knights lined up at the southern border of the field, and ladies in the crowd encouragingly waved their handkerchiefs. As each knight prepared to take his turn, a herald would loudly proclaim his chosen fictitious medieval name such as the "Highland Chief" or the "Knight of the Red Beard"—two men who sadly were not victors for the day. Neither was "The Black Prince," who was "clad in black, with vizor down and helmet surmounted with white plumes. His horse was the finest on the ground—a magnificent dark grey steed, with flowing white tail and mane." While not a winner of the competition, the prince might have won if there'd been best in show.

Each knight was given three tries to obtain the ring. Points were awarded if the rider either hit or carried off the ring (no points if they missed it). The poor Knight of Berkeley missed all three attempts and rode away completely defeated. The Knight of Scampton, who unadorned was commonly known as David Humphreys from Jefferson County, triumphed as victor with two rings and a hit. He rode forward and claimed Kate Sappington of Charlestown as his chosen queen. When she arrived to the stage, the king-at-arms took a flower crown and holding it above her head ceremoniously proclaimed, "Fair lady! Here, in the presence of this assembly of brave men and beautiful women, and at the behest of your true and victorious Knight, I, the most devoted of your subjects, crown you Queen of Love, of Beauty, and of Chivalry . . . long may you reign." Next were second-, third-, and fourth-place knights, who each chose their ladies. Each maid received a wreath to commemorate the title. More trumpets signaled the tournament's end, and guests returned to the hotel for a "sumptuous dinner."[24]

The mock tournament left an indelible mark on Emma, who felt the palpable emphasis on the heroics of an all-male competition, and she later wrote *Miriam the Avenger* in which she re-created the tournament, making a mockery out of the mock tournament. The rich and controlling Commodore Nicholas Waugh, who has no offspring, wants his best friend, Professor Grimsby, to inherit his estate on his death. Yet he vainly desires his own bloodline to continue his lineage. Enter his fifteen-year-old niece, Jacquelina L'Oiseau, who has lived with her mother Mary in an isolated cottage in the woods. Instead of learning appropriate middle-class etiquette, Jacquelina has learned to ride a horse and shoot a bow and arrow. Independent and feisty, with a mind of her own, Emma nicknamed her San Souci—French for "no worries." Waugh mistakenly believes he can reeducate her to be a good wife for the much-older Grimsby.

San Souci continues her mischievous ways. When she becomes ill after heroically rescuing Waugh from a house fire, he takes his family to Bentley Springs so that she can rest. Surrounded with plenty of fresh air and sunshine, San Souci quickly recovers, and she, along with the visitors at the resort, excitedly plan for the upcoming mock tournament. When the day arrives, San Souci complains that she is suffering from an excessively bad headache and can't come. Here, Emma has fun with her characters. She describes the mock tournament in the novel almost exactly like the one she had witnessed at Shannondale Springs—with one exception. In the middle of the competition, a newcomer arrives dressed in a beautiful silver armor, announcing himself as Prince Ariel of Fairyland and challenging the remaining contestants. The prince wins, takes the flower crown, and lays it at the feet of the angered and astonished Commodore Waugh. The silent crowd anxiously waits for the prince to remove his vizor. Emma playfully wrote, "Reader, have you ever doubted his identity for a single moment?" The crowd breaks into uproarious applause as the naughty San Souci removes her helmet to show that a woman has won the event.[25] On the one hand, Emma had learned to masterfully appease the male critic by lightly poking fun at the status quo. With her other hand, she created heroines who gave her female readers role models of fiercely independent women who had minds of their own. She was brilliant.

Emma also shined brilliantly during the last event of the Shannondale Springs season. The Fancy Ball was a masquerade party, occurring the day after the jousting tournament. Several hundred guests attended and were astounded by the beautiful ballroom that had been decorated with flowers and orange trees. The costumed orchestra played, and the ballroom became an enchanted world as if "the magic ring and the wonderful lamp of Aladdin . . . had been discovered."[26] Of course, Kate Sappington, the queen of the mock tournament, attended along with her three maids, all gloriously costumed to show off their beauty.

But they were not the real stars of the event. "The feature of the evening," wrote Dr. Wallis, "was the entrée of Mrs. Southworth." Re-creating

San Souci presents the crown to Waugh at the mock tournament in *Miriam, the Avenger.* (*London Journal* [1862], Google Books)

the cast from Shakespeare's *Midsummer Night's Dream*, Emma entered dressed as the Queen of the Amazons, Hippolyta, wearing a gold tiara adorned with jewels and flowers, a red jacket trimmed with gold lace, a lace skirt, and pink slippers. Following in tow was Lottie, who was Titania, Queen of the Fairies, wearing a white and silver gossamer dress and a winged crown. Clothed in a white robe and gold crown and carrying a gold scepter was Richmond, playing the part of Oberon, King of the Fairies. Nine other children dressed as fairies, likely neighboring guests recruited by Emma to attend the king and queen. Emma's troupe was greeted by a round of applause and admired for its creativity and design.[27] Not only did Emma gain admirers during the Fancy Ball, but her fanbase had been growing all summer. The enthusiastic Philos even wrote a poem dedicated to her:

To Mrs. Emma D.E.N. Southworth

Awake! My lyre—enlivened by a song
Of woman's worth—I'll sweep thy tuneful strings;
And thrilling echo shall thy notes prolong,
Until the stern, repentant critic sings—
Until his praise adds "fuel to the fire"
That warms my spirit and awakes my lyre.

Thou, who hast told of Hagar's changeful lot,
Of broken vows—of man's inconstancy!
Say, has thou felt the woe of vows forgot,
Or dost thou dream of such hypocrisy?
The traitor's kiss, the world's cold scorn,
Are there by feeling or by fancy drawn?

Spirit of sadness! From thy gloom awake;
In Christ's calm likeness by thy soul array'd,
Oh, that thy genius, like the troubled lake,
By God's behest might find its surge allay'd!

And then with holy unction wield thy pen
For God's own glory and the weal of men.

With life inspired, thy passion scenes portray
The demon-foes that riot in the heart,
The tinsel'd garb of guilt dost rive away,
And golden gleams to virtue dost impart,
Accept this simple lay to genius due,
This friendly wreath my muse has twined for you.[28]

As partygoers danced into the early morning hours, Emma discovered something very powerful during her magical summers at the Springs. She was a talented writer, capable of creating heroines who could influence the attitudes and dreams of her female readers. She could also create whatever version of herself she wanted—even if that meant stylizing herself as the demure and helpless Mrs. E.D.E.N. Southworth. But on that night at Shannondale, she was the Queen of Shannondale, admired and celebrated by those around her.

Chapter 6

Prospect Cottage—a Place to Call Home

It was a veritable reclusorium, silent by day except for a whispering breeze through the impaled clematis vines and the meditative rows of boxwood; lightness by night, unless you could imagine that reflected stars were candles in the windows, and that subdued lights from the Potomac bridge were a soft fire in the heart. A little house, yet it was a tremendous literary laboratory, where so many novels were written.[1]

"If you would do your best with your pen, Mrs. Southworth, you must give up society, and above all things stop boarding, and get a little home of your own, where you can command your time," advised *Godey's* magazine editor, Sarah Hale, when interviewing Emma for a book on distinguished women.[2] In 1852, Emma took Hale's counsel and purchased Prospect Cottage, once used as a hotel. She remodeled it, maintaining its picturesque beauty of quaint gables and a vine-covered exterior, surrounded by garden beds laden with brightly colored flowers. Perched at the top of Thirty-Sixth Street in Georgetown, Prospect Cottage provided a breathtaking view. It was one and a half stories with a spacious veranda that wrapped around three sides. From here, Emma looked at rowboats and steamships on the Potomac River, watched traffic crossing the Aqueduct bridge, and admired rolling hills that stretched to Arlington. Prospect Cottage became Emma's writing sanctuary—a place she loved "better than any place on earth."[3]

Prospect Cottage, Thirty-Sixth Street and Prospect Street NW, Georgetown. (*Willard Ross Postcard Collection, DC Public Library*)

At Prospect Cottage, Emma again began a feverish writing pace, producing novels simultaneously for both the *Post* and the *Era*. Her next serial for the *Post* was *The Curse of Clifton*, which ran from July 24 through December 25, 1852. She then began a new serial for the *Era* in January 1853 called *Mark Sutherland*, followed immediately by *The Lost Heiress* in August for the *Post*.[4] Emma's popularity soared. For the moment, Henry Peterson at the *Post* seemed well pleased, advertising her as "a writer who, in vigor and fertility of genius, [was] not surpassed by any, male or female, in the Union." This renewed energy for writing could only be attributed to Emma's love for her new home. "I have written in every room in this house, but my favorite was the library, from which I could see the river and the old Jesuit College," Emma fondly recalled. "In summer I preferred to write upon the piazza. The outlook from it is fine, and while evolving my thoughts I could leave my desk and walk up and down."[5]

Emma also revised previously serialized novels for book publisher Abraham Hart. After publishing *Virginia and Magdalene* in September, Emma negotiated with Hart to publish a collection of her short stories called *Old Neighbourhoods and New Settlements*. Emma wrote to Hart in October, "I accept the terms you have offered me for the Christmas book and I will forward the copy and the daguerreotypes on Monday next." In further communication to Hart, Emma showed her willingness to take Hart's advice as she questioned whether to include her story "Hickory Hall; or, The Outcast." She also included possible titles for each story as well as a dedication and offered to look over the proof sheets for the engravings. In return, she asked Hart whether she could have two copies of the book bound in "Turkey Morocco and gilt edges."[6] Emma was more than a writer. She was actively engaged in book revisions and negotiated terms in selling her copyrights. Her business acumen and knowledge of commerce was phenomenal in an age when women could not yet vote or shop in public without an escort.

Emma next negotiated with Hart for the copyright of *The Curse of Clifton* as she was still finishing it for the *Post*. She agreed to accept $200 in cash or notes and $25 worth of books that he published, sending him a list of the titles she wanted.[7] As Emma made enough money to support herself, she purchased many books for her library at Prospect Cottage—a collection that continued to grow throughout her life. In a rare photo of her working, Emma sat at her desk in the library with books piled around her and a floor-to-ceiling bookcase also brimming with books. When Emma signed her friend Alice Underwood Hunt's remembrance album, she listed her best-loved poets as Lord Byron, John Greenleaf Whittier, and Adelaide Proctor. Her favorite authors were Shakespeare, Sir Walter Scott, and Victor Hugo.[8]

Numerous guests to Prospect Cottage took particular notice of Emma's library. Nineteenth-century spiritualist Nettie Colburn Maynard closely observed, "It was an ideal apartment, three sides of which were lined with books, showing through the glass doors that reached nearly to the floor. The room was in perfect order." Martha D. Lincoln similarly remembered looking through the many books in Emma's library: "Southworth . . . gave wonderful insight into the contents of the books of her favorite author." Newspaper reporter Henry Cowell interviewed Emma, noting her love of reading and knowledge of new authors. "She talked of Kipling and Barrie and Jerome as if they were very near friends," Cowell observed. "She has read all of Barrie and of Kipling with intense enjoyment, and is now doing Jerome."[9]

Emma D.E.N. Southworth in the library at Prospect Cottage. (*William B. Becker Collection/Photography*)

Showcasing her home and library, Emma regularly hosted social gatherings, inviting senators, generals, scholars, and writers—in other words, the "world's brightest and best." On Sunday evenings, Emma entertained twenty to thirty guests, treating them to a supper in the dining room that consisted of biscuits, preserves, ham, and cold tongue. The party then moved into the parlor, where guests were entertained with music and songs. The evening always ended with a "unanimous request" for Emma to tell one of her ghost stories. The usual story line was one in which she would wander through each of the rooms at Prospect Cottage "in her white robe with a flickering taper, looking for ghosts." She kept up the "air of mystery" until the end, when she revealed that she was actually the "ghost" and that she had scared herself. She also hosted Friday evening literary salons called "Conversations." Often on the guest list were Orville Dewey, John Howard Payne, Gamaliel Bailey, James Smithson, Grace Greenwood, Lydia Maria Child, and Alice Cary.[10]

Unfortunately, Prospect Cottage didn't shield Emma from all troubles—one of which was her estranged husband, Frederick. By 1853, he had moved from California to Mexico, where he had taken out a ten-year patent on his invention to preserve oysters, shrimp, lobsters, and fish. He had obtained permission from the Mexican government to catch, pack, and ship seafood, presumably to the U.S. markets.[11] For the moment, Frederick's far-off business ventures, particularly those out of the country, posed no immediate threat to Emma.

Loving the public eye, however, Frederick habitually posed as the hero, making sure that the press knew anytime he had performed an altruistic act. One such incident occurred in September 1853 during one of Frederick's expeditions between the United States and Mexico. On board the steamship *Texas* was Judge Alfred Conkling, who had just finished his appointment as U.S. minister to Mexico. Conkling became ill during the trip, but Frederick informed the press that he had taken care of Conkling during his sickness on board. Once the steamer stopped in Jalapa, Mexico, Frederick continued his care until Conkling was well enough to resume travel to New Orleans. If unsuccessful in his business ventures, Frederick was masterful at making connections with important political figures, and he never let a good deed go unnoticed.

Emma had been careful in biographical accounts of her life to avoid using Frederick's name, which led to one reporter misidentifying her husband as S. S. Southworth, the editor of the *Sunday Atlas* and later the *New York Mercury*. A retraction in the magazine correctly identified Frederick as Emma's husband, which other papers picked up around the country.[12] This connection to Frederick is one that Emma would have preferred to be left alone.

Frederick was in the news again when he was aboard the steamer *San Francisco*, which was destroyed during a hurricane, making national headlines. On December 21, 1853, around 700 passengers boarded the steamship in New York bound for San Francisco. On Christmas Eve, the boat encountered a violent storm that flung 167 passengers overboard to their deaths. Three days later, 413 survivors were rescued by the *Three Bells* and the *Antarctic*—both vessels returning to New York with no further problems. A third steamer, the *Kilby*, took the remaining 120 passengers, one of which was Frederick. Unfortunately, the *Kilby* didn't have enough food for that many passengers and had also been severely damaged by the same storm. When the *Kilby* began sinking, survivors had to be transferred again to the *Lucy Thompson*. The ordeal finally ended on January 14 when the *Lucy Thompson* docked in New York and unloaded the cold and hungry survivors, who now numbered 108.[13]

Frederick was first in line to tell his story to reporters—and a fantastical story it was. He claimed that he was one of the passengers who had initially been swept overboard into the sea, along with his traveling companion James Stockwell. "When I arose to the surface of the ocean a harrowing sight was before me," Frederick claimed. "I was over a half mile from the steamer, and around me was about an acre of floating timber." He and Stockwell clung to pieces of the floating timber until Frederick managed to swim back to the ship, where he caught hold of a rope. Clinging to the line, he observed a man standing on the paddle wheel be swept into the ocean. Stockwell perished, but Frederick climbed back on board. "I was enabled at last to crawl upon the forward deck, and there with my hand, broke open a stateroom window, and crept into it half drowned," Frederick claimed. Along with a Mr. Rankin, he miraculously survived.[14]

Emma later wrote *The Island Princess*, in which she told the story of a shipwreck—one that questioned the authenticity of Frederick's tall tale. In Emma's plot, the *Queen Charlotte* encounters the "ill-fated *Mercury*," whose "masts had been snapped off, and with all their sails and shrouds had fallen forward upon the sand." The passengers and crew on board the *Queen Charlotte* watch as a mountainous wave throws the *Mercury* as well as its three remaining survivors into the sea. Members aboard the *Queen Charlotte* watch helplessly as two of the three drown until the hero of the story, Lord Montressor, takes action to save the last survivor. Along with the assistance of several crew members, he attaches a rope around his waist, throws himself into the sea, and reaches the man just in time, as "the strength of the poor wretch was exhausted." The men on board pull the rope and haul Montressor and the shipwrecked man onto the boat.[15] The similarities to Frederick's account and the ways in which Emma responds to them cannot be overlooked. None of the survivors in Emma's tale have the strength to swim back to the ship, let alone grab a rope and swing himself onto the deck. Even Montressor, who's physically fit and rested, requires the help of the crew to pull the rope and the men to safety, thus emphasizing the unlikelihood of Frederick's story.

The reappearance of Frederick was not Emma's only family trouble. She was at odds with Joshua Henshaw over the issue of slavery. On

Engraving of wreck of the *Mercury* in *Island Princess* (June 27, 1857). (*Falvey Digital Library, Villanova University, Pennsylvania*)

Dorothy's death, Emma inherited the slave Caroline, and Charlotte was given Mandy and Leonard Jr. Caroline continued to live with Susanna and Henshaw; Mandy lived with Emma from the time she was twelve until at least 1851. At some point, Charlotte agreed with Emma that slavery should end. In 1853, seriously ill with consumption, Charlotte drafted a will that stipulated what should happen to Mandy and Leonard following her death. She willed Leonard Jr. to Susanna, insisting that he be freed on Susanna's death. Mandy's freedom was to be more imminent. Charlotte asked that on payment of $300 to Susanna, Mandy was immediately to obtain her freedom.[16] Even though Charlotte rallied back to some semblance of health and lived for several more years, the intent was clear—Emma and Charlotte did not want to continue the legacy of slavery, which stood in direct opposition to what Henshaw wanted.

Although Charlotte's wishes regarding Mandy and Leonard were spelled out in a written will, what Emma wanted for Caroline became muddied. Before her death, Dorothy had sent Mandy, not Caroline, to live with Emma, while Caroline lived with Susanna and Henshaw. This arrangement led to Henshaw's belief that he owned Caroline and her two children by default. Emma disagreed, and the problem of ownership came to a head after an incident that occurred on March 17, 1854. Caroline had been working for Rev. J. C. Smith, who believed Caroline was a free black woman. On that Friday, Caroline took her oldest daughter, nine-year-old Annie, from Henshaw's house. The next day, a report surfaced that stated two or three slaves had been found hiding at Reverend Smith's residence.

On March 23, however, Henshaw reported to the press that he spoke with Smith and that no freed blacks were discovered there and that Smith was unaware that Caroline or her children were slaves. Apparently locating Caroline, Henshaw threatened to have her arrested in order "to obtain information where she had concealed the child." Henshaw implied that Emma had hidden Annie and that plans were underway for Caroline and her children to leave DC. "I should here state, that at the room of the woman, I found everything packed and ready for a start," Henshaw declared. "There are circumstances which lead directly to the door of proof, that some ten or twelve slaves, including this woman and her children, were to start on Saturday night last." Henshaw then claimed in the article that he had found "the child" before concluding that he did not want to pursue the case further.[17] Based on later published articles, Henshaw's claims become confusing, as later reports indicated that Annie was still missing.

In response to the first article that claimed two or three slaves had been taken from Smith's home, another account (presumably by Emma) asserted the two black people found at Reverend Smith's "were as free, as right as law can make them." The unnamed "runaways" were Caroline and possibly Annie and her sibling. In a continued escalation of this tit-for-tat, Henshaw again responded that no free blacks were at Smith's and that Emma's claim was a "brand of falsehood." He ended, "I shall not submit quietly and in silence to the reiteration of the charge that I have attempted to reduce to slavery one entitled to her freedom." Emma then released a series of advertisements called "A Warning to the Public," in which she claimed that Annie had once been her property, but she had recently freed her. Emma further claimed Annie had lived with Henshaw but had "disappeared from her friends." Fearing Annie had been "carried off . . . to be sold," Emma warned readers against purchasing Annie since she was a freed slave.[18]

The war heated up, and Henshaw and Emma started naming names. Henshaw responded to Emma's advertisement with one of his own in which he claimed that "Emma D.E.N. Southworth addressed to the public ostensibly for the protection of a mulatto girl whom she alleges was once her property." Henshaw claimed that Emma intended to "injure" him out of "bitter malignancy." He further asserted that, because Caroline had been in his possession for eighteen years and that Annie had been born and raised in his house, they were "absolutely of right and in law [his] property." Emma responded that she was "incapable of 'bitter malignancy'" and that she had permitted Henshaw "the use of these negroes for some time but by what name shall she characterize the act that seeks to use such permission to deprive her of her property." She published the legal record of her title to the slaves, reiterating that Annie was a free person and promising that she would no longer work this dispute out in the newspapers but rather in a court of law. Henshaw claimed Emma's legal documents were "not worth the paper upon which it was written" and that he denied "the existence of any title in law or equity to this property."[19]

Then the war between them vanished. No more claims or attacks appeared in the newspapers, nor was any claim brought before the courts. Because manumission records for 1854 are missing, it's unclear what happened to Caroline or her children. In later records, Susanna emancipated Leonard Sr., Alexander, and Leonard Jr., who were other members of the Taylor family.[20] But there's no mention of Caroline, Annie, or Mandy. There can be no doubt as to what Emma wanted: for the slaves she had inherited to have their freedom. The newspaper battle between Henshaw and Emma shows how difficult and complicated freeing slaves was at that time, even when Emma had a legal right to do so. She had to go head-to-head with the man who had raised her. Emma fiercely believed in abolishing slavery, even when it came at such a high cost.

In addition to family trouble, she continued to have problems in her writing career. Although she had a good relationship with her book publisher Abraham Hart, he retired in 1854, which left her in search of another publisher. By April, she had one: Theophilus Beasley Peterson, who was a first cousin of the *Post*'s Henry Peterson. Despite the family relationship, Henry disapproved of Emma's choice. "For in your books you reinstate sometimes what I had omitted," Henry chastised. "For this very reason, and no other, as the Appletons told us, they would not publish for you. And now that you have a publisher whose name will not uphold you in the least, you should be doubly careful as to what you write."[21] Henry did not respect T. B. and for good reason.

T. B. had become known as a publisher of "cheap sensational fiction," even advertising himself as the "Cheapest book house in the World." He purchased the plates of several of Emma's books from Abraham Hart and planned to republish them. He also wanted to buy Emma's latest serial, *The Lost Heiress*, and offered her $200, which Emma accepted. In 1854, he reprinted her short story collection *Old Neighbourhoods*, retitling it *The Wife's Victory, and Other Nouvellettes*. This practice of retitling previously published work was one that T. B. continually used—an unethical strategy of which Emma was aware. *The Wife's Victory* was advertised as "New

Books," increasing sales but at the expense of readers who might have already purchased *Old Neighbourhoods*.[22] As unethical as it was, selling books cheap allowed more readers the ability to buy books, increasing the inspiring messages Emma wanted to send to her female audience. Unlike Henry, T. B. didn't censor or change the stories.

Henry became increasingly critical of Emma's work for the *Post*, and her latest serial, *Miriam, the Avenger*, was no exception. Writing about the book's title in October 1854, Henry chastised, "Mrs. Stephens said recently that your titles often might be improved—as Miriam would be better than Miriam the Avenger."[23] Henry had already criticized Emma directly, but she refused to edit her stories, so he tried a different strategy—"other" people said. Ann Stephens was a respected editor and writer, and, through her, he hoped to bend Emma to his will.

In another letter, Henry was much more direct, clearly mandating, "I want you to alter the plot." Specifically, he was unhappy about the secret marriage between the characters Marian and Thurston, and he asked Emma to make Marian "sensible and noble, instead of a weak and foolish woman." Henry even resorted to threats. "Consider deeply on this matter before rejecting my advice, for you are standing at the parting of the ways . . . I *know* that I am correct," he scolded. "I stand between you and literary perdition." But Henry also knew the goldmine he had in Emma. He ended the letter with what can only be termed passive-aggressive abuse. "It is said that blessed are the wounds of a friend—may the wounds I inflict in this letter be blessed both to you and me," he cajoled. "You have given me a deal of *trouble* and anxiety I assure you."[24] If Henry were her friend, how terrified Emma must have been about her enemies.

Emma continued to have enemies in some of her critics, despite her growing popularity. Sarah Hale praised *The Lost Heiress* for presenting "some of the most noble and beautiful models of virtue, in private and in public life." John Rueben Thompson, however, quipped, "The admirers of Mrs. Southworth, and she had created many by her passionately sensuous style, will no doubt find the *Missing Bride* highly entertaining. For ourselves, we never sup on horrors with any satisfaction nor can we approve that class of fiction to which the previous works of this lady belong." In an effort to again squelch this negativity, Emma sought to downplay her books' controversial themes by continuing to market herself as a model of true womanhood, encompassing the virtues of submissiveness, domesticity, piety, and purity.[25]

Biographical sketches of Emma's life appeared in Sarah Hale's 1853 *Woman's Record* and in John Hart's 1855 *Female Prose Writers of America*. Although never lying in the biographical accounts, Emma softened or omitted many contentious aspects. Highlighting her ancestors' two hundred years of American patriotism, she didn't say that they were also slaveholders. She called Dorothy a "lady of the old school" and credited Henshaw for "all the education she received"—again omitting their slave ownership. She underscored her childhood loneliness and plainness, thereby eliciting sympathy from her readers. On her marriage, she wrote that it was an "overwhelming misfortune" and that she chose to "pass over in silence" that time in her life. Her message about her personal life was clear—she wrote because she had no other choice.[26] She had not abandoned true womanhood; it had abandoned her.

Despite Emma's efforts, Henry Peterson still harangued her work while simultaneously coaxing her to continue writing for the *Post*. Even though he wrote that he liked her proposed title "Sibyl's Secret" for her next novel, he then inserted that he really wanted her to simply call it "Vivia or Vivia; A Tale of ______," leaving Emma to fill in the blank with "some quiet phrase." He drew a comparison to one of Emma's favorite authors, Sir Walter Scott, saying that "Scott himself liked not a too suggestive title." Henry advertised the novel in January 1855 as "Vivia, a Story of Life's Mystery." Emma proved again that she was not going to be controlled. On the one hand, she seemed to take Henry's suggestion, but what she used to fill in his "blank" was anything but a "quiet phrase." When the novel appeared in the *Post*, it was called *Vivia; or, The Secret of Power*.[27] Emma continued to be "trouble" for Henry. For Emma, his continued attempt to control what she wrote was starting to wear thin.

It was becoming increasingly apparent that Henry needed Emma more than she needed him or the *Post*. In 1855, he advertised her as "the *Post*'s own exclusive contributor." Emma, however, was hardly "exclusive" with the *Post*. In 1853, London-based book publisher Clarke, Beeton and Company printed *The Curse of Clifton*, advertising it as "an American story, rich in variety of adventure, and not wanting either in tenderness of sentiment or force of description." In 1855, the *London Journal* serially published two of Emma's previous works, *The True and False Heiress* and "The Better Way; or, The Wife Victory." It's unclear the extent to which Emma knew her works were being published. Clarke, Beeton and Company advertised Emma as the author; however, the *Journal* published Emma's stories anonymously, except for the last installment of *The True and False Heiress*. In November 1855, an agent from the *Journal* met with both Ann Stephens and Emma, hoping to receive "the advance sheets of all their writings, without reservation, and on their own terms."[28] What deal Emma made is unclear, but she at least considered the agent's offer since she would later go on to write for the *Journal* for many years.

The *Journal* wasn't alone in wanting to promote their magazine by using Emma's name. Even though she hadn't written anything for the *Era* in more than a year, Bailey and Whittier still listed her as one of their contributors. T. B. Peterson continued republishing her books, putting out four of them in 1855, continuing his shady practice of retitling them. Another downright unethical way in which T. B. used Emma's name for profit was by slipping the name of an unknown author's work in a listing of her books. One such advertisement appeared in the *Vicksburg Daily Whig* in November 1855, which listed *The Initials, a Love Story* alongside *The Missing Bride*, *The Lost Heiress*, and *The Wife's Victory*. *The Initials* was actually written by Baroness Tautphoeus, who wrote three other books but remained relatively unknown. Another misuse of Emma's name occurred when Mrs. S. A. Southworth published *The Inebriate's Hut* and advertisements for her book conveniently left out her first name or initials, leaving readers to erroneously believe it was by Emma.[29]

Ironically, as more booksellers were capitalizing from Emma's name, the year 1855 proved to be Emma's least successful in producing new works. Despite Henry's promise in the *Post*'s 1855 Prospectus, Emma's novel *Vivia* didn't appear. In fact, once she finished *Miriam, the Avenger*, Emma's pen remained silent for the remainder of that year. The numerous battles Emma had fought, both personally and professionally, had taken their toll with "a distressing illness" and a "period of discouragement and depression." It wasn't until November that Emma finally broke her silence, explaining, "Sickness, death, litigation, the parting from friends . . . all followed close succession, until I am tempted to believe that the evil destinies had received permission to test the full strength of my human heart."[30] Nevertheless, Emma couldn't stay down for long—she still had to provide for Richmond and Lottie—and she had many more empowering stories to tell.

By January 1856, her serialized novels were appearing again in both the *Era* and the *Post*. One of Henry's continued criticisms was that her stories were too long, and he consistently asked her to shorten them, but Emma resisted by explaining, "The length of the next story can be managed if I write the whole of it before you begin to print it." Emma, however, was done with Henry even though she didn't outright tell him, saying, "as long as my work is worth anything to you, you shall have it." Still, the signs were plainly there for Henry to read. She boldly told him that she intended to write for Maturin M. Ballou's *Pictorial Drawing-Room Companion* as well as for Charles J. Peterson, who not only was T. B. Peterson's brother and Henry's cousin but also had previously owned the *Post* before starting his own publication, *Peterson's Magazine*. She further told Henry, "I waived an engagement with the *New York Ledger* and other papers for the present for want of time." Undeterred, Henry advertised that Emma wrote exclusively for the *Post* and would soon write a new story for them.[31] Not only was *Vivia* the last story she wrote for the *Post*, once her short story "The Brothers" was finished in April 1856, but she also no longer contributed to the *Era*. Emma was ready for a fresh start.

Emma struggled to find what she wanted to do next. In October 1856, Emma wrote for and edited a short-lived weekly paper in Philadelphia called the *Nation*, which lasted only five weeks. Then, in her eagerness to break from the *Post*, Emma overcommitted herself to write for other publications. By April 1857, Ballou reminded Emma of her promise to write a story for him. That promised piece never materialized. She also committed to Charles Peterson's magazine, and he excitedly advertised in November 1856 that his magazine would soon publish Emma Southworth. She wrote a new serial for it called *Love's Labor Won* in 1857, but the only other piece she wrote for *Peterson's* was "The Outcast," a revised version of the previously published "Hickory Hall."[32] Although Emma likely felt an obligation to produce works for Charles Peterson because of his familial relationship to T. B., both *Peterson's Magazine* and Ballou's *Pictorial Drawing-Room Companion* were monthly publications, meaning a smaller income than her usual work for weekly periodicals.

Emma finally received an offer that changed her writing career. Proprietor and editor for the *New York Ledger* Robert Bonner first approached Emma on October 10, 1856, to see whether he could get Emma to write exclusively for him. Understandably, she might have felt wary about "exclusive" deals after the way Henry Peterson had treated her, but Bonner's tone quickly set aside those doubts. "I have read several of your Tales," he wrote. "My wife has read all of them . . . and my own belief is that there is no female author . . . who can write so excellent a story." The idea that his wife was an avid fan likely piqued Emma's interest. Bonner dangled other famous authors she knew who had joined the *Ledger* as his exclusive writers, such as Fanny Fern and Alice Cary. Most appealing had to be what he was willing to pay her. "I think I can afford to pay you *your own terms*," Bonner explained. "At any rate, I am willing to give you *double* the amount that you have ever received for a Tale from any newspaper publisher—I care not what amount that may be."[33]

Emma wrote back to Bonner on October 21, explaining to him that she was neither "permanently" nor "exclusively" tied to another publisher but that she had to finish prior writing commitments. Bonner replied that he would never consider pursuing her if she weren't free but reiterated his offer to pay her well if she would agree to write exclusively for his paper. He spent a lot of money to advertise his authors' works; he only asked in return for their commitment to his paper. The earliest Emma could submit a story to the *Ledger* would be November, and Bonner told her he'd be happy to get one whenever she could. He ended his October 22 letter with a request to visit her in person.[34]

Emma invited Bonner to Prospect Cottage, and the meeting had far-reaching ramifications. "The first day that you entered my little cottage, was a day blessed beyond all the other days of my life," she told him. "I was dying from the combined effect of overwork and underpay, of impiety and of actual privation." Bonner proved true to his word. He

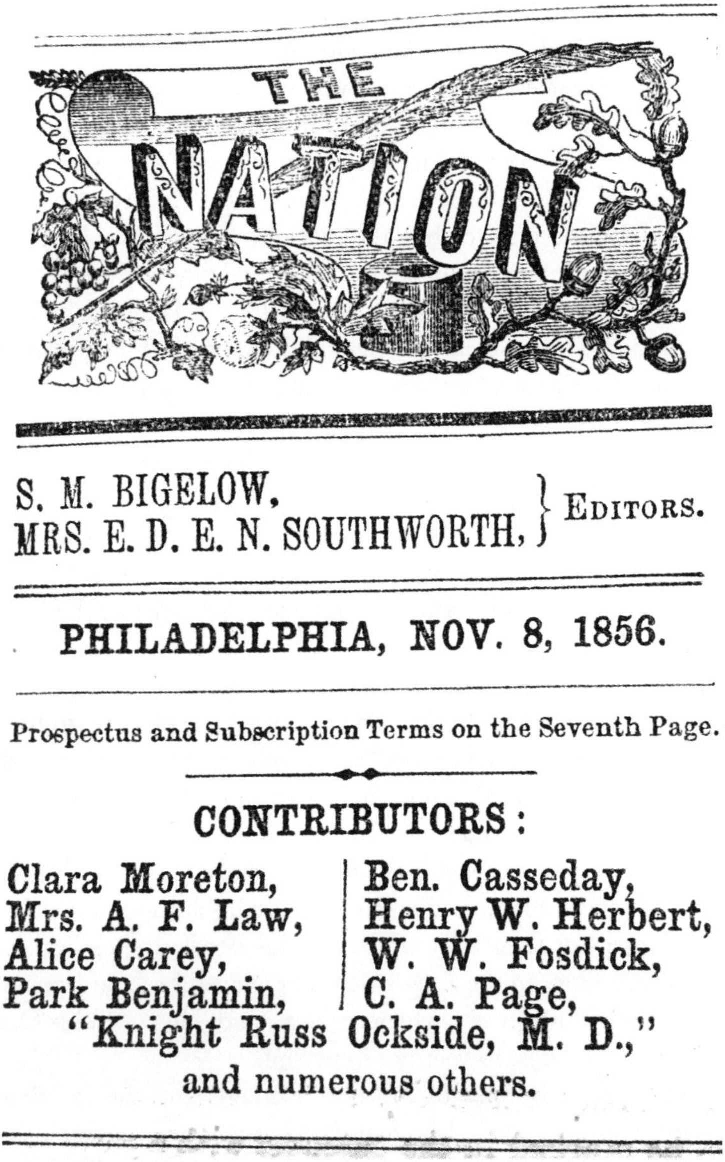

THE NATION

S. M. BIGELOW, MRS. E. D. E. N. SOUTHWORTH, } EDITORS.

PHILADELPHIA, NOV. 8, 1856.

Prospectus and Subscription Terms on the Seventh Page.

CONTRIBUTORS:

Clara Moreton,
Mrs. A. F. Law,
Alice Carey,
Park Benjamin,
Ben. Casseday,
Henry W. Herbert,
W. W. Fosdick,
C. A. Page,
"Knight Russ Ockside, M. D.,"
and numerous others.

E.D.E.N. Southworth as coeditor for the *Nation* (1856). (*American Antiquarian Society*) not only paid her better for the work she produced but also allowed her the freedom to write what she wanted. Emma was truly grateful. "Every improved circumstance around me, every comfort in my home, every attainment of my children, speak of your kindness and liberality to us," she noted.[35] Bonner and his family became her lifelong friends.

Bonner wasted no time publicizing the news that Emma had joined his team of elite writers. In December 1856, he advertised in DC's *Evening Star* that his list of popular authors included Mrs. Emma D.E.N. Southworth. Another advertisement in the *Era* stated that, after January 1, 1857, she would publish only in the *Ledger*. Henry couldn't have missed Emma's declaration to leave the *Post*, and he had no intention of letting her go. Henry asked whether she would "honor" her previous letter to write for the *Post*. Hearing nothing, he wrote to her again, this time attaching the announcement that she was now writing for the *Ledger*. "I now wish to know whether you positively refuse to comply with your engagements to us, and through us to a large portion of the public," Henry threateningly demanded. He continued to advertise in March 1857 that Emma was writing a new novel for the *Post*.[36] Clearly, she no longer had plans to produce such a novel, and Henry went after Emma's reputation.

Unlike Emma's previous battles with Henry, she was no longer alone, as Bonner came to her defense. "Our readers will find a calm, dignified, and convincing statement by Mrs. Southworth, relative to her withdrawal from the *Saturday Evening Post*," he explained. "When a lady deems it expedient to expose the misrepresentations of men who, so long as they could get her to write for them, extolled her productions, but now, seeing she is engaged to write only for the *Ledger*, assail her, we cheerfully yield her the use of our columns to set the matter right." Considering that Emma had not yet written anything for the *Ledger*, the offer to allow her unlimited space in his paper to respond to Henry's attacks showed Bonner's generosity. And respond, Emma did. "Having been importuned by Mr. Henry Peterson to write a novelette for the *Post*, I had given a verbal and conditional promise to do so," she explained. "The letters tell the rest." She then published the letters between herself and Henry, the

Robert Bonner, owner/editor of the *New York Ledger*. (*Famous American Men and Women*, 1896, 141)

last letter asking him "to withdraw my name from the list of your contributors."[37] She then laid down her pen to let the readers decide.

Henry expected Emma's statement to appear in the *Ledger*, and he responded with his own article in the *Post* the same day. He acknowledged that the *Post* had no written contract with Emma but that, "sometime after October," their assistant editor overheard a conversation between them in which Emma said she would still write the story "in addition with the *New York Ledger*." Not only had Henry now resorted to hearsay, but his vagueness regarding the date of the conversation along with once again noting that Emma had no exclusive arrangement with the *Post* did not work in his favor to convince his readers of Emma's wrongdoings. He concluded his argument with an emotional plea: "Our only complaint is that in '*cutting one of her heart strings, and letting go the sweetest and dearest associations of her literary life*,' she should have done it in so ruthless a manner."[38] As Henry emphasized in italics Emma's own words against her, he failed to mention how far their relationship had deteriorated from January to April. During those months, Emma realized she had no choice but to cut those strings with the *Post*, as Henry's tone became increasingly patronizing, demoralizing, and threatening.

The battle that was played out between Henry and Emma in the newspapers solidified her decision to join Bonner at the *Ledger*. In what can only be described as bitter fruit, Henry falsely asserted, "It appears that at the very time that we were advising Mrs. S. to complete an engagement with the *New York Ledger*, that paper was anxiously striving to wrest from us the 'prize' which we were exerting ourselves to obtain."[39] While Emma was a prized writer, Henry's statement revealed the heart of the problem: he failed to realize until too late that Emma had a mind of her own. She didn't need to be "advised," nor was she a "prize" to be won. Going forward, she would write for Robert Bonner's *Ledger*. Not only had Emma found a place to call home in her move to Prospect Cottage, but she also found a new literary home with the *Ledger*, where she would have more freedom and space to write what she wanted to say.

Chapter 7

Robert Bonner and the *New York Ledger*

> *But if you ask me what offices [women] may fill; I reply—any. I do not care what case you put; let them be sea-captains, if you will. I do not doubt there are women well fitted for such an office. . . . I think women need, especially at this juncture, a much greater range of occupation than they have, to rouse their latent powers.*[1]

Emma's first novel for the *Ledger* was *The Island Princess*, which began serially on May 30, 1857. Bonner gave Emma the freedom she needed to write about issues that were important to her, and this time she again chose to address the Woman Question—specifically, employment for women outside the domestic sphere. In the epitaph of chapter 15, Emma quoted women's rights activist Margaret Fuller's 1845 *Woman in the Nineteenth Century*, the first major feminist work in the United States. Like Emma, Fuller worked as a teacher before writing for the *Dial* and then the *New York Tribune*. Fuller lived an unconventional (albeit brief) life that showed what women could do if they cast aside traditional expectations that limited women's choices, and Emma aligned her position with Fuller's in *The Island Princess.*

Emma created one female heroine who put into practice the famous line Fuller wrote a decade earlier to "let them be sea-captains, if they will." Barbara Brande is the daughter of a sea captain, who teaches her how to navigate a sailing vessel. The stage is set for Barbara to become a sea captain herself after her father and older brothers are killed at

THE NEW YORK LEDGER

DEVOTED TO CHOICE LITERATURE ROMANCE THE NEWS COMMERCE

VOL. XIII. R. BONNER, EDITOR AND PROPRIETOR. NEW YORK, MAY 30, 1857. TERMS, $2 PER ANNUM, IN ADVANCE. NO. 12.

THE ISLAND PRINCESS.

A ROMANCE OF THE OLD AND NEW WORLD.

BY EMMA D. E. N. SOUTHWORTH.

CHAPTER I.

E.D.E.N. Southworth's *Island Princess* in the *New York Ledger* (May 30, 1857). (*Falvey Digital Library, Villanova University, Pennsylvania*) sea. She serves as a foil to the actual main character, Estelle, a refined aristocratic lady who was duped into an illicit marriage, scorned by her parents, and tried in the court of public opinion. She is on the run from her true love, whom, she believes, she cannot legitimately marry because of her past mistake. In short, Estelle has allowed herself to be ruled by everyone around her, whereas Barbara allows herself to be ruled by none. Estelle books passage aboard Barbara's ship and finds Barbara's chosen profession "a strange and trying life for a woman." Barbara responds that she would rather face the fiercest storm "than stand before the footlights of a stage, face a mixed audience, and act out a part in a play, during a whole evening—as I find even cultivated women sometimes do in this city of yours."[2] Estelle has indeed acted the part of the traditional woman who obeys those around her—the result of which has left her alone and in hiding.

Estelle's true love Montressor has been searching for her and boards Barbara's ship later in the novel. He is similarly surprised to find Barbara in command and hesitates to take passage aboard a vessel run by a woman. Montressor questions "whether some more proper feminine occupation might not have been found." To which Barbara retorts, "I thought so! There it is again! What, precisely, do you call proper feminine occupation?—sewing? teaching? acting? keeping boarders? selling goods?" She explains to Montressor that she has neither training nor desire for any of these "feminine" occupations. No, Barbara insists, "I am born to freedom, independence, and domination!"[3] Clearly siding with Fuller, Emma still wrote with a hidden hand. Knowing too well the criticisms she would face if she were as overtly outspoken and radical as Fuller, Emma hid Barbara Brande's character within the layers of plots and subplots. Even as Barbara shows up time and again to rescue and draw together the star-crossed lovers, she remains a minor character—the only one to literally and figuratively sail into the final pages of the novel, independent and free to live her life as she pleases.

Like Barbara Brande, Emma was getting her first taste of a greater freedom and being well paid for it—all thanks to her new editor and friend Robert Bonner, who worked hard to establish the *Ledger* as one of the leading literary magazines in the nation. He advertised big and paid

Barbara Brande as sea captain in *Island Princess*, in the *New York Ledger* 13, no. 19 (July 18, 1857). (*Falvey Digital Library, Villanova University, Pennsylvania*)

his writers well, but the investments paid off. He paid anywhere from $5,000 to $25,000 weekly for advertising, and his subscriptions would eventually rise to more than three hundred thousand copies a week. He also spared no expense to get the best authors to write exclusively for the *Ledger*. In 1856, he wooed Fanny Fern away from the *Post*, paying her $1,000 for her first story. He reportedly paid Henry Ward Beecher $30,000 for his novel *Norwood*, $3,000 to Charles Dickens for his short story "Hunted Down," and $3,000 to Henry Wadsworth Longfellow for his poem "The Hanging of the Crane," the largest sum ever paid for a single poem.[4] Bonner's success increased as Emma joined his team of stellar writers.

When Emma finished writing *Island Princess* in September 1857, she had already formulated her next novel, *Bride of an Evening*. In June, Bonner sent her usual weekly fee of $40 along with a note: "'The Bride of an Evening' is a capital title. *Do not mention it to any one*, lest somebody might steal it." His advice stands in stark contrast to the battles she had faced with Henry Peterson, who constantly asked her to change what she wrote and suggested alternate titles. Bonner also excitedly asked Emma, "About what time do you think you will be able to commence it?" Again, unlike Peterson, Bonner didn't question her about the content or the length. In December, Bonner heavily advertised this story, taking out an entire column in both the *New York Herald* and the *New York Times*. Emma was also listed among Bonner's other prized writers such as Fanny Fern, Sylvanus Cobb Jr., Emerson Bennett, and Alice Cary in advertisements he placed across the country. "Now is a good time to subscribe," the advertisement touted. "Mrs. Southworth's new story *The Bride of an Evening* will be commenced in the *Ledger* on the first of January."[5]

The story began on January 2, 1858, and Bonner wasted no time. On January 6, he bought two columns in the *New York Times* and printed the first two chapters. Emma was masterful at cliff-hanger endings, and the excerpt ended with a group of young people gathered around the table reading fortune cards. When the hero of the story, Mr. Dulanie, draws his card, the fortune teller foresees, "Disgrace and ill and shameful death are near!" It was then that "an irrepressible cry broke from the pallid lips of Honora," Dulanie's love interest, who exclaims, "It is wicked this tampering with the mysteries of the future." To read more, readers had to subscribe to the *Ledger*.[6] Emma's story was sensational and page-turning, but she was once again tackling tough social issues—this time advocating against capital punishment, particularly when the criminal had been convicted based on circumstantial evidence.

Not only was *The Bride of an Evening* attracting new subscribers to the *Ledger*, but it had also gained the attention of budding playwright and actor Harry Watkins, the director of amusements at P. T. Barnum's American Museum in New York. The plays performed at the museum brought in little money, and Barnum considered closing the theater. Watkins, however, convinced Barnum to give him two weeks to produce a new play, an astonishing feat that he accomplished by producing *The Pioneer Patriot*. Its success prompted Barnum to issue a new challenge to Watkins: write a five-act play in eight days. In February, he accepted and approached Bonner about adapting one of Emma's works. Bonner decided to furnish Watkins with proof sheets while the *Ledger* was still publishing chapters of *The Bride of an Evening*. The task was more difficult for him than he had imagined. On February 22, he wrote in his diary, "Mrs. E.D.E.N. Southworth is about the best among the female authoresses of this country, but her novels, although dramatic among the reading, are not stagey. It would be a much easier job to write an original play than to construct one from a story of hers."[7] The pressure mounted for him to finish the play within the eight-day time frame.

Nevertheless, Watkins completed the task on March 7, and, after a quick casting of parts, the play was ready on March 10, even before subscribers read the ending in the *Ledger*. Emma was excited to see the play performed, and, on March 19, Watkins met her in New York; however, his description of her was less than flattering. "In appearance Mrs. Southworth is not very prepossessing—indeed she is what would be termed a homely woman," Watkins wrote in his diary. "She has a careworn look, sallow complexion, prominent nose and dull blue eyes. Her age, I should judge, is the wrong side of forty-five. I should take her to be a woman of strong nerve and not easily governed." Emma was thirty-nine at that time, but he was correct—she was not easily governed. She had a mind of her own, and, luckily for him, she was not privy to his diary record. On March 26, Emma attended the play, and Barnum paid her $100 for the use of her name.[8] From her private box, she rose after the performance and made a short and barely audible speech, praising Watkins for his dramatization of her story:

> Ladies and Gentlemen,
>
> I thank you for the honor you have conferred upon me and for the popularity and flattery with which the *Bride of an Evening* has been favored—a popularity greatly enhanced by the effective manner in which the drama has been produced. For indeed, the novelist can but present abstract images to the *mind*. The dramatist breathes into them the breath of life and making them live and move before the *eye*. . . . The object, however, of both novelist and dramatist is not only to amuse. If therefore the presentation of this piece should lead one earnest mind to consider more deeply the question of convictions upon merely circumstantial evidence, then indeed the holiest purpose of the humble author will have been blessed with success.

The theater gave two performances a day for five weeks—a good showing for Emma's first book performed on stage.[9]

Emma D.E.N. Southworth (ca. 1860). (*Harvard Art Museums*)

Another ten months passed in which Emma's pen was silent. Multiple possibilities exist as to why Emma took such a long break. By 1858, Frederick certainly needed financial help. No evidence remains on how successful his Mexican fishing endeavor had been, but during the time he was there, constant political upheaval led to the Mexican Reform War. It seems unlikely that Frederick could continue to run a successful export business during such civil unrest. He returned to Brazil, and in August he had his next venture ready. Advertising in newspapers across the United States, he claimed he had discovered a new inflammable material he called "illuminating clay," which he reported could give seven cubic feet of gas to the pound, much better than coal, which gave half that amount. There's no way Emma could have missed seeing what he was doing. He advertised in DC's *Evening Star* on the front page on August

26. A news report surfaced in December that the Brazilian government had granted Frederick a thirty-year exclusive right to manufacture rosin oil in Bahai.[10] One problem remained for Frederick, just as it had in 1840 with his waterwheel. He had the idea. He had the permission from the government. What he needed was capital—and a lot of it—probably more than even Emma could give him.

Emma was now making more money with half the amount of effort. Bonner not only paid her twice what she had earned at the *Post* but also often gave authors bonus checks when their work sold well. And Emma's works had made the *Ledger* a lot of money. T. B. Peterson also continued turning her serials into books, even if he was quite stingy in buying her copyrights. In January 1858, he wanted Emma's novel *Love's Labor Won*. "We will give you $500 for it," Peterson wrote. "There has never been such hard times in the book business." Emma apparently wasn't swayed by Peterson's lowball offer, since the novel was not published as a Peterson book until 1862. Still, Peterson did publish two other books in 1858, *The Three Beauties* and *The Two Sisters*—again previously serialized books with new names. In addition to title switching and reselling books as "new," Peterson continued his previous trick of advertising books as those written by Mrs. Southworth when they were actually written by unknown authors.[11] While Emma benefited from selling Peterson her copyrights, his nefarious business practices did not go unnoticed. *Evening Star* editor W. D. Wallach noted:

> These purported to be "new novels" by the authors and are elaborately noted as such . . . but it requires but a glance at their contents to detect two old acquaintances, viz: Mrs. Southworth's "Shannondale" and Mrs. Lasselle's "Annie Grayson." The Petersons are reputed to be wags [archaic term for disreputable people] as well as fast publishers, and we dare say are laughing in their sleeves hugely at the success of their experiment upon the credulity of the public and the newspaper folks, but we incline to the opinion that they will find that in the long run "honesty is the best policy" in book publishing as well as other pursuits.[12]

Nevertheless, Emma continued to do business with T. B. Peterson, indicating that she didn't mind too much that his business practices were deceptive. It still meant she was making money.

Having a better income might explain Emma's extended break from writing. She simply wanted a long vacation. In August, a Georgetown correspondent known as "Spectator" spotted Emma at Piney Point, a popular vacation spot near her ancestral home at St. Mary's. The reporter noted that she seemed "sprightly," indicating she was in good health despite her previous bouts with lung infections.[13] Because the resort was known for offering health benefits, Emma could have been visiting with her sister Charlotte, who had battled consumption for years and by 1858 was nearing the end of her life. Also, considering that Charlotte had for the past several years spent her time traveling between Washington, DC, and Natchez, Mississippi, for her health, it's not out of the question that she and Emma spent part of the fall at their uncle's plantation, Clermont Hall.

By the end of the year, Emma and Charlotte were back in Washington, and Emma was busily writing what would become her biggest hit, *The Hidden Hand*, clearly using Clermont Hall as the setting. "The estate is surrounded on three sides by a range of steep, gray rocks, spiked with clumps of dark evergreen, and called, from its horseshoe form, the Devil's foot," Emma wrote. When comparing her description to the land plats of the 1840s, Clermont did lie along the bottom side of a horseshoe bend in the Mississippi River. Another indication was her description of a landmark:

> Beneath that range of rocks, and between it and another range, there was an awful abyss or chasm of cleft, torn and jagged rocks, opening as it were from the bowels of the earth, in the shape of a mammoth bowl, in the bottom of which, almost invisible from its great depth, seethed and boiled a mass of dark water of what seemed to be a lost river or a subterranean spring. This terrific phenomenon was called the Devil's Punch Bowl.

At the edge of Clermont Hall was another Devil's Punch Bowl. It was a jungle of vines and trees with a two-hundred-foot plunge into the river below. Mississippi legend claims it's where river pirates hid, murdering those who stood in the way of their dastardly deeds before throwing them into the overgrown bluffs below. Emma used this legend in *The Hidden Hand*. It becomes the hideout of the notorious outlaw Black Donald.[14] Emma wouldn't have wanted to draw attention to the Mississippi Punch Bowl, especially since her uncle owned a large slave plantation there and the country was on the verge of a civil war over slavery. Yet the mysterious setting of Clermont Hall was perfect, so Emma put it in Virginia as a less offensive location.

Even if Emma changed the location to a fictitious place in Virginia, her familiarity with the settings in Natchez helped her create her most successful novel to date despite ongoing health issues. "I was in wretched health at the time," Emma later wrote. "My sister was dying of consumption, and yet in the midst of these depressing circumstances the brightest and gayest of my novels came to me." She traveled each morning from western Georgetown to the eastern end of Washington to visit Charlotte, so she got into the habit of writing from noon until midnight. "Anxious as I was about my sister," Emma remembered, "when I took up my pen I became possessed of the spirit of Capitola, and care and sorrow left me."[15] The fetters that had kept Emma bound to acceptable norms fell away, thanks to the care and encouragement of Bonner. Emma's heroine Capitola was carefree, adventurous, and unafraid of tackling any challenge.

Emma claimed that the idea for Capitola Black came to her from a newspaper article about a nine-year-old girl who dressed in boy's clothing in order to sell newspapers and who was arrested in New York. Emma, however, likely softened the realities of what actually happened. In March 1858, a story was widely publicized in numerous newspapers across the United States about a sixteen-year-old girl who had been traveling on the train cars between Cairo and Centralia, Illinois. She, along with a group of boys, had been doing well selling papers along the route, none of them suspecting that the "good-looking" newsboy was in fact a girl in disguise. "She . . . played billiards, smoked cigars, swore and drank whisky, as easily and naturally as a newsboy might be expected to do," the news article reported. Once the girl's identity was discovered, it turned out that she was actually twenty, and the reason for her masquerade remained unknown.[16] Using such a scandalous woman as the heroine for her novel wouldn't do, but the story planted the seeds for the raucous and wild tomboy named Capitola.

Emma used other stories she'd heard to create a novel filled with intrigue and mystery. She remembered a story from her childhood in which a nurse had been kidnapped by two disguised men and taken to a house where a woman was about to give birth. They tried to bribe the nurse to kill the newborn child, but she adamantly refused. Apparently, the young mother's family was displeased with her illicit pregnancy. Perseverance by the mother prevailed, and the child grew up in the city of Washington. Similarly, in *The Hidden Hand*, Nurse Nancy Grewell tells a fantastic tale of being kidnapped by two masked men and taken to a house where a young, blindfolded mother has just given birth to twins, one girl and a stillborn boy. The mother begs the nurse to give the dead baby to them and smuggle the newborn girl away from her kidnappers. Nurse Grewell agrees, and the mother gives her a wedding ring that was inscribed with two words: *Eugene* and *Capitola*. Grewell names the baby Capitola and discovers a strange birthmark in the middle of her left palm that was "the perfect image of a crimson hand."[17] It stood to reason that a girl possessed of extraordinary capabilities like Capitola needed to have extraordinary and mysterious birth origins. Emma had set the stage for some outrageous and often hysterical situations for her bold little Cap.

Emma also gleaned other characters and story lines from situations she had read about or experienced in real life. "My stories always have a foundation in fact," Emma wrote. She described her character Old Hurricane as "liberal, kind-hearted, but blustering and overbearing in manner—you might meet him any time among Maryland and Virginia planters." But, in actuality, Old Hurricane, who becomes Capitola's benefactor, was modeled after her uncle John Baptiste Nevitte from Clermont Plantation. Capitola's "sparkling speeches to Old Hurricane were taken from conversations which occurred between my sister and a Mississippi uncle," Emma confessed.[18] It seems likely, however, that most of these conversations were between Uncle Nevitte and Emma, as she is clearly more like her heroine Capitola than Charlotte.

From one such conversation, Emma recalled a real-life adventure of a Mississippi girl who had been taken advantage of by a British officer. She appealed to her brothers to avenge her honor, but they wouldn't take the matter seriously. She challenged the officer to a duel, which he took as a joke and ignored her. She met him anyway, armed with real bullets, and shot him, leaving him severely wounded. She gave herself up to the authorities, and once the case was investigated, she was released. Emma used this incident to create one of the most rip-snorting scenes in the novel.

The villain Craven LeNoir had previously tried to seduce Capitola, but she outwits his wicked designs. He then spreads rumors that she is a loose girl. After the village men refuse to defend her honor, Capitola challenges Craven to a duel, takes two pistols from Old Hurricane's cabinet, and waits for Craven on a lonesome road in the woods. He takes it all as a big joke, but she shoots him no fewer than six times. Capitola returns to the village, turns herself in, and shows the men where Craven was shot. After being taken to the doctor's office, Craven—thinking he's dying—confesses all that he's done to Capitola. Once the doctor examines Craven's "wounds," however, he discovers that he wasn't shot with bullets but with dried peas and was virtually uninjured. The tables are turned, and Craven becomes the laughingstock of the village.[19] Using satire as her weapon, Emma unhands the foolishness of the patriarchal duel, showing instead how women could save themselves and defend their honor by using their own acumen and wits.

It was just the kind of story women wanted, and when *The Hidden Hand* appeared on February 5, 1859, it became an instant success, helped by Bonner and his advertisements. By April, he released the first couple of chapters to more than one thousand newspapers at a cost of around $30,000. Then, in the middle of the serialization of *The Hidden Hand*, Emma did something quite surprising—at least to her readers. On May 9, Emma went to the State Department to apply for a U.S. passport. Widely publicized in newspapers was the news that she would be sailing on the next steamer to make a tour of Europe. Hidden in the report was the primary reason. "Mrs. S. has by her talents made a handsome fortune," one article reported. "Her husband, a worthless scamp, left her some three years since with two children, and quite destitute—but out of this cloud came the silver lining which has developed her brilliant talents, and been of profit to herself and pleasure to the public."[20] Clearly, Frederick had been snooping around for money the previous year—the year of her silence—and she wasn't going to give it to him. No, she was going to England.

She was going, with Bonner's blessing, not only to escape Frederick but also to secure copyrights for her works still being pirated in the London press. Emma and Bonner had decided who would publish her work in England.[21] Already having ties to the *London Journal*, editor George Stiff was eager for Emma to write exclusively for him. Stiff believed that if Emma lived in England, British copyright law would give him the sole rights to publish her works against other publishers who were pirating the stories from the *Ledger*. Even though Emma despised the fact that her works were being stolen, she had still made a handsome income at the time she departed for England. One report estimated that Bonner was paying her $2,000 a year, along with a similar amount of $2,000 from the *London Journal*, plus an undisclosed sum from book publishers and playwrights.[22] At an estimated $5,000 to $6,000 per year (approximately $187,000 to $224,000 in 2024 dollars), Emma was doing quite well for herself—and she and Bonner made the decision to go with the *London Journal*, most likely a result of a better financial offer.

While the reasons for Emma's departure for England were multifaceted, the trip was one that Emma, Bonner, and Stiff had obviously planned. When she left New York bound for Liverpool, the serialization of *The Hidden Hand* was in the middle of production in the *Ledger*. Chapters continued being published weekly for another six weeks, however, indicating that Emma had left the rest of the book with Bonner before she boarded the steamer on May 28, 1859. Emma, eighteen-year-old Richmond, and fifteen-year-old Lottie were among 154 passengers aboard the steamship *Vigo*. Prior to departing, Emma might have seen her dear old friend Gamaliel Bailey—perhaps even traveling together from DC to New York. Bailey departed for Europe the same day as

Emma, but he had passage aboard the steamer *Arago*. It would be the last time she would see him. On board, Bailey became increasingly ill and died mid-voyage on June 5.[23] Still on board the *Vigo*, it would be some time before Emma learned of her benefactor's fate.

The *Vigo* was a relatively new steamer, and Emma now had the money to purchase first-class cabins. The quality of the rooms and food equaled that of a good hotel, but accommodations were hardly luxurious. To save space, the saloon and staterooms were in the back of the ship, which made passengers profoundly feel the ocean waves, thus increasing motion sickness. Two berths were in each room, one above the other and around two feet in width and only a stool's width between the beds and the closet. Even though the rooms might contain a wash basin, there were no baths, unless a passenger wished to be hosed off by the boatswain washing the deck in the early morning.[24] Sailing across the ocean in 1859 was not for the faint of heart, even for first-class passengers.

Emma also described first-class accommodations in *The Bride's Fate*. When the two characters Anna and Drusilla come aboard the steamer *Hurona*, they are shown a first-class drawing room in which they see "velvet carpets, satin damask curtains, heavily gilded cornices, cheval mirrors, and all the showy appointments of the place." The steward shows Drusilla her berth, "a clean, cozy den, with an upper and lower berth, and a sofa, wash-stand, shelves and drawers, and all that was required for convenience." Anna and her husband Dick's accommodations seem even nicer and larger than Drusilla's, but being closer to the rear of the vessel meant that they "would be harassed by every motion of the ship."[25]

The *Vigo* was also one of the first steamers to offer third-class accommodations, but conditions for steerage passengers were horrible. Third-class quarters were in the belly of the ship, where the machinery was housed. Unlike first-class cabins, passengers in third class not only had to provide their own bedding but also had rows of bunk beds quartered closely together. The steamship companies provided food, but it was often poor quality and rationed. No plates or eating utensils were provided, meaning that passengers needed to bring their own and wash up after their meals. To make matters worse, water was also rationed, leading to unclean conditions and poor health. There were not enough bathrooms aboard, so passengers used chamber pots, and with such overcrowding, the smell below became overwhelming. The stench increased when the ventilation hatches had to be closed during bad weather. Even after the United States and Britain passed Passenger Acts in 1855, conditions only slightly improved because the laws were hard to regulate.[26] Nothing highlighted social class disparity better than the passage conditions aboard transatlantic steamers.

A keen observer of her surroundings, Emma wrote about them in *The Fortune Seeker*, describing the *Star of the West*, which served as a microcosm of the wealth disparity at large. Of the lowest class of citizens on board, she wrote:

> But of the three ranks of voyagers in the first, second, and third cabins, that in the third cabin or steerage contained the greatest element of human interest, I had nearly said, of tragic dignity. For here were none of the superficial votaries of wealth, fashion, or pleasure, seeking money, fame, or excitement. Here were crowded together hundreds of poor emigrants, earnest men, women, and even children sent out by the company—the homeless to seek a home, the famishing to seek food, the perishing to seek the means of living—to seek them through toil, danger, and suffering.

Further showing the terrible conditions for the poor, Emma created as her main hero twelve-year-old Welby Dunbar, an orphan working aboard the ship to pay the fare. He had spent many days "in the confined quarters of the lower deck, unable to look far out at sea, unable to look out anywhere except at a segment of the dark sky." He felt like he was riding aboard "a moving prison," as steerage passengers were not allowed to be on the main or upper decks.[27]

Two weeks of closely observing the differences between first- and third-class passengers weighed heavily on Emma's mind as she and her children arrived in the Old World. The *Vigo* docked in Liverpool on June 11, 1859. Then they took the railway to London, and what a world Emma witnessed once she arrived. Victoria was queen, and the city was filled with contrasts. The affluent wealth could be seen in the new constructions. Big Ben had just opened in May, and the Houses of Parliament had recently been rebuilt after a fire in 1837. The glitz of these buildings, however, was overshadowed by smog-filled streets from numerous coal factories and a polluted Thames River bursting with raw sewage. The air was thick and heavy, and the stench was often unbearable. The rapid growth in population from one million to six million—mostly poor immigrants who had left their farms for work in the city—furthered London's housing problem. As a result of the 1848 Potato Famine in Ireland, more than one hundred thousand starving Irish fled their homeland to settle in London, leading to even greater numbers of slum housing.[28] As Emma stepped off the train, she was overwhelmed by the glaring differences between the rich and the poor. She certainly had a lot to write about, which readers could buy in both Stiff's *Journal* and Bonner's *Ledger*.

Chapter 8

Under the Green Shadows of Old English Homes

Now, dear reader, my pleasant task is ended. Day and night have I wrought at it, cheered by your appreciation and by the goodness of the best publisher I have ever read. But my strength is not great nor my health good, and this week I go, with my two children, to recruit under the green shadows of old English homes. And in leaving my native shore I feel like begging from you all, a kind "God bless you."[1]

Even though Emma ended *The Hidden Hand* with the above note in the *Ledger* on July 9, 1859, she had already been living in London for several weeks. Not only was she working for George Stiff, but, at his invitation, she, Richmond, and Lottie were also living with him at his home Beulah Spa Villa in Upper Norwood, located around four miles south of London in the borough of Croydon. Once the site of the Royal Beulah Spa, the area was known for its healing spring water and twenty-five-acre garden. It was once a popular resort for the rich and famous, visited by well-known writers such as Charles Dickens and William Makepeace Thackeray as well as dukes, duchesses, and even Queen Victoria. In 1854, Beulah Spa declined in popularity, as tourists preferred the sights at the nearby Crystal Palace. With the addition of the Queen's Hotel in 1854, the Norwood area held its posh status, as the wealthy from abroad favored this location. Mansions were built along the Beulah Hills

Road, and the area became known as the fashionable place to see and be seen.[2] It was here that Stiff lived along with his servants, and, at first glance, it would seem that Emma was recuperating under the green trees of the English estates.

Stiff bought Beulah Spa Villa as a way to enjoy the money he earned after years working in the publishing business. He started as an engraver for Herbert Ingram's *Illustrated London News* in 1842. Ingram noticed that readership went up when issues contained woodcut engravings along with the written text, and his publication was the first to use these pictures in its standard layout. In 1845, Stiff started the *London Journal*, using the same kind of woodcut engravings and layout as Ingram's publication. The *Journal* reached monumental success, attaining a circulation of five hundred thousand by the mid-1850s. Despite Stiff's achievements, his lavish lifestyle was problematic for him. His obvious need for money reached a tipping point in 1857, and he made a surprising sale to his former boss for a whopping £300,000. Ingram failed to maintain the *Journal*'s success, however, likely because he put it in the hands of his friend Mark Lemon, who reserialized novels of bygone authors and drastically redesigned the layout. These changes proved to be a dismal failure, losing half the publication's subscribers by 1858. In June 1859, Stiff started two new papers: the *Guide* and the *Daily London Journal*. Ingram charged Stiff with plagiarism and took him to court, but because Ingram's *Journal* no longer looked anything like Stiff's, the judge dismissed the plagiarism charges. Perhaps as a way to end the court battle and appease the irate Ingram, Stiff bought back the *London Journal* for £3,500 more than he sold it.[3] It was into this competitive, dog-eat-dog world that Emma entered when she arrived in London—so much for relaxing under shade trees.

Helping Emma navigate the tangled limbs of the English publishing world was Robert Bonner, who understood the complexities of copyright laws. He had regularly taken a subscription to the *Journal*, and he turned the *Ledger* into a highly circulating literary publication by using the same layout with woodcut engravings and reprinting stories by popular British writers. Although republishing stories without paying the author seems unethical today, it was a common practice during the nineteenth century, both in the United States and abroad. Copyright laws really extended only to publishers and printers, and once they owned the copyright, authors no longer had to be paid for their work. If there was no copyright on a story, it was considered fair game to be used by other publishers. As middle-class readership grew, publishers rushed to gain subscribers by selling as cheap as possible. Being able to reprint stories without paying authors was one way to cut costs. Publishers also lowered subscription prices, sometimes selling cheaper than the cost to print, hoping that if they sold enough copies, they could break even. These practices led to the Book Wars of the 1840s, but the model, of course, was unsustainable and threatened to put them all out of business.[4] Publishers had to take matters into their own hands to secure the best and most profitable writers.

In order to protect the mutual interest of both publishers and authors, courtesy trade agreements, in which two publishers agreed to provide advance copies of a writer's work, became popular. John Cassell, who was vying for better international copyright laws, hoped to secure a trade agreement with Bonner to publish Emma's work in *Cassell's Illustrated Family Paper*, and yet Bonner chose Stiff, possibly because he had already published the first chapters of *The Hidden Hand* anonymously as *The Masked Mother* in the *Guide*. After repurchasing the *Journal*, Stiff merged it with the *Guide*, and he needed to secure first publishing rights with popular writers such as Mrs. Southworth. The trade agreement was beneficial for Bonner and Stiff. Bonner could still claim Emma as his exclusive writer in the United States while safeguarding that she would be well paid by the *Journal*. For Stiff, making Emma Southworth his "special star" helped ensure the steady regrowth of the *Journal*.[5] Other publishers, however, continued reprinting her work without paying her for it. The dark shadows of greed ran deep within the publishing world, and one of the first places she observed it was with the playwright success of *The Hidden Hand*, both in the United States and in England.

The serialization of *The Hidden Hand* had no sooner been completed on July 9 in the *Ledger* than it appeared as a play in New York on July 16. The immediacy of the play's release just a week after its completion in the *Ledger* suggests that Bonner had negotiated on Emma's behalf the rights for the book to be produced as a play, much as he had done for

Bride of an Evening. This time, playwright George L. Aiken wrote the script and played the part of Old Hurricane, both in Burton's Theatre in New York and in the Metropolitan Theatre in Buffalo, where it met with "splendid success."[6] Aiken's play continued to run throughout the rest of 1859; however, it was only one of many theatrical renditions of *The Hidden Hand.*

In September 1859, British actor and playwright James Burdett Howe produced a version of Emma's story called *Capitola; or, The Hidden Hand.* He starred in the role of Black Donald, playing to sold-out crowds in Pittsburgh, Baltimore, and Washington, DC, throughout 1859 and 1860. Bearing an uncanny resemblance to the famous John Wilkes Booth, Howe experienced several instances in which he was mistaken as one of the Booths. Not only was John Wilkes an actor, but brother Edwin and father Junius Brutus were as well. Howe's resemblance to the Booth family might explain why later in life Emma told reporters that John Wilkes Booth had played the part of Black Donald at the Grecian Theatre in London.[7] Howe had returned to England by 1862 and acted in several plays in London theaters, so Emma could have seen him perform and confused him with Booth. At any rate, John Wilkes Booth was never in London, and no records exist that prove he played the part of Black Donald.

Another playwright to capitalize on Capitola was a familiar face to Emma and Bonner—Harry Watkins, who had turned *Bride of an Evening* into a theater production. This time, Watkins opened *The Hidden Hand* at the Marshall Theatre in Richmond, Virginia. Watkins played in blackface the minstrel character Wool, the slave-servant of Old Hurricane; today's audience would consider this caricature offensive, but theatergoers of the nineteenth century viewed it as comic relief. Watkins's wife Rose Howard played Capitola. When Watkins's troupe played at the National Theatre in Philadelphia, audiences were "moved to tears and convulsed with laughter." After playing in the United States, Watkins took the play to England. Emma must have noticed advertisements that Harry Watkins and Rose Howard were performing *The Hidden Hand.* They appeared in 1861 and 1862 at the Victoria Theatre in London, the Royal Colosseum Theatre in Liverpool, and the Standard Theatre in Shoreditch.[8] Capitola

J. B. Howe (stage actor and John Wilkes Booth look-alike). (*Bijou Theatre, Australia*)

John Wilkes Booth (actor and presidential assassin). (*Library of Congress*)

fever had spread in theaters across the United States and the United Kingdom.

Shortly after Emma's arrival in London, she went to see the play at the Royal Grecian Theatre, presumably after it was advertised in *Lloyd's Weekly Newspaper* as a "great hit." A Mr. Mead played the role of Black Donald, and a Miss Coveney played Capitola. When it appeared in Southampton at the Theatre Royal, however, one critic gave it a less-than-stellar review, saying that the ominously named work "has not met with that success a new piece generally attracts . . . but as it has pleased the audience, we suppose that is all that is required of it." The play had continued success across London during the time Emma lived there, also appearing at the Marylebone and Olympic theaters.[9] While the numerous theater productions propelled Emma into international fame, her heroine Capitola soon spread beyond fiction and into real life.

Less than a year after the completion of *The Hidden Hand*, Capitola became a role model for women. Nineteenth-century cultural expectations were that middle- and upper-class women be submissive and fragile. Traits such as physical strength and emotional fortitude were unwomanly. Many women, particularly in America, questioned this image of the ideal woman as the country became fraught with economic uncertainty and rumors of war. More women realized they needed to be able to take care of themselves—Capitola was the fictitious heroine who could show them how to do so.[10] Prior to *The Hidden Hand*, Emma's female heroines embodied similar qualities of bravery and independence, such as Hagar Churchill in *The Deserted Wife* (1849), Harriette Joy in *Shannondale* (1850), Nettie Starbright in *The Discarded Daughter* (1851), and Helen Wildman in *Vivia; or, The Secret of Power* (1856). Although these characters rode horses, shot game with bows and arrows, rowed boats, and climbed trees, it was the over-the-top antics of Capitola that truly resonated with Emma's female audience, and it started a craze for all things "Capitola."

The satiric gender-bending capers of Capitola delighted women who secretly wanted to be more like her. The real joke is how Emma hid her true intent through her tongue-in-cheek commentary. "Reader! I do not defend, far less approve, poor Cap!" Emma feigned. "I only tell her story and describe her as I have seen her, leaving her to your charitable interpretation." Readers' approval soon became apparent. In September 1859, a racehorse named Capitola appeared on a Tennessee course and, "like her namesake in Mrs. Southworth's 'Hidden Hand,' she is hard to beat." True to predictions, Capitola was a winning horse. By the next year, a "fine new steamer *Capitola*" traveled the Ohio River, and one young girl Lulu Hall even convinced her father to name a seaside town in California after Capitola.[11] Naming towns, boats, and horses after the popular heroine was only the beginning of the influence she had on women.

Soon, the hot new fashion was the Capitola hat, a part of the heroine's riding habit. In the novel, Capitola rescues the fair Clara Day, who is being forced to marry Craven LeNoir. When Capitola discovers Craven's plan, she convinces the guard to let her into the house where Clara is being held against her will. Because the young women are relatively the same build, Capitola convinces Clara to switch clothing, allowing her to walk out unnoticed. It's more than the clothes that allow Clara's escape, however; it's the way she wears the hat and riding habit, requiring a lesson from Capitola: "Pull your cap over your eyes . . . throw back your head; walk with a little springy sway and swagger, as if you didn't care a damson for anybody, and—there! I declare, nobody could tell you from me." Clara's friend Marah later observes, "You must have contracted . . . Capitola's ways, from putting on her habit."[12] Being like Capitola was exactly what young women wanted.

Stores advertised a "fine selection" of Capitola hats with "Plumes, Velvet and Lace." One fashion reviewer pronounced that the "new headgear" was "a jaunty saucy little hat and feathers, and when worn by the girls it is, to our way of thinking, the most becoming fashion lately hit upon." He also instructed women how the hat should be worn: "It ought not, however, to be worn too much on the face, which gives the wearer a bold look. The idea is to droop the hat and feather a little, so as not to lose sight of that modesty without which a woman, young or old, is—leather and prunella." The reviewer had obviously not read the book—wearing the hat was all about achieving a bold look, which Emma wrote comes with a "sway and swagger." The hats were a big hit, and in one newspaper article about a man who had performed a tightrope act between

Engraving of Capitola on horseback in *The Hidden Hand* (April 30, 1859). (*Falvey Digital Library, Villanova University, Pennsylvania*)

two buildings, his feat was overshadowed by his audience. The reporter observed, "The ladies turned out to witness the occurrence in great numbers, and the streets and windows were 'chock full' of bright faces and gay Capitola hats."[13] If only the reporter had interviewed at least one of the hat wearers to see what they were thinking. Perhaps a few dreamed of walking the wire themselves.

Even if these women couldn't dream of such boldness for their own lives, they passed the hope of such daring bravery onto their daughters. In a sad story published in 1861, a reporter told of a young female servant who had "loved not wisely but too well" and became pregnant. "Here is the old story!" the reporter repined. "Women are weak and must love; men will play the villain—and this erring one was frail." Frail as the pregnant woman might have been, she named her daughter Capitola. The name *Capitola* grew in popularity throughout the nineteenth and twentieth centuries. Emma's heroine challenged normative behavior on how women should dress and behave, leading to tomboyism in America.[14]

While enjoying the popularity of *The Hidden Hand*, Emma had come to London to challenge copyright law in an effort to be paid by plagiaristic publishers. Not only had she seen her novel performed in theaters, but booksellers were also printing and selling it. As it had only just finished serialization in the *Ledger*, Emma hadn't sold the copyright to any book publisher, either in the United States or in England. It wasn't just *The Hidden Hand* being reprinted without her permission. On August 13, 1859, the *Ledger* began serializing *The Doom of Deville*. A week later, London's *Parlour Journal* was advertising the same story. In December 1859, Emma filed an injunction against the publication, citing that they were stealing it from Edward Forester Hyde, Stiff's employee at the *Journal*. Stiff printed *Doom of Deville* in pamphlet form to establish that it was being published in England, suggesting the *Parlour* was violating copyright law. However, because *Doom of Deville* had appeared in the *Ledger* before the pamphlets or the *Parlour*, no one had violated the law. The court felt it "was bound to dissolve the injunction," and the case did not proceed further.[15]

Despite the controversy surrounding Emma's serialization of *Doom of Deville*, its popularity in England led to a humorous incident with one of her fans. As the novel had been signed E.D.E.N. Southworth, it was unclear whether the author was a man or a woman. Impressed by the novel, a Yorkshire squire invited Emma to spend some time shooting on his estate. He explained that he was a bachelor and there were no ladies in the house except his housekeeper. "I laughed very much when I received this note," Emma wrote. "[I] need hardly tell you I did not shoot the preserves that autumn."[16]

Although she didn't visit the squire, she met famous and wealthy people (some of them aristocratic) who resided in the old English homes. Emma's favorite acquaintance was Anne Isabella Noel Byron, former wife of the famous poet Lord Byron. Prior to Emma's arrival, Harriet Beecher Stowe wrote a letter of introduction to Lady Bryon, describing Emma as a "very good and worthy woman who has led a suffering faithful life." She continued, "She is one of the many victims of man's cruelty—her husband a monster."[17] Both Emma and Lady Byron were separated from their husbands and reared their children alone. Lady

Byron had left her husband after reports of his numerous affairs and raised their only daughter, Ada, by herself. Because leaving one's husband was considered scandalous at the time, Stowe, who had met Lady Bryon in 1853, later defended her in *Lady Byron Vindicated* (1870). Similarities aside, Emma had hoped to meet Lady Bryon since seeing a picture of her in the frontispiece of Lord Byron's works many years earlier.[18] Byron was one of Emma's favorites—she frequently featured lines from his poems in her novels' epigraphs.

In June 1859, Emma walked along a row of three-story brick houses near Regent's Park before arriving at Lady Byron's home at St. George's Terrace. "The prospect of a presentation to Queen Victoria or Empress Eugenie would not have interested me nearly so much as the anticipation of a meeting with the poet's widow," Emma wrote. "I felt like one in a dream." She was surprised when greeted by the smartly attired butler, who looked more like a divinity student. Other servants she met were similarly clothed. Unlike other upper-class aristocracy, Lady Byron preferred that her servants dressed in ways that didn't highlight their domestic positions. Emma was also surprised at Lady Byron's appearance. "I had 'in my mind's eye' the image of a lady, tall, stately, queenly, richly arrayed," Emma recalled. Instead, she met a small, frail, silver-haired woman simply dressed in a plain black silk gown with a black crape shawl over her shoulders and a black and white widow's cap on her head. "Any betrayal of emotion is considered very 'bad form' in good society," Emma believed. "I hope and trust I did not show what I felt when I clasped the hand Lord Byron had so often pressed!"[19] Emma had met her real-life heroine, who had overcome many obstacles with intelligence, grace, and dignity.

Emma and Lady Byron also discovered they shared a commitment to the antislavery movement. Stowe told Lady Byron that Emma was "a thoroughly Southern woman tho [*sic*] a strong antislavery one." Lady Byron had attended the 1840 World Antislavery Convention in London, and she found Emma's intimate knowledge of slavery interesting. Wanting to learn more, Lady Byron invited Emma to lunch, and they continued to discuss their friend Harriet Beecher Stowe as well as the turbulent political climate in America.[20]

Another socially challenging issue on which Emma and Lady Byron agreed concerned capital punishment. Both believed that the death penalty was not a correct sentence even if the perpetrator had committed murder. Broaching the subject, Lady Byron asked Emma whether she had read Dinah Maria Mulock's 1856 novel *A Life for a Life*. When Emma affirmed that she had, Lady Byron said, "But not the last edition, probably, for it is just out." The latest version of the novel had just been released in August 1859. Central to the book was the murder committed by the main character, Max Urquhart. In the first version, Mulock indicated that the death was accidental, causing Max to work as a surgeon during the Crimean War as reparation for the life he took. "There was not much significance in the remorse of a man who had not intended to kill his deadly foe," Lady Byron said before advising Mulock to change the murder scene to one in which Max had meant to kill his adversary. In the reprinted edition, Lady Byron felt the novel was much improved. "This reading only could explain the life-long bitter expiation of him who had yielded to an impulse of murderous rage, and this only could carry the lesson intended to go to the heart of the most hopeless penitent as well as to the consciousness of the most arrogant Pharisee," she concluded.[21] This first meeting solidified an ongoing, albeit brief, friendship.

Emma last saw Lady Byron in December 1859, shortly after the hanging of John Brown, the American abolitionist who led a slave revolt at Harpers Ferry. Emma was now a well-known visitor and was immediately shown into the drawing room, where she met Lady Byron's longtime friend, the educationalist Mary Carpenter. She and a maid were packing a complete mourning outfit to be sent to John Brown's widow. Lady Byron explained, "All of this clothing has been made up by my school girls under the direction of Miss Carpenter." Both Carpenter and Lady Byron shared an interest in common education. Lady Byron founded Ealing Grove School, where working-class males received not only a classroom education but also practical skills such as carpentry or gardening. The school became a model for later industrial schools. Mary Carpenter likewise opened a reform school for delinquent children and wrote books on educating the poor. Emma later helped start similar schools when she returned to DC. After this visit, Lady Byron soon left

London for her country home. They corresponded until Lady Byron died in May 1860. "She was the most intimate friend I had in England," Emma wrote.[22]

In addition to Lady Byron, Emma met the Duchess of Sutherland, another outspoken advocate for abolishing slavery in the United States. In 1853, she organized an antislavery event at Stafford House, which under the duchess's influence became a center of social events and philanthropic undertakings. Stafford House was a palatial mansion in the St. James district, known for its grand staircase and ballroom as well as its impressive art collection. It was certainly one "old English home" that afforded Emma the opportunity to meet many among the rich and famous, which also included visits from Queen Victoria. The duchess had close personal ties to the queen and served as the Mistress of the Robes, who was responsible for Her Majesty's clothing and jewelry.[23] While it's unclear whether Emma ever met the queen, Emma ran in some pretty lofty circles.

Emma also encountered several famous British writers and religious leaders who sought to improve educational opportunities and living conditions for the poor. Among them were Charles and Henry Kingsley, brothers who were well-known historians and novelists; feminist author and lecturer Harriet Martineau and her brother James, a religious philosopher and Unitarian historian; and Arthur Helps, an author who had gained the confidence and respect of Queen Victoria.[24] Listening to the ideas of these new friends not only gave Emma insight into social class structures and the disparity between the rich and the poor but also served as fodder to create characters and plots for her next novels.

Emma enjoyed meeting diverse and interesting people, but she missed home and was eager to hear news about family and friends. She had grown especially close to Robert Bonner and his wife Jane. In Emma's letters, she regularly asked about Jane as well as the Bonners' sons: Andrew, Robert Jr., and Freddy. When the Bonners welcomed a daughter into their family in October 1859, they named her Emma Jane and asked Emma to be her godmother. News from home was not always joyful, however. After a long illness, Emma's beloved sister Charlotte died on November 10, 1859, and was buried in DC's Congressional Cemetery.

Their closeness was evident, as she left Emma "my Pictorial Bible as a testimony of my undying love for her."[25] The loss was magnified by the fact that Emma could not be at Charlotte's deathbed or her funeral.

Charlotte's death was not the only painful problem happening back home. After fourteen years of estrangement, Frederick finally came after her money. He had discovered "Illuminating Vegetable Turf" in Brazil a year earlier and had heavily advertised the benefits of using his oil, but, as always, he needed investors. By late 1859 and early 1860, Frederick traveled several times to Philadelphia, New York, and DC in what appeared to be an attempt to speak with Emma's publishers to procure money from the sale of her books.[26] He had no idea of the business relationship she had with T. B. Peterson or the personal relationship she had with Bonner, who closely protected her financial and business interests.

Legally, Frederick was entitled to Emma's earnings, but her publishers refused to comply with his demands, so Frederick went to the press. In February 1860, several U.S. newspapers reported a "family quarrel" in which Frederick had "obtained an injunction inhibiting Mr. Robert Bonner, of the *New York Ledger*, and all other publishers, from accepting or publishing any manuscript furnished by his wife—Mrs. E.D.E.N. Southworth." Making matters worse was what Frederick said about their marriage:

> Between Mr. and Mrs. Southworth an unfortunate feud has existed for the last eighteen years—originating in incompatibility of temperament. The husband has constantly sought the society and marital duty of the wife; the wife has performed what she has deemed her proper duty and both parties have strictly declined going into Doctors' Commons for divorce. Mr. Southworth is an opulent merchant of Rio de Janeiro, and his wife has secured, through her literary labors, a fortune for herself. Neither party is actuated by the lust of money.

A second article stated that they were "both rich and undivorced."[27] Several clues belie Frederick's slanderous attacks. By his own admission, they had a long-standing separation, so he had no need to stop her from earning a living, as it would be his financial responsibility if she didn't.

Because Frederick desperately needed money, he used the injunction as retributive blackmail in hopes that she would cave to his demands. Emma would have been further horrified about Frederick's claim that they still had sexual relations. No evidence exists that they had spent any time together since he'd left her. Emma hadn't procured a divorce, but she likely didn't want the publicity such legal proceedings would raise in the press. Because of Frederick's abandonment, she had grounds. Frederick didn't and would have wanted to stay married to Emma, as she was becoming increasingly wealthy—a wealth he now sought to obtain.

In addition to using the press to blackmail Emma, he went after her book copyrights. From January through April 1860, Frederick registered copyrights of eighteen of Emma's novels in the Southern District of New York. This action can only be seen as a frantic attempt to legally own her work in order to sell the novels to other book publishers. This desperation becomes increasingly clear when examining the titles of the books he registered—several were the same novels with different titles. He also registered a novel titled *Kathleen Vernon*, which wasn't even the title of a novel but the name of the heroine in *The Curse of Clifton*. Frederick's rash action demonstrated how little he knew of Emma's writing and copyright laws. Because her books were already copyrighted, his attempts to own her published works were meaningless.[28]

Emma was appalled by what Frederick was doing, and, in March 1860, T. B. Peterson printed a collection of previously published short stories called *The Haunted Homestead*, which included "An Autobiography of the Authoress," placed prominently at the beginning of the work. Advertisements for the new book focused on Emma's life story.[29] Emma realized that if she could sell a lot of copies to readers, she could portray her life the way she wanted. In the fourteen-page biography, Emma retold much of what had appeared in previous biographical sketches; yet, regarding her marriage, she wrote:

> Let us pass in silence over the disastrous days of Emma's fatal marriage, and come at once to the period when, three years after, Mrs. Southworth found herself broken in health, spirits and fortune, a widow in

> fate though not in fact, with two babes looking up to her for the support she could not give them.[30]

In one sentence, Emma said it all. She completely debunked Frederick's claims that she was his dutiful wife. Perhaps the greatest insult to the narcissistic Frederick was that she never even mentioned his name. Hidden in the brevity was the silently endured pain that she intended to keep buried, private, intensely personal. These were "disastrous days" for her—an insignificant blip in her life's story. She considered herself widowed; he was most certainly dead to her.

Ridding herself of Frederick for the moment, Emma finally wrote a new story that would appear simultaneously in the two publications under different titles. On May 19, the first chapters in the *Ledger* appeared as *Rose Elmer*; a week later, the same chapters appeared in the *Journal* as *Laura Etheridge*—the main female characters of the novel. Emma had paid close attention to women she had met who were rich as well as those who were poor, observing limitations placed on women regardless of social class—a theme Emma plays out in the novel. A deathbed confession reveals two women had been switched at birth (one was rich, the other poor), and they decide to right the wrong and switch to their birth roles. As Laura relinquishes her fortune and title, she flounders in her new surroundings because she has no concept of the value of money or how to get it. She eventually uses the education she received while a wealthy heiress as a stepping-stone to earn her living as a writer, reinstating herself into an upper-class social realm. As Rose becomes the rich heiress, she struggles to fit in because she has lacked educational opportunities, but Rose uses her strong work ethic to learn the social skills to fit into the aristocratic world of her birth.[31] Emma chose *Rose Elmer* as the title in the *Ledger*, indicating that Rose's character modeled the American Dream that hard work led to success. Emma's point was clear—whether rich or poor, in order for women to be successful, they needed education and a strong work ethic.

As a mother, Emma instilled these lessons in her daughter, sending seventeen-year-old Lottie to Bedford Ladies' College, which was only a mile from the *Journal*'s office.[32] Harriet Beecher Stowe, Harriet

Martineau, and Lady Byron recommended the school, as it offered a liberal and progressive education that elevated "the moral and intellectual character of women, as a means to an improved state of society." The goal of the institution was "to provide for ladies, at a moderate expense, a curriculum of liberal education. The instruction is given on the same plan as in the public universities, of combined lectures, examinations, and exercises." While no evidence has been found indicating specific classes Lottie took, subjects such as English literature, ancient and modern history, mathematics, natural science, astronomy, geography, Latin, German, French, Italian, elocution, vocal music, and drawing were available. Students could choose anywhere from one to eighteen lessons, and most classes met twice a week. The college founder, Elizabeth Reid, hoped that women in the future would have freedom to use their knowledge for a greater good.[33]

Emma also emphasized the same values of education and hard work to her nineteen-year-old son Richmond. Shortly after arriving in London, Emma helped Richmond get a job at the *Journal.* Learning the printing business, he rotated through the composing department, the machine room, the editor's office, and the accountant's office under the guidance of George Stiff and his staff. Emma additionally hired a tutor for Richmond, and he spent his evenings studying. The printing business didn't suit him, so, in November 1860, Emma sent him to take care of business for her in Georgetown, Philadelphia, and New York, one of which was getting checks cashed from T. B. Peterson. At times, Richmond encountered problems, writing to Bonner, "I shall, also, be thankful to you if you will advise me how to get the money for the check, as all the banks have suspended payment."[34] Considering Frederick's interference in her book copyright, he likely also had spoken with Emma's bankers. Stepping in as a surrogate father, Bonner helped Richmond get the checks cashed.

In England, Emma faced more challenges as she wrote the Rose Elmer / Laura Etheridge novel. Getting material submitted on time for two publications separated by a vast ocean was no easy task. After failing to secure British copyright for the *Doom of Deville*, Emma suggested to Bonner that they publish first in England. Publishing in the *Ledger* before the *Journal* was giving British publishers like the *Glasgow*

Times the edge to publish *Laura Ethridge* before the *Journal.* Stiff had little recourse despite petitioning the courts to make the *Glasgow Times* cease its publication. At some time during serialization, the novel began appearing in the *Journal* before the *Ledger*, demonstrating that Bonner valued Emma's opinions.[35] She was a shrewd and savvy businesswoman who looked out for her best interests.

Also looking out for Emma's best interests was Bonner. Prior to leaving for England, Emma knew that her money would not be safe from Frederick in the banks, so she left her earnings in Bonner's hands. Not only had he written checks to Richmond, but Bonner also wrote checks to Susanna, who was paying bills at Prospect Cottage in Emma's absence. Emma also trusted her good friend Henry Hardy to get cash for her, and Henry and Bonner worked together to get Emma the most money for her copyright of *Bride of an Evening*. Although T. B. Peterson wanted it, he was as stingy as ever. "If T. B. Peterson won't give six hundred dollars for it . . . let the N.Y. publishers have it," Emma told Bonner. "T. B. Peterson ought to give eight hundred for it—but I know he will not give one dollar more than he can help. I know you will do the best you can for me and with whatever you may do I shall be pleased and grateful." The best deal Bonner and Henry could secure was from T. B. Peterson, who paid a paltry sum of $400.[36] Emma lived during a time when she had to rely on men to help her with financial affairs; still, she knew a lot about the publishing business and what her novels were worth—even if she didn't always get it.

Emma also faced difficulties ensuring that her manuscript chapters made it safely from London to New York. In February 1861, she sent the first forty-six pages of her new novel *Eudora* to Bonner. "It has been so long a time since I received a letter from you that I cannot make it out at all," Emma pondered. Even in the best of circumstances, steamers transporting mail between the two countries took approximately two weeks. Factoring in conditions like bad weather, wrecks, and broken vessels, the trip could take longer. Some steamers were lost in the Atlantic. Emma needed to know that manuscripts had arrived safely and on time, but this plan didn't always work. On March 24, Emma received word that Bonner had received the second installment but not the first. "With your letter I also got a letter from mother, in which she complains of not having received a letter from me—although I posted one to her on the same day that I posted copy to you," Emma replied. The lost mail traveled aboard the *Australasian*, which had been missing since March 14. Emma wrote Bonner, "I hope that the steamer and her freight of human souls is safe!" Three weeks later, the vessel, which had been damaged during a storm, returned, and the passengers and mails were redirected to the *Arabia*.[37] Despite the good news, the delay set production of *Eudora* back a couple of months.

By April 1861, Bonner had received three installments, and Emma and Stiff waited for word from Bonner about when he would start in the *Ledger* so that the *Journal* could closely match that date. Publishing simultaneously for journals separated by an ocean was trying Emma's patience, and as the two-year marker of Emma's stay in England approached, she longed to come home. "I am very homesick and I mean to return at the close of this novel," she bemoaned. Unfortunately, more mail mishaps lay ahead. Trying to ensure the most efficient delivery, Emma had Bonner send mail to her home in Norwood and then to the *Journal* office before finally trying the Ladies' College, each time hoping that mail would get to her more quickly. Her impatience made mail delivery even worse. Emma complained to Bonner about a letter debacle at the Ladies' College: "But just think of it—by the carelessness of a servant that cleared off the teacher's desk the letter was burned before I could see it and so I do not know a line that was in it." Emma still had no way of knowing when to start publishing *Eudora*, which required more waiting. Finally, serialization began on June 27, 1861, in the *Ledger* and on July 29 in the *Journal*.[38]

By August, Emma was once again exhausted. Her doctors advised rest; however, she needed to finish *Eudora* first. "I am so homesick that I do think my heart will break, before this novel which detains me here, is done," Emma opined to Bonner. "But when it is finished—'Westward Ho!' If we live and God wills, I will fly home joyously as an Eagle to her eyrie!" In addition to Emma's homesickness, the problems with Frederick had reached a boiling point. "I do not believe that there is one chance in a million of Southworth's annoying you anymore, but still I would not risk

THE

LONDON JOURNAL:

And Weekly Record of Literature, Science, and Art.

FOR THE WEEK ENDING JULY 20, 1861 [PRICE ONE PENNY.

EUDORA.

BY E.D.E.N. SOUTHWORTH

CHAPTER VIII

E.D.E.N. Southworth's *Eudora* in the *London Journal* (July 30, 1861). (*Google Books*) that millionth chance where the *Ledger* is concerned," Emma retorted. "I fancy his next descent, if he has life enough left to make one, will be upon my London publisher;—and if he does Mr. Bonner—if he does—it will be the last time he ever troubles anybody in this world. And that you may take my word for it."[39] Emma didn't have to make good on her threats, as Frederick's days were numbered.

Even though no reports were given at the time of Frederick's illness, years later, a friend of the Rountree family, Judge Hough, stated that Frederick had suffered from "softening of the brain." Little was known about the cause or treatment for this ailment, but Frederick might have suffered from encephalomalacia, softening of brain tissue due to a brain injury, as a result of the 1854 shipwreck. Bearing in mind his frequent travels to Brazil and Mexico, he also might have developed neurocysticercosis, a parasitic brain infection caused by pork tapeworm larvae. On ingestion, the larvae form cysts, which cause few symptoms until the larvae die, triggering inflammation and brain swelling. Both diseases would explain his erratic and frenzied behavior of 1859 and 1860. Encephalomalacia and neurocysticercosis sufferers exhibit severe headaches, memory loss, and mood swings. To be close to his brother A. B., Frederick returned to California, where he died on August 23, 1861, at the age of forty-five.[40] Even though he and Emma had lived together for only three of their twenty-one years of marriage, it was finally over for good. He would no longer cause Emma angst and worry. He would no longer hound her for money. She was, at long last, a widow in fact.

Emma didn't know the exact day of Frederick's death, as she had traveled to Scotland in August for that much-needed rest. After visiting clerical friends, Emma and Lottie traveled to the Highlands—the setting that appears later in *The Brothers; or, The Earl and the Outcast.* On Emma's short tour, she took a path from Edinburgh to the Trossachs National Park, taking mental photographs of what she heard and saw along the way. A few miles west of Edinburg lay Linlithgow Palace and Linlithgow Loch. Once used as a palatial retreat of kings and queens, it had burned in 1746, but the ruins were a popular tourist destination. For Emma, it became the familial name of the title characters of her book. Another well-known tourist spot was Stirling Castle, the heart of the Scottish kingdom for centuries and the gateway to Trossach National Park. Emma based her fictional castle on that of Sterling Castle. "Trosach [*sic*] Castle was one of those ancient strongholds of the Western Highlands, closely associated with national history," Emma wrote.[41] Emma's vacation to Scotland was the first real rest she had in the United Kingdom, although her fertile mind continued to craft scenes and stories that she would save for another day.

Emma and Lottie next traveled to Brighton, staying in a posh townhouse at 8 Regency Square, a short stroll to the sea. Since the coming of the railroad in 1840, Brighton had become a favorite seaside resort. Tourists enjoyed walking onto the Chain Pier, 350 feet out over the ocean. The pier had once been used by steamers to deliver passengers and goods to the town. By the time Emma arrived, it was lined with souvenir and refreshment shops, catering to the needs of tourists. Underneath the pier were bathhouses for both men and women so that vacationers could wade in the water. Doctors advised patients to take seawater baths as a restorative health treatment. Another favorite tourist spot was the Royal Pavilion, a lavish oriental palatial estate built by King George IV. Queen Victoria had sold the property to Brighton in 1850, and the citizens opened it to the public. In addition to tours, the estate was often used as the location for fetes, balls, and exhibitions.[42] Brighton was a place where Emma could get what her doctor had ordered—fresh air, restorative baths, and interesting entertainments.

Still, Emma never stopped working for long. In Brighton, she finished *Eudora*, which had been delayed six weeks. "I have sent you all the proofs except the 16th number which was incomplete by half a column," Emma reminded Bonner. "But . . . I have finished [it] this week and will send by the next mail." In addition to finishing the novel, she visited Dr. William King, one of her "most esteemed friends." Emma and King had much in common regarding education. King founded the Mechanics' Institute and published a periodical called the *Co-Operative*; both advocated educating working-class citizens as a way to improve the social conditions for all.[43] King's ideas on education were particularly interesting to Emma, who would one day help create educational facilities based on these principles.

By the end of 1861, Emma and Lottie returned to London. Stiff's overspending finally caught up with him, and, unable to repay his loans, he faced debtor's prison. His ruin meant it was time for Emma to finally return home. While she had been in England, the United States finally succumbed to a civil war, and she was concerned that England and France would intervene by raising a blockade of the Southern ports as a way to protect their interests in U.S. cotton. She had nothing good to say about France's leader. "There never was such a toad eater in this world as Louis Napoleon," she wrote. "He is toadying to the British Government all the time. He shakes in his shoes if the British lion does but roll his eyes. He knows the treacherous instability of his own position and looks to England to help at a strait." With these international tensions, steamer travel was dangerous; however, Emma had few options. Richmond escorted his mother and sister home, and, in late March, they boarded the *Asia*, arriving in New York on April 12, 1862.[44] Instead of the joyous homecoming Emma had anticipated, she arrived in the midst of a prolonged and bloody war—a war that would take place virtually on the doorstep of Prospect Cottage—a war into which she would be drawn.

Chapter 9
Mrs. Southworth's War at Home and Abroad

Some of the enthusiastic old confederate sympathizers hung out the stars and bars, but the old flag with its hues of heaven was swung from the flag-staff of Prospect Cottage, far above its roof, that all might know that the loyal native of "Maryland, my Maryland," did not sympathize with the old, or the new incipient rebellion.[1]

When Emma returned in April 1862, Washington and Georgetown looked very different. Over the course of the previous year, Abraham Lincoln had been elected the sixteenth president, and South Carolina seceded from the Union. Additional states joined their southern sister state, forming the Confederate States of America and electing Jefferson Davis as their president. When the Confederacy fired on Fort Sumter, the American Civil War officially began. Lincoln expanded the army by calling for an additional forty-three thousand volunteers, and Georgetown's Union supporters responded. Emma's stepfather Joshua Henshaw formed Company C of the Union Regiment, which was assigned to the Seventh Battalion of the DC Militia.[2]

A majority of Georgetown residents, however, considered themselves Southerners. Recognizing the proximity to the Capitol, Lincoln sent thousands of troops to be quartered at Georgetown College (now Georgetown University). First to arrive was the Sixty-Ninth New York

Division of the Irish Brigade, who were quiet and well behaved, but the Seventy-Ninth New York Highlanders drank and damaged college property. As many as fifteen thousand troops came, many exhibiting rowdy behavior, and the once quiet streets of Georgetown were no more.[3]

In addition to the rowdiness, Emma found neighbor against neighbor as each household drew lines on which side they supported. Emma flew the Union flag over her house. "Whoever comes to my door," she proudly declared, "will have to pass under that." Just a few blocks away was Miss English's Seminary for Young Ladies. At the helm was Miss Lydia Scudder English, who had educated the daughters of Washington's elite for forty years. The Union army confiscated the school and turned it into a hospital for the sick and wounded. An avid secessionist, Miss English became so distraught at seeing the Union flag displayed on her beloved school that she moved around the corner so she wouldn't have to look at it. Across the street from the Seminary Hospital was another Confederate supporter, Dr. Grafton Tyler, who was so agitated by the sight of the flag that he kept his windows shuttered tight, even in the stifling heat of Georgetown summers.[4] After a year of battles with no end in sight, tension and anger had mounted based on long-held beliefs about the definition of freedom.

This antagonism between neighbors and friends was far from the homecoming Emma dreamed about during her three-year stay abroad. After battling English publishers and stressing over an unpredictable mail service, Emma wanted the comfort and normalcy of home. Arriving just in time for Richmond's twenty-first birthday, Emma was determined to throw him a party. "Although the house was still in much confusion," Emma wrote, "we managed to get our dining room . . . in some order to receive a few of [Richmond's] friends in the evening." She hosted around twenty-five guests, feeding them supper before they spent the night playing parlor games, listening to music, and chatting. A few days later, Emma hired workmen to install gas and water pipes. She also repapered and painted the parlor.[5] She wanted a return to order, a sense of being settled. However, her life was far from those things, and she had hardly unpacked before she would have to make some difficult decisions.

One of the most heart-wrenching decisions was what to do about her relationship with Henry Hardy. She had met him when she was a teacher and he was the principal of the school where she first taught. For eighteen years, he had been there—a friend, confidant, advisor. After his wife Mary died, he moved with his three children to Jefferson County, home of Shannondale Springs.[6] So, when Emma had spent summers in Shannondale Springs, Henry was near. When Emma prepared for England, Henry helped her get a passport. Henry helped negotiate a book deal and wrote letters while Emma was abroad. Henry was waiting for her when she returned.

Henry's actions over the years indicated that he loved her, and yet when he ultimately asked Emma to marry him, she turned him down. "I have not seen Mr. Hardy, nor is it likely that I shall see him," Emma told Bonner in May 1862. "There is no one in the world I esteem and honor more than I do Henry Hardy—a man as near Christian perfection as any human being could approach, I do think. But it is not likely that we shall ever meet again, nor do I wish it. I only wish to hear of his welfare." Emma deeply cared for Henry; however, she couldn't chance marriage again. Henry took Emma at her word, and he moved on, marrying Susan Oxley in August. Emma had found comfort in Henry's friendship but avoided making a commitment while legally married to Frederick. With Frederick's death, she couldn't hide behind that legality anymore. A war raged inside Emma's heart. Rejecting Henry was hard, but remarrying would jeopardize the persona she'd worked so hard to hide behind. Her image had protected her, provided security, ensured her success—everything a husband should have done. She decided she was better off making her own way in the world. "As for myself," she assured Bonner, "I shall always remain as I am—E.D.E.N. Southworth. So, you will never lose your contributor by her change of name."[7]

Another decision Emma had to make was what to do with Richmond, who'd now reached adulthood and needed a profession. "It's not well for him to have no special business," Emma told Bonner. "It is better that he should work regularly for little or nothing than not at all." Even though Lincoln had not yet instituted a mandatory draft, Emma and Richmond were living in the midst of thousands of volunteers who'd enlisted to fight; the most obvious choice for Richmond was to join the military. Whether Confederate or Union, the popular sentiment was that young men should serve their country.

Emma's younger half brother Henry Clay Henshaw, who was only about a year older than Richmond, enlisted in DC's Seventh Battalion Infantry on April 17, 1861. Emma was torn between her love of country and the preservation of her child. She had fought long battles to ensure that her only son, who had grown up in poor health, would live to adulthood. Richmond had become a man, but he was small and thin with delicate features, kind eyes, and an inquisitive appearance. Emma had given Richmond the best education she could afford. From age thirteen to sixteen, he was enrolled at Georgetown College, where he finished three years at a preparatory school and one year studying humanities.[8] He had a tutor in England, and Emma thought his education was finished. She hadn't anticipated a civil war. By July 1862, Emma and Richmond had a plan—one that would keep Richmond out of the line of fire but would allow him to serve by helping the sick and wounded. He was going to medical school. He would become a physician.

Richmond enrolled in New York's College of Physicians and Surgeons, which had recently joined with Columbia University. He was one of 254 students attending medical school that year, with lectures and clinics in obstetrics, chemistry, and anatomy, as well as the new addition of military surgery, a need brought about by the increased cases of wounded soldiers in the Civil War. In addition to class lectures, students observed and practiced alongside their preceptors at New York's public and charitable hospitals.[9] For the present, Emma was assured that Richmond was safe, far from the fields of battle.

Emma also had to assist Susanna and Henshaw, who were strapped for money. When Bonner gave Emma an unexpected bonus check, she vented to him about her divided feelings between loyalty to family and anger over being used. "And often when I feel overburdened by the mass of helpless—I had nearly said—good-for-nothing people—that lean on me," Emma wrote, "here comes some unexpected and unearned kindness from you to reconcile me." She also expected something in return from Susanna. On April 16, President Lincoln signed DC's Emancipation

Richmond Southworth. (*Gladys Goud Estate*)

Act of 1862, compensating slave owners who freed their slaves. The District of Columbia was the only part of the United States to do so. More than three thousand slaves lived in the district, and Lincoln set aside $1 million, paying up to $300 per slave as long as their owners proved ownership and pledged loyalty to the Union. On May 31, Emma went with Susanna to the Circuit Court to certify that she owned three slaves: Leonard Taylor, age seventy; Alexander Taylor, age thirty-five; and Leonard Taylor Jr., age twenty-nine. On June 2, Emma served as a witness to Susanna's loyalty pledge.[10] The money came at a much-needed time for the Henshaws, but finally freeing the rest of the Taylor family was an act Emma considered long overdue.

Other battles remained for Emma; she might have left England, but England had not left her. Emma's opinion of George Stiff worsened when, facing debtor's prison, he sent two of his young employees, John Madigan and Edward Hyde, to the United States so that they couldn't testify against him. Madigan and Hyde had only enough money for passage to New York, believing Stiff was sending money for their living expenses. When they arrived, no money was there. Hyde turned to Emma for help. "I invited them to come and stay with us until Mr. Stiff forwarded their remittances," Emma wrote. Madigan subsequently heard from his father, who said that Stiff was to have a second hearing before the bankruptcy court on July 24. "He looks ill and depressed—unfit to struggle with adverse fate," Madigan's father reported. "And his enemies do all that is possible to annoy and distress him." Three months later, Hyde wrote to Stiff asking when they could come home, but, instead of sending an answer, Stiff wrote to Emma, saying that the young men needed to stay where they were.[11] Emma's patience with Stiff was growing thin.

By August, Emma wrote to Bonner for advice. "They are either totally abandoned by their employer, or else they are purposely kept here out of money lest they should return home," Emma explained. Even though Madigan and Hyde were of the highest character, they were a burden not only on Emma's finances but also on the space and quiet she needed to write. She was kind to her friends, who both longed to go home, particularly Hyde, who had a poor mother and two sisters who depended on him. "I think I never heard of such an artful and villainous piece of work," Emma surmised, especially after Hyde received a letter from his mother, who said, "Mr. Stiff is living in magnificent style, in a villa . . . with carriages, horses, servants, etc."[12] Madigan and Hyde were expendable pawns in Stiff's war with his creditors and the courts.

Although Stiff's antics were hard for Emma, she faced a literal civil war occurring on her back doorstep. On August 28, the Second Battle of Bull Run began near Manassas, Virginia. With Prospect Cottage perched high on the hill looking across the Potomac, Emma had a bird's-eye view of the battle less than thirty miles away. For days, rumors that Confederate troops were close to Washington flourished, and tensions grew as residents feared their city might be attacked. On the third morning of the battle, Emma observed:

> We started out of our morning sleep and went upon the large porch that overlooks the river. There a scene met our eyes that must remain forever engrafted upon our memories. The great range of Virginia hills on the opposite side of the river, so silent, some hours before, were covered with hastily pitched tents and lighted up with the red glare of the campfires—it was McLellan's [McClellan's] army who had marched throughout the night and had halted there to cook their breakfasts. It was the advance columns on their march to Manassas, and still they came on and on until the whole shore was alive with the men and the earth grew soldiers instead of trees.[13]

Georgetown citizens gathered in Emma's backyard to see whether the Union with General McClellan's army or the Confederacy led by Stonewall Jackson would triumph.

As horrifying as it was for Emma to see the coming battle across the Potomac, even more alarming was the scene that intensified on the hillside behind her porch. Emma emphasized:

> It was awful—neighbors living side by side and standing there glared at each other with undying hatred—Upon a little more provocation they were ready to take each other by the throats. Two she-rebels were on my hill, outside of *my* fence however—parading the secession colors

> and openly proclaiming their sentiment. I felt my human nature rising above my education and had to come in least I should forget myself and fall upon them. But if they appear there again, I will take our water hose and douche them. There is nothing on earth I hate with a hatred so intense as I do a she-rebel—and there are thousands and thousands of them in the District of Columbia.[14]

Like the rest of Georgetown who'd gathered on the hill, Emma had also taken sides and was ready to go to battle.

What made Emma the angriest were Georgetown women who sided with the Confederacy—those she called the "she-rebels," and for Emma it was solely the issue of slavery that caused such great emotions. Instead of spraying them with a water hose, she tried reasoning with them through the portrayal of her latest heroine, Astrea, in the novel by the same name, running in the *Ledger* from August 2 to December 6, 1862. Kidnappers have drugged the rich heiress Astrea, and, to make sure she will not be discovered, they dye her hair and skin in order to pass her off as a quadroon (a person with one-quarter African blood who could still be sold into slavery by law). Astrea is put aboard a steamer headed to New Orleans before being sold to a plantation owner. Once Astrea regains consciousness, she tries to explain who she really is, but no one believes her. Even worse, because Astrea is a very beautiful woman, the plantation owner buys her for his own sexual pleasures.[15] Emma's message was clear for her wealthy Southern female readers—only their affluence and whiteness protected them from those horrors of slavery. For black women, rape was perhaps the most horrific, habitually resulting in children born from unwanted sex with the plantation owners—evidenced by the continued lighter-colored skin of the slaves.

No doubt the problems with slavery helped incite the Civil War; unfortunately, the result was intense fighting and huge numbers of wounded and dead. The Second Battle of Bull Run was no different. Even though it was a decided victory for the Confederacy, the number killed and injured was great on both sides. Emma had heard rumors that as many as forty thousand soldiers lay on the battlefield, and although that number was greatly exaggerated, the scene was certainly gruesome.

Close to fourteen thousand Union troops and more than eight thousand Confederates needed to be either transported to hospitals or buried, with an estimated total of twenty-two thousand casualties. Help was desperately needed from every able-bodied person. "Posters appeared all over Washington and Georgetown," Emma described, "calling upon the benevolent among men to volunteer to go to the battleground and help to take care of the wounded and bury the dead."[16]

Emma was no different from other Georgetown citizens who wanted to help, but what she really wanted was to fight. "I wish I were a man; I wish I was with the army," Emma told Bonner. "It was heart-rending last night to see the rear of McClellan's army—sick, fevered, weary and exhausted men, some who had not been out of the saddle since Wednesday." Emma later played out her desire to be a soldier in *Britomarte, the Man-Hater*, in which two female heroines don soldiers' uniforms in order to fight for their cause—Britomarte Conyers for the Union and Alberta Goldsborough for the Confederacy. Both women characters disguise themselves as men since women weren't allowed to enlist. While Alberta is eventually killed in battle (she is, after all, fighting on what Emma considered the wrong side), she and Britomarte exhibit bravery and triumph in battle, even leading their male counterparts to victories. Women did fight during the Civil War; however, the number of female soldiers has been difficult to determine. One estimate suggests that as many as 400 to 750 women fought in various battles.[17]

A more common way women helped during the Civil War was volunteering to nurse the sick and wounded in the numerous hospitals that sprang up in Georgetown and Washington. One was Louisa May Alcott, author of *Little Women*, who volunteered as a nurse at Georgetown's Union Hospital until she contracted typhoid fever and went home after six weeks of service. She would later record her experience in *Hospital Sketches*. Like Alcott, Emma volunteered but at Georgetown's Seminary Hospital located behind the Union Hospital and just a few blocks from Prospect Cottage. Formerly Miss English's Seminary for Young Ladies, the hospital was a three-story brick building with forty-five rooms; thirty-two were converted into wards, with the remainder used as a kitchen, laundry, storeroom, and sleeping quarters for nurses. Most wards were small, with only three to four beds; the two larger wards had twenty beds each. During the summer months, with the doors and windows opened to provide proper ventilation, the hospital could accommodate as many as 190 patients, but in colder weather, that number was reduced to 123 to lessen the spread of communicable diseases in confined spaces.[18]

When the Second Battle of Bull Run occurred, the Seminary Hospital specifically treated officers, as it had gained a good reputation for providing top-notch bandaging and wound care as well as clean wards and bedding despite being understaffed. Dr. Joseph R. Smith, four assistant surgeons, and seven nurses were the only full-time staff at the hospital, so volunteer nurses like Emma and Lottie were highly important to its success. One wounded officer who arrived at the Seminary Hospital was James Valentine Lawrence from the second regiment of the New York Heavy Artillery unit. At Bull Run Bridge, James had been wounded before rushing to secure the regimental colors from his fallen sergeant and leading retreating troops to safety.[19] He was a dashing young officer at nineteen with brown hair, sideburns, and a full moustache, and eighteen-year-old Lottie soon became smitten. With his stellar military service, Emma approved of young James as a suitor to her daughter.

In *Britomarte*, the similarities between the real-life James Lawrence to Emma's fictional hero Justin Rosenthal leave little doubt that James is Justin. Like James, Justin enlists in the Union army as a private before quickly rising through the ranks "for gallant and Meritorious conduct." Justin's love interest is the heroine Britomarte, who dresses as a man in order to watch over Justin. Furthering the comparison, Emma dedicated the first of the two-volume printed book "to you, my dear, only daughter, Lottie."[20] While Justin serves as the prototype of male heroism, Emma also offered an equal counterpart in the heroine Britomarte, who becomes a soldier, spy, and battlefield nurse.

One of the most famous battlefield nurses was Clara Barton, who was called the "Angel of the Battlefield" for her field work during the war. She later founded the American Red Cross. In *Britomarte*, Emma modeled the character of Erminie Rosenthal after Barton, as the soldiers Erminie tends refer to her as the "Angel of the Hospitals." There were indeed many hospital angels during the war; more than twenty thousand

James Valentine Lawrence. (*Daniel and Carol Ann Kindberg*)

women are listed in the Carded Services Record. This number, however, represents only women who received pay and does not include the scores of other women who volunteered their time both in the hospitals and at home. The potential to contract disease as a result of their hospital work in close, crowded rooms was just one danger these nurses faced, and Emma played out that scenario through Erminie, who becomes seriously ill after contracting one of the many fevers from volunteering at the hospitals.[21]

Smallpox was one of the most hideous and feared diseases in the war. Symptoms of the disease included high fever, headaches, vomiting, and rash. As the illness progressed, the rash spread throughout the body, particularly the mouth and throat, before forming into pus-filled blisters and then scabs. Thirty percent of those who contracted smallpox died, and those who survived were frequently left with disfiguring scars and blindness. In October 1862, Emma became one of the volunteers who contracted smallpox, becoming so ill that Hyde dictated letters to Bonner for her. As the lesions grew on her face and body, Emma suggested Bonner find a ghostwriter to continue *Astrea*. On October 8, Hyde wrote to Bonner, not dictating but writing the letter himself. "The doctor who attends only broke to her on Sunday the true nature of her disease," Hyde explained to Bonner. "She has suffered much, but I am happy to think that the worst is over now."[22] Realizing the seriousness of Emma's condition, Bonner found a ghostwriter. In just a few weeks, Emma resumed writing, finishing *Astrea* by the end of the year.

By the end of November, Madigan and Hyde finally received the long-awaited news that they could go home to England. Madigan once again sent a request for money to his father, who suggested his son should borrow it from Emma. She knew that paying for the boys' passage home meant she would never be repaid. She was additionally "stiffed" by Stiff, who had not paid her for advance sheets. Emma told Bonner, "As far as my experience goes, that set over there, are a set of very *sharp practitioners* to say the most charitable thing of them." Finally, Madigan's father sent his son fare for passage home. Hyde still waited for a line of credit from his mother, and he told Emma that once he returned, he would never work for Stiff again. Hyde's letter of credit finally arrived, and both young men went home.[23] Their stay was longer than any of them had expected; still, Emma formed deep attachments to them, especially Hyde, who had helped her so much.

Emma had grown to despise Stiff. While in debtor's prison, he started the *7 Day's Journal*, and since he had no money to pay authors, he just stole what he liked from American papers, including work by Emma, with whom he supposedly had a contract. "I am firmly resolved never to let him have another [story]—never!" Emma emphatically told Bonner. "My opinion of that party has undergone a thorough revolution since the facts brought to light in there [*sic*] law-proceedings." Emma wanted to write for Cassell in England: "I had rather feel my soul at ease in being connected with honorable parties, even at a smaller remuneration, than have anything whatever to do with literary sharpies."[24] Any more dealings with London publishers would have to wait, however, as Civil War problems drew Emma away from her work.

The district was crowded not only by Union troops stationed across the city but also by African American slaves who came into Washington and Georgetown as they fled from their owners in Southern states, with an estimated ten thousand living there by 1863. To combat the Fugitive Slave Act of 1850 that required fleeing slaves to be returned to their masters, Union officials listed the slaves as property, because enemy property could be confiscated and not returned. Former slaves became known simply as Contrabands.[25] Most of the refugees were women, children, and the infirm, who were sent to camps like Duff Green's Row, Camp Barker, and Freedman's Village—dismal places filled with disease and lack of nutrition. By the end of January, the National Association for the Relief of Destitute Colored Women and Children was formed with the intent of finding decent living quarters with adequate food, clothing, and education for indigent black women and children. In two weeks, their charter was granted by Congress and approved by President Lincoln.

Three committees were formed in order to delegate the work: administrative, investigating, and ways and means. The ways and means committee raised money and collected donations of food, clothing, and supplies. Harriet Beecher Stowe and Jane Swisshelm joined Emma as part of that thirty-two-member committee. Money was initially raised by collecting membership dues for those joining the association, with basic dues of $2, annual dues of $5, and lifetime dues of $50. Emma contributed $2 in her own name and another $2 in Lottie's. The National Freedman's Relief Association of New York donated a whopping $1,000.[26] With war on her doorstep, Emma's philanthropic efforts expanded beyond the pages of her books.

Perhaps as a way of procuring donations for the association, Emma entertained many of the Washington elite and military at Prospect Cottage. Attending one of these social gatherings was Nettie Colburn Maynard, a noted spiritualist. With thousands of soldiers dying far from home, family members never had closure in burying their dead sons, so, looking for answers, many turned to spiritualism. Spiritualists held séances in which they would enter a trance-like state and claim to be possessed by a dead soul who wanted to communicate with a participant in the séance circle. Even the president's wife, Mary Todd Lincoln, hoping to communicate with her deceased sons Eddie and Willie, held séances with Nettie.[27] Although Emma was likely not the devotee that Mrs. Lincoln was, Emma loved a good ghost story, and she was fascinated with mediums and the idea of communicating with the spirit world. Yet, on a wintry night in February 1863, Emma was unaware that Nettie was a spiritualist who would be attending.

While in Washington, Nettie became friends with Anna Mills Cosby, a well-known socialite, giving Nettie some inroads to be invited to Emma's party. When Mrs. Cosby learned that Nettie was a huge Southworth fan, they made plans to attend. "Nothing would give me more pleasure than to meet her," Nettie told Mrs. Cosby. "But I never expected to realize my desire." Mrs. Cosby replied with a smile, "Why not, when she lives in Georgetown! If you would so much like to meet with her, I will send her a note this morning, asking her to appoint a time to receive us." Emma invited them to attend her reception the next evening. When Mrs. Cosby and Nettie arrived, they were shown into the drawing room filled with ladies in brilliant evening dresses and gentlemen in army and navy uniforms. Seated at the piano was a beautiful girl with fair skin, deep brown eyes, and golden-brown hair that hung in long curls down her shoulders. She was surrounded by a court of young officers—one of whom no doubt was James Lawrence. For, indeed, the center of attention was Lottie.

It was nine o'clock before Emma made her entrance. She wore her dark hair parted down the middle with a low bun coiled low at the back of her neck. Her gown was black velvet with old lace at the sleeves and neck held together by a beautiful diamond pin. Working her way through the room, Emma warmly greeted her friend Mrs. Cosby. "This is one of the queer people," Mrs. Cosby whispered to Emma. "Indeed!" Emma exclaimed. "But you did not tell me that in your note, or I would have had you visit me more privately." Emma escorted them down a narrow

Lottie Southworth Lawrence. (*Daniel and Carol Ann Kindberg*)

hall into the book-filled library, where a dark green carpet lay across the oak floor and a table stood in the middle of the room.

Emma asked Nettie to put her hand on the center table and give a reading. "I obeyed her and was instantly conscious of the presence of a tall, majestic-looking man, who impressed me as being one born to command, and with power to execute any purpose he might desire to achieve," Nettie recalled. As the table in question was once owned by Emma's beloved late father, Emma seemed pleased. She then recounted a story of when she, Lottie, and a hired man were alone on the eve of the Second Battle of Bull Run. Emma worried that they had no way of protecting themselves from invasion. She said half aloud, "There are but three of us here." What Emma said she heard next was straight out of the pages of one of her own ghost stories:

E.D.E.N. Southworth (ca. 1863). (Nettie Maynard, *Was Abraham Lincoln a Spiritualist?*, 1891, 147)

I distinctly heard a voice say as if in response, "There are four," and I immediately became aware that standing at the end of the sofa was what I can only describe as a grand majestic presence. I did not see him, but felt he was there. Who it was, I do not know. I can only tell you that my feelings instantly changed, and I became calm and collected, and from that moment all fear left me. I felt a sense of protection scarcely to be described, and from that moment to this, have felt the utmost confidence in a Protective Power, whatever it may be.

Emma said she thought it was the same presence Nettie had described when she placed her hand on the table.

Emma then led Nettie to her bedroom. Clothes had been carelessly thrown across the four-poster bed, and at the back of the room was a large mirror and dressing table scattered with a glittering profusion of jewelry. There was a toilet basin with a row of shelves above, and perched on one of the shelves was half of a frosted cake, partially covered with a white napkin and a silver knife beside it. Emma asked Nettie to read the room. "I seemed to sense, in a manner I cannot describe, that where we then stood had been enacted a scene of violence," Nettie remembered. "I am satisfied," Emma replied, explaining that the house had once been a tavern.

Emma wasn't quite finished with Nettie for the evening and asked whether she would agree to a séance with her guests. Of course, Nettie agreed—it was her chosen "profession"—and they reentered the drawing room. As music softly played, Nettie was entranced and, for more than an hour, gave readings for Emma's guests. Nettie claimed she awoke to applause from the crowd, many of whom were eager to know more about her "peculiar gift." It proved to be a good business move for Nettie, as many wanted her to call on them for a private sitting in order to get more information about beloved family members from beyond the grave.

Nettie was also pleased at meeting her favorite author, saying, "I shall ever remember the pleasure and satisfaction I experienced in meeting with her whom I had learned to love through her writings, and who to my youthful mind seemed something beyond the common order of humanity."[28] In Emma's novels, when she told a ghost story, she almost always concluded it by giving a plausible explanation for the supposed supernatural event, so the extent to which she actually believed Nettie's spiritual abilities seems questionable. Yet Emma was a most gracious host to Nettie and found her presence the centerpiece of a particularly enjoyable evening—a most welcome delight in the midst of civil war.

By March 1863, Emma once again became concerned for Richmond's safety when Lincoln signed into law the Enrollment Act, requiring men between the ages of twenty to forty-five to register for a draft. Men were selected at random through a lottery system. The Enrollment

Act still allowed some to be exempt from service, and Bonner offered to help Emma keep Richmond off the battlefield. "Richmond and myself both thank you earnestly for your generous offer to help to buy him a substitute in the event of his getting drafted," Emma replied. As much as she was grateful for Bonner's offer, she struggled to accept it. Working in the Seminary Hospital and living in the midst of military camps, Emma saw plenty of young men who were willing to fight. Understandably, the policy in which a man could buy his way out of service became very unpopular, especially for poor immigrants who began referring to the Civil War as the "rich man's war, poor man's fight." Tensions mounted, especially in New York, and in July, riots erupted between poor Irish immigrants and freed African Americans, who were in direct competition for low-paying jobs. The immigrants were particularly angry with the Enrollment Act that exempted freed blacks from the draft because they were not recognized as U.S. citizens.[29] As Emma's novels often centered on disparities that existed in the social classes, she had much empathy for these working-class poor.

Because Emma was a widow, Richmond qualified for an exemption as her only son. Emma's conscience still struggled with this solution. Other mothers cared just as deeply for their enlisted sons as she did. When Richmond returned home in June after finishing his first year of medical school, he found a way to help with the war effort. "Today, Richmond has enlisted in the medical service of the U.S.A. for three months," Emma reported to Bonner. "He gets no pay; but I am glad to [know] he will be useful." As an acting medical cadet, Richmond helped hospital surgeons with duties such as dressing wounds, assisting with postmortem examinations, and performing administrative duties. Particularly useful in severely understaffed hospitals, Richmond also gained valuable experience toward earning his medical degree. He volunteered during the summer as a medical cadet until the end of the war.[30]

Richmond's service wouldn't have prevented him from contracting the many communicable diseases that ran rampant in the hospitals, but he never did, perhaps because he served during the summer when opened doors and windows provided better air ventilation. Overcrowding, poor hygiene, and inadequate nutrition worsened in the winter, and these poor conditions caused approximately 63 percent of Union soldiers to die from diseases such as malaria, smallpox, and typhoid. Doctors had limited knowledge about diagnosing or treating these illnesses; however, they knew they needed to be quarantined from wounded soldiers. One quarantined soldier was Lottie's betrothed, James Lawrence, who had contracted typhoid and was sent to the Kalorama Hospital, also referred to as the "eruptive fever hospital." Horrifically overcrowded, patients regularly caught several diseases before they died. Emma was not going to let James suffer the same fate, and she went to Kalorama to get him. "Adjutant Lawrence is with us and is ill with typhoid fever," Emma wrote. "I had to bring him over from the fever side of the river, as the only means of saving his life."[31] Typhoid was a serious illness marked by high fevers, weakness, headaches, and mental confusion. At Prospect Cottage, James had the best chance of recovery, with clean bedding, nutritious food, and personal care from Emma and Lottie.

James wasn't the only resident of Prospect Cottage to suffer from disease in the fall of 1863. In addition to caring for James in their home, Emma and Lottie continued to volunteer at the hospital, where Emma contracted influenza and Lottie became ill with erysipelas, a type of wound infection. During the war, little was understood about how to properly treat wounds. No matter how slight the wound, chances were high that infection would occur. Caregivers often reused sponges and didn't wash their hands while cleaning and bandaging wounds. Tetanus, gangrene, pyemia, and erysipelas were the four most common wound infections of the war. Erysipelas was a serious and painful streptococcal infection, causing a bright red rash, high fever, fatigue, headaches, and vomiting. Caregivers were also susceptible to contracting the infection if they had an open cut on their hands when they treated the wound.[32]

Emma credited the use of Hostetter's Bitters for the recovery from the illnesses in her household, and, in 1863, the proprietors of the medicinal bitter were happy to have the famous Mrs. Southworth endorse their product. In the advertisements, Emma claimed:

> I had come to the conclusion that nothing but a total change of residence and pursuits would restore my health, when a friend

> recommended Hostetter's Bitters. I procured a bottle as an experiment. I required but one bottle to convince me that I had found at last the right combination of remedies. The relief it afforded me has been complete. It is now some years since I first tried Hostetter's Bitters, and it is but just to say that I have found the preparation all that it claims to be. It is a Standard Family Cordial with us, and even as a stimulant we like it better than anything else; but we use it in all nervous, bilious, and dyspeptic cases, from fever down to toothache. If what I have now said will lead any dyspeptic or nervous invalid to a sure remedy, I shall have done some good.

Hostetter's Bitters no doubt made Emma's family briefly feel better, but temperance-minded Emma was obviously unaware of what she actually promoted. Hostetter's was 47 percent alcohol, which is 97 Proof. It was even sold in saloons by the glass.[33]

As the war dragged on, Americans needed things to make them feel better, which might have been Emma's intent when she retold a story she heard to John Greenleaf Whittier, her former editor at the *Era* and a prestigious poet. In September, Emma's neighbor C. S. Ramsburg told her and Richmond about a ninety-year-old woman named Barbara Frietchie from Frederick, Maryland, who was so distraught at Stonewall Jackson's army parading through her town that she grabbed a bullet-torn Union flag, stood in front of her house, and defiantly waved it at the passing troops. "What a fine subject for a poem by Whittier," Richmond said to his mother. "It ought to have fallen into better hands," Whittier replied. "But I have just written out a little ballad of 'Barbara Frietchie.'"

Consisting of thirty verses, the ballad appeared in the October 1863 edition of the *Atlantic Monthly* with the famously quoted lines, "Shoot if you must this old gray head, / But spare your country's flag, she said." Controversy over the facts of the incident began shortly after publication. While there was a ninety-year-old woman named Barbara Frietchie who found her yard filled with rebel soldiers one afternoon, some argued that she never waved a flag at them, instead saying, "Get up, you dirty fellows, and let me in."[34] Additionally, Stonewall Jackson's troops never marched through Frederick, so it's unclear which rebels

Barbara had even confronted. Nonetheless, the poem inspired hope for Union supporters that the war would turn in their favor for a victory.

Emma hoped her next novel would be inspirational, too, and, in 1863, she began *Self-Made; or, Out of the Depths*. "This story is different in character to any that I have ever written before, and as such may be considered as an experiment," Emma told Bonner. "In former stories, I have catered to what I believed to be the popular taste; but in this I have a higher aim—popular good."[35] Emma's experiment in her new story was using a male character as the main hero—a risky move in a largely female reading audience. Emma must have believed a quintessential hero was desperately needed for her novel—one who epitomized the ideal portrayal of the American Dream that, through hard work and perseverance, freed people could realize their true potential. Continuing serialization for a little over a year, *Self-Made* became Emma's favorite work.

With the conclusion of *Self-Made*, Emma had another reason to celebrate. On May 2, 1864, Lottie married James, who had been promoted to the rank of captain. That beautiful spring Saturday, three hundred guests gathered on the lawn at Prospect Cottage and awaited the entrance of the bride—the backdrop for the ceremony was a breathtaking view of the Potomac River. The bride and her three bridesmaids entered to the "Wedding March," played by the New York Second Artillery band. Lottie wore a white glace silk dress covered with tulle. Her wreath and bouquet were orange blossoms. Emma thought of everything, including the fact that the bridesmaids and groomsmen formed a "pleasing gradation of age." After the ceremony, a wedding breakfast was served as the band continued to play for the guests. The newlyweds left for their honeymoon to New York, where they planned to visit James's parents.[36] As progressive as Emma was in her own life and writing, she was traditional about what she wanted for her daughter—safety, security, home, family.

Safety and security were greatly desired as the Civil War continued relentlessly into its fourth year, even after the reelection of President Lincoln for a second term on November 8, 1864. Lincoln was sworn into office on March 4, 1865, and hosted a grand inaugural ball on March 6. Tickets were sold at $10 each, which included an elegant supper with the proceeds earmarked to help soldiers' families. An estimated four thousand guests were expected to attend. The ball took place at the Patent Office—the walls of which were still lined with small-scale patented inventions, one of which might have been the Tide and Current Water Wheel that Frederick had proudly displayed there so many years earlier. In 1862, the Patent Office had been used as a hospital for soldiers, but on the night of the ball, all vestiges of previous pain and suffering had been cleared away.

In the north saloon, blue and gold sofas were carried in for the presidential ball. Gas jets were installed, and flags draped the walls. The supper room was set up in the west wing, and long tables with meats, oysters, salads, jellies, desserts, and coffee were prepared. Elaborate confectioner displays were constructed. One was of the army, showing a combat between calvary and infantry. A second was the navy with a replica of David Farragut's flagship, the admiral strapped to the mast. The grand centerpiece was a sugar model of the Capitol. No expense was spared to welcome in the second term of Lincoln and the hoped-for end of the long Civil War.

Abraham Lincoln's Second Inaugural Ball. (*National Portrait Gallery, Smithsonian Institution*)

As guests arrived and mingled in the promenade halls, Lillie's Finley Hospital Band played. Reporters noted the arrival of the distinguished guests, including cabinet members, diplomats, generals, Admiral Farragut, and the talented authoress Mrs. E.D.E.N. Southworth escorted by Richmond. How far Emma had come from a desperately poor schoolteacher to an esteemed and honored guest at a presidential inaugural ball. Unlike the brightly festooned ladies, Emma wore a heavy black velvet dress, trimmed in black lace, making her stand out in stark contrast to the frivolity. At 10:30, dancing stopped as the band played "Hail to the Chief" and President and Mrs. Lincoln entered. With so many guests, the ballroom became so packed that dancing became almost impossible.

Shortly after midnight, the Veteran Reserve Corps played music, and as guests shifted into the west wing, a melee erupted as a hungry four thousand attendees expected to be fed. Tables had been planned to accommodate three hundred at a time. Unfortunately, guests rushed at once, grabbing what they could and taking it to corners of the room, where they made their own picnics. Smashed glass and discarded food were strewn across the floor. Although the confectioner display of the Capitol had been safely removed, the army and navy displays were ransacked by souvenir hunters. Despite the unseemly behavior of their guests, President and Mrs. Lincoln stayed with many of the other distinguished guests into the wee hours of the morning.[37] No doubt Emma disapproved of the supper debacle, but she was one to enjoy a good party and was known to stay until daybreak.

In another month, the Union celebrated as Lee surrendered, but less than a week later, Lincoln was assassinated. A president was dead. Conspirators were dead. There had been four years of death—from wounds, disease, and starvation. An exhausted America was ready for the senseless killing to end. Once the blood cleared from the rivers and battlefields, an estimated 620,000 to 750,000 Union and Confederate soldiers had died. Factoring in an untold number of civilian deaths, losses on both sides were staggering. Emma felt the pain of the Civil War for the rest of her life. "I shrink with deepest pain from the recollections of our civil war, with all its unimaginable horrors and sorrows," Emma later wrote. "For with near relatives and dear friends in both opposing armies, who fell in battle on both sides, my heart was bleeding all the time."[38] Reconstructing a deeply wounded people wouldn't be easy. Difficult days lay ahead, but Emma sought to improve her country and its people.

Chapter 10

Coming Out from Behind the Pages

Let us reverently pass over that awful calamity of April the fourteenth, which followed so swiftly upon the winged feet of Victory, quenching all her lights of joy and of triumph in darkness and in blood. The Nation's holy sorrow is too sacred a subject to be treated here.[1]

Emma said little about Abraham Lincoln's death and the end of the Civil War, but she captured her sentiment in the previous lines from her serialized novel *Britomarte, the Man-Hater*, which began publication in the *Ledger* on October 14, 1865, six months after the assassination. In the novel, she navigated through the trials and tribulations of the entire war, carefully presenting both sides in an effort to evoke unity instead of continued hostility. Emma also worked to reconcile a nation when her 1862 serialized novel *Astrea* was published by T. B. Peterson in book form as *The Fortune Seeker*. On March 1, 1866, Emma dedicated her book "to Mrs. Judge John C. Underwood of Virginia, tried and true, in the darkest days of her country's woe: this work is inscribed, with the earnest esteem and affection of the author."[2] Prior to her marriage, Mrs. Underwood was Maria Gloria Jackson, a cousin of the famous Confederate general Stonewall Jackson. Her husband was a radical antislavery New York lawyer, appointed by Lincoln as a federal judge for the eastern district of Virginia. He confiscated estates owned by Confederates in what he called "retributive justice." After the war, he advocated for African Americans' and women's right to vote. Maria Underwood represented many Americans who were quite literally torn between two sides of her family—her abolitionist husband on one side and her Southern family heritage on the other.

Emma often hid progressive ideas in the pages of her books, but after the Civil War, Emma stepped outside of those boundaries, advocating her reconstructionist views in the real world. On March 18, 1867, Emma wrote Robert Bonner, "I take great pleasure in introducing to you, General Benjamin Ewell, late of the Confederate Army and now President of William and Mary College, Virginia." With the war's end, Ewell eagerly sought funding to repair damages incurred to the campus during its closure. "President Ewell is deeply interested in the cause of general education," Emma explained, "and he is anxious to cooperate with all true patriots in the work of reconstruction and reconciliation." Emma hoped that Bonner could connect him with Northern supporters who might offer donations. Realizing that Ewell had played a prominent role in the Confederacy, Emma used her reputation as collateral, introducing Ewell to Senator Henry Wilson in Washington. "He looks more like a doctor of divinity than a fire-eating rebel leader, doesn't he?" Emma said of Ewell.[3] Wilson was a radical Republican who strongly opposed slavery, but he had worked as a schoolteacher before becoming a senator and was interested in education reforms. His political influence could help Ewell fund the college.

Reconstruction wasn't Emma's only agenda, and she continued to help her family, especially her children, even though Lottie was now married. Lottie's husband James Lawrence took a job with the U.S. postal service, negotiating mail agreements between the United States and foreign countries. He traveled to Brazil, Great Britain, China, and Japan, which meant long absences from home. Even while home, he worked on earning a law degree from Columbia University. Much to Emma's delight, Lottie continued to live at Prospect Cottage, where she and James welcomed their first child, whom they named Emma Southworth Lawrence on March 23, 1865. Little Emma was soon joined by William H. Lawrence on October 28, 1866, and Gladys Rose on May 11, 1869. Emma's children were everything to her, and her grandchildren were no different. "This is our Willie's birthday," Emma told Bonner.

"And as soon as I have done this [week's copy], I am going to get a big wagon and take him and his mother & sisters out into the beautiful woods for a holiday." Emma also helped Lottie through her greatest tragedy on April 23, 1871, when baby Gladys Rose died, just shy of her second birthday.[4] Emma didn't just want to help Lottie and her family; she needed to be with them.

Richmond was still in medical school once the war ended, and Emma was desperate to bring him home. After Richmond finished his degree at Columbia Medical School in 1866, he hoped to establish his own practice in New York, and Bonner offered to help Richmond buy a practice there. "The old physician has declined to sell his practice, so I cannot get that," Richmond told Bonner, admitting defeat. "I intend to open an office in Washington and make a specialty of the microscope." By June 1867, Richmond set up his office at the corner of High and Lingan in Georgetown, only a couple of blocks from Prospect Cottage, where he remained living with his mother. In addition to his practice, Richmond worked at the Columbia Hospital for Women as an analytical chemist.[5] Given Emma's passion for helping women, Richmond's choice was heavily influenced by her. After years of hardships, she used her controlling influence to keep Richmond close. After all, she was his mother; she knew what was best.

Emma also believed she knew what was best for other members of her family, especially her half siblings. Henshaw died on September 14, 1866, followed by Susanna on December 10, 1869. Emma felt it her duty to care for her half siblings: Frances (whom Emma nicknamed Pinkie), Edith, and Henry. Emma was sixteen to twenty years older than they were, so she felt more like a surrogate parent than a sister. She was proud of her little brother Henry, who had commanded a revenue cutter during the war, but he had married Gertrude White and moved to Frederick, Maryland, to oversee his wife's family agriculture business. Henry really didn't need her, but the care she gave to her spinster sister Edith, who lived at Prospect Cottage, was obvious, as Emma dedicated *The Changed Brides* "with the love of her sister" in 1869.[6]

Pinkie, however, was the sister Emma helped the most. Pinkie aspired to become a writer like her big sister, and Emma helped her get her first short story published. "I enclose another short sketch from Mrs. Baden; at your disposal, if you like it," Emma wrote to Bonner. "It is good." It really wasn't, but in deference to his star writer, Bonner published Pinkie's story. In "Willful Lottie; or, What Will She Do Next," Pinkie sought Emma's approval, naming the major characters "Lottie" and "Richmond Worth," obviously replicas of Emma's children. In the story, Lottie's aunt (clearly Pinkie) gives Lottie advice, which turns out to be bad advice, proving that Lottie knew what was best.[7] Bonner continued to publish Pinkie's story, giving her space on page 6 of the *Ledger*—a small price to pay to keep Emma content.

Emma could afford to help her family financially, as she was now internationally famous. By 1868, she was earning $4,500 a year (approximately $99,000 in 2024 dollars), and although her income paled in comparison to heavy hitters like Rev. Henry Ward Beecher, who earned five times Emma's salary, or Jay Gould, president of Erie Railway, who earned $150,000 that same year, when newspapers reported the earnings of famous Americans, Emma was the only woman who made the list. Even her critics had a hard time not recognizing her success. "Mrs. Southworth is still the novelist most in demand in the circulating libraries," literary critic Bayard Taylor wrote. "Yet, notwithstanding this fact, it is pretty certain that the lowest point of literary demoralization had been reached and passed."

Her fans disagreed. "It is common to account for her success by calling her stories sensational, but if anybody thinks it an easy matter to write successful sensation stories, or any other kind, for twenty-six years continuously, let them try it—or let them try one, even!" wrote an enthusiastic reporter. "But let anyone review the Southworth novels and he will be surprised by the small amount of sensation matter in them . . . she seems likelier to be a writer of the Martineau order than of the imaginative style."[8] What the reporter observed was that Emma had become a more confident writer during and after the Civil War, no longer hiding her progressive views. Her relationship with Bonner changed everything, as he gave her freedom to write what she wanted, and as she became more outspoken in her novels, her readers responded by buying even more copies of her books.

Emma was eternally grateful to Bonner and his wife Jane for their generosity and support, which grew after the war. In 1867, Bonner drew up a new five-year contract, increasing her salary from $50 to $75 per week. Bonner's contract made practical business sense, as Emma's stories made him a lot of money, but his generosity extended beyond his profit margin. In January 1869, when Emma became sick with pneumonia, Bonner reassured Emma that he would pay her the promised weekly salary during her illness. "Heaven forbid that I should ever so heavily tax your unbounded benevolence," Emma responded. "Heaven grant that I may write and *write well* for the *Ledger* as long as we both live;—and that in my best way I may serve your best interests, as you have always promoted mine." Emma was also close to Jane, who treated Emma like family, inviting her to stay with them while in New York. As a token of appreciation, Emma dedicated *The Bride of Llewellyn* "to Mrs. Robert Bonner of New York, this book is inscribed, as a tribute of esteem and affection, from her friend, the Author." Jane was delighted with the kind gesture, but Emma wished she could do more to show her appreciation. "It was not half as good as the good things with which she nourished and comforted me when I was with her—but it was the best I could do," Emma wrote. "There was nothing in the world else that *I* could have offered her, that *she* the wife of a very wealthy man could not have got far richer and better for herself."[9]

Emma pledged to Bonner that she would never leave the *Ledger*. In 1868, she was approached by R. S. Davis and James Elverson, owners of the *Philadelphia Saturday Night*, a weekly paper that was a *Ledger* competitor. They were republishing *The Curse of Clifton*, a story that had originally appeared in 1852. The older work was obviously selling well because Davis and Elverson offered her the enormous sum of $10,000 to write a new story for *Saturday Night*. Even though Emma had no control over her novels once she'd sold the copyright, she reassured Bonner, "God who sees me knows that I was not tempted for an instant, even to wish to accept the offer. . . . I am not worth much; but such as I am, the associated press of the whole world is not rich enough to buy me from the *Ledger*."[10] Emma had worked for some bad publishers before and appreciated how Bonner cared for his writers. More important, she wouldn't compromise the relationship she had with the Bonners, even for such an exorbitant offer.

Because of this valued friendship, Bonner asked Emma's opinion on financial issues. He was proud that he could sell his weekly paper at an affordable price, $2 per year or roughly 4¢ per issue. By 1863, the cost of paper had risen by 50 percent, but Bonner pledged to keep his prices the same. However, in 1865, Bonner raised the price for a yearly subscription to $3 or 6¢ per issue. He worried about some of his competitors who were offering lower rates. In 1869, thc *Post* advertised *The Lady's Friend* for just $2.50 a year or 5¢ per issue, which was a penny less than the *Ledger*. Plus, the *Post* promoted a second deal in which subscribers could buy both *The Lady's Friend* and the *Post* for $4 per year, which meant getting two weeklies at just 4¢ each. Other weeklies sold for much less, such as the *Weekly Sun* at a $1.50 per year and the *Weekly Tribune* at $2.50 per year. "I think a small difference in the price makes very little differences in the circulation of a popular story paper—in fact I think it makes no difference," Emma reassured Bonner. "If . . . all the other story papers in the United States were to come down to 4 cents the *Ledger* would still hold all its readers at 6 cents—though some might grumble at having to add a penny to their half dime."[11] Bonner took Emma's advice and kept the cost of the *Ledger* at his higher rate, and the paper continued to do well.

Emma also followed Bonner's advice about money, especially when he regularly gave her bonus checks each Christmas. Bonner had stopped being Emma's "banker" after she returned from England. At first, Emma was quite ignorant about how to manage money. In 1867, Bonner finally asked her what she was doing with all the checks he sent weekly, as none of them had been cashed. "I had not the slightest idea that it inconvenienced you for me to keep the checks uncashed. I kept them as a matter of economy," Emma reasoned. "I thought that until I cashed a check the money could not be wasted—but just as soon as I do cash a check—whew!—the money flies in all directions." Bonner advised her to become more prudent with her money, and by 1873 she followed his direction, investing in U.S. bonds.[12] In the event that anything ever happened to Bonner or the *Ledger*, Emma would still have means of a modest income to support herself, though perhaps not her family.

Emma also became a more focused and intentional writer after the war. With Bonner's increase in her salary, she didn't need to write in such a rapid frenzy, nor did she need to continue to battle the English publishers. In 1867, she was still writing for both the *Journal* (now owned by William Johnson) and the *Reader* (Stiff's new publication), but they were up to their old tricks. "[They] have the monopoly of their line of publication in England," Emma told Bonner. "And the choice between them is the old choice between 'the witch and the devil.'" However, there was a third option—stop doing business with them altogether. In 1869, both publishers wanted advance sheets of Emma's new novel, *The Hallow-Eve Mystery*. Bonner knew how frustrated Emma had become regarding the English publishers, and he decided to stop sending advance sheets to England. No more of Emma's works appeared in the *Reader*, and only one republished story appeared in the *Journal*.[13] Cutting ties with the English publishers freed Emma's time to concentrate on her work for the *Ledger* and with T. B. Peterson.

Over the next decade, Emma produced one serial novel a year for the *Ledger*, which T. B. Peterson quickly bought and printed in book form. Peterson had purchased all of her books—except one—and he was desperate to get his hands on it. By 1867, *The Hidden Hand* was still as popular as it had been eight years earlier, with numerous publishing houses attempting to steal it. "I enclose you a letter from T. B. Peterson. You will see by the post-script, that some house in Boston is bringing out a book under the 'Hidden Hand,'" Emma complained to Bonner. "The title was mine and you copyrighted it with all the other content of the *New York Ledger*. About two years ago, the title was stolen in Paris and in London for a vile French play." Emma knew the value of her most popular serial and realized that the title was as important as the story itself. "I know that *my* 'Hidden Hand' is constantly called for in the bookstores, and I think that circumstance has tempted the Boston House to bring out a spurious book under that popular title," Emma wrote. "Of course, it will very much injure my copyright. You see T. B. Peterson wants to bring mine out immediately; but I don't wish him to do it."[14] Emma had another plan.

After writing novels for almost twenty years, Emma recognized that *The Hidden Hand* was worth far more than miserly Peterson would ever pay. "T. B. Peterson has applied for it about twice a year, ever since it first appeared in the *Ledger*," Emma wrote. "I told him I was not ready to publish it in book form." What Emma wanted was for the story to have another run in the *Ledger*; her readers wanted it, so it made sense that it would help sell subscriptions. "I have considered the copyright *pledged to you* for as long as you might wish to use it," Emma told Bonner. "Either for a limited or an unlimited time." On September 28, 1867, Bonner bought the copyright and paid Emma handsomely for it: $1,000. Bonner then reserialized *The Hidden Hand* in the *Ledger* from September 5, 1868, to February 6, 1869. As usual, he heavily advertised its release throughout the country. "In regard to that lavish expenditure in advertising the 'Hidden Hand,' I hope and trust that you have got back your money with interest," Emma wrote. "To me it seemed a fearful risk. How kind it was of you too, to tell me of the increase of the circulation since that advertisement."[15] Bonner took risks but only those he believed would make him money, and *The Hidden Hand* was a goldmine.

Even though Emma wisely invested much of her profits, she also spent a lot. She enjoyed opening her home, and she continued hosting literary gatherings, fashionable parties, and even weddings for her family and friends. One event that Emma looked forward to the most was Ulysses S. Grant's inauguration as the eighteenth president of the United States. Bonner was delighted when Emma invited him to stay with her for the inauguration.[16] No doubt, Emma had Prospect Cottage looking its finest when Robert and Jane came to stay.

Given how famous and well connected Bonner and Emma were, they had no problems securing the required tickets for admission to the inauguration at the Capitol or tickets to the Treasury Department, where the reception was to be held. On March 4, 1869, the parade route along Pennsylvania Avenue was lined with Chinese lanterns decorated in red, white, and blue with the word *Union* emblazoned across them. Crowds lined the streets early in the day with onlookers opening up umbrellas to keep out of the drizzly rain. Wealthier onlookers paid exorbitant prices to secure windows and balconies that gave the best views, while boys and men climbed trees, posts, and rooftops in hopes of watching the presidential festivities. At 11:00 a.m., the umbrellas were put away as the skies cleared just in time for the procession to begin. Escorted by the first division of the U.S. military, Ulysses S. Grant and General John Rawlings rode in an open carriage. Eight U.S. divisions paraded the route along with bands, fire brigades, and police—the grandest yet for any U.S. president.

The parade ended at the Capitol, where the Senate gallery was already packed to capacity, with more than half of the seats being occupied by women. After Schuyler Colfax was sworn in on the Senate floor, congressional members and Senate-gallery ticket holders proceeded to the east portico to witness Chief Justice Salmon P. Chase administer the oath of office to President Grant, while a packed crowd watched from below. Grant then gave a brief inaugural address, covering three basic points. The first two highlighted the importance of law enforcement and the need to pay off Civil War debt, but of utmost significance to Emma was Grant's third point—his approval of passing the Fifteenth Amendment, giving all citizens the right to vote. The concept of "suffrage" was a broad scope that included not only newly freed black men but also black and white women. However, whether the ratification of the Fifteenth Amendment would include all citizens or only men was indeed, as Grant stated, "likely to agitate the public."[17]

Congress had passed and ratified the Thirteenth Amendment of the Constitution in 1865. Section 1 of this very short amendment was concise and to the point: "Neither slavery nor involuntary servitude, except as a punishment for crime whereof the party shall have been duly convicted, shall exist within the United States, or any place subject to their jurisdiction." Because women were denied equal privileges such as the right to vote or equal opportunity in the world of commerce, many felt that they fell into the category of "involuntary servitude," thus giving women hope that the next amendment would give all citizens full rights accorded by law. It was one thing to be "free"; it was quite another to be equal. Making a strong case for women's rights, Emma wrote *Britomarte* for the *Ledger* from October 14, 1865, to September 15, 1866, before being printed by T. B. Peterson in two volumes in 1868 and 1869.[18] In the novel, Emma

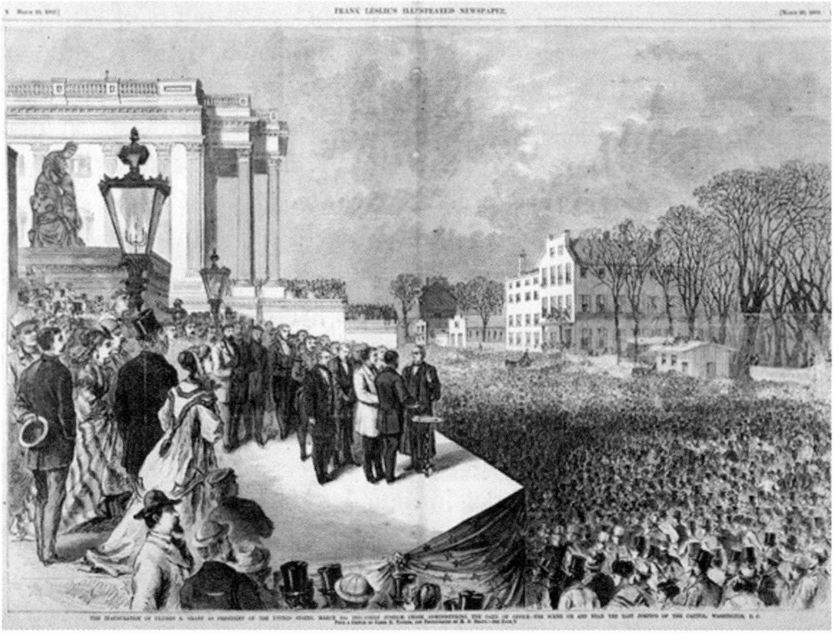

President Grant's inauguration (1869). (*U.S. Senate Collection*)

argued that women could perform equally at jobs that were available only to men—even as doctors and soldiers. It was no accident that the timing of both the serial and the book publications coincided with the political fight to secure equal rights for women.

As outspoken as Emma was in *Britomarte*, she made an even bolder move by stepping outside the pages of her books to openly advocate women's rights. In the fight for equality, African Americans and white women had been closely tied, and they cheered together with the passage of the Thirteenth Amendment, which made slavery illegal. Because this amendment ensured freedom for both black men and women, the hope was that future amendments, including one about voter's rights, would include women. "If that word 'male' be inserted," activist Elizabeth Cady Stanton wrote, "it will take us a century at least to get it out."[19] Emma agreed, and, in 1868, she joined the District of Columbia Woman Franchise Association, a part of the National Woman Suffrage Association. On June 25, 1868, the District Franchise Association petitioned the

Britomarte as a soldier in *Britomarte*, in the *New York Ledger* (1866). (*Falvey Digital Library, Villanova University, Pennsylvania*)

House of Representatives to pass a bill presented by Henry D. Washburn for women's right to vote. Emma was one of eleven women who signed a memorial, which noted

> the fact that congress had freed 3,000 slaves, and enfranchised 8,000 colored men of the district, both of which experiments had worked well, notwithstanding conservative predictions to the contrary; and showing that, while the former experiments, on a small scale comparatively, had yielded rich results, so the enfranchisement of half the adult population would produce vast good.[20]

Despite this petition, Congress ratified the Fourteenth Amendment on July 9, 1868, which granted citizenship to both men and women born in the United States but recommended that only "male citizens" over the age of twenty-one be allowed the vote. This amendment was monumentally devastating to women, as it was the first time in constitutional history that Congress specifically mentioned gender, thus excluding women from the right to vote.

Any hope that this exclusion would be abolished in the Fifteenth Amendment was dashed with its passage on March 30, 1870. The amendment was short and to the point: "The right of citizens of the

United States to vote shall not be denied or abridged by the United States or by any State on account of race, color, or previous condition of servitude." It was ambiguous at best. Women could argue that they had been in a "previous condition of servitude" by laws that had historically denied them rights to own property or to vote. Women's rights activists were divided on whether to support the amendment, and the suffragists fractured into two groups—the National Woman Suffrage Association (NWSA), led by Susan B. Anthony and Elizabeth Cady Stanton, and the American Woman Suffrage Association (AWSA), led by Lucy Stone. The AWSA believed they should support the amendment and that a new amendment would soon be passed that granted women the right to vote. The NWSA was more radical, however, believing instead they should protest the new law. Emma and her friends aligned with the NWSA.

In April 1871, voters prepared to elect new city officials—male voters, of course. Principal of the Spencerian business college Sara J. Spencer and physician Susan A. Edson organized a petition to present to city officials asking that they be allowed to register to vote. In the petition, the women who signed declared the following:

> We, the undersigned, citizens of Washington, D.C. believing it to be our solemn duty—a part of the allegiance we owe to our Maker, to our country, and to our homes—to exercise the right of the elective franchise, hereby earnestly petition that our names be registered as qualified voters in our several districts.

Sara J. Lippincott (whose pen name was Grace Greenwood) and Emma Southworth were at the top of the list of petitioners. Grace and Emma had been longtime friends, working first as writers for the *Era* before moving to the *Post* and then to the *Ledger*. When Sara Spencer gave Grace the petition, she promptly signed it before asking her mother whether she would like to sign it. "Yes!" the ninety-year-old mother said. "Write it twice." When the petition was handed to Emma, she signed it without question. "It *must* come," Emma told Sara Spencer. "They may as well accept that situation gracefully," to which Sara remarked, "But they say we women don't want to vote." Emma responded, "Oh, to be sure. They said the negroes didn't want freedom, you know. But where is my pen? I have had the *penophobia* for two weeks. Ah! Here it is." And Emma signed the document with determination. In all, sixty-seven women signed the petition.[21]

The petition was just the starting point. On April 14, Emma, along with the other women petitioners, marched to City Hall, despite board members' suggestion to meet the ladies at a different place. They wanted to register in the same way and in the same place as the men. What a sight to see: sixty-seven women clad in the various fashionable dresses of the day—layers of ruffles, braids, tassels, ribbons, and lace; big flouncy bustles protruding from behind; intricate bonnets trimmed with flowers, ribbons, and feathers—each woman dressed in different brightly colored hues of purples, pinks, blues, and yellows. To hear their silvery voices nervously and excitedly chatting with each other as they climbed the steps, their skirts rustling and swishing as they vied to enter the building. These were sights and sounds likely not seen before at City Hall—sights and sounds that would have stood in stark contrast to the businessmen of the day who wore simple dark-colored frock coats, plain white shirts, and gray trousers.[22]

The chairman of the board, Mr. Crocker, allowed the women to fill out the applications to vote, but they were refused registration, as the registrars unanimously decided that only men could vote under the existing laws. While the women expected this outcome, they were not sorry they had done it. "They have proven that intelligent Christian women in Washington feel it their duty to exercise the elective franchise," a reporter observed. "They have taken the first steps toward securing a legal recognition of their citizenship."[23] It was a good step, but other steps were needed to reach their destination—women's equality and the right to vote.

As disappointing as the failure to win women's right to vote was, another event happened that disappointed Emma more. After years of working for the U.S. Postal Service, Emma's son-in-law James was ready to do something different. In 1873, he decided to join his brother Fred in Yonkers, New York, and establish the Lawrence Brothers Lumber Company. This meant Lottie and the grandchildren would be a considerable distance from Georgetown. James built a large family home at 107 Buena Vista Avenue in Yonkers—a place Emma would visit often.[24]

Emma still had Richmond at Prospect Cottage, with his own Georgetown medical practice where he specialized in the microscope. In December 1871, Richmond, along with fellow Georgetown physician Horace T. Porter, made improvements to the eye-piece portion of the microscope, making it simpler and cheaper to produce and less eye fatiguing, while still equal in accuracy to its predecessors. Their invention was recognized by their peers in the *American Journal of Science and Art*. Emma was proud of Richmond, who had inherited the best part of his father Frederick—a love of invention and a talent for mechanical devices that would improve and modernize industry. In addition to having a medical degree, in May 1873, Richmond graduated from Columbia Law School, proving that he was an intelligent and capable young man.[25] He didn't need his mother hovering over him, but Emma remained overbearing.

While on a visit to Yonkers to visit Lottie, Emma received news that instantly alarmed her. "You see, I heard that Richmond was very sick and I flew off at once, like a hen to the rescue of her chicken," Emma wrote. "And when I got here, I found Richmond about as well as ever. He had the toothache for two days, and that originated the 'black crow' story of his serious illness."[26] Richmond was thirty-two years old, a physician and a lawyer. Even if he had been ill, as a doctor, he hardly needed his mother, but this evidence indicates the fervor with which Emma was rushing back and forth at a moment's notice at the mere hint that she might be needed by one of her children or grandchildren.

Emma had once again put too much on her plate, and it was bound to catch up with her. In addition to frequent trips from Georgetown to Yonkers, she was writing novels, negotiating new deals for previous works, helping her sister Pinkie with her writing, and working with the women's rights movement. By November 1875, she was exhausted to the point of mental and physical collapse. She had recently finished *Only a Girl's Heart* for the *Ledger* and had immediate plans to begin *The Lost Lady of Lone*. Emma had also just returned from a visit to New York when she began to feel the effects of her fast-paced life. Despite being unable to eat or sleep throughout the weekend, she promptly planned another trip to New York. Before she could leave her house, however, she fainted on the stairs. Richmond called in physicians James J. Porter and J. Hampton Porter, the father and brother of his colleague Horace Porter, to make a diagnosis. "We are entirely agreed in believing your nervous system to be much affected," they explained. "In so great a degree in fact, that a longer continuance in your present state of health would involve permanent disease."[27] Emma understood that she needed to slow down and rest, but her obsessive and unnecessary worries over her grown and independent children interfered with her ability to take proper care of herself.

Emma formed a plan that she put into effect at once. She wrote to Bonner about her illness, asking him to continue paying her for three months while she rested. Embarrassed by her request, she implored Bonner to "*never let anyone not even my own son or daughter* know that I have made this appeal to you." Naturally, he agreed. Emma graciously thanked him: "I think you have saved my life, and given me a new lease of life. . . . Anxiety added to mental and physical prostration would soon have done its work upon me—a woman with the lifelong double burden of man and woman laid upon me." Without the additional burdens of travel and philanthropic work, it didn't take long before Emma felt like writing again. "This slow convalescence that keeps me in the house and the cold weather that keeps people away, give me a solitude and quiet that is highly favorable to my work," Emma explained to Bonner. "The consequence is that I am writing my very best."[28]

Emma's confinement proved one thing to her—she had to slow down, but her obsession to have her children and grandchildren close to her continued, which meant more changes were needed. With James firmly planted in Yonkers in his new business with his brother, there was little hope they would move back to Georgetown. Perhaps she could convince Richmond to move to New York. He had wanted to remain there to practice medicine. If Emma could find a quiet, peaceful house in which to write that was close to Lottie, she could greatly reduce her travel. She could still do her philanthropic work with occasional trips to Georgetown. She had the money to keep Prospect Cottage and rent another house in Yonkers. Bonner and his family were in New York, so visits with them would require much less effort. Yes, Emma formed a plan. She and Richmond would move to New York.

Chapter 11

From Prospect Cottage to Birds Nest

He makes you love your children [but] He loves them a thousand times better than you do—be sure of that—and feels for their sufferings too, when He cannot give them just what He would like to give them—cannot for their good, I mean.[1]

Even as Emma underlined and starred the above passage in her copy of Rev. George Macdonald's *Annals of a Quiet Neighborhood*, she seemed powerless to overcome her one great obsession and sin—a need to remain close and ever vigilant to Lottie and Richmond, even now that they were grown with careers and lives of their own. She convinced Richmond to relocate with her to Yonkers. One thing was certain: Emma's children were devoted to their mother, and Emma had all her chicks together again—even naming her new rented home "Birds Nest," which was at the corner of Warburton Avenue and Locust Street. Other than moving in with Lottie, "Birds Nest" was in the best location possible, as it was only a ten-to-fifteen-minute walk to Lottie's two-story Victorian-style home that looked out over the Hudson River. Even though Emma had her own place, she spent much time visiting her daughter and grandchildren.

The house at 103 Warburton Avenue was also convenient for Richmond, who had a position at St. John's Riverside Hospital only two blocks from their home. By this time, Emma had recovered sufficiently from her extreme bout of mental and physical exhaustion. She told Bonner, "I never was so near death before, but for leaving my children I think I should have been glad." While her focus remained on caring for her grown children, at the age of fifty-seven, she morbidly considered her own mortality. "I feel at times, such a vivid realization of that higher, freer, better life which is beyond," she pondered. "It is the aspiration of the *caged bird*, for the open air."[2] The idea of the caged bird being free might have inspired her to name the house Birds Nest. Whether intentional or not, referring to it by this title seems metaphorically pertinent.

In truth, Lottie did have a growing number of children. The oldest, Emma, named after her grandmother, was eleven; Lottie and James had four more children, and they would add another four in the years Emma lived in Yonkers. "Mrs. Southworth has a troop of grandchildren," one reporter noted, "who come to her for ginger-bread and salute her as 'Grandma Emma.'" James was busy with the Lawrence Brothers business, selling lumber, coal, wood, brick, and lime. He was also active in the community. In March 1876, James ran on the Democratic ticket for mayor of Yonkers. Even though he didn't win, he remained active in politics and was also a longtime member of the local Board of Education.[3] With so much on James's plate, there were plenty of grandmotherly duties for Emma, and Lottie appreciated having her mother nearby.

Richmond wasted no time establishing his own life separate from his mother. Emma said, "Richmond is devoted to his profession and spares me very little time either as a visitor or as a correspondent." Richmond heavily advertised his doctor services in both the *Yonkers Gazette* and the *Yonkers Statesman*. By all accounts, he was a respected member of the medical community. When a mysterious death occurred across the street from his home at Dr. George B. Upham's residence, Richmond was called in to perform an autopsy. It was rumored that the young Upham had been either poisoned or shot. On completion of the autopsy, Richmond released a statement to reporters: "We found no evidence of any injury by gunshot wounds nor of any other violence. The autopsy was a complete vindication of the family, and contradicted all the published stories. I will not name the cause of death except to the coroner."[4] Richmond, who not only was a doctor but also had earned a law degree, understood the delicate nature of the case and used the utmost caution when dealing with reporters.

Richmond was also popular with his medical colleagues. The New York State Medical Association appointed him as the chosen state delegate at the American Medical Association that met in Washington, DC. His practice thrived to the point that he added a brick wing to the rear of the Warburton home to use for his office, which allowed him not only to treat patients but also to invite guests for presentations. On one occasion, he gave a lecture on chemistry. With his nineteen-year-old nephew William Lawrence acting as assistant, Richmond performed a series of experiments for his guests. "The discourse was both highly instructive and entertaining and was replete throughout with humorous diversions," the *Yonkers Gazette* enthusiastically reported. "The presence of Mrs. E.D.E.N. Southworth was most enjoyable, and the occasion one of the red-letter days in the history of the society."[5] Richmond was a successful man in his own right, but ever in his mother's shadow.

Even though Emma was fully involved in her children's lives, she made new acquaintances and entertained guests at her home in Yonkers. When Mrs. Roswell A. Roberts and Mrs. Willard H. Brownson invited 300 guests to an elegant afternoon tea, Emma was one of 130 people who attended. It was a gathering exclusively for the who's who of Yonkers. Another of Emma's friends was the celebrated Shakespearean actor George C. Miln, whom Emma invited to stay at Birds Nest when he performed in Yonkers. Miln opened to a large audience at the Yonkers Opera House, where he played Shakespeare's Hamlet. In attendance was Samuel J. Tilden, New York's twenty-fifth governor and Democratic presidential candidate in the 1876 election. Jay Gould, American railroad magnate and one of the wealthiest men during the nineteenth century, was also in attendance, as was American actress Clara Morris, who in 1869 had played the part of Capitola Black on stage.[6] Emma loved to entertain and be entertained—an aspect of her life that remained the same in Yonkers.

Emma hadn't forgotten about Georgetown or her beloved Prospect Cottage, and she retained ownership of her home throughout her years in New York. She left the cottage in the very capable hands of Amanda Taylor—her beloved maid Mandy, who had cared for Emma and the children during her darkest days. By the mid-1850s, Mandy no longer lived with Emma, and where she'd spent the past twenty years is unknown. She appeared again when a reporter came to Prospect hoping for an interview with the famous authoress. "Well, I found the cottage kept by an intelligent, good looking colored woman, who spoke pure English and had a once-a-week letter from Mrs. Southworth in her pocket," the reporter wrote. "The woman who takes care of the cottage . . . was brought up in the family and has spent the most of her life with her mistress."[7] Long after the end of slavery, Emma left Mandy in charge of the one possession that meant the most to her—Prospect Cottage.

Mandy was not taking care of an empty house while Emma was in Yonkers; in fact, the house was filled to the brim with Emma's half sisters Edith and Pinkie, Pinkie's husband Thomas Baden, and Pinkie and Thomas's six children. Emma financially helped the family, even though Thomas was capable of working. "My brother-in-law Mr. Baden has lost his office under the government, in consequence of retrenchment. He has not saved one dollar. How could he with a family of eleven, six of whom are young children and only fourteen hundred dollar's salary?" Emma defended him to Bonner, adding, "In the hundreds of clerks that have been discharged from office and seeking employment it seems almost impossible for Mr. Baden to get anything to do, though he is a very accomplished pen-man and bookkeeper, and bears the highest character."[8] Finding employment seemed permanently beyond Baden's reach, as Emma continued to financially provide for him and his large family for the next fourteen years.

In order to achieve some semblance of financial stability, Pinkie tried to contribute, and to this end, Emma pitched in to help. Pinkie had written enough short stories to have a collection printed in book form, but Pinkie didn't have Emma's celebrity status. So Emma wrote a short story called "The Artist's Love," which became the title of the book, enabling Peterson to advertise the book as being written by Mrs. E.D.E.N. Southworth. With Emma's name attached, the book met with some success, so, in 1877, Peterson asked Emma to again write the first story for a second collection of Pinkie's short stories—but this time, he marketed it as an original Southworth novel. He placed one advertisement stating that "The Fatal Secret" by Mrs. Emma D.E.N. Southworth had "never before been issued in any form whatever"—a far cry from what the book actually was. He did add in smaller type that the book was "admirably supplemented by a collection of brief and interesting stories by Mrs. Baden, a sister of Mrs. Southworth"; however, the majority of the "Entire New Book by Mrs. Southworth" was written by Pinkie. Even though it was false advertising, Emma allowed it since the headlines helped bring in money for Pinkie's family. Emma also let Peterson use her name for a third collection, *The Phantom Wedding* (published in 1878).[9] A number of possibilities exist as to why no more were published after that year: Pinkie might have had no more short stories to sell; Peterson might have realized he wasn't able to make a profit with them; or Emma realized that allowing Pinkie's stories to be marketed and sold under the brand name of Mrs. E.D.E.N. Southworth was negatively affecting her readership numbers.

As Emma carefully negotiated her new contract with Bonner in 1878, other publishers pursued her. "All preceding propositions of this sort I have promptly disposed of, by replying that 'I have an exclusive engagement with the *New York Ledger*,'" Emma told Bonner. "But this has come after our contract dated Nov. 1, 1872 has expired. Of course, I take it for granted that we shall make a new contract . . . yet I cannot give my correspondence a definite answer until I hear from you, on the matter." Emma was still an author in high demand, and she knew it. Bonner quickly responded the next day with a new contract, offering her the same terms as the previous one. Emma signed it without dispute but with one caveat: "Yet—will you permit me to say—in all good feeling and friendliness that in one respect I am disappointed. I had hoped or, rather, I had much desired an increase of salary."[10]

While Emma claimed it was to save more for retirement, she also needed it for the continued support of Pinkie's brood. As Bonner was always generous, he no doubt gave her the raise. Even then, Emma often found herself needing more money. "I have been under heavy expenses and I wish to pay some debts before I leave the city," Emma wrote Bonner from DC. "Will you be so good to me as to advance the price of 2 numbers of my coming story?" Over the next several years, Emma made at least six more similar requests.[11] By Emma's own admission, she liked to spend money, but her greatest weakness had been giving money to family.

Half sisters Pinkie and Edith weren't the only reason Emma came back to visit Georgetown and Washington; she also continued to advocate for women's rights. Emma remained active in DC's Woman Franchise Association, serving with well-known physicians Susan Edson and Caroline Winslow and future presidential candidate Belva Lockwood. During the 1876 association election, Emma's friend Sara J. Spencer was elected president, with Emma and Caroline B. Winslow serving as vice presidents. This association was connected to the National Women's Suffrage Association led by well-known women's rights advocates Matilda Gage, Lucretia Mott, Elizabeth Cady Stanton, and Susan B. Anthony. Together, they presented a "Memorial of Women, Citizens of the United States" before the Senate in which they asked to be granted the right to vote, and they also formed the following "Woman's Plank" for the 1876 election year:

> That principles of justice and the welfare of the nation alike demand that every obstacle in the way of the exercise of the right of suffrage by the women citizens of the United States shall be speedily removed, and that we pledge ourselves to secure this end. On this one hundredth anniversary of the independence of the men of the United States we claim that the women of this country should receive something more than a mere promise of "respectful consideration." It is proper to say in this connection, that in 1872 the Republican convention "recognized the services of the loyal women of America," and acknowledged "that their demand for additional rights should receive respectful consideration."

While they were again unsuccessful in achieving the vote for women, they made strides toward that end.[12] Although Emma didn't live to see the day when women in the United States gained the right to vote, her daughter Lottie; granddaughters Rose, Vallie, Edith, and Mary; and all of Pinkie's daughters were able to go to the ballot boxes and let their voices be heard.

Emma also served on the board of trustees of a proposed school for wayward girls. In January 1876, Sara Spencer asked Congress to fund the land and building for a reform school. Helping her friend Sara, Emma presented evidence describing the horror of extreme poverty. Women who had children outside of marriage were often abandoned by men who took advantage of their youth and inexperience. Ostracized by friends, family, and their communities, these women, who were typically uneducated and from poverty-stricken backgrounds, were unable to find employment. Infanticide was sadly their last option. Emma described the gruesome details of a dead baby found along the shores of Rock Creek. Its throat had been cut and a stone attached to its little body before being thrown in the river. It landed on the shore instead of in the water and was thus discovered and taken to the police. "A hurried inquest—it was only a baby and nobody's baby at that—and the body was being taken to the hole that had been dug for it," Emma lamented. "Oh, pitying angels! Who bent from your radiant home to receive this little human soul, could you not send down one ray of kindly feeling to touch the head of the father, whose blood is in those frozen veins, to touch the heart of a cruel world which suffers such things to be and passes by 'on the other side?' A baby's funeral!"[13] To avoid such a dreadful outcome, the school offered a way for poor, uneducated, young women to receive job training and support until they could find employment.

The trustees went to the newspapers to show the public not only a need for a girls' reform school but also examples of the good that was being done with the current boys' industrial school. They argued that there was no place for young destitute mothers to go except to the workhouse or jail and that out of sheer desperation these women were driven to the despicable crimes of abortion and child murder. Pointing to existing laws, the girls' reform school trustees stated that men who had seduced innocent and unprotected women into having sex were able to abandon them once they became pregnant. The reform school could train these women as skilled workers so they could then feed, clothe, and protect their children and then raise them to be productive members of society. "The long delay in making provisions for these classes of persons," the trustees stated, "has led to terrible suffering among young women and to fearful slaughter of infant life." The final plea was for citizens to implore Congress to pass the girls' reform school bill, which allowed for monies to build the school. It was signed by the board of trustees, with Sara Spencer as president and E.D.E.N. Southworth as vice president.[14]

Emma was also one of the managers for the aforementioned boys' industrial school. In addition to attending school, boys were taught useful skills that would help them find jobs. A newspaper report stated, "Enabling these waifs of the community . . . to attend school and learn trades contributes to the public good quite as much as to the usefulness, respectability and happiness of the individual." If good could be accomplished at the industrial home school for boys, similar results could surely be achieved by building a girls' reform school. Congress finally approved the funds for the school in 1892, with the first school opening in 1893.[15] The time Emma had spent in England with educational reformists Lady Byron, Mary Carpenter, and William King influenced many of the ideas implemented in these DC reform schools.

Problems that arose from wealth disparity had always been an important cause for Emma, a societal ill often addressed in her novels. Published in the *Ledger* from July 1876 to March 1877, Emma's novel *Em* addressed poverty and how characters' lives were changed when given opportunities to improve. Two minor characters, John and Susan Palmer, have spent their lives in extreme poverty. John works hard at blue-collar jobs and Susan is a laundress, but they struggle to feed and clothe their numerous children. They send their children to school in the hope that a better education might give them greater opportunities, but the real change in their lives comes from an unknown benefactor who gives John an overseer job on a large farm estate in the country. Finally, their children have plenty of fresh air, horses to ride, and lots of garden food to eat. John and Susan have a good amount of farm work to do, but, compared to the stench and poor living conditions on Laundry Lane in the city, their new life seems like paradise.[16]

Sadly, Emma's own life was often not a paradise, especially when a series of tragedies occurred, affecting her deeply. The first was the death of Robert and Jane Bonner's fifteen-year-old daughter Mary on March 11, 1878. As she was the youngest of the Bonners' children, the blow was heart wrenching. "I do wish to give your dear brother and sister a thought that helped us in our sorrow," Emma comforted her goddaughter Emma Jane Bonner. "It was uttered by a minister of the Lord, just before turning away from the grave where a mother had laid the earthly form of her child. After the prayers were over, he said this: 'Now having performed the last earthly office of love to our dear one, by committing her mortal body to the dust from whence it came—*we leave it there, where she has left it, and follow her, by faith, to her eternal home*'" (emphasis Emma's).

Mary's death resurrected Emma's own loss seven years earlier when her infant granddaughter Gladys died. In *Em*, the death of one of her own characters caused her to momentarily slip into an authorial voice. "Now, if any should doubt that such an angel child ever lived, let me tell them that we ourselves had a little seraph with a heart like Em's, but that, as might have been expected, she went to heaven at two years old," Emma reminisced. "From her we learned how angelic a child might be."[17] Like her granddaughter, Emma had known Mary since her birth, and she felt the girl's death deeply.

A mere three weeks later, on April 2, 1878, Bonner's beloved wife Jane died at only forty-nine from tuberculosis. At the time of Mary and Jane's deaths, tuberculosis was commonly referred to as consumption or the "Great White Plague" because of how extremely pale its sufferers became. Caused by airborne bacteria, it was often spread through close and constant contact with infected family members. Mary and Jane had been invalids for several years with the disease. Emma and her sister Charlotte also suffered from it. Although people could live a long time, there was no cure. Remedies were crude, such as one in which hot plasters were placed on the skin in order to cause blistering, and then the fluid was drained from the blister. Emma was not a fan of this treatment. "I am sorry that dear Mrs. Bonner has been suffering so much, but blisters are the most barbarous things, worthy only of the darkest ages of medical practice," Emma emphasized. "They are not only very painful but very exhausting." When Mary and Jane died from the disease, Emma grieved even as she tried to comfort Bonner. "[Jane] was one of the angels of this earth without the least selfishness in her pure heart, which was full of warmest affection for her family and friends and good will to all creatures," Emma mourned. "I never realized how much I loved her until she left us. I was very fond of Mamie too; she was from infancy up, one of the brightest, sweetest little girls I ever knew."[18] Bonner and his children remained inconsolable.

The coming months were difficult for the Bonner family. By May 1878, two of Bonner's sons, Allie (Andrew) and Fred (Frederic), also became ill. "I have to report that Allie has not been at all well. His liver has been troubling him very much; but he has been improving for two or three days," Bonner wrote to Emma. "Fred has also been sick—so that he had to leave college and come home." Emma advised Bonner to take the children on an extended trip abroad. "I know what would be good for you and your children and if I were your physician with authority to counsel you, I should say go to Europe . . . in order to break up this morbid and unhealthy state into which your double bereavement has thrown you all," Emma strongly urged. Bonner didn't follow Emma's advice to go to Europe, but he did take some time off work, telling Emma, "I write mainly to say that I am not going down to the office today, *as I am going up to the farm again*."[19] Bonner's emphasis showed where he found the most comfort for his overwhelming grief—taking care of his beloved horses.

As grief and suffering finally subsided in the Bonner household, tragedy struck Emma's own family. Lottie's two-year-old daughter Alice fell gravely ill on May 22, 1878, with scarlet fever, and, as the family physician, Richmond was called in to help. Not only was he Alice's uncle, but he'd also suffered from the same childhood illness when he was seven. Doctors knew what the disease was, but it would still be years before antibiotic treatment was used to stop the infection. The treatment was to feed patients a liquid diet, keep cool rags about the head, and apply Epsom Salts, ammonia, carbonate, and nitrate silver, which were believed to counteract the poison from the fever. Such treatmnts were rarely successful, and six days after contracting scarlet fever, baby Alice died. Many Americans turned to their religious faith to help them with grief. Emma was no exception. "Our little Alice did not die, your dear Mamie did not die. *No* one ever really dies. They fall into the last delicious sleep; but they wake in the higher life," she fervently told Bonner.[20]

In the midst of tragedy, one event was a cause of celebration: Richmond found a bride. He and Emma had long been acquainted with the Porter family in Georgetown. Richmond began his medical practice alongside Horace Porter, and together they had worked on improving the microscope. Horace's father, James, and brother, John, had been Emma's attending physicians when she became ill before moving to Yonkers. Also among the family members was their sister Blanche, and it was she to whom Richmond had proposed. During the nineteenth century, the average age of marriage was twenty-two for women and twenty-six for men. At thirty-six, Richmond was considered a "confirmed bachelor," and Blanche was coined either an "old maid" or a "spinster" at thirty-eight. Their ages might explain the expedited nature of their marriage. On February 13, 1878, a brief announcement of their engagement appeared in DC's *Evening Star*, and a month later, on March 25, they were married. Unlike Lottie's elaborate wedding, Blanche and Richmond had a small ceremony without even a brief honeymoon. When the grieving Bonner sent a gift to the newlyweds, Emma was deeply touched. "It was so very kind and so deeply affecting that you should think of Richmond and Blanche in the midst of your own heavy sorrows," Emma told him. "It brought tears to our eyes."[21]

Although 1878 had been a year of emotional highs and lows, Bonner and Emma returned to business matters. Emma's book publisher, T. B. Peterson, had reprinted more than thirty of Emma's previously serialized novels, often in two-volume sets, and by 1876 he had all of her works except one—*The Hidden Hand*, which he remained ever vigilant to get. "Is there any way that you could get Mr. Bonner to let us issue the 'Hidden Hand' in uniform style with your other books published by us?" Peterson questioned Emma in 1877. "You may give him the privilege of running any 12 of your books he may know through the *Ledger* at any time he may please." Peterson knew the only way to print the book was if Bonner allowed it as the copyright owner. Believing *The Hidden Hand* would never run a third time in the *Ledger*, Peterson thought Bonner had no use for it. In February 1883, Peterson made one final plea to Bonner: "Is there no arrangement at all that we can make with you, whereby you will allow us to publish [it]?"[22] Bonner knew the moneymaker he had with *The Hidden Hand* and refused to sell.

Bonner's refusal caused Peterson's blood to boil and was the final tipping point in ending the printing relationship Emma had with Peterson. Because Bonner prided himself on paying his best authors very well, he loathed Peterson's tactics of lowballing authors for their copyrights as well as changing the serialized titles of books and then advertising them as original works. When Emma's serialized novel *Self-Made* went to press, she asked Peterson to keep the same title so that people would recognize the book. Instead, he published it in two volumes under the titles of *Ishmael; or, In the Depths* and *Self-Raised; or, From the Depths*. A more egregious error appeared in an advertisement in which Peterson stated, "Ishmael, the self-made man of mind (as distinguished from the lower class, who are 'made of money') stands above every other person in the tale."[23] Bonner saw the offhanded comment as a personal insult, as he had begun life in poverty but was now a man of extreme wealth. Even if Peterson's side-swipe attack was caused by his frustration over not getting *The Hidden Hand*, it was too much for Bonner.

Emma tried to justify Peterson's behavior as a result of the unexpected loss of his only son. Named after his father, Theophilus Peterson Jr. died suddenly at the age of twenty-four. Having groomed his son to take over his printing business, Peterson was devastated. Emma tried to smooth things out with Bonner on his behalf:

> Expressing your very natural indignation at the conduct of Peterson, in regard to "Self Made," I was shocked and grieved when I saw that advertisement in the New York papers. It was entirely unjustifiable . . . but just as that thing appeared, he was heavily stricken in the death of his son . . . said to have been "his right hand." I have more than one fault to find with him at that time but I could not do it then. Indeed, every angry feeling gave way before a great pity.[24]

Peterson had done too much damage, and while he managed to publish a few more books using Emma's title story to sell Pinkie's short stories, he never again published Emma's novels.

Sample of T. B. Peterson's Uniform Editions of Southworth novels. (*Author photo*)

After the break with Peterson, Emma wrote thirteen new serial novels for the *Ledger*. When negotiating a new contract in 1883, Bonner was so generous that Emma felt no need to ask for a raise as she had in 1878. She shared the good news with Blanche and Richmond. Emma, who had once again been feeling the effects of overexertion, was relieved by Bonner's lavish contract. "I believe this elixir is a very fine tonic," Emma told Richmond. "I am feeling so much stronger." Richmond replied, "I reckon it is Mr. Bonner's letter that is the tonic." Newspapers in the mid-1880s varied widely regarding her reported income. The *Times-Picayune* claimed she earned $8,000 per year from the *Ledger* alone. Another report in the *Brooklyn Times* estimated much higher, saying she earned $10,000 from the *Ledger* and another $15,000 from the sale of her forty books.[25] At any rate, Emma was doing very well for herself financially, even without the added income from Peterson.

Having secured such a handsome contract, Emma took longer breaks between novels, anywhere from three to five months at a time, and returned more often to Prospect Cottage and Georgetown. Her friends and family celebrated her visits with parties hosted in their homes. Sara Spencer hosted one reception that included music and dancing, and many of Emma's family and friends attended. Dr. and Mrs. George Mitchell held a similar reception at their home. Emma's friends also received warm welcomes at Prospect Cottage. Sara Spencer and American Red Cross founder Clara Barton planned one such visit. "If agreeable to you I will call to drive you to Prospect Cottage about 5 or 5–30 p.m. If possible, we want to catch the sunset from the wierd [*sic*] old cottage porch, and interview the ghosts that rise as darkness gathers, for you know the house is haunted. We won't stay long unless you wish," Sara told Clara. A frequent visitor to Prospect Cottage, Sara remembered Emma's comfort and friendship when her baby Rossie had died.[26] Emma missed the kind of relationships she had established with women like Sara Spencer.

Emma's bond with Sara Spencer helped her decide to become a member of the Swedenborgian Church. The Swedenborgian movement began from the teachings of Emanuel Swedenborg, whose aim was to discover profound meanings in the Bible that would lead members to deeper spiritual growth and understanding of self. The Swedenborgians established a congregation in DC in 1846, and Sara and her husband Henry had been members since 1869. Emma had been familiar with the church long before she became a member. On May 10, 1876, she hosted one of the social meetings of the Washington Society of the New Jerusalem at Prospect Cottage. The topic that evening was "Centennial Echoes." On July 1, 1883, Emma was officially baptized into the church and paid the annual dues of $25. Emma found attractive the doctrine that every soul was spiritually connected to a specific soul partner to whom they would be eternally united in the afterlife. Considering Emma's unhappy marriage to Frederick and her equally unhappy rejection of Henry Hardy, Emma found comfort in having a soul partner in heaven. In her view, "[The church is] adapted to the needs of human beings in their present state of advanced enlightenment."[27] Emma's new church ties gave her more reasons to return home.

Not everything that happened in DC was pleasing. One man in particular who got under Emma's skin was bookseller Joe Shillington, who told a tall tale of knowing Emma before she published her first story—a story that he published in local papers. He described Emma as a timid and nervous woman who frequented his shop, lurking through the books and magazines. He claimed she was always dressed in black. "One day 'the queer woman' approached me very cautiously, looking around to see that no one observed her," Shillington said, "and took from under her black shawl a big bundle of manuscript, and told me it was a story she had been writing, and asked me to have it printed in the *Sun*." He reportedly took it to the editor of the *Sun*, who then passed it on to *Saturday Visiter* editor Dr. Snodgrass. The clincher of his wildly outlandish claim was that he set up a meeting among Emma, Snodgrass, and Gamaliel Bailey of the *Era* and that Snodgrass and Bailey decided there was some merit in Emma's story but that it was "crude and ungrammatical" and needed much revising. This work, Shillington said, turned into *Retribution*. "Indeed I never even saw the periodical dealer spoken of in the article until long after 'Retribution' was published—two or three years fully," an astonished Emma said. "The only bookstore where I went at that time and was well acquainted was Robert Farnum's. . . . I never possessed 'a roll of MSS' in my life. You know I wrote from pen to printer."[28]

Despite men who wanted to capitalize on Emma's fame, she had many loyal fans. Her books were published all over the world and translated into French, Spanish, and German. When one New York reporter asked what books were most checked out at area libraries, novels by Mrs. E.D.E.N. Southworth topped the list. Another New York paper claimed that Emma had begun her sixty-fifth novel in her sixty-fifth year, while a third reported that at least 150 baby girls had been named after Emma's heroines. Though most of her fans were female readers, she had male admirers as well. "I think 'Ishmael' and 'Self-raised' the two finest books I ever read, and I think if any young man will take 'Ishmael' for an example, and follow his precepts, he is sure to succeed," said J. E. Cowan of Dixon Valley, Wyoming.[29]

Despite Emma's success, eventually, there had to be an end. The beginning of the end came as Bonner's sons took over at the *Ledger* and listened to those pesky critics that Bonner and Emma had learned to ignore long ago. In New York, the superintendent of one of Buffalo's public libraries put Emma's novels at the top of the suggested books to remove from the shelves. "The quality of her fiction . . . compares unfavorably with its quantity," another critic wrote. "It abounds in improbable plots, impossible personages, stagey dialogue, and stilted narrative. No young, impressionable reader will turn from its pages more content with life's realities." Not that this criticism was inaccurate; Emma favored sensationalism because she felt that was what her readers wanted.[30]

For thirty years, Robert Bonner had given Emma carte blanche to write whatever she pleased, and her pen flowed freely—with novels sometimes extending from six months to a year's run in the *Ledger*. As Allie, Eddie, and Fred Bonner hired younger editors and proofreaders, their father put increased pressure on Emma to streamline her work, but it was to no avail. "Close attention to details is a quality I share with the best authors and not with inferior writers who are careless," she wrote Bonner. "When I commence a story, I am caught up in its current and carried on and cannot get out of it; while it lasts. I must go the way it takes me, doing as well as I can."[31] Emma completely missed that readers' tastes were changing, and she seemed powerless to adapt the style of her writing.

Finding new material was also increasingly difficult, and Emma produced only three more novels after Bonner's 1883 contract. Instead, she revised some of her older stories to be reserialized, such as *The Hidden Hand*. Editing her own work proved as impossible for her as cutting down on details in her original novels. Nonetheless, *The Hidden Hand* made a third run in the *Ledger* from 1883 to 1884, but it had still not been printed in book form. The necessity to stock bookstores with *The Hidden Hand* became apparent in 1887 when a younger author, Emma Garrison Jones, asked for a copy so that she could write a new story from it. Emma appallingly expressed to Bonner, "I am told that she made this statement and this request with as much nonchalance as if she had asked for a pattern for embroidery or a recipe for a pudding, as if to ask for it

LEDGER BUILDING.

Engraving of the *New York Ledger* building in 1876. (*Fairmount Park*, 1876, 243)

and to get it was a matter of course and the demand quite a compliment to me!" Bonner and his sons finally made an agreement with G. W. Dillingham to print *The Hidden Hand* in book form in 1888, ensuring that the story belonged exclusively to Emma.[32]

Emma hadn't written any new material since the completion of *A Deed without a Name* in 1886, but she continued trying to revise *Only a Girl's Heart*. Its first serialization in the *Ledger* ran weekly for more than a year. Despite its excessive length, she could find nothing to condense. "I have read it with such perfect satisfaction that, after all, I dislike to have any part of it cut out," Emma explained. "I would like to ask you to publish the whole story unabridged." Bonner acceded to her wishes, and it was reserialized from November 6, 1886, to December 24, 1887. *Only a Girl's Heart* was the last serialized novel printed in the *Ledger* for several years.[33] Emma's time at the *Ledger* had come to an end.

Initially, she refused to admit her writing career was over. "Richmond gave me your message—to the effect that now is the time to write a good old-fashioned story to let people know that I am not being played out," Emma exasperatedly wrote to Bonner. "Now—what in the—*Dexter* do you mean by—'played out' in the remotest connection with me? I tell you what Brother Bob! When all the rest of me is played out, my heart and brain and hand will do it well while ever they have work to do." Despite her protests, Emma knew she was, in fact, played out. She had bought a typewriter in 1886 but still had not produced any new material by 1889, and she regarded "the pen as an old, tried friend." She had two gold pens that she favored, and by March 1888, she made an important decision that signified, even if she wouldn't acknowledge it aloud, she knew in her heart that her career was over. Emma melted the pens into gold rings, one for Lottie and one for Richmond—her children were the only things on earth that meant more to her than her writing. "It is supposed that she will confine her story-telling hereafter to her grandchildren," one reporter observed.[34]

Emma should have signed a new contract in 1888, but it took Bonner another year before telling Emma the fatal news—the *Ledger* wasn't giving her one. She took this final blow very hard. Her heartbreak was obvious when she told Bonner:

> You write that you have done no wrong. I will not discuss the point. God will judge. Thirty-two years ago, in 1857 I came back into your life with "The Peace Child." What we have been to you in all these years, you know. Now in 1889 his Heavenly Father has taken him to Heaven and you have lost me. I am not angry, I bear no malice. As I have prayed for you and yours, ever since your one great sorrow, so I shall still pray daily. This is all. Goodbye.[35]

Emma's "Peace Child" was her writing, and it was the one great gift she had given Bonner, who had become not just a trusted friend but also the brother she never had. Each novel was a "Peace Child"—a part of her that she nurtured and grew and birthed just as she had her two biological children. For thirty-two years, she handed each of these precious novel children to Bonner to be sent into the world through the *Ledger*. She was forced to admit there would be no more children. The "Peace Child" had died.

The news that she would no longer write for the *Ledger* was the last in a line of grievous events that occurred in 1889 and had a devastating consequence on Emma's already fragile health. The first was the sudden death of Pinkie's twenty-eight-year-old son Frank Baden. He worked as a telegraph operator for the Baltimore and Ohio railroad and was riding the train to work at the Lee Street tower on February 17. As the train reached a sharp curve, Frank stepped off and was thrown headfirst onto the track. Three weeks later, Emma's younger half sister Edith died at Prospect Cottage. Along with the death of her "Peace Child" in December, it was simply too much.

By February 1890, Emma became so critically ill that her family thought she would never recover, but in April she rallied enough that she had only one thought—she wanted to return to Prospect Cottage.[36] Lottie had just had her last child, Mary, in August 1889; the older grandchildren were grown, or almost so, and were old enough to visit their grandmother in Georgetown by themselves. There was no question about Richmond and Blanche; naturally, they would return with Emma so that, as her physician, Richmond could care for his mother. She had come to Yonkers to keep all her chicks close in her nest, but she was now tired and had only one wish. She wanted to go home.

Chapter 12

Going Home

> *Yes, we are nearer and nearer every day to re-union with our loved ones who are gone before—nearer to the time when you shall meet your mother, wife and daughter, and I shall meet my own dear ones too, and we shall look into each other's happy faces and say—"We hardly could believe this, when we were on earth—could we?"*[1]

Emma wrote the above note to Robert Bonner when Jane and Mary passed away, and as she recovered from her latest illness, thoughts of a reunion with her loved ones in heaven were ever present. She had considered where she wanted to die and returned to her beloved Prospect Cottage in May 1890. A contentious matter developed with Pinkie and her family, who had lived in Emma's home for fourteen years but had recently been forced to find another place to live. Although the 1890 census listed Pinkie's husband Ned as an inventor and Pinkie as an authoress, they were not making enough to support a family.[2] As Emma no longer had a contract with the *Ledger* and her health was poor, she couldn't keep providing for them.

Pinkie threw a fit after she moved out, and her behavior following Emma's return to Prospect Cottage led to a rift between the sisters from which Emma never recovered. Although Emma had regularly sent money to the Badens, Prospect Cottage was in dire need of repair. But there were other problems. Emma had left a large trunk in the attic filled with bedsheets, pillowcases, tablecloths, and blankets, but when Blanche went to retrieve them, she found the trunk filled with nothing but old, torn rags. Emma had also left two complete sets of rosebud china in her glass bookcase, but when she went to use the dishes for their afternoon tea, she found only two rosebud cups with broken handles and one black and white cup. "In short, everything trusted had been destroyed," Emma reported to Lottie. "I had left a most comfortably furnished home and I came to a desolation as far as fittings and furniture was concerned."[3]

As dismayed as Emma felt over the loss of her things, Pinkie's attacks became more heartbreaking. The day after Emma, Richmond, and Blanche returned, a letter arrived at their door, supposedly from Ned Baden, but Emma suspected Pinkie had dictated the message. "It was not the letter of a decent man or woman," Emma relayed to Lottie. "It was the letter of a low, blackguard. Full of insulting epithets, such as none but the lowest of the low and most spiteful of the vicious could have written." Emma asked Richmond to send a letter asking Pinkie and her family to leave them alone. Instead, another letter arrived, this one worse than the first. "She called Richmond vile names, the lightest of which was a 'crank,'" Emma told Lottie. "Said he had a sickly brain and a malicious nature and that he had written a cruel and insulting letter to his dying aunt—all her own wicked lies." Those lies cut Emma deeply. She had cared for Pinkie and her family in their most dire need. She gave them a home and a regular income when Ned became unemployed. She had been there for them when Pinkie's son Frank and then their sister Edith had died so close to each other. Considering that Pinkie had taken money from Emma for years, it was laughable that Pinkie spread rumors that Emma would be impoverished.

For Emma, the final blow was what she'd heard from her friends about the rumors circulating around town. An exasperated Emma exclaimed, "*May the just God requite her! She has reported all over the city that Richmond cruelly and vehemently neglected me and ill-treated me during my long illness*" (emphasis Emma's). She was beyond distraught, having loved her half sister Pinkie with a motherly affection—only to be betrayed at the deepest level. Emma asked Lottie not to respond to any correspondence that Pinkie might send her. Emma felt that the best solution was to completely cut ties with Pinkie and her family. The unforgivable cut was her allegation that Emma's most beloved children had treated her cruelly.

In the end, Pinkie didn't change anyone's opinion. Mrs. Southworth was a beloved sister of Georgetown. On the day of Emma's return, her friends Sara Spencer and Alice Underwood visited her, as did Blanche's brother Hampden, with Emma's granddaughter Rosie in tow. There was one visitor in particular whom Emma was very happy to see. "Lastly when all the rest were gone, dear Mr. Hardy. When his name was brought up to me, I was undressing to lie down," Emma fondly recalled. "But I quickly dressed myself and went downstairs to the library where he and Richmond were sitting. I went to him and held out both hands. He met me with all his old warm friendship and stayed talking with us until eleven o'clock."[4] Even though Emma and Henry had moved on with separate lives, they remained friends. Emma enjoyed regular visits from family and friends as she settled into her familiar surroundings.

Emma seemed content with a quiet life and preferred spending most of her time in seclusion. Richmond and Blanche were completely devoted to her. She was much slower now, preferring to sleep until early afternoon and never seeing visitors until after five o'clock, but the truth was that she had always been quite the night owl. Those who were lucky enough to see her in later years described a woman who still had a commanding presence. Her dark brown hair was now tinged with silver, and she kept it pulled into a bun at the back of her head. Her blue eyes were full of kindness and lit up when she told a story. She was not only a great conversationalist but also a good listener. She preferred to spend most of time in her library, often retiring to her porch to look out at the commanding view of the Potomac. "You know I have seen a great many people and visited a great many scenes," Emma told reporter Henry Cowell. "I have traveled from the very north of Canada to Mississippi and through the West, and I was three years in Europe."[5] Now she was ready to spend more time resting, but only a few months after returning to Prospect Cottage, she faced one more crisis.

In September 1890, a Marian Crandall Southwick from Olema, California, insisted that she wrote the novel *Self-Made*—a claim made worse by the fact that this novel was Emma's favorite. Emma was used to having stories stolen from her. "I have from the first suffered from plagiarism—not in pocket, nor in reputation, but in *mind*," Emma told Bonner. Being accused of plagiarism was new territory, however. Thirty-nine-year-old Marian Southwick and her father, William Osborne Crandall, told the outlandish story to their physician, George Frederick Morgan, who believed their claims and went to the press:

> In 1868 a talented young lady of this place sent to the editor of the *New York Ledger* [a] manuscript, which, if placed in book form, would make a volume of 500 pages. She heard nothing of it for nearly a year, at the expiration of which time she received a letter from the *Ledger* offering to buy out all rights to the book for $100. The offer was accepted and the cash was forwarded to her. Shortly afterward the book appeared in serial form in the *Ledger* under the very name the young lady had given it. To it was appended the name of Mrs. Emma D.E.N. Southworth as author.

Emma was dismayed, and the day the article appeared in the *New York Herald*, Emma reached out to Robert Bonner for help. "This looks like a device to provoke a newspaper controversy and thus get up a free advertisement of the book in question, and so should be suffered to die silently of its own imbecility," an exasperated Emma claimed. "Yet, as it assaults your honor as Editor and Publisher and mine as author, it should be put down."[6] Because Emma and Bonner were famous, the story spread through the newspapers like wildfire.

Emma and Bonner quickly stepped in to squash the rumors. The next day, Emma reached out to the *Washington Star*. "It was a popular story; so much so that after a short interval Mr. Bonner reprinted it in the *Ledger*," Emma told the reporter. "This was at a time when the *Ledger* had a circulation of 400,000, and why this charge should have lain dormant so long is more than I could understand if there was the slightest doubt about authorship." Giving further authenticity, Richmond testified, "I carried all the copy for the *Ledger* to the post office. While mother was writing the story in question, I went every week and I saw the whole thing from beginning to end." Bonner also quickly responded to the accusation. "Permit me to state that there is not one word of truth in what

Dr. Morgan, of California, is reported to have said about 'Self-Made,'" Bonner wrote. "I will forfeit $10,000 to any charitable society the *New York Herald* may designate if I cannot prove that Mrs. Southworth wrote 'Self-Made; or, Out of the Depths,' and that what Dr. Morgan says about my having bought the manuscript from any person in California is false."[7] Still, Morgan wasn't giving up so easily.

When Morgan saw the newspaper reports from Emma and Bonner, he wrote a scathing letter to the *Star* in what was quickly becoming a "he said/she said" debate. More concrete proof was needed, and Emma and Bonner had it. Instead of printing Morgan's article, the *Star* publisher brought it to Emma, as she had long been one of the newspaper's own contributors. She made a second plea to Bonner to stop these reports once and for all:

> Only you can silence them. Oh, I know Mr. Bonner, that it is asking a great deal of you. . . . But if you would only insert in the *San Francisco Chronicle* a card to the effect that *Self-Made* or *Out of the Depths* was written by me and commenced in the N.Y. *Ledger* March 21st, 1863—five years previous to the date at which Morgan claims that the other woman sent the manuscript to you—You would then kill the venomous libel in the very nest in which it was hatched.

It was the very fact needed to end the false allegations. *Self-Made* began in the *Ledger* in 1863 and was reprinted in 1874. Peterson printed it in two volumes as *Ishmael; or, In the Depths* and *Self-Raised; or, From the Depths* in 1876.[8] Morgan and Southwick were out of their depth. When *Self-Made* was first published in 1863, Marian Crandall Southwick was only twelve years old. Furthermore, the novel had never been published in 1868, nor had Southwick made any previous claim to authorship despite the numerous times the novel had been published.

Much to Emma's relief, the false allegations finally stopped once Bonner released the details to the press. "I thank you more than I can express for your card," Emma told him. "I wish I had a dozen copies of it to scatter among Californians. It is a 'stunner.'" When the news reached Morgan, he was embarrassed. "I am forced to the conclusion that

Mrs. Southworth must be the real author of the book in dispute—*Ishmael*," Morgan apologized to her. "For if Mrs. Southwick claims to have written it in 1868, while the same thing appeared in print five years before and did not appear in print in the year that she claims, then the conclusion is self-apparent and *inevitable*!" Morgan further promised to write an apology to Bonner as well as to correct his error with a letter to be printed in the *San Francisco Chronicle*.[9] While no such letter appeared in the *Chronicle*, the bogus claims made by Morgan and Southwick vanished, and Emma was firmly established as the rightful author of her favorite novel.

Even though Emma never published another novel once she returned to Prospect Cottage, she continued to write for the next several years. "I shall not write any more books," Emma told reporter Henry Cowell. "Haven't I done enough?" Instead, she returned to what she wrote at the beginning of her career—the short story. From 1889 to 1891, she continued her tradition of writing a Christmas story, and, like many of her others, one theme prevailed—they were stories in which Emma reminisced about the past. "I do not believe with Longfellow in any 'dead past,'" Emma told Lottie. "No! The past is all alive in our memories and is all our own! No one can take that from us! And if its memory is free from self-reproach, it is happy—for even sorrow is softened and lightened by distance."[10]

When Samuel Thomas Pickard asked her to contribute to a biography he was writing about John Greenleaf Whittier, Emma was happy to write about memories she had made with her friend and editor from her long-ago days at the *Era*. "That is a task indeed! My hands so cramped and chopped with the cold that I can hardly write a letter," Emma explained. "Dearest Lottie, *I live in the past*." She wrote about her memories of Whittier but was not happy with the results. "I am pleased that you liked the 'Reminiscences,'" Emma told Pickard. "But I think you spoke more favorably of them than they deserved."[11]

Another project that kept Emma busy was her desire to write a preface to each novel she had written, which again kept her mind tied to bygone days. "She calls them the 'Stories Underneath the Stories,'" Richmond told a reporter. "[She] tells in them how each novel was written and where the characters came from, and how much of truth and how much of fiction there is."[12] Emma had lived a rich and full life, and during her later years at Prospect, her best days were those in which she could tell stories about those exciting and wonderful times—the good, the bad, and everything in between.

Although writing about the past was enjoyable for her, it wasn't profitable. She had given away much of her fortune taking care of extended family, and while she had saved money for her retirement years, she didn't have the income she once did. Newspapers repeatedly claimed she had a $10,000 annual income, but Emma argued those numbers were exaggerated. Still, she had several sources of continued income. She was getting paid for her short stories. And Robert Bonner's sons had expanded the business beyond the *Ledger* into book publishing. After Emma's break with Peterson, she hadn't had her serialized novels printed in book form and still owned the copyrights. Beginning in 1890, Robert Bonner's Sons reprinted in book form many of the novels Emma had originally written for the *Ledger*. They also reserialized *Only a Girl's Heart* and *The Widows of Widowville*.[13] Robert Bonner and his sons Allie, Eddie, and Fred had not forgotten about Emma and her many years of devotion and friendship. Perhaps she couldn't contribute new serials, but her fans still enjoyed reading her stories again and again.

Emma was as popular as ever and had become an iconic figure of American literature. "Her novels are household words in this country; every schoolboy and girl has read and reread them," one reporter noted. "More than one adult has in his more mature years followed the fortunes of her heroes and heroines, and had his sympathies aroused by following trials of the human heart, which she so well knows how to depict." Her novels were in high demand at public libraries across the country. She remained an "immensely popular" novelist at the Enoch Pratt Free Library in Baltimore, Maryland. Also, when librarians in Atlanta, Georgia, requested novels by Emma D.E.N. Southworth, Robert Bonner's Sons sent them a collection as a gift. Emma autographed and wrote a sentiment in many of them for her readers. She was inducted into the Woman's National Press Association and given a reception at Willards in 1892. "I was not well enough to go so I wrote a letter to them," Emma recalled. "Richmond took it down on the evening of the meeting." Emma's friend and president of the association, Martha D. Lincoln, read the letter during the reception and sent Richmond home with two large bouquets of flowers for the celebrated Mrs. Southworth.[14]

Emma had written for nearly a half century and had influenced more than one generation of readers. Her books were more than sensational stories; hidden within the page-turning chapters were messages of empowerment and hope and inspiration. Fans didn't just want to read her books; they wanted to see and talk with the author too. Many readers appeared at her doorstep once she'd returned to Prospect, and as long as her health allowed, she greeted them with generosity and kindness. One guest Emma found interesting was Fanny Kelly, who had achieved notoriety after being captured by the Sioux Indians in July 1864. After her return, she moved to Washington DC, where she wrote a book called *Narrative of My Captivity among the Sioux Indians*. Mrs. Kelly was surprised that Emma had never heard of her or of her book. "I seldom looked at the news from the Frontier and so had missed them," Emma explained. "I should certainly like to hear all about them."[15] She enjoyed learning about her guests as much as they enjoyed having the opportunity to meet her.

Another fan whom Emma found intriguing was the poet and travel writer Charles Warren Stoddard, and after his first trip to Prospect Cottage, they became friends. Around the same age as her children, he had been an avid fan since he was sixteen years old. "Of all the contributors to the *Ledger* of that period there was one who was queen of my heart," he wrote. "It seemed to me, when I first began to read her, that she was the greatest writer of—well, of all time." In spring 1893, Stoddard finally had the opportunity to meet his beloved authoress through a mutual friend. When he saw Emma at Prospect Cottage, he thought she seemed like a romantic vision who had stepped out of one of the pages of her plantation novels. She was still tall and slender but a little bent from old age. Her hair was silver, her eyes sympathetic, and her voice low and sweet. "[She gave] one the impression of softest silk, old laces and sweet lavender," Stoddard recalled. "O! school-boy days and school-boy dreams, how the memory of you rushed back upon me and turned me hot and scarlet and struck me dumb!"

The feelings were mutual. Emma had a special place in her heart for her new young friend, and the two corresponded with each other. "We are Souls. I felt as I sat near you in closer contact with a soul than ever before in my life," Emma fondly told him. "But you are comparatively a young man and you may come to think it a bore for an aged woman to write to you very often." She regularly addressed him as her "Light at Eventide," adding, "That is what you are to me, who have outlived—on this earth at least—all my dear friends of childhood, of youth, of middle age!" As a travel writer, Stoddard was frequently on "vacations" (as Emma called them), and she eagerly read about his adventures to Egypt, the South Sea Islands, and the Leper Isle of Molokai. "You have a magician's power of taking me with you wherever you go. Time, space, locality are annihilated," Emma visualized. "No longer an invalid in the hut on the hill, I am a wanderer dreaming amid the tropical beauty of the Southern isles, under the splendor of Southern skies." In return, she sent him autographed copies of *The Hidden Hand* and *The Missing Bride*. "These are the two sprightliest books I ever wrote," Emma explained after reading his book *South Sea Idyls*. "I concluded that you had had tragedy and melodrama enough in your real life."[16] She treasured Stoddard's friendship for the rest of her life.

Another friend and fellow author visiting Prospect Cottage was Martha D. Lincoln, who became widely known by her pen name "Bessie Beech." Along with other women journalists, she founded the Woman's National Press Association in 1882 and became president of the American Society of Authors for Washington in 1892, and she ensured that Emma was inducted into both organizations. Writing about a visit in August 1893, Emma recalled, "As we walked around the porch, I whispered to Mrs. Lincoln that the good of staying home in hot weather in a cool place like this is that one can *walk around in their shimmytails* at which she laughed heartily."[17] Soon afterward, Martha Lincoln wrote an article for the *Washington Post*, fondly recalling her bygone days at Prospect Cottage:

> Memories uniting the past to the present, glimpses of the glad, golden days of vanished years, all come back to me as I stood on the portico of Prospect Cottage. In the old days we roamed through the library and found the books of every clime and country in the niches about the wall. . . . And the suppers in that spacious old dining room! Such biscuits and preserves; such delicate ham and cold tongue; such unstinted hospitality when from twenty to thirty guests gathered about the board on these delightful Sunday evenings![18]

On that Sunday evening so many years later, the two friends stood on the porch remembering those bygone times that had brought so much joy.

As much as Emma enjoyed visits, the number of people who showed up at her doorstep could overwhelm her, especially hungry young journalists trying to make a name for themselves by getting an interview with the famous author. On one particular occasion, she wanted to sit outside on her porch in solitude. Instead of spending a peaceful evening looking out over the Potomac, Richmond appeared with a reporter in tow. "Mother," he said, "here is a young lady who wishes to see you." Emma agreed to be interviewed. Despite Richmond's warning not to overtax his invalid mother, the aspiring journalist, who introduced herself as Miss Sherman from Virginia, overstayed her welcome. "She stayed 2 mortal hours and asked unnumbered questions upon every subject she could think of from literature to personalities," a frustrated Emma wrote. "It would be easier to tell what she didn't ask than what she did ask. For instance, she did not ask me how many times I went to the water closet." Feeling incredibly sorry for the inexperienced reporter, Emma allowed the interview to continue. "Just think of a poor fragile little mite—I am glad I answered all her questions if it did make me weak. And I must see what is to become of her. Her little face haunts me!"[19] Whatever became of Miss Sherman is unknown, for if she did write a story, she didn't receive a byline for it, and Emma never mentioned her again. The time she spent patiently answering Miss Sherman's questions, however, was indicative of the kindness given, even to strangers.

At other times, Emma was so weak she was confined to her bedroom. Even then, she instructed Richmond and Blanche to give fans a tour of

Prospect Cottage, taking great care to tell stories about the parlor, the portraits, and the library. After two Southworth enthusiasts were shown through the house, they told Richmond it was the best treat they'd had since visiting Washington. Another party who came to see Prospect Cottage was delighted at having the opportunity to shake hands with Emma's son and daughter-in-law. "It is almost as good as seeing Mrs. Southworth herself," one guest exclaimed. Blanche ran upstairs to see whether Emma could get out of bed. As the fans left the house, Richmond told them they could see Mrs. Southworth from her bedroom window. "I went to it and kissed my hand to half a dozen ladies and gentlemen," Emma touchingly remembered. "They returned the greeting and bowed and filed away."[20]

As loyal as Emma was to her fans, her children and grandchildren remained first and foremost in her heart. She increasingly fretted over Richmond's health, which had steadily worsened since returning to Georgetown. Likely the result of his untreated scarlet fever, he suffered bouts of rheumatic fever, joint inflammation, shortness of breath, and fatigue. Richmond told Emma that he had a spinal disease, perhaps hoping to cause her less worry. "Richmond, poor Richmond is no better. His nervous system seems completely broken down," Emma explained to Lottie. "He will not call a specialist because he says that he understands his case as well as any one of them and knows how to treat himself." Richmond gave up his medical practice as a result of battling his chronic disease. He was only fifty years old. Emma was in no better shape, and Blanche became their caregiver. "Poor dear Blanche is almost worn out, and no rest is left her," Emma sympathetically wrote.[21]

As beloved as Blanche was, Emma missed Lottie and longed to hear from her daily. When Emma returned to Prospect Cottage, she had believed her death was near, but as the months turned into years, she was brokenhearted at not having Lottie with her. "I cried over it, to feel that we should not be together on this Christmas Day nor on my birthday," Emma bemoaned to Lottie on that first Christmas apart. Lottie had spent most of her life close to her mother and felt the stinging loss every time she drove past Birds Nest. When she told Emma how much she missed her, her mother advised, "Oh! my dear, I am so sorry that you should have that pain . . . comfort yourself with your dear husband—for he *is* a very dear husband—and your pretty girls and lovely boys." Lottie and James, who had eight living children, came as frequently as they could to Georgetown, usually bringing the younger children with them. The older grandchildren visited on their own. Emma loved having her grandchildren visit, and she told Lottie, "I wish one of your children might be with me all the time. You have so many of them I think they might, and I should feel nearer to you if one of yours were with me."[22] In truth, one or more of them regularly stayed at "Grandmother's House."

As the 1890s drew to a close, Emma's health steadily deteriorated, and while she was eager to hear from Lottie and her grandchildren, her letters to them became less frequent—her handwriting increasingly difficult to read. She rarely went into Georgetown and was increasingly confined to bed. In those last few years, she thought about the afterlife and had visions of her deceased grandchildren. In 1892, James and Lottie lost a third child, twenty-four-year-old Willie, from tuberculosis. "I have often felt Willie near me," Emma told Lottie. After another dream, she wrote, "Alice will be with me now I know to the last. I do so deeply feel her sweet presence—a fair girl who has grown up with Gladys in Heaven." Fewer visitors came, and she spent her days imagining the afterlife, where she could spend an eternity with her beloved daughter, whom she missed desperately. "Oh! What are you not to your good mother!" Emma exclaimed. "And when I remember that, though we are parted now, we shall spend *Eternity* together, I feel unutterably happy!" It was a far cry from what she imagined when she teased Bonner about his age in 1877. "What do you mean by saying that *you* are growing old? *You* should not think of growing old until you have passed your eightieth birthday," Emma had told him twenty years earlier. "I am five years your senior, and *I* am not growing old and I should be extremely angry with any idiot who should suggest that I was." Neither of them saw their eightieth birthdays—Bonner passed away when he was seventy-five.[23] On December 26, 1898, Emma quietly celebrated her seventy-ninth birthday.

As the final year of the century began, Emma's health continued to worsen, and Georgetown's extreme summer temperatures would deliver the fatal blow. "The heat has been horrible in Washington. . . . Public offices had to be closed at midday," Emma had previously noted of one hot summer. "We all suffered from the heat. All three of us . . . could not sleep at night and consequently lost flesh and strength and I am afraid temper too." By June 1899, Emma became so weak that she ate and drank very little. "I wish my soul would leave this tired body," she sighed. They would be the last words she uttered. Richmond sent word for Lottie and James to come and, along with Blanche, took up a constant watch by Emma's bedside. As newspapers from across the country caught word of the author's failing health, reporters clamored for information.

Releasing a statement to the press, Richmond reported, "Mrs. Southworth is gradually sinking and while I do not anticipate any immediate fatal result, I hardly think that she will last much longer." Emma rallied briefly that afternoon and into the next day. She was resting easy and free from any pain, but on June 30, 1899, newspapers reported that her death was hourly expected.[24] On Friday evening—the hour Emma usually put down her pen after a week's work—the sun was slowly setting over the Potomac River, a scene of beauty Emma had witnessed many times. In that moment, she breathed her last, finally joining family and friends in the heavenly sphere. The end of Emma's life was reminiscent of one of the characters in her novels; it was as if she had written her own death scene.

News of the famous author's death spread internationally across newspaper telegraph wires. Fans had been reading novels and short stories by Mrs. E.D.E.N. Southworth for more than fifty years; she had influenced generations, and the world grieved the loss of America's favorite author. Funeral plans were made. Rev. Frank Sewell, minister of the Swedenborgian Church, would speak. Without the watchful eye of the press, a small family service would be held in the beautiful chapel at Oak Hill Cemetery in Georgetown; her remains would be placed in the grave that contained her deceased granddaughter, Gladys. For several days, her body lay in the library of Prospect Cottage, where friends and fans came to pay their respects. One group of visitors showed just how beloved Emma was.

Late on Sunday evening, a quiet knock was heard at the front door, and four timid little girls asked whether they could come in. No one knew who they were. Each little girl carried a small bouquet of roses, and, when admitted into the library, they put their offerings on top of

E.D.E.N. Southworth's headstone in Oak Hill Cemetery, Georgetown. (*Chris Haugh*)

the coffin. One by one, they knelt on each side of the casket and recited the prayer of the Angelical Salutation. As silently as they came, they

Renwick Chapel, Oak Hill Cemetery, Georgetown. (*User APK, Wikimedia Commons*)

withdrew.[25] To them, Emma was more than a famous author. She was the creator of all their heroines—Hagar, Nettie, Jacquelina, Miriam, Vivia, Britomarte, and Capitola. These tiny readers had romped through the woods with their heroines—riding horses, shooting arrows, climbing trees, and rowing boats. All the things society told little girls they shouldn't do, she showed them that they could. For these little girls and millions of others like them, Emma was not just another novelist. She was their friend.

Chapter 13

A Hidden Legacy Rediscovered

In this, the centennial anniversary year of the birth of Mrs. E.D.E.N. Southworth, it is a fitting and graceful tribute that the Columbia Historical Society pays the gifted authoress, to meet in her honor this evening. Mrs. Southworth is the city's pioneer novelist. She was also perhaps, the most prolific writer of fiction in America for nearly fifty years.[1]

Dr. Sarah Huddleson, one avid reader of Emma's novels, gave the above tribute on April 22, 1919, in a speech delivered to the Columbia Historical Society. One reason for the continued success of Emma's novels well into the twentieth century was because Lottie kept reprinting them. T. B. Peterson's publishing company went out of business soon after his death in 1891, which left those copyrights available for Lottie to renew. Robert Bonner's sons were unable to keep the *Ledger* or their book publishing business afloat. They folded in 1903, leaving additional copyrights available. As Lottie was the sole beneficiary of Emma's property, she was granted the copyright to at least forty-five novels, which she retained until her death in 1939. A. L. Burt printed uniform editions of many of Emma's novels, which readers kept buying.

Throughout the early twentieth century, bookstores advertised dozens of E.D.E.N. Southworth novels alongside the works of Charles Dickens, Alexandre Dumas, and Victor Hugo. In the 1920s, her novels were published as part of the American Home Classics series, which included writers like Nathaniel Hawthorne, James Fenimore Cooper, Rudyard Kipling, and Harriet Beecher Stowe. Even in the 1930s, booksellers advertised Emma's novels as "old-fashioned stories that are always new." A Canadian bookshop noted they had books "written by women authors for women readers," with Mrs. Southworth's novels at the top of their list. In 1921, Fox Productions made a silent movie called *Hearts of Youth* based on Southworth's favorite novel, *Ishmael.* In 1930, Emma made the list of a popular parlor game called Game of Authors, which was similar to today's game of Go Fish. "I remember seeing Uncle Abner with a royal flush consisting of Bulwer-Lyon, E. P. Roe, Felicia Hemans, Willkie Collins and Mrs. E.D.E.N. Southworth," a gameplayer recalled.[2] Even though Emma had died thirty years earlier, new readers and admirers continued to have a great deal of respect and reverence for her, as she had become an iconic symbol of Americana.

In addition to the resale of her novels, Prospect Cottage remained a favored pilgrimage for readers when they visited the nation's capital. Visitors were still greeted by Richmond and Blanche until Richmond's death in July 1900, a little over a year after his mother's passing. Blanche soon left to live with her siblings. For a short time, Southworth's half sister Frances Baden Henshaw—the infamous Pinkie—lived in the house and gave tours. However, in 1901, as the beneficiary of Prospect Cottage, Lottie wanted to sell it, advertising in the *Evening Times*. Unable to find a buyer, she leased it to various tenants. In 1902, the building was used as a boardinghouse. By 1905, P. A. Dempsey leased and remodeled it into a delicatessen and ice cream parlor. Visitors and Southworth enthusiasts could consume a "café parfait or Buffalo Sunday [*sic*] in the dear, low-ceiled old drawing room devised by Mrs. Southworth, or demolish coffee and ham sandwiches in the library adjoining, where the dear old lady did her best work." Perhaps worse yet was that these "holiday makers began cutting splinters out of the side of the house, clawing up growing plants, and even capturing butterflies, grasshoppers and hop toads" in the hopes they might take away some small souvenir or memento of Southworth's home.[3] Unfortunately for the preservation of Emma's beloved home, it had become commercialized.

Harold Goodwin as Ishmael Worth and Lillian Hall as Beatrice Merlin in *Exhibitor's Herald*, June 18, 1921, 74. (*Internet Archive*)

Everyone near the cottage was out to make a buck from the fame of the late authoress. One newspaper reporter interviewed an Italian fruit stand owner who set up next to the cottage and, for a price, claimed, "The old lady never sitta up and writes; she lay right down on her stomach on the porch, yes she did, lady. I see her do it; kicka her feet in the air."

E.D.E.N. Southworth's Prospect Cottage used as a deli (ca. 1905). (John DeFerrari, *Streets of Washington* [blog])

Another street urchin said he had a story—again, for a price: "She used to walk around the garden lots when she was alive, and now at night people often see her walking up and down and wringing her hands." The lad continued, "One night a boy and me coming home from an entertainment happened to look up at the window where she used to live, and there she was, honest, lady, looking out. Just bet we run home fast."[4] As Emma had enjoyed telling a good ghost story, she might have smiled favorably, not only at the boy's storytelling ability but also at his entrepreneurial enthusiasm.

With commercialism at its center and enthusiasts slowly prying away its parts, Prospect Cottage fell into decay by the late 1910s. If something wasn't done soon, the iconic landmark of America's favorite authoress would soon be no more. In 1921, Sarah Huddleson bought Prospect Cottage. She was an avid "collector of Southworth first editions, relics of the authoress and perhaps the most devoted of Southworthians in the world." She knew the true worth of Prospect Cottage couldn't be measured in dollars; instead, it should be a place to honor Southworth's memory as one of the most popular American novelists of the nineteenth century. "The city of Washington should ever preserve [Prospect Cottage] as one of its greatest literary shrines," Huddleson argued. "Let us preserve this literary landmark for the pride of the city, and the good of coming generations."[5]

Huddleson's mission was to find an organization that could buy the house from her and restore it as a historic landmark. In 1927, the National League of American Penwomen purchased Prospect Cottage with this goal in mind, intending to remodel it as a part of the league's new national headquarters. They wanted to use Southworth's library as the central focus of the building, which would house a complete collection of her novels. Penwomen president Mrs. Clarence Bush remarked, "We are likely to make some changes, though these will come slowly. Whatever we do we shall always keep intact the room that was the library of the old Southworth home, in which she did most of her writing for many years." Three board members presented a bust of Southworth to be displayed in the new library. Most of the house was in such bad shape that much of it would have to be taken down, but the library remained the main focus. Architectural plans were made in which a two-story brick colonial structure would be built around the library. It included a roof garden that overlooked the Potomac as well as a formal garden, an auditorium to seat four hundred, offices, and a kitchen. Construction was set for spring 1929 with an estimated cost of $45,000.[6] With the support of Huddleson and the Penwomen, the future of E.D.E.N. Southworth's cherished library at Prospect Cottage seemed secured.

The Penwomen began a national fund-raising campaign to raise money for their new headquarters. Well-known women like Mrs. Henry Ford and Mrs. Edith Rockefeller each contributed $100 toward the endeavor. Despite the early vigor, enthusiasm for such a large project soon waned. Reporter Elisabeth Poe lamented, "Too bad that the plans of the League of American Penwomen did not materialize to the extent of saving this literary landmark for future generations." After remaining empty for ten years waiting for renovations to begin, Prospect Cottage's fate seemed certain. In 1939, the Penwomen found that the Georgetown site was no longer "suitable" and sold it to fund their new headquarters' location.[7] Prospect Cottage, once such a vibrant and inspiring

NEW BUST OF MRS. SOUTHWORTH

This bust of Mrs. E. D. E. N. Southworth, novelist, who wrote much of her work in Georgetown, was brought to Washington yesterday for presentation to the National League of American Pen Women. In the photograph, left to right: Lilla Wood Daniels, Ohio State vice president; Mrs. Frank Wade, publicity director, and Mrs. Rachael McDonald, vice president. —Star Staff Photo.

Bust of E.D.E.N. Southworth by National League of American Pen Women (1929). (*Evening Star* [Washington, DC], April 12, 1929, 5)

Georgetown landmark, was finally demolished in 1942 to make way for a newer, colonial-style brick home.[8] Today, a marker exists there, but it's not about Prospect Cottage. Instead, it shows horror movie fans the spot where the infamous stairway scene occurred in the 1973 film *The Exorcist*.

Along with the demolition of Prospect Cottage, a new wave of literature called modernism had established firm roots, and Emma's popularity declined. Modernist literature focused on a conscious break from traditional modes of storytelling, and proponents of this new literary form were particularly critical of the domestic sensational literature of the nineteenth century. Even as early as 1901, critics claimed Mrs. Southworth's literature was old-fashioned compared to the newer modes of American realism. Twentieth-century journalist and author Willa Cather cautioned readers to be respectful of their predecessors, who lived in a much different era. "We should be duly humble, and never forget that our grandparents were entirely convinced that the fiction of Mrs. Southworth was more engaging, more elevating, and of far higher literary merit than the stories of Master Edgar Allen Poe," Cather wrote. "We must remember that Mrs. Southworth was not always the butt of jests as now, particularly the jests of the newly emancipated in the matter of literary taste, who are eager to attest their emancipation."[9] However, after a global world war, the Spanish flu pandemic, and the Great Depression, American readers became less sympathetic to literature rife with improbable plots that led to happily-ever-after endings. In the world of the twentieth century, life was filled with shattered dreams, and as a second world war loomed, American youth favored literature that more closely mirrored the lives they led.

Events of the late 1930s and 1940s came together in a perfect storm that virtually wiped away the public's knowledge of most of the nineteenth-century domestic sensational writers, who were mainly women. In July 1939, Lottie died at the age of ninety-five, and Emma's books ceased being published. Furthering Emma's burial in the trash bin of history were newspaper critics—mostly men—who wrote scathingly negative commentaries about her novels. As America entered World War II, book drives were held across the country in order to send reading material to the troops overseas. Regarding books like Southworth's, one reporter scolded, "Don't give them to the soldiers. All these may have been good reading forty years ago. But there isn't one soldier or sailor in a thousand who wants to read them now."[10] The reporter was partly correct. While Emma had a few men who enjoyed reading her novels, she had always written primarily about women and for women.

Unfortunately, her progressive views on women's rights and social equality somehow got lost in the modernists' crusade to throw away all things historical. A reporter turned college professor, Herbert Ross

Brown, wrote a dissertation titled "The Sentimental Novel in America, 1789–1860," which gave "an account of the light reading of our ancestors." To argue his position, Brown referred to a quote by Nathaniel Hawthorne. By the 1940s, Hawthorne's work was held up in college classrooms as the example of "good" literature for its excessively detailed passages and inflated word choice. In truth, Hawthorne's work might have been well received by twentieth-century critics, but he made little money during his lifetime. He blamed his lack of popularity on domestic sensational women writers. "America is now wholly given over to a damned mob of scribbling women," Hawthorne protested to his editor. Brown named the "mob" of these most successful women, with Southworth's name at the top of the list.[11]

After World War II, Emma's critics continued to trash her novels. Journalist Charles Honce noted that three of Emma's novels had sold more than two million copies in her lifetime, but he still condemned her work. "Mrs. Southworth was no great shakes for quality," he argued, "but she certainly provided quantity." Another critic, William McCann, snidely suggested that she was perhaps never that popular at all, and publishers merely printed large quantities of her novels. "How else can one account for copies in every used-book store, every furniture and antique shop?" He rudely postulated, "But is it possible that a great number of Americans once read 'The Missing Bride' by Mrs. E.D.E.N. Southworth?"[12] Much like in Emma's day, these criticisms fall flat when held next to the facts about her continued popularity.

When one reader of the *Austin American* asked in 1948 what best-selling books of all time were written by women, Southworth's *Ishmael* and *Self-Raised* were among the top five, alongside Louisa May Alcott's *Little Women*, Harriet Beecher Stowe's *Uncle Tom's Cabin*, Margaret Mitchell's *Gone with the Wind*, and Betty Smith's *A Tree Grows in Brooklyn*. By 1955, Emma still topped the list of best sellers with *Ishmael* and *Self-Raised*, alongside James Fenimore Cooper's *The Last of the Mohicans*, Louisa May Alcott's *Little Women*, Mark Twain's *Tom Sawyer*, Marion Hargrove's *See Here, Private Hargrove*, Betty Smith's *A Tree Grows in Brooklyn*, and Wendell Willkie's *One World*. By the 1960s, however, Emma's novels became harder to find in used bookshops, and fans had to be more creative in procuring them. Under the "Wanted to Buy" section of American newspapers, advertisements appeared by those seeking to find one of Emma's novels.[13] Though perhaps not as popular as in the nineteenth century, Emma still had readers who enjoyed her novels, but as they became increasingly harder to find, knowledge of her or her books was almost lost.

By the 1970s and 1980s, a slow resurgence began in colleges and universities as more women earned PhDs in American literature. While Emma Southworth's novels had virtually faded from the general reading public, female professors began asking why women writers weren't often anthologized in college textbooks. One professor at Dominguez Hills State College in California, Dr. Claudia Buckner, offered a college course studying soap operas, comparing them to serialized novels by Mrs. E.D.E.N. Southworth, Caroline L. Hentz, and Sylvanus Cobb. Much like these serializations, Buckner posited, "Millions of listeners and viewers have found mirrors of their own lives and solutions to their own problems."[14]

Numerous other university professors began a more serious reassessment of Southworth's novels. They didn't have much scholarly evidence to work from, except for James Mason's master's thesis "Mrs. E.D.E.N. Southworth" (1935) and Regis Louise Boyle's dissertation "Mrs. E.D.E.N. Southworth, Novelist" (1939). Literary analysis of Southworth's works appeared in Nina Baym's *Woman's Fiction* (1978) and *Novels, Readers and Reviewers* (1984), as well as Annette Kolodny's *The Land before Her* (1984). Joanne Dobson wrote an introduction for an edited republication of Southworth's famous *The Hidden Hand* in 1988. As the first novel reprinted in the twentieth century, this reprint inspired other scholars to examine Southworth's other works.

During the late twentieth and early twenty-first centuries, interest in Southworth increased in university classes throughout the country. In 1990, Susan Harris called *The Deserted Wife* Southworth's "spiritual biography," one that portrayed women who submit to traditional marriage roles while overcoming adversity and taking charge of their lives. Other notable scholarly works include Amy Hudock's dissertation "No Mere Mercenary" (1993), Lyde Cullen Sizer's *The Political Work of*

Northern Women Writers and the Civil War (2000), Karen Tracey's *Plots and Proposals: American Women's Fiction, 1850–90* (2000), Joyce Warren's *Women, Money and the Law* (2005), Michelle Ann Abate's *Tomboys: A Literary and Cultural History* (2008), and Melissa Homestead and Pamela T. Washington's *E.D.E.N. Southworth: Recovering a Nineteenth-Century Popular Novelist* (2012). Editors Homestead and Washington have categorized twelve scholarly essays into four areas of study: serialization, genres, intertextuality, and marriage and the law. Although these university professors have helped renew interest in Southworth and the domestic sensational novel, their work is largely confined to academic settings, with ongoing debates about Southworth's value in the canon of American literature.

But what and who decides literary value? Surely the very act of being popular should make a work "good." Whether it's a book, movie, or work of art, shouldn't the individual be able to determine whether something is "good" based on whether they enjoyed it? Do we need "experts" to tell us what we value? Versions of the domestic sensational novel still exist today. Think of Harlequin romances, soap operas, or Hallmark movies. Like other genres, sensational fiction gives modern readers and viewers not only entertainment but also a chance to see themselves in these stories. Nineteenth-century readers didn't listen to the expert critics tell them what they should value or read. They enjoyed the domestic sensational novels because they were page-turners with improbable plots, cliff-hanger endings, and love stories that ended happily. But more than that, these novels helped women readers figure out their place in the world. These books educated them on how to be more empowered, more self-aware, more assertive. And no author was more masterful at creating these kinds of novels than E.D.E.N. Southworth.

As one of the most famous women writers of the nineteenth century, E.D.E.N. Southworth deserves to be remembered as a part of who we are as a nation and as a people. She had more than fifty books to her credit, and while her goal was most certainly to make money from her pen, she also wanted to make the world a better place for women and all those who were disempowered. Much like in her stories, she lived a life full of hardships, struggles, and adversity, and she wrote stories that told women how to overcome those obstacles. Like the rest of us, she was far from perfect. Nonetheless, she lived a fascinating life. She traveled the world, made her own living, and took bold and daring chances during a time that confined most women to homemaking and the domestic sphere. She was an iconic literary figure who should be properly placed in American history. Emma Southworth lived a life worth telling—a life that has been hidden for far too long.

Acknowledgments

This book never would have been possible without the help of Dr. Pamela T. Washington, who first introduced me to Southworth in 2007 when I took her "Nineteenth-Century American Women Writers" class. She then graciously agreed to be my advisor and chair as I completed my master's thesis—"E.D.E.N. Southworth: A Little Learning Is a Dangerous Thing"—in 2012. Her mentorship continued as she joined Dr. Caroline Franklin in helping me complete my dissertation—"E.D.E.N. Southworth and the Power of Her Pen: Impacting Female Education in the Nineteenth Century"—at Swansea University in 2016. These women were instrumental in teaching me how to research, and I so appreciate the friendships that have grown from this process. As Pam Washington and I learned more about Southworth's life, we decided to write this biography, enjoying many research trips together, until cancer took her too soon before we had a chance to put words to paper. My hope is that she will look down from the heavenly sphere and be pleased that I carried this book to fruition.

There have also been numerous archivists who have provided assistance at institutions across the country, most notably the Southworth papers at the Library of Congress, the Clifton Walter Barrett Library at the University of Virginia, and the Rubenstein Library at Duke University. A special thank you to Jerry McCoy, special collections librarian/archivist at the District of Columbia Public Library's Washingtoniana Division and Peabody Room, who's an avid Southworth fan and was always available to answer any questions I had.

I also owe many thanks to Melissa Homestead and Vicki Martin for their published research "A Chronological Bibliography of

E.D.E.N. Southworth's Works Privileging Periodical Publication" in the 2012 *E.D.E.N. Southworth: Recovering a Nineteenth-Century Popular Novelist*. Southworth's novels were first serialized in weekly periodicals before being printed in book form, and oftentimes years would pass between the serialization and the book release. Understanding the order of her writing was further complicated given that the title of the book often changed from the serialized version. Their research has been invaluable in helping me tell Southworth's story.

I was further honored to be able to meet several of Southworth's great-great-granddaughters: Pat Force, Pam Costantini, Nancy Magill, and Carol Ann Kindberg. I have so appreciated your time and effort in providing pictures, memorabilia, and stories of your family history, and I have thoroughly enjoyed getting to know you all.

Of course, I would be remiss if I did not thank my own family. To Chris, for countless hours of proofreading. From my master's thesis to my doctoral dissertation, and on to this biography, your dedication to this project has been unmatched. To my daughter, Jessica, and her husband, Josiah White; my son, Michael Wilton; and my stepchildren and their spouses, Travis and Kate Neal, Brett and Cheska Neal, and Erin and Ryan McInally, for listening to my Southworth stories for the past decade. Your patience, loyalty, and support have not gone unnoticed.

And, finally, to Brittany Stoner, who has been the most kind and helpful editor. I appreciate her patience in walking me through the publishing process and her editorial skills as we had to make the project a more manageable size. Also, a special thank you to my production editor Patricia Stevenson and publicist Chloe Hummel for your suggestions, advice, and quick responses to my numerous questions. Thank you to everyone at Lyons Press for taking a chance on this newbie author and believing in this biography.

Notes

Foreword

1. Mikaela Lefrak, "She Was One of America's Most Successful 19th-Century Writers and Largely Forgotten, Until Now," DCist, January 3, 2020, https://dcist.com/story/20/01/03/she-was-one-of-americas-most-successful-19th-century-writers-and-largely-forgotten-until-now/.

2. Ann Beebe, "E.D.E.N. Southworth's Civil War Washington," *Washington History* (Fall 2015), 39.

3. Eliza McGraw, "The Best-Selling Washington Writer You've Never Heard Of," *Washington Post Magazine*, March 3, 2016, https://www.washingtonpost.com/lifestyle/magazine/the-best-selling-washington-writer-youve-never-heard-of/2016/03/02/ddb63ef2-b40d-11e5-a76a-0b5145e8679a_story.html.

Introduction

1. E.D.E.N. Southworth, *The Hidden Hand; or, Capitola the Madcap*, ed. Joanne Dobson (New Brunswick, NJ: Rutgers University Press, 2009), 111–12.

2. Southworth, *The Hidden Hand*, 121.

3. Alison Scott and Amy Thomas, "The Hidden Agenda of *The Hidden Hand*: Periodical Publication and the Literary Marketplace in Late-Nineteenth-Century America," in *E.D.E.N. Southworth: Recovering a Nineteenth-Century Popular Novelist*, ed. Melissa J. Homestead and Pamela T. Washington (Knoxville: University of Tennessee Press, 2012), 52, 65.

4. Joanne Dobson, introduction to *The Hidden Hand; or, Capitola the Madcap*, by E.D.E.N. Southworth, ed. Joanne Dobson (New Brunswick, NJ: Rutgers University Press, 2009), xl; Amy E. Hudock, "No Mere Mercenary: The Early Life and Fiction of E.D.E.N. Southworth" (PhD diss., University of South Carolina, 1993; Ann Arbor, MI: University Microfilms [ON9400225]), 186; Regis Louise Boyle, *Mrs. E.D.E.N. Southworth, Novelist* (Washington, DC: Catholic University of America Press, 1939), 13.

5. Frank Luther Mott, *Golden Multitudes: The Story of Best Sellers in the United States* (New York: Macmillan, 1947), 122.

Chapter 1

1. E.D.E.N. Southworth, *Vivia; or, The Secret of Power* (Philadelphia, PA: Peterson, 1857), 27.

2. Louisa May Alcott later parodied her use of initials in *Little Women* when Jo adopts the pen name S.L.A.N.G. Northbury. See Lucy M. Freibert and Barbara A. White, eds., *Hidden Hands: An Anthology of American Women Writers, 1790–1870* (New Brunswick, NJ: Rutgers University Press, 1994), 68.

3. "Mrs. E.D.E.N. Southworth," *Representative* (Fox Lake, WI), April 17, 1891, 2; John Hart, "Emma D.E.N. Southworth," in *Female Prose Writers of America: With Portraits, Biographical Notices and Specimens of Their Writings* (Philadelphia, PA: Butler, 1855), 211.

4. "The Authors of Washington: Who They Are and Something about Them," *Evening Star* (Washington, DC), January 6, 1872, 1; Hart, "Emma D.E.N. Southworth," 211; "In Chancery, Jan. 3, 1801," *Telegraph and Daily Advertiser* (Baltimore, MD), February 3, 1801, 4; "In the Case of Charles Nevitte, an Insolvent Debtor," *National Intelligencer and Washington Advertiser* (Washington, DC), August 24, 1804, 3; "Be It Known," *Alexandria Gazette* (Alexandria, VA), March 3, 1810, 3; "In Common Council," *Alexandria Gazette,* July 28, 1810, 3; "In Common Council," *Alexandria Gazette* (Alexandria, VA), August 10, 1810, 3.

5. Even though most of Emma Southworth's early biographies list Charles Nevitte's age as forty-five, this age is likely in error. Nevitte's obituary lists his age at his death in 1832 at forty-six, which would make him thirty-five and not forty-five when he married Susanna. "Died," *Daily National Intelligencer* (Washington, DC), April 9, 1823, 3.

6. "Died," *National Intelligencer* (Washington, DC), August 24, 1813, 3; Beverly Schwartzberg, "'Lots of Them Did That': Desertion, Bigamy, and Marital Fluidity in Late Nineteenth-Century America," *Journal of Social History* 3737, no. 1 (Spring 2004): 574; Timothy Gilfoyle, "The Hearts of Nineteenth-Century Men: Bigamy and Working-Class Marriage in New York City, 1800–1890," *Prospects* 19 (October 1994): 135–60.

7. Dorothy Wailes received her husband George's estates upon his death in either 1797 or 1798, consisting of six Negroes, two horses, a debt owed to him from Levin Wailes of forty-four pounds, eight shillings, and the balance of his estate; Susan Johanson, "Johanson Family Tree-Roots Spreading from Sweden, Medieval England, Massachusetts, and South Carolina," Roots Web: Finding Our Roots Together, February 26, 2014, http://wc.rootsweb.ancestry.com/cgi-bin/igm.cgi?op=GET&db=johanson&id=I70271.

8. "Petition 2098060 Details," Race and Slavery Petitions Project, accessed March 1, 2017, http://library.uncg,edu/slavery/petitions/details.aspx?pid=16758.

9. Donald R. Hickey, *The War of 1812: A Forgotten Conflict* (Champaign: University of Illinois Press, 2012), 109–10; "To Thomas Jefferson from Henry Dearborn, 31 July 1807," Founders Online, National Archives, accessed November 28, 2021, https://founders.archives.gov/documents/Jefferson/99-01-02-5981; F. L. Brockett and George W. Rock, *A Concise History of the City of Alexandria, VA., from 1669–1883 with a Directory of Reliable Business Hours in the City* (Alexandria, VA: Gazette Book and Job Office, 1883), 23–24; Harvey W. Crew, William B. Webb, and John Wooldridge, *Centennial History of the City of Washington DC* (Dayton, OH: United Brethren, 1892), 208; "Charles L. Nevit in the U.S. War of 1812 Service Records, 1812–1815," Ancestry, accessed April 13, 2018,

https://www.ancestry.com/family-tree/person/tree/43882184/person/12718707316/facts; Joe Krone, *Land of the Free: Wartime Rules for North America 1754–1815* (New York: Osprey, 2014), 174; Spencer C. Tucker, ed., *The Encyclopedia of the War of 1812* (New York: ABC-CLIO, 2012), 750.

10. William G. Glasson, *Federal Military Pensions in the United States* (New York: Oxford University Press, 1918), 108; 1820 US Census, Washington, District of Columbia, digital image s.v. "Dorothy Wailies," Ancestry, accessed April 10, 2024, https://www.ancestry.com/imageviewer/collections/7734/images/4433158_00121?pId=660158.

11. T. H. Y., "Biographical Sketch of the Author," in *The Haunted Homestead, and Other Novelettes, with an Autobiography of the Author*, by E.D.E.N. Southworth (Philadelphia, PA: Peterson, 1860), 30–31; Susan K. Harris, *Nineteenth-Century American Women's Novels: Interpretative Strategies* (New York: Cambridge University Press, 1990), 128.

12. Kathleen Wiengand, Parish Registration at St. Peter's on Capitol Hill, e-mail to Rose Neal on January 22, 2018, confirms date of baptism; Hart, "Emma D.E.N. Southworth," 212.

13. T. H. Y., "Biographical Sketch of the Author," 30–31.

14. When Dorothy's husband died, she inherited six slaves. His will lists the first names of these slaves, one of which was Biggs, in Will of George Wailes, of Prince George's Co., SMC, JJ2, 208, 4/2/1797–5/9/1798.

15. T. H. Y., "Biographical Sketch of the Author," 33–34; Hart, "Emma D.E.N. Southworth," 213.

16. Glasson, *Federal Military Pensions in the United States*, 108; "War of 1812 Discharge Certificates," Military Records, National Archives, accessed December 3, 2021, https://www.archives.gov/research/military/war-of-1812/1812-discharge-certificates/discharge-certificates.html; Hart, "Emma D.E.N. Southworth," 213; T. H. Y., "Biographical Sketch of the Author," 31–34.

17. E.D.E.N. Southworth, *The Three Beauties; or, Shannondale*. Philadelphia, PA: Peterson, 1878, 147.

18. Hart, "Emma D.E.N. Southworth," 213; T. H. Y., "Biographical Sketch of the Author," 35–36.

19. Hart, "Emma D.E.N. Southworth," 213; "Joshua Laurens Henshaw," Hinshaw Family Association, 1997–2015, accessed February 9, 2015, http://www.rawbw.com/~hinshaw/cgi-bin/id?9883; E.D.E.N Southworth (E.D.E.N.) to Lottie Southworth Lawrence (Lottie), undated (box 1), LOC; T. H. Y., "Biographical Sketch of the Author," 35.

20. Regis Louise Boyle, *Mrs. E.D.E.N. Southworth, Novelist* (Washington, DC: Catholic University of America Press, 1939), 4; "Prospect Cottage: The Historic Building in Georgetown," *Evening Star* (Washington, DC), June 4, 1904, 22; T. H. Y., "Biographical Sketch of the Author," 35.

21. "Mrs. Emma D.E.N. Southworth," *Wisconsin State Journal* (Madison, WI), May 1, 1878, 1; "Prospect Cottage," 22.

22. "A Woman Who Writes: A Chatty Talk with Mrs. Southworth, the Author," *Washington Post* (Washington DC), March 27, 1879, 2; "Female Seminary and Boarding

School," and "Alexandria Female Academy and Boarding School," both published in the *Alexandria Gazette* (Alexandria, VA), September 2, 1836, 2.

23. "A Woman Who Writes," 2; Cornelius J. Heatwole, *A History of Education in Virginia* (New York: Macmillan, 1916), 126–30.

24. "A Woman Who Writes," 2; "Mrs. Southworth: Personal Recollections of the Wonderfully Prolific Novel Writer," *Winfield Courier* (Winfield, KS), August 3, 1882, 4; "Traveling on the National Road," National Park Service, U.S. Department of the Interior, accessed December 13, 2021, https://www.nps.gov/articles/national-road-travel.htm.

25. "Springfield Ohio," Touring Ohio in the Heart of America, Ohio City Production, accessed December 13, 2021, http://touringohio.com/southwest/clark/springfield/springfield.html.

26. Charles Theodore Greve, *Centennial History of Cincinnati and Representative Citizens* (Prospect: Biographical Publishing Company, 1904), 1:617; "Catharine Beecher," Walnut Hills Historical Society, accessed December 18, 2021, https://walnuthillsstories.org/stories/catherine-beecher/; "Scenes from *Uncle Tom's Cabin*: Harriet Beecher Stowe Found Many of Them during Her Stay in Cincinnati," *Times Union* (Brooklyn, NY), August 1, 1896, 11.

27. Louis L. Tucker, "The Semi-Colon Club of Cincinnati," accessed January 2, 2022, http://earthpa.us/Harriet/SCclub/OHC_semi-Colon.pdf.

28. "Mrs. Southworth: Personal Recollections," 4. Although the reporter lists Susan B. Anthony, Elizabeth Cady Stanton, and Elizabeth Blackwell as the girls Southworth met there, neither Anthony nor Stanton lived in Ohio during this time; however, Blackwell did. Given the likelihood of newspaper reporter error, I argue that Southworth did meet Blackwell, Harriet Beecher Stowe, and Alice Cary at a meeting of the Semi-Colon Club.

29. "Peaceful End: Death of Mrs. E.D.E.N. Southworth, the Novelist," *Evening Star* (Washington, DC), July 1, 1899, 10; "Harriet Beecher Stowe Slavery to Freedom Museum," Kentucky Department of Tourism, accessed January 2, 2022, https://www.kentuckytourism.com/maysville/attractions/museums/harriet-beecher-stowe-slavery-freedom-museum; "*Uncle Tom's Cabin*," *Evening Star* (Washington, DC), September 25, 1921, 44; "Scenes from *Uncle Tom's Cabin*," 11; Sarah M. Huddleson, "Mrs. E.D.E.N. Southworth and Her Cottage," *Records of the District of Columbia Historical Society* 23 (1920): 71.

30. "Elizabeth Blackwell: First Woman Doctor in the United States," History of American Women, accessed January 2, 2022, from https://www.womenhistoryblog.com/2006/06/elizabeth-blackwell.html; Elizabeth Blackwell, *Pioneer Work in Opening the Medical Profession to Women: Autobiographical Sketches*. London: Longmans, Green, 1895, 10–14; Blackwell Family, Blackwell Family Papers: Elizabeth Blackwell Papers, Manuscript/Mixed Material, https://www.loc.gov/item/mss1288000957/.

31. June Edwards, "The Cary Sisters," Dictionary of Unitarian & Universalist Biography, March 20, 2003, https://uudb.org/articles/carysisters.html.

32. "Frederick Hamilton Southworth," Ancestry, accessed January 4, 2022, https://www.ancestry.com/family-tree/person/tree/43882184/person/12718709615/facts; "New

Invention," *Newark Daily Advertiser* (Newark, NJ), June 18, 1838, 2; "Water Wheel," *Biblical Recorder* (Raleigh, NC), November 16, 1839, 4.

33. Greve, *Centennial History of Cincinnati and Representative Citizens*, 901; U.S. Passport Applications, 1795–1925, digital image s.v. "Frederick H. Southworth" (age 27), Ancestry, accessed April 10, 2024, https://www.ancestry.com/imageviewer/collections/1174/images/USM1371_2-0022?pId=726224.

34. E.D.E.N. Southworth, *The Haunted Homestead, and Other Nouvellettes* (Philadelphia, PA: Peterson, 1860), 48–51.

35. "Southworth's Improved and Premium Feather Dresser," *Commercial Advertiser and Journal* (Buffalo, NY), July 31, 1839, 1; "Notice," *Commercial Advertiser and Journal* (Buffalo, NY), August 5, 1839, 3.

36. Unsigned and undated article found at the League of American Pen Women in the files in Washington, DC, accessed March 23, 2018. The article also makes an unsubstantiated claim that Emma was a governess for Susan B. Anthony's family and taught her siblings; however, no other evidence exists to help support this claim.

37. Southworth, *The Haunted Homestead*, 52, 109.

38. "Tide and Current Water Wheel," *Ohio Statesman* (Columbus, OH), October 9, 1839, 3; "Mechanical," *Baltimore Sun* (Baltimore, MD), December 6, 1839, 2.

39. "F. H. Southworth, Water Wheel, No. 1,478, Patented Jan. 23, 1840," accessed January 5, 2022, https://patentimages.storage.googleapis.com/91/53/cd/b20da25ef17f83/US1478.pdf; "Tide and Current Water Wheel," *Washington Globe* (Washington, DC), February 15, 1840, 3; "National Gallery of Manufactures, Inc.," *Native American* (Washington, DC), November 28, 1840, 3; "Report from the Commissioner of Patents, Showing the Operations of the Patent Office during the Year 1840," *Public Documents Printed by Order of the Senate of the United States, during the Second Session of the Twenty-Sixth Congress, Begun and Held at the City of Washington, December 7, 1840, and in the Sixty-Fifth Year of the Independence of the United States* 4, no. 152 (1840): 1.

40. "Marriages," *National Intelligencer* (Washington, DC), January 30, 1840, 3; E.D.E.N. Southworth, *The Deserted Wife* (Philadelphia, PA: Peterson, 1886), 247; Southworth, *The Haunted Homestead*, 110.

Chapter 2

1. T. H. Y. "Biographical Sketch of the Author," in *The Haunted Homestead, and Other Novelettes, with an Autobiography of the Author*, by E.D.E.N. Southworth (Philadelphia, PA: Peterson, 1860), 86.

2. John Hart, "Emma D.E.N. Southworth," in *Female Prose Writers of America: With Portraits, Biographical Notices and Specimens of Their Writings* (Philadelphia, PA: Butler, 1855), 213.

3. Matt Fenton, "The Baltimore and Ohio Railroad's Washington Branch: The First Rail Link to the Nation's Capital," ASCE Library, May 16, 2012, https//doi.org/10.1061/40759; "Washington Branch Railroad," *Native American* (Washington, DC), March 28, 1840, 4.

4. Stephen Campbell, "Panic of 1837," Economic Historian, November 12, 2020, https://economic-historian.com/2020/11/panic-of-1837/.

5. This novel was first serialized as *Mark Sutherland; or, Power and Principle.* T. B. Peterson later published it in book form as *India: The Pearl of Pearl River* (1856). This excerpt is from the book form: E.D.E.N. Southworth, *India: The Pearl of Pearl River* (Philadelphia, PA: Peterson, 1875), 251.

6. "Port of Louisville," *Courier-Journal* (Louisville, KY), March 6, 1840, 2; "A Woman Who Writes: Mrs. Southworth Tells about Her Own Literary Work," *Evening Star* (Washington, DC), September 6, 1890, 14.

7. Southworth, *India*, 250–53.

8. Jonathan Henry Evans, "Some Reminiscences of Early Grant County," *Wisconsin Historical Society Proceedings*, 1909, 234, https://genealogytrails.com/wis/grant/history_reminiscences.html.; "From the New York *Evening Star*: Letter from Wisconsin," *Wisconsin Express* (Madison, WI), August 29, 1840, 2.

9. "From the New York *Evening Star*," 2; Evans, "Some Reminiscences of Early Grant County," 236, 242; Consul Wilshire Butterfield, *History of Grant County* (Chicago, IL: Western Historical Company, 1881), 920–21.

10. Southworth, *India*, 262.

11. "Industrialization: Marriage, Family, The Bourgeois Family as a Model," in *Marriage and Family Encyclopedia*, accessed November 1, 2021, https://family.jrank.org/pages/872/Industrialization.html.

12. "Mrs. Southworth—Personal Recollections of the Wonderfully Prolific Novel Writer," *Winfield Courier* (Winfield, KS), August 3, 1882.

13. "From the New York *Evening Star*," 2; "Women and the Law," Harvard Business School: Women, Enterprise, and Society, 2010, https://www.library.hbs.edu/hc/wes/collections/women_law/.

14. Verne S. Pease, *The Life Story of Major John H. Rountree: The Public Career of a Colonial Gentleman on the Frontier in Wisconsin* (Baraboo, WI: Sauk County, 1928), 38; "Mrs. Southworth—Personal Recollections," 4. No remnants of this building remain today. What was then Court Street is now Southwest, and much of the ravine and the area in which the log cabin would have been is today a part of the University of Wisconsin in Platteville.

15. Southworth, *India*, 265.

16. Southworth, *India*, 268; "John H. Rountree," Wisconsin Historical Society, Wisconsin Local History & Biography Articles; Grant County News; Platteville, Wisconsin; December 30, 1927; https://www.wisconsinhistory.org/Records/Newspaper/BA3206.

17. Southworth, *India*, 273.

18. "Mrs. Southworth—Personal Recollections," 4.

19. Evans, "Some Reminiscences of Early Grant County," 234–35; "Mrs. Southworth—Personal Recollections," 4; Southworth, *India*, 288.

20. Richard P. Thiel, *The Timberwolf in Wisconsin: The Death and Life of a Majestic Predator* (Madison: University of Wisconsin Press, 1993), 189–90; Southworth, *India*, 290.

21. "Mrs. Southworth—Personal Recollections," 4; Southworth, *India*, 304.

22. "From the New York *Evening Star*," 2; Butterfield, *History of Grant County*, 690.

23. Todd Stevens Gernes, "Recasting the Culture of Ephemera: Young Women's Literary Culture in Nineteenth-Century America" (PhD diss., Brown University, 1992), 58–59, 66.

24. Lydia Southworth Rountree friendship album (box 4, folder 1), JHR.

25. Lisa Reid Ricker, "(De)Constructing the Praxis of Memory-Keeping: Late Nineteenth-Century Autograph Albums as Sites of Rhetorical Invention," *Rhetoric Review* 29, no. 3 (2010): 241.

26. Lydia Southworth Rountree friendship album (box 4, folder 1), JHR.

27. "List of Letters," *Natchez Weekly Courier* (Natchez, MS), August 13, 1840, 4.

28. Holford, 523; "Advertisement," *Grant County Witness* (Platteville, WI), May 2, 1872, 2.

29. Butterfield, *History of Grant County*, 690; "Advertisement," *Northern Badger* (Platteville, WI), January 8, 1842, 3–4; *Northern Badger* (Platteville, WI), January 29, 1841, 3; *Northern Badger* (Platteville, WI), February 19, 1841, 4; *Grant County Witness* (Platteville, WI), January 13, 1876, 1; Hon. J. W. Murphy, "Early Schools of the City," *Platteville Witness* (Platteville, WI), October 4, 1922, 1.

30. Southworth, *India*, 306–7.

31. Henry C. Campbell, *Wisconsin in Three Centuries* (New York: Century History, 1906), 4:187; Dumas Malone, ed., *Dictionary of American Biography* (New York: Scribner, 1935), 17:414.; Murphy, "Early Schools of the City," 1; "Platteville School," *Northern Badger* (Platteville, WI), January 8, 1841, 4.

32. Abbey Pignatari, "Celebrating Rachel, Formerly Enslaved by John Rountree," Exponent: University of Wisconsin-Platteville, May 2, 2019, https://uwpexponent.com/features/2019/05/02/celebrating-rachel-formerly-enslaved-by-john-rountree/.

33. Laura Rountree Smith, "When Platteville 'First' Began to Appear on Map," *Platteville Journal and Grant County News* (Platteville, WI), July 26, 1922, 2.

34. *Grant County Witness* (Platteville, WI), January 13, 1876, 1.

35. Southworth, *India*, 305, 309.

36. Southworth, *India*, 374.

37. "Richmond Joseph Southworth," Ancestry, accessed March 29, 2024, https://www.ancestry.com/family-tree/person/tree/43882184/person/12718723159/facts.

38. Southworth, *India*, 381.

Chapter 3

1. T. H. Y., "Biographical Sketch of the Author," in *The Haunted Homestead, and Other Novelettes, with an Autobiography of the Author*, by E.D.E.N. Southworth (Philadelphia, PA: Peterson, 1860), 36–37.

2. Previous biographical accounts of Emma's life have her returning to DC much later in 1843–1844; however, Frederick's tin business had clearly failed by summer 1841, and considering their financial circumstances, it's not likely they stayed in Platteville.

3. 1840 United States Census, Washington, District of Columbia, digital image s.v. "JL Henshaw," Ancestry, accessed April 10, 2024, https://www.ancestry.com/imageviewer/collections/8057/images/4411221_00169?pId=1622153; 1840 United States Census, Washington, District of Columbia, digital image s.v. "Dorotha Wailes," Ancestry,

accessed April 10, 2024, https://www.ancestry.com/imageviewer/collections/8057/images/4411221_00259?pId=1623388. (Comparing the two census records, the Henshaws were clearly living in a separate residence from Dorothy.)

4. T. H. Y., "Biographical Sketch of the Author," 30–31; E.D.E.N. Southworth (E.D.E.N.) to Lottie Southworth Lawrence (Lottie), June 22, 1895 (box 1), LOC. (In this letter, Emma claimed that Henshaw later had thrown them out of Dorothy's house, so it stands to reason that they moved into Dorothy's house on returning from Platteville.)

5. I've drawn this conclusion from a variety of sources—a difficult task, as 1840 records list only the head of the household by name, using tick marks and age ranges for all other household residents. Analyzing the 1840 census records of Joshua Henshaw and Dorothy Wailes (see note 4), Dorothy had four slaves living in her household, one of whom is likely Leonard Taylor Sr., as his age in 1840 matches one of the slaves named Leonard whom Dorothy inherited from her husband in 1798. See Will of George Wailes, of Prince George's Co., SMC, JJ2, 208, 4/2/1797–5/9/1798. Another slave record from 1833 showed Dorothy purchasing a woman named Cassy and her young children Caroline, Amanda, and Leonard, who later all use the surname Taylor. See Liber W.B., no. 44, folios 325 and 326 in the National Archives. Again, the ages of Cassy, Amanda, and Leonard in the 1840 census match the record from 1833. Additional records after Dorothy's death shows Susanna giving manumission papers to three slaves: Leonard Sr., Leonard Jr., and Alexander Taylor. See Records of the U.S. District Court for the District of Columbia Relating to Slaves, 1851–1863, microfilm serial M433, microfilm roll 1, National Archives and Records Administration (NARA), Washington, DC. Cassy's third child Caroline was likely living with Joshua and Susanna Henshaw, as the 1840 census lists one female slave aged ten to twenty-three. This information will become more important in later chapters of Emma's life.

6. "F. H. Southworth's Patent Lard Lamps," *Springfield Republican* (Springfield, MA), October 15, 1842, 4; "F. H. Southworth Lard Lamp, patent no. 2,703, patented July 2, 1842," Patent Images, accessed January 7, 2022, https://patentimages.storage.googleapis.com/92/f8/37/68f2243835f5d2/US2703.pdf; "Southworth's Patent Lard Lamp," *Baltimore Sun* (Baltimore, MD), October 31, 1842, 3; "Mr. F. H. Southworth," *Massachusetts Spy* (Worcester, MA), December 28, 1842, 3.

7. "Southworth's Patent Lard Lamp," *Boston Traveler* (Boston, MA), February 17, 1843, 3; *Journal of the House of Representatives of the United States: Being the First Session of the Twenty-Eighth Congress Begun and Held at the City of Washington, December 4, 1843, in the Sixty-Eighth Year of the Independence of the United States* (Washington, DC: Blair and Rives, 1844), 274.

8. "F. H. Southworth, Mar. 7, 1844," *Index to the Reports of the Committees, 28th Congress, First Session*, vol. 1, rep. no. 280.

9. U.S. Passport Applications, 1795–1925, digital image s.v. "Frederick H. Southworth," (age 27), Ancestry, accessed April 10, 2024, https://www.ancestry.com/imageviewer/collections/1174/images/USM1371_2-0022?pId=726224; "Reciprocity—from Trade," *Courier Journal* (Louisville, KY), April 20, 1844, 2.

10. E.D.E.N. to Lottie, June 22, 1895 (box 1), LOC; Sarah M. Huddleson, "Mrs. E.D.E.N. Southworth and Her Cottage," *Records of the District of Columbia Historical Society* 23 (1920): 61.

11. "Letter(s) Received from Southworth, F H," Letters Received from Commissioned Officers Below the Rank of Commander and from Warrant Officers, 1802–1886, U.S. National Archives and Records Administration, accessed January 13, 2022, https://catalog.archives.gov/id/132287524; "Naval," *Evening Post* (New York, NY), March 23, 1844, 2; "Naval," *New York Daily Herald* (New York, NY), April 17, 1844, 1.

12. I'm basing this conjecture on a letter she wrote to Henry Wise, U.S. minister to Brazil from 1844 to 1847, in which she implies that she expected Frederick to send for his family. In Emma D.E.N. Southworth to Hon. Henry A. Wise (box 8, folder 9), CRAL.

13. E.D.E.N. to Lottie, January 19, 1894 (folder 1), LOC.

14. E.D.E.N. to Lottie, June 22, 1895 (folder 1), LOC.

15. J. Ormond Wilson, "Eighty Years of the Public Schools of Washington—1805 to 1885," *Records of the Columbia Historical Society* 1 (October 30, 1896): 122.

16. Huddleson, "Mrs. E.D.E.N. Southworth and Her Cottage," 60; T. H. Y., "Biographical Sketch of the Author," 36; "Election of Public School Teachers," *Daily Madison* (Washington, DC), April 11, 1845, 2; "Fourth District School," *Daily National Intelligencer* (Washington, DC), August 29, 1845, 1.

17. E.D.E.N. to Lottie, June 22, 1895 (folder 1), LOC; T. H. Y., "Biographical Sketch of the Author," 36.

18. E.D.E.N. Southworth, *The Lady of the Isle; or, The Island Princess* (Philadelphia, PA: Peterson, 1886), 451–52.

19. Charles L. Nevitte to My Dear Daughter, undated (folder 1), LOC.

20. E.D.E.N. to Lottie, June 5, 1895 (folder 1), LOC; Beverly Schwartzberg, "'Lots of Them Did That': Desertion, Bigamy, and Marital Fluidity in Late Nineteenth-Century America," *Journal of Social History* 3737, no. 1 (Spring 2004): 574; T. H. Y., "Biographical Sketch of the Author," 36.

21. "Knowledge Boxes: The First Public Schools of the City of Washington," *Evening Star* (Washington, DC), April 10, 1897, 19.

22. Huddleson, "Mrs. E.D.E.N. Southworth and Her Cottage," 59–60; E.D.E.N. Southworth, *The Missing Bride; or, Miriam, the Avenger* (Philadelphia, PA: Peterson, 1874), 383, 304–5.

23. E.D.E.N. Southworth to Mary Lawrence, October 10, 1895 (folder 1), LOC; Thomas Woody, *A History of Women's Education in the United States* (New York: Science Press, 1929), 1:488–91; E.D.E.N. Southworth, *Fair Play; or, The Test of the Lone Isle* (Philadelphia, PA: Peterson, 1868), 122–23.

24. T. H. Y., "Biographical Sketch of the Author," 37.

25. John C. French, "Poe and the Baltimore *Saturday Visiter*," *Modern Language Notes* 33, no. 5 (May 1918): 257. Snodgrass's father Robert Snodgrass owned four slaves. See 1830 U.S. Census, series M19, roll 189, p. 246, Family History Library Film 0029668, Berkeley, Virginia; Melissa J. Homestead and Vicki L. Martin, "A Chronological Bibliography of E.D.E.N. Southworth's Works Privileging Periodical Publication," in *E.D.E.N. Southworth: Recovering a Nineteenth-Century Popular Novelist*, ed. Melissa

J. Homestead and Pamela T. Washington (Knoxville: University of Tennessee Press, 2012), 294; J. E. Snodgrass, "A Pioneer Editor," *Atlantic Monthly* 17 (June 1866): 749.

26. Snodgrass, "A Pioneer Editor," 749; T. H. Y., "Biographical Sketch of the Author," 37; Regis Louise Boyle, *Mrs. E.D.E.N. Southworth, Novelist* (Washington, DC: Catholic University of America Press, 1939), 8.

27. "Baltimore *Saturday Visiter*," *Vermont Union Whig* (Rutland, VT), April 22, 1847, 2; "American Progress," *Star of Freedom* (Leeds, West Yorkshire, UK), March 6, 1847, 27; "Letter from Lewis Tappan, Washington, Feb. 28, 1847," *Green-Mountain Freeman* (Montpelier, VT), March 25, 1847, 1; E.D.E.N. Southworth, "Reminiscences of the Poet, John Greenleaf Whittier," June 17, 1893 (box 11), PW.

28. Huddleson, "Mrs. E.D.E.N. Southworth and Her Cottage," 62; Homestead and Martin, "A Chronological Bibliography of E.D.E.N. Southworth's Works," 294; Snodgrass, "A Pioneer Editor," 749; Southworth, "Reminiscences" (box 11), PW.

29. Homestead and Martin, "A Chronological Bibliography of E.D.E.N. Southworth's Works," 294; E.D.E.N. Southworth, *The Wife's Victory, and Other Nouvellettes* (Philadelphia, PA: Peterson, 1854), 31–83.

30. "From Rio de Janeiro," *New York Daily Herald* (New York, NY), October 13, 1847, 4; E.D.E.N. to Wise, March 1850 (box 8, folder 9), CRAL.

31. Martha D. Lincoln, "Prospect Cottage," *Washington Post* (Washington, DC), October 1, 1893, 16.

32. Lincoln, "Prospect Cottage," 16; T. H. Y., "Biographical Sketch of the Author," 39; E.D.E.N. to Lottie, June 3, 1894 (folder 1), LOC.

33. E.D.E.N. Southworth, "Sybil Brotherton; or, the Temptation," in Southworth, *The Wife's Victory*, 85–154.

34. Homestead and Martin, "A Chronological Bibliography of E.D.E.N. Southworth's Works," 295; Mary Kay Ricks, "Escape on the *Pearl*," *Washington Post* (Washington, DC), August 12, 1998, H01.

35. Grace Greenwood, "An American Salon," *Cosmopolitan: A Monthly Illustrated Magazine*, February 1890, 438; "City of Washington," *Washington Union* (Washington, DC), April 20, 1848, 2; Ricks, "Escape on the *Pearl*," H01.

36. Greenwood, "An American Salon," 439; Ricks, "Escape on the *Pearl*," H01.

37. "The Case of the *Pearl*," *Liberator* (Boston, MA), August 11, 1848, 4; Hampden, "Beauties of the Slave System," *Green Mountain Freeman* (Montpelier, VT), September 28, 1848, 1; "The Pearl Prisoners," *Vermont Journal* (Windsor, VT), September 1, 1848, 3.

38. Huddleson, "Mrs. E.D.E.N. Southworth and Her Cottage," 59, 64; "The Schools in 1849," *Daily National Republican* (Washington, DC), June 3, 1873, 2; T. H. Y., "Biographical Sketch of the Author," 40; "Knowledge Boxes," 19.

39. Huddleson, "Mrs. E.D.E.N. Southworth and Her Cottage," 64–65.

40. Greenwood, "An American Salon," 440, 443; Southworth, "Reminiscences" (box 11), PW.

41. Southworth, "Reminiscences" (box 11), PW.

Chapter 4

1. John Hart, "Emma D.E.N. Southworth," in *Female Prose Writers of America: With Portraits, Biographical Notices and Specimens of Their Writings* (Philadelphia, PA: Butler, 1855), 215.

2. Hart, "Emma D.E.N. Southworth," 214; Gilberta S. Whittle, "Traits of Two Authors: Richard Malcolm Johnston and Mrs. E.D.E.N. Southworth," *Times* (Philadelphia, PA), June 4, 1893, 22; Sarah M. Huddleson, "Mrs. E.D.E.N. Southworth and Her Cottage," *Records of the District of Columbia Historical Society* 23 (1920): 64.

3. Hart, "Emma D.E.N. Southworth," 214; "Scarlet Fever," *Alexandria Gazette* (Alexandria, VA), January 9, 1849, 2.

4. Hart, "Emma D.E.N. Southworth," 214; "Office of the Board of Health," *Daily Republic* (Washington, DC), July 9, 1849, 3; Whittle, "Traits of Two Authors," 22.

5. Melissa J. Homestead and Vicki L. Martin, "A Chronological Bibliography of E.D.E.N. Southworth's Works Privileging Periodical Publication," in *E.D.E.N. Southworth: Recovering a Nineteenth-Century Popular Novelist*, ed. Melissa J. Homestead and Pamela T. Washington (Knoxville: University of Tennessee Press, 2012), 65–66.

6. "The Authors of Washington: Who They Are and Something about Them," *Evening Star* (Washington, DC), January 6, 1872, 1.

7. E.D.E.N. Southworth, *Retribution: A Tale of Passion* (Philadelphia, PA: Peterson, 1856), 158.

8. "The Authors," 1.

9. Southworth, *Retribution.*

10. Washington, DC, Slave Emancipation Records, 1851–1863, digital image s.v. "Susanna G Henshaw, enslaver (May 31, 1862)," Ancestry, accessed April 10, 2024, https://www.ancestry.com/imageviewer/collections/2171/images/31555_217981-00920?pId=2331; Southworth, *Retribution*, dedication page.

11. An example of the numerous booksellers advertising Emma's book can be found in the *Hartford Courant* (Hartford, CT), September 8, 1849, 3; "New and Valuable Works," *Evening Post* (New York, NY), August 25, 1849, 2; "New Books," *Daily Union* (Washington, DC), September 7, 1849, 2; Harriet Marion Stephens, "Retribution," *Alexandria Gazette* (Alexandria, VA), December 20, 1849, 1.

12. "New Books—Retribution," *Buffalo Morning Express* (Buffalo, NY), October 19, 1849, 2.

13. Huddleson, "Mrs. E.D.E.N. Southworth and Her Cottage," 66; Homestead and Martin, "A Chronological Bibliography of E.D.E.N. Southworth's Works," 295.

14. E.D.E.N. Southworth, *The Deserted Wife* (Philadelphia, PA: Peterson, 1886).

15. Southworth, *The Deserted Wife*, 92, 94; Henry Peterson to E.D.E.N. Southworth, September 10, 1849, Southworth (folder 1), RL.

16. E.D.E.N. to H. Peterson, September 10, 1849 (folder 1), RL; Huddleson, "Mrs. E.D.E.N. Southworth and Her Cottage," 66.

17. Homestead and Martin, "A Chronological Bibliography of E.D.E.N. Southworth's Works," 295; "A New Novel by Mrs. Southworth!" *Baltimore Sun* (Baltimore, MD), November 23, 1849, 2.

18. H. Peterson to E.D.E.N., October 15, 1849 (folder 1), RL.

19. "Books and Stationery," *Alexandria Gazette* (Alexandria, VA), November 14, 1849, 4; Catalog Record #67900, American Antiquarian Society, accessed February 2, 2022, https://catalog.mwa.org; "Books and Stationery," *Alexandria Gazette* (Alexandria, VA), September 12, 1850, 4.

20. E.D.E.N. Southworth, "Mrs. Southworth's Letter, Washington City, Jan. 24, 1850," *Pittsburgh Saturday Visiter* (Pittsburgh, PA), February 9, 1850.

21. E.D.E.N. Southworth, "Washington Letters—#1, Washington City, Thursday, January [*sic*] 7, 1850," *Pittsburgh Saturday Visiter* (Pittsburgh, PA), February 16, 1850.

22. "Pittsburgh Saturday Visiter," *National Era* (Washington, DC), February 28, 1850, 3; "Mrs. Southworth," *Pittsburgh Saturday Visiter* (Pittsburgh, PA), March 9, 1850.

23. "Women and the Law," Women, Enterprise, and Society, Harvard Business School, accessed February 7, 2022, https://www.library.hbs.edu/hc/wes/collections/women_law/.

24. Donna Young, "Divorce in Nineteenth-Century Washington County, District of Columbia," Gender and Legal History in American Papers, Georgetown Law Library, Georgetown University, 1985, http://hdl.handle.net/10822/1051416.

25. E.D.E.N. Southworth to Henry Wise, March 1850 (box 8, folder 9), CRAL.

26. Jane Swisshelm, *Half a Century* (Chicago, IL: Jansen, McClurg, 1880), 125; Jane Swisshelm, "Daguerreotype of Daniel Webster," *Anti-Slavery Bugle* (Lisbon, OH), May 18, 1850, 1; Jane Swisshelm, *Crusader and Feminist: Letters of Jane Grey Swisshelm*, ed. Arthur J. Larsen (St. Paul: Minnesota Historical Society, 1934), 7.

27. Swisshelm, *Half a Century*, 129; "Mrs. Southworth," *Pittsburgh Saturday Visiter* (Pittsburgh, PA), August 10, 1850.

28. Southworth, "Washington Letters."

29. "Infamous Outrage," *Peru Miami County Sentinel* (Peru, IN), August 1, 1850, 1.

30. "Shannondale Springs in Jefferson County, VA, 5 Miles from Charleston," *Richmond Enquirer* (Richmond, VA), August 9, 1839, 4; "Shannondale Springs for Sale," *Baltimore Sun* (Baltimore, MD), February 23, 1847, 3.

Chapter 5

1. E.D.E.N. Southworth, "Letters from Shannondale Springs," *Virginia Free Press* (Charleston, VA), August 23, 1850, 2.

2. William D. Theriault, "History of Shannondale Springs," Research Gate, 2009, 15, https://www.researchgate.net/publication/265103728_History_of_Shannondale_Springs.

3. "Shannondale Springs, Five Miles from Charlestown, Jefferson County, VA," *Baltimore Sun* (Baltimore, MD), August 11, 1849, 3, 6, 9–10; "Mrs. Southworth," *Evening Post* (Philadelphia, PA), August 3, 1850, 1.

4. "Mrs. Southworth," 1; "Shannondale; or, The Nun of Mount Carmel," *Saturday Evening Post* (Philadelphia, PA), August 3, 1850, 1.

5. Jon Gjerde, *Catholicism and the Shaping of Nineteenth-Century America*, ed. S. Deborah Kang (New York: Cambridge University Press, 2012), 1–7.

6. E.D.E.N. Southworth, *The Three Beauties; or, Shannondale* (Philadelphia, PA: Peterson, 1878), 54–60. (The serialized version was published in the *Saturday Evening Post* from August 10 to November 30, 1850; see Melissa J. Homestead and Vicki L. Martin,

"A Chronological Bibliography of E.D.E.N. Southworth's Works Privileging Periodical Publication," in *E.D.E.N. Southworth: Recovering a Nineteenth-Century Popular Novelist*, ed. Melissa J. Homestead and Pamela T. Washington (Knoxville: University of Tennessee Press, 2012), 296.) Theriault, "History of Shannondale Springs," 14–15.

7. Homestead and Martin, "A Chronological Bibliography of E.D.E.N. Southworth's Works," 296; An Admirer of Shannondale, "Shannondale Springs," *Virginia Free Press* (Charlestown, VA), September 25, 1875, 2; Theriault, "History of Shannondale Springs," 11; Southworth, "Letters from Shannondale Springs," 2.

8. "D. Appleton & Co. Publish," *New York Tribune* (New York, NY), December 19, 1850, 1; "September 3d, Received at the Book Store This Day," *Wilmington Journal* (Wilmington, NC), September 13, 1850; "*The Deserted Wife*," *Sandusky Register* (Sandusky, OH), October 4, 1850, 2; *Louisville Daily Courier* (Louisville, KY), October 31, 1850, 3; "*Saturday Evening Post* and Mrs. Southworth," *National Era* (Washington, DC), November 14, 1850, 2.

9. H. C. H., "Washington City—Mrs. Southworth," *National Era* (Washington, DC), October 17, 1850, 2; John R. Thompson, ed., "Notices of New Works: *The Deserted Wife*," *Southern Literary Messenger: Devoted to Every Department of Literature and the Fine Arts* 16, no. 12 (December 1850): 111.

10. "Mrs. Southworth's Story," *National Era* (Washington, DC), December 26, 1850, 2; "A Woman Who Writes: Mrs. Southworth Tells about Her Own Literary Work," *Evening Star* (Washington, DC), September 6, 1890, 14.

11. "Mrs. Southworth's Story," 2; "Prospectus of the *National Era*, Vol. V—1851," *National Era* (Washington, DC), February 13, 1851, 4; Homestead and Martin, "A Chronological Bibliography of E.D.E.N. Southworth's Works," 296–97.

12. "Prose Fiction: *The Deserted Wife*," *Southern Quarterly Review* 3, no. 5 (January 1851): 293; "Critical Notices: *Shannondale*," *Southern Quarterly Review* 3, no. 6 (April 1851): 566; "Review 18—No Title," *International Monthly Magazine of Literature, Science and Art* 2, no. 2 (January 1, 1851): 181; John R. Thompson, "Notices of New Works: Shannondale," *Southern Literary Messenger: Devoted to Every Department of Literature and the Fine Arts* 17, no. 2 (February 1851): 128; John R. Thompson, "Notices of New Works: *The Mother-in-Law; or, The Isle of Rays*," *Southern Literary Messenger: Devoted to Every Department of Literature and the Fine Arts* 17, no. 6 (June 1851): 390.

13. *Saturday Evening Post*, March 8, 1851.

14. E.D.E.N. Southworth, "Leaves from Shannondale: Stage Coaches," *Saturday Evening Post* (Philadelphia, PA), July 19, 1851, 1.

15. Southworth, "Leaves from Shannondale: Stage Coaches," 1.

16. F., "From an Occasional Correspondent," *Daily Union* (Washington, DC), July 16, 1851, 3.

17. Gamaliel Bailey, "Letter from the Editor," *National Era* (Washington, DC), July 17, 1851, 2; E.D.E.N. Southworth, "Leaves from Shannondale, Number III," *Saturday Evening Post* (Philadelphia, PA), August 2, 1851, 1.

18. Mary J. Windle, "Summer Sketches—No. 1," *Southern Press* (Washington, DC), July 19, 1851, 4; Mary J. Windle, "Summer Sketches—No. 2," *Southern Press* (Washington, DC), July 23, 1851, 4.

19. Southworth, "Leaves: Stage Coaches," 1.

20. E.D.E.N. Southworth, "Leaves from Shannondale, Number II," *Saturday Evening Post* (Philadelphia, PA), July 26, 1851, 1.

21. Southworth, "Leaves, Number III," 1.

22. "Shannondale Springs," *Southern Press* (Washington, DC), August 26, 1851, 2; Mary J. Windle, "Summer Sketches—No. 8," *Southern Press* (Washington, DC), August 14, 1851, 2; B. V. W., "Shannondale Springs, Jefferson County, VA., July 31, 1851," *New York Herald* (New York, NY), August 5, 1851, 2; E.D.E.N. Southworth, "Leaves from Shannondale, Number IV," *Saturday Evening Post* (Philadelphia, PA), August 16, 1851, 1.

23. Mary J. Windle, "Summer Sketches—No. 6," *Southern Press* (Washington, DC), August 5, 1851, 2; B. V. W., "Shannondale Springs," 2; E.D.E.N. Southworth, "Leaves from Shannondale, Number V," *Saturday Evening Post* (Philadelphia, PA), August 23, 1851, 1; Windle, "Summer Sketches—No. 8," 2; B. V. W., "Shannondale Springs, Jefferson Co., Va., Aug. 9, 1851," *New York Herald* (New York, NY), August 19, 1851, 6.

24. W., "The Watering Places, Fashion in Virginia," *New York Herald* (New York, NY), September 8, 1851, 3; E.D.E.N. Southworth, "Leaves from Shannondale, 'The Tourney,'" *Saturday Evening Post* (Philadelphia, PA), September 27, 1851, 1.

25. E.D.E.N. Southworth, *The Missing Bride; or, Miriam, the Avenger* (Philadelphia, PA: Peterson, 1874), 211–19.

26. W., "The Watering Places," 3.

27. Southworth, "Leaves, 'The Tourney,'" 1; W., "The Watering Places," 3.

28. Philos, "Lines, To Mrs. Emma D.E.N. Southworth, Author of the Deserted Wife, &c., &c.," *American Telegraph* (Washington, DC), September 12, 1851, 1.

Chapter 6

1. Michael Earls, S. J., *Manuscripts and Memories: Chapters in Our Literary Tradition* (Freeport, NY: Books for Libraries Press, 1935), 24.

2. Gilberta S. Whittle, "Mrs. Southworth and Her Novels: How Her Famous Literary Career Was Begun," *Times* (Philadelphia, PA), October 28, 1894, 12. From 1837 to 1877, Sarah Hale was the editor of *Godey's*, the leading publication dedicated to women's fashion and domestic life. Hale influenced the success of writers by publishing prose and poetry in her magazine.

3. Sarah M. Huddleson, "Mrs. E.D.E.N. Southworth and Her Cottage," *Records of the District of Columbia Historical Society* 23 (1920): 76; Mary S. Lockwood, *Historic Homes in Washington: Its Noted Men and Women* (New York: Belford, 1889), 263; Martha D. Lincoln, "Prospect Cottage," *Washington Post* (Washington, DC), October 1, 1893, 16; Whittle, "Mrs. Southworth and Her Novels," 12.

4. Melissa J. Homestead and Vicki L. Martin, "A Chronological Bibliography of E.D.E.N. Southworth's Works Privileging Periodical Publication," in *E.D.E.N. Southworth: Recovering a Nineteenth-Century Popular Novelist*, ed. Melissa J. Homestead and Pamela T. Washington (Knoxville: University of Tennessee Press, 2012), 297.

5. "Mark Sutherland," *National Era* (Washington, DC), April 28, 1853, 2; "The *Saturday Evening Post*," *Loudon Free Press* (Loudon, TN), January 15, 1853, 4; Whittle, "Mrs. Southworth and Her Novels," 12.

6. E.D.E.N. Southworth to Abraham Hart, October 1852, CWBL; E.D.E.N. to Hart, January 24, 1853, CWBL; E.D.E.N. to Hart, October 12, 1852, GM.

7. E.D.E.N. to Hart, November 17, 1852, GM; E.D.E.N. to Hart, December 15, 1852, BPL.

8. Melissa J. Homestead and Pamela T. Washington, eds., *E.D.E.N. Southworth: Recovering a Nineteenth-Century Popular Novelist* (Knoxville: University of Tennessee Press, 2012), frontispiece; Huddleson, "Mrs. E.D.E.N. Southworth and Her Cottage," 75–76.

9. Nettie Colburn Maynard, *Was Abraham Lincoln a Spiritualist; or, Curious Revelations from the Life of a Trance Medium* (Philadelphia, PA: Hartranft, 1891), 148–49; Lincoln, "Prospect Cottage," 16; Henry Clayton Blackwood Cowell, "A Noted Novel-Writer: Produced One Book for Nearly Every Year of Her Life," *Washington Post* (Washington, DC), December 2, 1894, 17.

10. "Writer of 80 Novels: Mrs. E.D.E.N. Southworth at the Age of Seventy-Four," *Washington Post* (Washington, DC), January 7, 1894, 14; Lincoln, "Prospect Cottage," 16; Daisy Fitzhugh Ayers, "Memories of Mrs. Emma Dorothea Eliza Nevitte Southworth," *Times Democrat* (New Orleans, LA), August 6, 1905, 25; "Mrs. Southworth, Favorite Novelist in Grandmother's Day," *Evening Star* (Washington, DC), August 28, 1921, 55.

11. "Further from Mexico," *Times-Picayune* (New Orleans, LA), September 27, 1853, 2; "America," *Manchester Weekly Times and Examiner* (Manchester, UK), November 30, 1853, 2; "Mexico," *Guardian* (London, UK), November 30, 1853, 2.

12. *Times-Picayune* (New Orleans, LA), September 13, 1853, 2; "Retribution; or, The Vale of Shadows," *Literary World* 5, no. 141 (October 13, 1849): 315; "Publisher's Circular," *Literary World* 5, no. 143 (October 27, 1849): 363; *Buffalo Courier* (Buffalo, NY), December 6, 1855, 2; *Daily American Organ* (Washington, DC), December 7, 1855, 2.

13. "Arrival of More of the Passengers of the *San Francisco*," *Connecticut Courant* (Hartford, CT), January 21, 1854, 1; "The *San Francisco*—Additional Particulars," *Boston Courier* (Boston, MA), January 16, 1854, 2.

14. "Further from the *San Francisco*," *Newark Daily Advertiser* (Newark, NJ), January 16, 1854, 2; "Arrival of More of the Passengers of the *San Francisco*," 1.

15. E.D.E.N. Southworth, "Ch. IX, Shipwreck," in *The Island Princess: A Romance of the Old and New World*, *New York Ledger* 13, no. 16 (June 27, 1857): 2.

16. Emma claimed that the title to the slaves willed to her could be found in Liber W.B. 49, folios 198–99 in Washington County, DC; Mississippi, Wills and Probate Records, 1780–1982, digital image s.v. "Charlotte L. Nevitt (will dated Dec. 1, 1853)," Ancestry, accessed April 10, 2024, https://www.ancestry.com/imageviewer/collections/8995/images/005818325_00103?pId=1504217.

17. "Runaways," *Evening Star* (Washington, DC), March 20, 1854, 3; J. L. Henshaw, "The Late Runaway Case," *Daily Evening Star* (Washington, DC), March 23, 1854, 2.

18. "Correction,—Gentlemen," *Evening Star* (Washington, DC), March 21, 1854, 3; Henshaw, "The Late Runaway Case," 2; "A Warning to the Public," *Daily National Era* (Washington, DC), March 22, 1854, 3. Note: This advertisement continued to run in the *Era* as well as the *Daily National Intelligencer* through March 30.

19. J. L. Henshaw, "To the Public," *Daily National Intelligencer* (Washington, DC), March 23, 1854, 2; E.D.E.N.S., "A Warning to the Public," *Evening Star* (Washington, DC), March 24, 1854, 2; Henshaw, "To the Public," 2.

20. "Washington, DC, Slave Emancipation Records, 1851–1863," digital image s.v. "Susanna G. Henshaw (May 31, 1862)," Ancestry, accessed April 10, 2024, https://www.ancestry.com/imageviewer/collections/2159/images/31556_217987-00950?pId=4008.

21. "Hart, Abraham," in *Appletons' Cyclopædia of American Biography*, ed. James Grant Wilson and John Fiske (New York: Appleton, 1888), 3:102; Henry Peterson to E.D.E.N. Southworth, December 24, 1854, RL.

22. Michael Denning, *Mechanic Accents: Dime Novels and Working-Class Culture in America* (New York: Verso, 1987), 88; T. B. Peterson to E.D.E.N. Southworth, April 12, 1854, RL; "New Books! New Books!" *Nashville Union and American* (Nashville, TN), February 11, 1855, 3.

23. H. Peterson to E.D.E.N., October 30, 1854, RL.

24. H. Peterson to E.D.E.N., December 24, 1854, RL.

25. Sarah Hale, "Novels, Serials, Pamphlets, Etc.," *Godey's Lady's Book* 49, no. 26 (December 1854): 555; John Reuben Thompson, "Notices of New Works: *The Missing Bride, or Miriam the Avenger*," *Southern Literary Messenger: Devoted to Every Department of Literature and the Fine Arts* 21, no. 7 (July 1855): 455–56; Barbara Welter, "The Cult of True Womanhood: 1820–1860," *American Quarterly* 18 (Summer 1966): 152.

26. Hale, "Novels, Serials, Pamphlets, Etc.," 793–94; John Hart, "Emma D.E.N. Southworth," in *Female Prose Writers of America: With Portraits, Biographical Notices and Specimens of Their Writings* (Philadelphia, PA: Butler, 1855), 211–15.

27. H. Peterson to E.D.E.N., October 30, 1854, RL; "Prospectus for 1855," *Lancaster Intelligencer* (Lancaster, PA), January 2, 1855, 3; Homestead and Martin, "A Chronological Bibliography of E.D.E.N. Southworth's Works," 298.

28. "Prospectus for 1855," 3; "Literature," *Morning Post* (London, UK), October 28, 1853, 3; Homestead and Martin, "A Chronological Bibliography of E.D.E.N. Southworth's Works," 294; "Orders for American Authoresses," *Richmond Dispatch* (Richmond, VA), November 19, 1855, 1.

29. John Greenleaf Whittier, "The Era's Contributors," *National Era* (Washington, DC), February 1, 1855; "Bulwer's and Mrs. Southworth's New Novels!" *Vicksburg Daily Whig* (Vicksburg, MS), November 17, 1855, 3; "Literary Notices," *National Era* (Washington, DC), January 25, 1855, 2.

30. Whittle, "Mrs. Southworth and Her Novels," 12; Emma D.E.N. Southworth, "To the Readers of the *Saturday Evening Post*," *Saturday Evening Post* (Philadelphia, PA), November 3, 1855.

31. E.D.E.N. to H. Peterson, August 30, 1856, letter reprinted in "Mrs. Southworth Again," *Saturday Evening Post* (Philadelphia, PA), May 2, 1857, 2; "Editor's Table," *Peterson's Magazine* 30 (November 1856): 338.

32. "The Nation," *Spirit of Democracy* (Woodsfield, OH), December 31, 1856, 2; "If You Want a Good Paper," *Bellevue Gazette* (Bellevue, NE), June 11, 1857, 4; Maturin M. Ballou to E.D.E.N. Southworth, April 20, 1857, RL; "Editor's Table," *Peterson's Magazine*

30 (November 1856), 338; Homestead and Martin, "A Chronological Bibliography of E.D.E.N. Southworth's Works," 298.

33. Robert Bonner to E.D.E.N. Southworth, October 10, 1856, RL.

34. Bonner to E.D.E.N., October 22, 1856, RL.

35. E.D.E.N. to Bonner, December 26, 1869, RL.

36. "Mrs. Emma D.E.N. Southworth," *National Era* (Washington, DC), December 11, 1856, 4; H. Peterson to E.D.E.N., March 21, 1857, RL; "Prospectus," *Saturday Evening Post* (Philadelphia, PA), March 28, 1857, 2.

37. "Mrs. Southworth's Statement," *New York Ledger* (New York, NY), May 2, 1857, 4; "To All Interested," *New York Ledger* (New York, NY), May 2, 1857, 4.

38. "Mrs. Southworth Again," *Saturday Evening Post* (Philadelphia, PA), May 2, 1857, 2.

39. "Mrs. Southworth Again," 2.

Chapter 7

1. Margaret S. Fuller, *Woman in the Nineteenth Century* (New York: Greeley & McElrath, 1845), 159.

2. E.D.E.N. Southworth, "Ch. XV: The Girl Captain," in *The Island Princess: A Romance of the Old and New World*, *New York Ledger* 13, no. 19 (July 18, 1857): 5.

3. Southworth, "Ch. XV: The Girl Captain," 6.

4. Matthew Hale Smith, "Robert Bonner and the *New York Ledger*," in *Sunshine and Shadow in New York* (Hartford, CT: Burr, 1868), 608–12; "Robert Bonner Is Dead," *New York Times* (New York, NY), July 7, 1899, 1; "Robert Bonner," Ramelton Tidy Towns, accessed April 23, 2022, https://sites.google.com/site/rameltontidytowns1/robert-bonner.

5. Robert Bonner to E.D.E.N. Southworth, June 20, 1857, RL; "Literature," *New York Herald* (New York, NY), December 24, 1857, 5; "Mrs. Southworth's New Story," *New York Times* (New York, NY), December 24, 1857, 5; *Star of the North* (Bloomsburg, PA), December 23, 1857, 2; *Memphis Daily Appeal* (Memphis, TN), December 29, 1857, 2; *Monmouth Democrat* (Freehold, NJ), December 17, 1857, 2; *Weekly Raleigh Register* (Raleigh, NC), December 23, 1857, 3; *Wisconsin State Journal* (Madison, WI), December 28, 1857, 3.

6. "The Bride of an Evening," *New York Times* (New York, NY), January 6, 1858, 5.

7. Amy E. Hughes and Naomi J. Stubbs, introduction to *A Player and a Gentleman: The Diary of Harry Watkins, Nineteenth-Century US American Actor*, by Harry Watkins (Ann Arbor: University of Michigan Press, 2018), 12, 288; Maud Skinner and Otis Skinner, *One Man in His Time: The Adventures of H. Watkins, Strolling Player 1845–1863 from His Journal* (Philadelphia: University of Pennsylvania Press, 1938), 227–29.

8. Hughes and Stubbs, introduction to *A Player and a Gentleman*, 288–89; Skinner and Skinner, *One Man in His Time*, 230–31.

9. E.D.E.N., Speech for *Bride of an Evening*, miscellaneous (box 2), LOC; "Barnum's American Museum," *New York Tribune* (New York, NY), March 26, 1858, 1.

10. "Important Discovery," *Alexandria Gazette* (Alexandria, VA), August 23, 1858, 2; *Louisville Daily Journal* (Louisville, KY), August 24, 1858, 3; *Georgia Telegraph* (Macon, GA), August 31, 1858, 2; *Buffalo Daily Republic* (Buffalo, NY), August 24, 1858, 2;

Monmouth Democrat (Freehold, NJ), August 26, 1858, 2; *Detroit Free Press* (Detroit, MI), August 25, 1858, 1; "A New Species," *Evening Star* (Washington, DC), August 26, 1858, 1; "Brazil and La Plata," *Charleston Courier* (Charleston, SC), December 21, 1858, 4.

11. T. B. Peterson to E.D.E.N. Southworth, January 20, 1858, RL; Melissa J. Homestead and Vicki L. Martin, "A Chronological Bibliography of E.D.E.N. Southworth's Works Privileging Periodical Publication," in *E.D.E.N. Southworth: Recovering a Nineteenth-Century Popular Novelist*, ed. Melissa J. Homestead and Pamela T. Washington (Knoxville: University of Tennessee Press, 2012), 298; "Phinney & Co.'s Advert's," *Buffalo Daily Republic* (Buffalo, NY), March 25, 1858, 3.

12. "Book Notices," *Evening Star* (Washington, DC), March 5, 1858, 2.

13. "Spectator Abroad," *Evening Star* (Washington, DC), August 20, 1859, 2.

14. E.D.E.N. Southworth, *The Hidden Hand; or, Capitola the Madcap*, ed. Joanne Dobson (New Brunswick, NJ: Rutgers University Press, 2009), 7, 15, 212; "U.S. Indexed Early Land Ownership and Township Plats, 1785–1898," Ancestry, accessed September 23, 2018, www.ancestry.com/interactive/Print/2179/30656_100110-00; Walt Grayson, "Focused on the Mississippi: The Devil's Punchbowl," WJTV, posted on June 26, 2020, accessed May 13, 2022, https://www.wjtv.com/news/focused-on-mississippi-the-devils-punchbowl/.

15. Gilberta S. Whittle, "Mrs. Southworth and Her Novels: How Her Famous Literary Career Was Begun," *Times* (Philadelphia, PA), October 28, 1894, 12.

16. Whittle, "Mrs. Southworth and Her Novels," 12; "A Good-Looking Newsboy," *Mount Carmel Register* (Mount Carmel, IL), March 5, 1858, 2.

17. Whittle, "Mrs. Southworth and Her Novels," 12; Southworth, *The Hidden Hand*, 15–29.

18. Whittle, "Mrs. Southworth and Her Novels," 12.

19. Whittle, "Mrs. Southworth and Her Novels," 12; Southworth, *The Hidden Hand*, 108–18, 349–77.

20. "The Hidden Hand," *Muscatine Weekly Journal* (Muscatine, IA), April 8, 1859, 1; U.S. Passport Applications, 1795–1925, digital image s.v. "Emma D.E.N. Southworth," Washington, D C, May 9, 1859, Ancestry, accessed May 19, 2022, http://search.ancestry.com/cgi-bin/sse.dll?db=uspassports&h=1515708&ti =0&indiv=try&gss=pt; "Mrs. Southworth, the Novelist," *Wisconsin State Journal* (Madison, WI), May 27, 1859, 2.

21. E.D.E.N. Southworth to Robert Bonner, [ca. 1860], RL. Because the letter has only a date listed as Christmas morning, the Duke librarians have noted a possible date as circa 1860; however, clues within the letter indicate that the actual date was 1858. Emma had listed Prospect Cottage as her address, and in 1860, she was living in England. Because she discussed her plans for publishing in both countries, she hadn't departed for her trip, thus dating letter December 25, 1858.

22. "A Woman Writer: The Remarkable Career of Mrs. E.D.E.N. Southworth," *Times* (Philadelphia, PA), August 26, 1888, 11; "Mrs. Southworth," *Chicago Tribune* (Chicago, IL), June 3, 1859, 2.

23. "Travel to Europe," *Baltimore Sun* (Baltimore, MD), May 30, 1859, 2; "Death of Gamaliel Bailey, ESQ," *Liberator* 29, no. 26 (July 1, 1859): 103.

24. "Steam to All Parts of Ireland, England and Scotland," *Charleston Mercury* (Charleston, SC), June 1, 1859, 3; "Passenger Ships—19th Century," Global Security, accessed May 20, 2022, https://www.globalsecurity.org/military/systems/ship/passenger-19.html; "Inman Line/Liverpool and Philadelphia Steamship Company/Liverpool, New York and Philadelphia Steamship Company," Ships List, accessed May 19, 2022, https://www.theshipslist.com/ships/lines/inman.shtml.

25. E.D.E.N. Southworth, *The Bride's Fate: A Sequel to "The Changed Brides"* (Philadelphia, PA: Peterson, 1869), 94–95.

26. Thomas W. Page, "The Transportation of Immigrants and Reception Arrangements in the Nineteenth Century," *Journal of Political Economy* 19, no. 9 (November 1911): 738.

27. E.D.E.N. Southworth, *The Fortune Seeker* (Philadelphia: Peterson, 1866), 27–28.

28. "Liverpool," *Guardian* (UK), June 11, 1859, 4; "Victorian London," British Express: Passionate about British Heritage, accessed May 26, 2022, https://www.britainexpress.com/London/victorian-london.htm.

Chapter 8

1. E.D.E.N. Southworth, final installment of *The Hidden Hand* in the *New York Ledger* 15, no. 18 (July 9, 1859): 2.

2. Gilberta S. Whittle, "Mrs. Southworth and Her Novels: How Her Famous Literary Career Was Begun," *Times* (Philadelphia, PA), October 28, 1894, 12; 1861 England Census, digital image s.v. "E.D.E.N. Southworth" (Croydon, Surrey, England), Ancestry, accessed April 10, 2024, https://www.ancestry.com/discoveryui-content/view/6902673:8767?ssrc=pt&tid=43882184&pid=12718707314; Chris Shields, *The Beulah Spa, 1831–1856: A New History* (Morrisville: Lulu Press, 2019), 48–96; "Upper Norwood, Croydon," Hidden London, accessed June 28, 2022, https://hidden-london.com/gazetteer/upper-norwood/.

3. Christopher Hibbert, *The Illustrated London News' Social History of Victorian Britain* (Sydney: Angus & Robertson, 1975), 11; Andrew King, *The* London Journal, *1845–1883: Periodicals, Production and Gender* (New York: Routledge, 2004), 82, 112, 132–35.

4. Jessica Nelson, "The Gilded Page: How International Copyright Law Helped Create Mark Twain's International Success," *Journal of Publishing Culture* 17 (May 2017): 3–4.

5. Nelson, "The Gilded Page," 5; King, *The* London Journal, *1845–1883*, 133, 136.

6. "Theatre," *Buffalo Daily Republic* (Buffalo, NY), July 16, 1859, 3; "*The Hidden Hand*," *Buffalo Commercial* (Buffalo, NY), July 18, 1859, 3; "Theatre," *Buffalo Daily Republic* (Buffalo, NY), July 19, 1859, 3.

7. J. B. Howe, *A Cosmopolitan Actor: His Adventures All over the World* (London: Bedford, 1888), 74, 93, 97–98; "The Pittsburg Theatre," *Pittsburgh Daily Post* (Pittsburgh, PA), September 14, 1859, 1; "Baltimore Museum," *Baltimore Sun* (Baltimore, MD), December 24, 1859, 2; "Amusements, Washington Theatre," *Evening Star* (Washington, DC), January 9, 1860, 2; "A Reminiscence," *Great Bend Register* (Great Bend, KS), December 6, 1906, 4.

8. "Richmond Theatre," *Richmond Dispatch* (Richmond, VA), December 7, 1859, 2; Allston Brown, *A History of the New York Stage: From the First Performance in 1732 to 1901* (New York: Dodd, Mead, 1903), 1:469; "Amusements," *Public Ledger* (Philadelphia,

PA), April 10, 1860, 3; "Victoria Theatre," *Era* (London, UK), March 17, 1861, 8; "Royal Colosseum Theatre," *Liverpool Mercury* (Liverpool, UK), October 4, 1861, 1.

9. "Royal Grecian Theatre, City-Road," *Lloyd's Weekly Newspaper* (London, UK), July 24, 1859, 6; "Southampton. Theatre Royal," *Era* (London, UK), November 13, 1859, 12; "Marlyebone Theatre," *Era* (London, UK), August 26, 1860, 8; "February," *Era* (London, UK), January 5, 1862, 14; "Marlyebone Theatre," *Era* (London, UK), September 21, 1862, 8.

10. Michelle Ann Abate, *Tomboys: A Literary and Cultural History* (Philadelphia, PA: Temple University Press, 2008), 4–5.

11. Southworth, *The Hidden Hand*, 121; "Woodlawn Course," *Republican Banner* (Nashville, TN), September 23, 1859, 2; "The River," *The Wheeling Daily Intelligencer* (Wheeling, WV), October 26, 1860, 3; "A Brief History of Capitola," City of Capitola, California, accessed June 29, 2022, https://www.cityofcapitola.org/capitola-museum/page/brief-history-capitola#:~:text=Lulu%20and%20S.%20A.%20Hall%2C%20Frederick%20Hihn%2C%20and,of%20four%20incorporated%20cities%20in%20Santa%20Cruz%20County.

12. Southworth, *The Hidden Hand*, 306–7, 326.

13. "Jockey Hats, Capitola Hats, Equestrian Hats," *Baltimore Sun* (Baltimore, MD), August 21, 1860, 2; "The Capitola," *Louisville Daily Journal* (Louisville, KY), July 26, 1860, 1; "The Wire Walking Yesterday—a Great Feat and a Great Crowd," *Wheeling Daily Intelligencer* (Wheeling, WV), August 15, 1860, 3.

14. "Capitola," *Louisville Daily Courier* (Louisville, KY), March 22, 1861, 1; Abate, *Tomboys*, 23.

15. "*The Hidden Hand*," *Daily News* (London, UK), August 5, 1859, 8; "Parlour Journal," *Lloyd's Weekly Newspaper* (London, UK), August 21, 1859, 10; "Southworth vs. Taylor," *Morning Post* (London, UK), December 23, 1859, 6.

16. "The Authors of Washington: Who They Are and Something about Them," *Evening Star* (Washington, DC), January 6, 1872, 1.

17. Harriet Beecher Stowe to Lady Byron, April 9, 1859 (box 5, no. 246), BSFP.

18. E.D.E.N. Southworth, "With Lady Byron: Mrs. Southworth's Memorable Visit to the Poet's Widow," *Evening Star* (Washington, DC), October 25, 1890, 13.

19. Southworth, "With Lady Byron," 13.

20. Stowe to Lady Byron, April 9, 1859, BSFP; "Annabella Byron," Spartacus Educational, accessed July 3, 2022, https://spartacus-educational.com/Annabella_Byron.htm.

21. Southworth, "With Lady Byron," 13.

22. Caroline Franklin, *The Female Romantics: Nineteenth-Century Women Novelists and Byronism* (New York: Routledge, 2013), 122; Frank Prochaska, "Carpenter, Mary (1807–1877)," *Oxford Dictionary of National Biography* (Oxford: Oxford University Press, 2004), http://www.oxforddnb.com/view/article/4733; Southworth, "With Lady Byron," 13.

23. "The Authors of Washington," 1; Lloyd C. Sanders, "Leveson-Gower, Harriet Elizabeth Georgiana," in *Dictionary of National Biography*, ed. Sidney Lee (New York: Macmillan, 1893), 33:152–53.

24. "The Authors of Washington," 1; "Mrs. Southworth: Talk with the Eminent Novelist," *National Republican* (Washington, DC), April 29, 1882, 1.

25. "Mrs. Southworth: Personal Recollections of the Wonderfully Prolific Novel Writer," *Kansas City Times* (Kansas City, MO), July 3, 1882, 3; Mississippi, Wills and Probate Records, 1780–1982, digital image s.v. "Charlotte L. Nevitt (probate Feb. 1860)," Ancestry, accessed April 10, 2024, https://www.ancestry.com/imageviewer/collections/8995/images/005818325_00103?pId=1504048.

26. "Arrivals at the Principal Hotels, Girard House," *Philadelphia Press* (Philadelphia, PA), November 10, 1859, 3, and March 6, 1860, 3; "Arrivals at the Hotels," *Evening Star* (Washington, DC), April 13, 1860, 4.

27. "A Family Quarrel," *Evergreen City Times* (Sheboygan, WI), February 4, 1860, 1; "Mr. Southworth," *Grant County News* (Platteville, WI), February 23, 1860, 2.

28. Melissa J. Homestead, *American Women Authors and Literary Property, 1822–1869* (New York: Cambridge University Press, 2005), 47.

29. "*The Haunted Homestead*," *Racine Democrat* (Racine, WI), April 18, 1860, 3.

30. E.D.E.N. Southworth, *The Haunted Homestead, and Other Nouvellettes* (Philadelphia, PA: Peterson, 1860), 36.

31. E.D.E.N. Southworth, *The Bridal Eve* (Philadelphia, PA: Peterson, 1864).

32. In a letter to Robert Bonner on March 24, 1861, Southworth asked him to address his correspondence for her to "Lotty at her school address." On April 23, 1861, she wrote to Bonner and listed the "Ladies' College" as the return address, RL. In an unpublished thesis, James Mason claims that Lottie went to a school in Brixton, but his source was from correspondence between another researcher Bernice Grieves and Southworth's grandson-in-law. James Mason, "Mrs. E.D.E.N. Southworth" (master's thesis, George Peabody College for Teachers, 1935), Jean and Alexander Heard Library, Vanderbilt University, Nashville, TN. Research on women's colleges during the time Southworth was there finds only one college called the Ladies' College, located in Bedford Square, indicating Lottie was a student at the Bedford Ladies' College in London.

33. Sybil Oldfield, "Reid, Elisabeth Jesser (1789–1866)," in *Oxford Dictionary of National Biography* (Oxford: Oxford University Press, 2004), https://www.oxforddnb.com/view/article/37888; Margaret Tuke, *A History of Bedford College for Women, 1849–1937* (New York: Oxford University Press, 1939), 20–25, 319–21.

34. E.D.E.N. to Bonner, April 25, 1862, RL; Richmond Southworth to Bonner, November 30, 1860, RL.

35. E.D.E.N. to Bonner, July 20, 1860, RL; "How Tales Are Got Up," *Bradford Observer* (Bradford, UK), September 6, 1860, 3; Melissa J. Homestead and Vicki L. Martin, "A Chronological Bibliography of E.D.E.N. Southworth's Works Privileging Periodical Publication," in *E.D.E.N. Southworth: Recovering a Nineteenth-Century Popular Novelist*, ed. Melissa J. Homestead and Pamela Washington (Knoxville: University of Tennessee Press, 2012), 299.

36. E.D.E.N. to Bonner, July 20, July 27, and August 10, 1860, RL.

37. E.D.E.N. to Bonner, February 18 and March 24, 1861, RL; "The Missing Steamship *Australasian*," *New York Daily Herald* (New York, NY), March 14, 1861, 5; E.D.E.N. to Bonner, March 24, 1861; "Safety of the Steamer *Australasian*," *Evening Star* (Washington, DC), March 18, 1861, 2.

38. E.D.E.N. Southworth to Robert Bonner, April 9, 1861 and April 23, 1861, RL; E.D.E.N. to Bonner, September 17, 1861, CWBL; Homestead and Martin, "A Chronological Bibliography of E.D.E.N. Southworth's Works," 299.

39. E.D.E.N. to Bonner, April 25, 1861, RL; Robert Gallup, "More Letters of American Writers," *Yale University Library Gazette* 37, no. 1 (1962): 32.

40. "Judge Hough," *Appleton Crescent* (Appleton, WI), June 15, 1872, 1; "Mr. F. H. Southworth," *Sonoma County Journal* (Petaluma, CA), September 6, 1861, 2.

41. E.D.E.N. Southworth, *The Lost Heir of Linlithgow* (Philadelphia, PA: Peterson, 1872), 23.

42. "Chain Pier," Brighton Museums, accessed July 11, 2022, https://www.brightonmuseums.org.uk/discover/2012/07/05/chain-pier; "Short History of the Pavilion," Brighton Museums, accessed July 11, 2022, https://www.brightonmuseums.org.uk/royalpavilion/history/short-history-of-the-royal-pavilion/.

43. E.D.E.N. to Bonner, September 17, 1861, CWBL; Martin Purvis, "King, William (1786–1865)," *Oxford Dictionary of National Biography* (Oxford: Oxford University Press, 2004), http://www.oxforddnb.com/view/article/15608.

44. Passenger Lists of Vessels Arriving at New York, New York, 1820–1897, Microfilm Publication M237, 675 rolls, NAI 6256867; Records of the U.S. Customs Service, Record Group 36, National Archives, Washington, DC.

Chapter 9

1. Mrs. E. N. Chapin, *American Court Gossip; or, Life at the National Capitol* (Marshalltown, IA: Chapin & Hartwell, 1887), 85.

2. "Civil War Timeline," Gettysburg National Military Park, accessed July 15, 2022, https://nps.gov/get/learn/historyculture/civil-war-timeline.html; "History: Lost Capitol Hill: Company C of the Union Regiment," The Hill Is Home, January 4, 2016, accessed July 15, 2022, https:// thehillishome.com/2016/01/lost-capitol-hill-company-c-of-the-union-regiment.html.

3. "The Civil War in Georgetown," Chesapeake & Ohio Canal National Historical Park, accessed July 15, 2022, https://www.nps.gov/choh/learn/historyculture/the-civil-war-in-georgetown.htm.

4. Emily Edson Briggs, *The Olivia Letters* (Washington, DC: Neale, 1906), 339; "Georgetown Civil War Walking Tours," Chesapeake & Ohio Canal National Historical Park, accessed July 15, 2022, https://www.nps.gov/choh/learn/historyculture/georgetowncivilwarwalkingtour.htm.

5. E.D.E.N. Southworth to Robert Bonner, April 25, 1862, RL.

6. "Henry Hardy," Ancestry, accessed July 15, 2022, https://www.ancestry.com/family-tree/person/tree/155639486/person/422053456074/facts.

7. E.D.E.N. to Bonner, May 28, 1862, RL; "Henry Hardy"; E.D.E.N. to Bonner, May 28, 1862, RL.

8. E.D.E.N. to Bonner, April 25, 1862, RL; "Soldiers—Henry C. Henshaw," The Civil War, National Park Service, U.S. Department of the Interior, accessed July 22, 2022, https://www.nps.gov/civilwar/search-soldiers-detail.htm?soldierId=33E6CBA7-DC7A-DF11-BF36-B8AC6F5D926A.; "Capt. Henshaw Dead," *News* (Frederick, MD),

March 12, 1903, 5; *Catalogue of the Officers and Students of Georgetown College, District of Columbia for the Academic Year 1853–1854* (New York: Settle, 1854); *Catalogue . . . 1854–1855* (New York:. Settle, 1855); *Catalogue . . . 1855–1856* (New York: Settle, 1856); *Catalogue . . . 1856–1857* (New York: Settle, 1857).

9. *College of Physicians and Surgeons in the City of New York Medical Department of Columbia College. Fifty-Sixth Annual Catalogue of the Officers and Students of the College. Session of 1862–63* (New York: Baker & Goodwin), 8–12.

10. E.D.E.N. to Bonner, undated circa 1862, RL; C. R. Gibbs, "DC Emancipation Day," DC.gov, accessed July 23, 2022, https://emancipation.dc.gov/node/105922; Jessica Parr, "The Compensated Emancipation Act of 1862," We're History: American Then for America Now, April 16, 2018, https://werehistory.org/the-compensated-emancipation-act-of-1862/; Washington, DC, Slave Emancipation Records, 1851–1863, digital image s.v. "Susanna G. Henshaw" (May 31, 1862), Ancestry, accessed April 10, 2024, https://www.ancestry.com/imageviewer/collections/2171/images/31555_217981-00920?pId=2331; Washington, DC, Slave Owner Petitions, 1862–1863, digital image s.v. "Susanna G. Henshaw" (June 2, 1862), Ancestry, accessed April 10, 2024, https://www.ancestry.com/imageviewer/collections/2159/images/31556_217987-00950?pId=4008.

11. E.D.E.N. to Bonner, August 19, 1862 and circa 1862, RL.

12. E.D.E.N. to Bonner, August 19, 1862, RL.

13. E.D.E.N. to Bonner, August 31, 1862, RL.

14. E.D.E.N. to Bonner, August 31, 1862, RL.

15. Melissa J. Homestead and Vicki L. Martin, "A Chronological Bibliography of E.D.E.N. Southworth's Works Privileging Periodical Publication," in *E.D.E.N. Southworth: Recovering a Nineteenth-Century Popular Novelist*, ed. Melissa J. Homestead and Pamela T. Washington (Knoxville: University of Tennessee Press, 2012), 299; E.D.E.N. Southworth, *The Fortune Seeker* (Philadelphia: Peterson, 1866), 192–93, 277–313.

16. "Second Manassas," American Battlefield Trust, accessed August 3, 2022, https://www.battlefields.org/learn/civil-war/battles/second-manassas; E.D.E.N. to Bonner, August 31, 1862, RL.

17. E.D.E.N. to Bonner, August 31, 1862, RL; Mrs. Southworth, "Britomarte, the Man-Hater," *New York Ledger* 22, no. 4 (March 24 and June 30, 1866): 4; "Female Soldiers in the Civil War," American Battlefield Trust, accessed August 3, 2022, https://www.battlefields.org/learn/articles/female-soldiers-civil-war; DeAnne Blanton and Lauren Cook, *They Fought Like Demons: Women Soldiers in the American Civil War* (Baton Rouge: Louisiana State University Press, 2002), 10, 169.

18. Ednah Dow Cheney, ed., *Louisa May Alcott: Her Life, Letters, and Journals* (Boston, MA: Roberts Brothers, 1892), 138; Daisy Fitzhugh Ayers, "Memories of Mrs. Emma Dorothea Eliza Nevitte Southworth," *Times Democrat* (New Orleans, LA), August 6, 1905, 25; Charles Smart, *The Medical and Surgical History of the War of the Rebellion*, part 3, vol. 1, *Medical History* (Washington, DC: Government Printing Office, 1888), 899.

19. "The Georgetown Hospitals," *National Republican* (Washington, DC), September 15, 1862, 3; Stephen Smith and George F. Shrady, eds., *The American Medical Times: Being a Weekly Series of the* New York Journal of Medicine, vol. 3, *July–December 1861* (New

York: Baillière, 1861), 128; Walter W. Spooner, "Lawrence, James Valentine," in *Westchester County, New York: Biographical* (New York: New York History, 1900), 153.

20. E.D.E.N. Southworth, *Fair Play; or, The Test of the Lone Isle* (Philadelphia, PA: Peterson, 1868), frontispiece.

21. Elizabeth Brown Pryor, *Clara Barton: Professional Angel* (Philadelphia: University of Pennsylvania Press, 1987), 99; E.D.E.N. Southworth, *How He Won Her: A Sequel to "Fair Play"* (Philadelphia, PA: Peterson, 1869), 321–96; Jane E. Schultz, *Women at the Front: Hospital Workers in Civil War America* (Chapel Hill: University of North Carolina Press, 2004), 20.

22. E.D.E.N. to Bonner, October 5, 1862, RL; Edward F. Hyde to Bonner, October 8, 1862, RL.

23. E.D.E.N. to Bonner, circa 1862; October 19, 1862; November 10, 1862, RL.

24. E.D.E.N. to Bonner, October 19, 1862; November 10, 1862, RL.

25. "Living Contraband—Former Slaves in the Nation's Capital during the Civil War," National Park Service, accessed August 10, 2022, https://www.nps.gov/articles/living-contraband-former-slaves-in-the-nation-s-capital-during-the-civil-war.htm.

26. *First Annual Report of the National Association for the Relief of Destitute Colored Women and Children* (Washington, DC: McGill & Witherow, 1864).

27. Alexandra Kommel, "Seances in the Red Room: How Spiritualism Comforted the Nation during and after the Civil War," White House Historical Association, accessed August 5, 2022, https://www.whitehousehistory.org/seances-in-the-red-room.

28. Nettie Colburn Maynard, *Was Abraham Lincoln a Spiritualist?; or, Curious Revelations from the Life of a Trance Medium* (Philadelphia, PA: Hartranft, 1891), 146–53.

29. E.D.E.N. to Bonner, circa 1862, RL; "New York Draft Riots," Civil War of the Western Border, Kansas City Public Library, accessed August 6, 2022, https://www.civilwaronthewesternborder.org/timeline/new-york-draft-riots.

30. E.D.E.N. to Bonner, circa 1863, RL; Guy Hasegawa, "The Civil War's Medical Cadets: Medical Students Serving the Union," *Journal of the American College of Surgeons* 193, no. 1 (July 2001): 81–89; *Catalogue of the Governors, Trustees and Officers, and of the Alumni and Other Graduates of Columbia College (originally King's College) in the City of New York from 1754–1882* (New York: Macgowen & Slipper, 1882), 120.

31. Lloyd Klein, "Infectious Diseases in the Civil War," *Hektoen International: A Journal of Medical Humanities*, March 31, 2022, https://hekint.org/2022/03/31/infectious-diseases-in-the-civil-war/; E.D.E.N. to Bonner, circa 1863, RL.

32. E.D.E.N. to Bonner, October 5, 1863, RL; Stanley B. Burns, "Wound Infection," PBS, accessed August 6, 2022, https://www.pbs.org/mercy-street/uncover-history/behind-lens/wound-infection/.

33. "Hostetter's Celebrated Stomach Bitters," *National Republican* (Washington, DC), October 29, 1863, 4; Ferdinand Meyer, "Jacob & David Hostetter—Dr. J. Hostetter's Celebrated Stomach Bitters," Peachridge Glass, October 30, 2018, https://www.peachridgeglass.com/2018/10/jacob-david-hostetter-dr-j-hostetters-celebrated-stomach-bitters/.

34. "Barbara Frietchie," *Indianapolis News* (Indianapolis, IN), August 30, 1899, 5; "A London Journal Writer," *London Journal and Weekly Record of Literature, Science, and Art*

19, no. 476 (January 28, 1893): 64; John Greenleaf Whittier, "Barbara Frietchie," *Atlantic Monthly: A Magazine of Literature, Art, and Politics* 12, no. 72 (October 1863): 495–97.

35. E.D.E.N. to Bonner, circa 1863, RL.

36. "Interesting Wedding," *Evening Star* (Washington, DC), May 9, 1864, 3.

37. Margaret Leech, *Reveille in Washington, 1860–1865* (New York: Harper, 1941), 371–72; "The Inauguration Ball," *Evening Star* (Washington, DC), March 7, 1865, 2; "The Inauguration Ball," *Cleveland Leader* (Cleveland, OH), March 10, 1865, 4.

38. Aaron O'Neill, "Number of United States Military Fatalities in Major Wars, 1775–2022," Statista, June 21, 2022, https:// www.statista.com/statistics/1009819/total-us-military-fatalities-in-american-wars-1775-present/; E.D.E.N. Southworth, *Her Love or Her Life: A Sequel to "The Bride's Ordeal"* (New York: Street & Smith, 1904), 336.

Chapter 10

1. E.D.E.N. Southworth, *How He Won Her: A Sequel to "Fair Play"* (Philadelphia, PA: Peterson, 1869), 480.

2. Melissa J. Homestead and Vicki L. Martin, "A Chronological Bibliography of E.D.E.N. Southworth's Works Privileging Periodical Publication," in *E.D.E.N. Southworth: Recovering a Nineteenth-Century Popular Novelist*, ed. Melissa J. Homestead and Pamela T. Washington (Knoxville: University of Tennessee Press, 2012), 300; E.D.E.N. Southworth, *The Fortune Seeker* (Philadelphia: Peterson, 1866), frontispiece.

3. E.D.E.N. Southworth to Robert Bonner, March 18, 1867, RL.

4. Walter W. Spooner, "Lawrence, James Valentine," in *Westchester County, New York: Biographical* (New York: New York History, 1900), 153–54; E.D.E.N. to Bonner, October 28, 1870, RL; "Charlotte Emma Southworth Lawrence," Ancestry, accessed August 25, 2022, https://www.ancestry.com/family-tree/person/tree/43882184/person/12718709622/facts.

5. Richmond Southworth to Bonner, June 27, 1867, RL; "Southworth, R. J.," *Washington, District of Columbia, City Directory* (1868), 121; "Southworth, R. J.," *Washington, District of Columbia, City Directory* (1874), 35; "Letters from Washington," *Baltimore Sun* (Baltimore, MD), September 23, 1867, 4.

6. "Henry Clay Henshaw," *Baltimore Sun* (Baltimore, MD), March 14, 1903, 8; E.D.E.N. Southworth, *The Changed Brides* (Philadelphia, PA: Peterson, 1869), frontispiece.

7. E.D.E.N. to Bonner, Christmas Day, 1867, RL; Frances Henshaw Baden, "Willful Lottie; or, What Will She Do Next," *New York Ledger* 24, no. 22 (July 25, 1868): 3.

8. "The United States," *The Times* (London, UK), May 20, 1869, 5; *Evening Star* (Washington, DC), December 27, 1875, 2; "The Authors of Washington: Who They Are and Something about Them," *Evening Star* (Washington, DC), January 6, 1872, 1.

9. Writing contract between E.D.E.N. and Bonner, September 28, 1867, RL; E.D.E.N. to Bonner, January 12, 1869, RL; E.D.E.N. Southworth, *The Bride of Llewellyn* (Philadelphia, PA: Peterson, 1866), frontispiece; E.D.E.N. to Bonner, circa 1867, RL.

10. E.D.E.N. to Bonner, January 5, 1869; E.D.E.N. to Bonner, circa 1869, RL.

11. "Prospectus for 1863," *White Cloud Kansas Chief* (White Cloud, KS), December 10, 1863, 4; "New York Ledger," *White Cloud Kansas Chief* (White Cloud, KS), December 29,

1864, 3; "The Lady's Friend," *Aegis & Intelligencer* (Bel Air, MD), September 24, 1869; "Books and Stationery," *Richmond Dispatch* (Richmond, VA), December 19, 1870, 3; E.D.E.N. to Bonner, circa 1869.

12. E.D.E.N. to Bonner, March 4, 1867; December 26, 1873, RL.

13. E.D.E.N. to Bonner, March 4, 1867, RL; Homestead and Martin, "A Chronological Bibliography of E.D.E.N. Southworth's Works," 301; "Periodicals," *Daily News* (London, UK), April 2, 1869, 8, RL.

14. E.D.E.N. to Bonner, circa 1869, RL.

15. E.D.E.N. to Bonner, September 28, 1867, RL; Homestead and Martin, "A Chronological Bibliography of E.D.E.N. Southworth's Works," 301; E.D.E.N. to Bonner, January 12, 1869, RL.

16. "Wedding at Prospect Cottage," *Evening Star* (Washington, DC), September 9, 1870, 1; "Our Society People," *National Republican* (Washington, DC), February 17, 1873, 4; "Mrs. Southworth," *National Republican* (Washington, DC), February 7, 1874, 4; E.D.E.N. to Bonner, February 28, 1869; Mrs. M. D. Lincoln, "Prospect Cottage," *Washington Post* (Washington, DC), October 1, 1893, 16.

17. "The Inauguration," *Evening Star* (Washington, DC), March 4, 1869, 1; "President Grant's Inaugural Address," *Evening Star* (Washington, DC), March 4, 1869, 1.

18. Homestead and Martin, "A Chronological Bibliography of E.D.E.N. Southworth's Works," 300.

19. Allison Lange, "The 14th and 15th Amendments," National Women's History Museum, 2015, accessed August 30, 2022, https://www.womenshistory.org/resources/general/14th-and-15th-amendments.

20. Elizabeth Cady Stanton, Susan Brownell Anthony, and Matilda Joslyn Gage, eds., *History of Woman Suffrage*, vol. 3, *1876–1885* (Rochester, NY: Anthony, 1886), 810.

21. "Justice for Women," *New National Era* (Washington, DC), April 20, 1871, 3.

22. Harper Franklin, "1870–1879," Fashion History Timeline, August 18, 2020, https://fashionhistory.fitnyc.edu/1870-1879/.

23. "Notes and Comments," *Vermont Watchman and State Journal* (Montpelier, VT), April 19, 1871, 2.

24. "Lawrence, James V.," *Curtin's Westchester County Directory, 1873–74*, 270, Ancestry, accessed April 10, 2024, https://www.ancestry.com/imageviewer/collections/2469/images/41199_1220706242_4278-00287?pId=1396791085.

25. R. J. Southworth, "On a New Micrometric Goniometer Eye Piece for the Microscope," *American Journal of Science and Arts* 2 (July–December 1871): 408; "Improvement of the Microscope," *Evening Star* (Washington, DC), January 4, 1872, 4; "Columbia Law School," *Evening Star* (Washington, DC), May 31, 1873, 4.

26. E.D.E.N. to Bonner, circa 1873, RL.

27. E.D.E.N. to Bonner, November 1875, RL; J. J. Porter and J. H. Porter to E.D.E.N., November 27, 1875, RL.

28. E.D.E.N. to Bonner, November 1875; November/December 1875; December 1875, RL.

Chapter 11

1. George Macdonald, *Annals of a Quiet Neighbourhood* (New York: Routledge, 1872), 202. Emma's annotated copy of Macdonald's *Annals of a Quiet Neighbourhood* is in the Peabody Room at Georgetown Public Library in Georgetown, Washington, DC.

2. 1880 US Census, Yonkers, Westchester, New York, digital image s.v. "E.D.E.N. Southworth," Ancestry, accessed April 4, 2024, https://www.ancestry.com/imageviewer/collections/6742/images/4243582-00674?pId=39509684; E.D.E.N. Southworth to Robert Bonner, June 1, 1876, RL.

3. "Mrs. E.D.E.N. Southworth," *Interior Journal* (Stanford, KY), March 17, 1885, 1; "Lawrence Brothers," *Yonkers Gazette* (Yonkers, NY), September 9, 1876, 4; "Democratic Nominations," *Yonkers Gazette* (Yonkers, NY), March 26, 1876, 2; "Board of Education," *Yonkers Statesman* (Yonkers, NY), August 1, 1899, 3.

4. E.D.E.N. to Bonner, May 1876, RL; "Special Notices," *Yonkers Statesman* (Yonkers, NY), July 28, 1877, 2; "Special Notices," *Yonkers Statesman* (Yonkers, NY), August 31, 1877, 4; "Special Notices," *Yonkers Statesman* (Yonkers, NY), August 31, 1877, 4; "Special Notices," *Yonkers Gazette* (Yonkers, NY), January 19, 1878, 2; "Young Dr. Upham's Death," *Sun* (New York, NY), May 26, 1882, 1.

5. "Dr. R. J. Southworth," *Yonkers Gazette* (Yonkers, NY), April 26, 1884, 3; "Dr. R. J. Southworth," *Yonkers Gazette* (Yonkers, NY), April 25, 1885, 3; "C.L.S.C.," *Yonkers Gazette* (Yonkers, NY), April 11, 1885, 3.

6. "Afternoon Tea," *Yonkers Statesman* (Yonkers, NY), November 28, 1883, 3; "George C. Miln," *Yonkers Gazette* (Yonkers, NY), August 1, 1885, 3; "Miln Captures Yonkers," *Bismarck Weekly Tribune* (Bismarck, ND), August 21, 1885, 1; "Mr. Tilden," *Yonkers Statesman* (Yonkers, NY), August 15, 1885, 3; "Theatre," *Daily Ohio Statesman* (Columbus, OH), January 26, 1869, 3.

7. M. L. Rayne, "The Cottage Where Mrs. E.D.E.N. Southworth Wrote Her Numerous Novels," *Detroit Free Press* (Detroit, MI), March 2, 1890, 8.

8. "Walks and Talks in the City," *New York Tribune* (New York, NY), December 4, 1884, 5; Mrs. E. N. Chapin, *American Court Gossip; or, Life at the National Capitol* (Marshalltown, IA: Chapin & Hartwell, 1887), 84; E.D.E.N. to Bonner, October 13, 1876, RL.

9. "The Fatal Secret," *Buffalo Sunday Morning News* (Buffalo, NY), February 25, 1877, 2; "An Entire New Book by Mrs. Southworth," *Daily Review* (Wilmington, NC), March 14, 1877, 4; "Literary," *Daily News* (Lebanon, PA), February 12, 1878, 2.

10. E.D.E.N. to Bonner, January 28 and January 30, 1878, RL.

11. "A Good Paper," *Swanton Courier* (Swanton, VT), January 12, 1878, 3; E.D.E.N. to Bonner, May 2, 1878; March 29, 1880; September 1, 1881; August 14, 1882; December 13, 1883; November 3, 1886.

12. "Memorial of Women, Citizens of the United States," in *The Miscellaneous Documents of the Senate of the United States for the First Session of the Forty-Fourth Congress* (Washington, DC: Government Printing Office, 1876), 40–41; "Woman Suffrage," *National Republican* (Washington, DC), April 15, 1876, 4; Elizabeth Cady Stanton, Susan Brownell Anthony, and Matilda Joslyn Gage, eds., *History of Woman Suffrage*, vol. 3, *1876–1885* (Rochester, NY: Anthony, 1886), 810–13.

13. Paige Mathieson, "Bad or Mad? Infanticide: Insanity and Morality in Nineteenth-Century Britain," *Midlands Historical Review* 4 (May 13, 2020), accessed October 3, 2024, https://www.midlandshistoricalreview.com/wp-content/uploads/2020/05/BadOrMadInfanticide.pdf; Mrs. Sara J. Spencer, *Argument before the Committee on the District of Columbia of the United States Senate, Friday, January 26, 1876, upon the Pending Senate Bill for the Purpose of a Site and the Construction of Buildings for a Girls' Reform School in the Capital of the United States* (Washington, DC: Beresford, 1876).

14. "The Girls' Reform School," *National Republic* (Washington, DC), December 13, 1876, 2.

15. "Industrial Home School," *National Republican* (Washington, DC), October 31, 1876; *The Executive Documents of the House of Representatives for the Third Session of the Fifty-Third Congress, 1894–95* (Washington, DC: Government Printing Office, 1895), 141.

16. Melissa J. Homestead and Vicki L. Martin, "A Chronological Bibliography of E.D.E.N. Southworth's Works Privileging Periodical Publication," in *E.D.E.N. Southworth: Recovering a Nineteenth-Century Popular Novelist*, ed. Melissa J. Homestead and Pamela T. Washington (Knoxville: University of Tennessee Press, 2012), 302; E.D.E.N. Southworth, *Em: A Novel* (n.p.: Bonner, 1892; repr., n.p.: Burt, 1904) and the sequel, E.D.E.N. Southworth, *Em's Husband: A Novel* (n.p.: Bonner, 1892; repr., n.p.: Burt, 1904).

17. E.D.E.N. to Emma Bonner, circa April 1878, RL; Southworth, *Em*, 188–89.

18. "Death of the Wife and Daughter of Robert Bonner," *Journal* (Evansville, IN), April 15, 1878, 1; E.D.E.N. to Bonner, March 1876 and April 8, 1878, RL.

19. Bonner to E.D.E.N., May 24, 1878; E.D.E.N. to Bonner, June 3, 1878; Bonner to E.D.E.N., circa June 1878, RL.

20. Alice N. Lawrence, certificate no. 769, *City of Yonkers Death Register*, 1875–1884, 56, Ancestry, accessed April 4, 2024, https://www.ancestry.com/imageviewer/collections/61535/images/61535_b1036868-00055?pId=80857740; Bonner to E.D.E.N., May 24, 1878, RL.

21. "Society," *Evening Star* (Washington, DC), February 13, 1878, 1; "Personalities," *Yonkers Gazette* (Yonkers, NY), March 30, 1878, 3; E.D.E.N. to Bonner, April 1, 1878, RL.

22. T. B. Peterson to E.D.E.N., September 12, 1877; T. B. Peterson to Bonner, July 6, 1874; March 8, 1876; July 30, 1877; August 14, 1878; February 20, 1883, RL.

23. E.D.E.N. to Bonner, March 8, 1876, RL; "Self-Raised; or, From the Depths," *Boston Globe* (Boston, MA), May 15, 1876, 3.

24. E.D.E.N. to Bonner, October 23, 1876, RL.

25. E.D.E.N. to Bonner, May 18, 1883, RL; "Mrs. E.D.E.N. Southworth," *Times-Picayune* (New Orleans, LA), May 3, 1885, 4; "Literary Chat," *Brooklyn Times* (Brooklyn, NY), July 23, 1887, 7.

26. "Mr. and Mrs. H. C. Spencer," *Critic* (Washington, DC), May 12, 1882, 4; "Dr. and Mrs. George Mitchell," *Times-Picayune* (New Orleans, LA), June 24, 1883, 12; Sara Spencer to Clara Barton, circa 1887, CBP.

27. *Social Meetings of the Washington Society of the New Jerusalem, Spring Series, 1876* pamphlet and *Washington Society of the New Jerusalem: Baptism, Confirmation, Marriage, Funeral & Membership Records*, archives at the Church of the Holy City, National Swedenborgian Church, Washington, DC; Gilberta S. Whittle, "Mrs. Southworth and Her Novels: How Her Famous Literary Career Was Begun," *Times* (Philadelphia, PA), October 28, 1894, 12.

28. "Mrs. Southworth's First Story," *Evening Bulletin* (Honolulu, HI), March 28, 1883, 1; "Mrs. Southworth, the Novelist: The Truth Concerning Her First Story," *Evening Star* (Washington, DC), February 24, 1883, 2.

29. Sarah M. Huddleson, "Mrs. E.D.E.N. Southworth and Her Cottage," *Records of the District of Columbia Historical Society* 23 (1920): 74; "A Peep into a Model Library," *Port Chester Journal* (Port Chester, NY), November 25, 1880, 2; "Women," *Buffalo Times* (Buffalo, NY), January 16, 1885, 2; "Mrs. E.D.E.N. Southworth," *Democrat and Chronicle* (Rochester, NY), May 31, 1888, 3; "Loyal Woman's Work: The Household, Conversation Club, Puzzles, etc.," *National Tribune* (Washington, DC), August 9, 1888, 7.

30. Whittle, "Mrs. Southworth and Her Novels," 12; "What Not to Read," *Brooklyn Union* (Brooklyn, NY), March 10, 1882, 1; "Our Advertisers," *Catholic Union and Times* (Buffalo, NY), December 22, 1881, 4.

31. E.D.E.N. to Bonner, March 24 and March 29, 1887, RL.

32. E.D.E.N. to Bonner, circa 1883 and June 13, 1887, RL; Homestead and Martin, "A Chronological Bibliography of E.D.E.N. Southworth's Works," 299.

33. E.D.E.N. to Bonner, October 7, 1886, RL; Homestead and Martin, "A Chronological Bibliography of E.D.E.N. Southworth's Works," 302, 304.

34. E.D.E.N. to Bonner, circa 1886, RL; "Current Topics," *Democrat and Chronicle* (Rochester, NY), May 14, 1889, 4; "Literary Notes," *Buffalo Evening News* (Buffalo, NY), March 12, 1888, 3.

35. E.D.E.N. to Bonner, December 30, 1889, RL.

36. "Georgetown," *Evening Star* (Washington, DC), February 18, 1889, 3; "Died," *Evening Star* (Washington, DC), March 12, 1889, 5; "Social Matters," *Evening Star* (Washington, DC), May 1, 1890, 2.

Chapter 12

1. E.D.E.N. Southworth to Robert Bonner, April 8, 1878, RL.

2. 1890 US Census, Washington, District of Columbia, digital image s.v. "Thomas E. Baden," Ancestry, accessed April 4, 2024, https://www.ancestry.com/imageviewer/collections/5445/images/4376859-00498?pId=3704.

3. "House with History: Prospect Cottage," *Evening Star* (Washington, DC), September 21, 1889, 9; E.D.E.N. to Lottie Southworth Lawrence (Lottie), May 2, 1890, LOC.

4. E.D.E.N. to Lottie, May 2, 1890, LOC.

5. Gilberta S. Whittle, "Mrs. Southworth and Her Novels: How Her Famous Literary Career Was Begun," *Times* (Philadelphia, PA), October 28, 1894, 12; "Mrs. Southworth—Personal Recollections of the Wonderfully Prolific Novel Writer," *Winfield Courier* (Winfield, KS), August 3, 1882, 4; "Mrs. Southworth: Talk with the Eminent Novelist," *National Republican* (Washington, DC), April 29, 1882, 1; Henry Clayton

Blackwood Cowell, "A Noted Novel-Writer: Produced One Book for Nearly Every Year of Her Life," *Washington Post* (Washington, DC), December 2, 1894, 17.

6. E.D.E.N. to Bonner, circa 1878 and September 1, 1890, RL.

7. "How the Story Was Written: What Mrs. Southworth Says about a Charge of Plagiarism," *Evening Star* (Washington, DC), September 2, 1890, 7; "Self-Made; or, Out of the Depths," *Osage County Times* (Scranton, KS), October 3, 1890, 8.

8. E.D.E.N. to Bonner, October 15, 1890, RL; Melissa J. Homestead and Vicki L. Martin, "A Chronological Bibliography of E.D.E.N. Southworth's Works Privileging Periodical Publication," in *E.D.E.N. Southworth: Recovering a Nineteenth-Century Popular Novelist*, ed. Melissa J. Homestead and Pamela T. Washington (Knoxville: University of Tennessee Press, 2012), 300, 302.

9. E.D.E.N. to Bonner, October 25, 1890, RL; Dr. G. F. G. Morgan to Eliza Nevitte, November 3, 1890, RL.

10. Cowell, "A Noted Novel-Writer," 17; Homestead and Martin, "A Chronological Bibliography of E.D.E.N. Southworth's Works," 305; E.D.E.N. to Lottie, July 9, 1890, LOC.

11. E.D.E.N. to Lottie, January 13, 1893, LOC; E.D.E.N. to Samuel Thomas Pickard, June 23, 1893, PW.

12. Richmond J. Southworth, "Snapshot Interviews," *Washington Times* (Washington, DC), February 18, 1897, 5.

13. "Household Matters," *Lafayette Advertiser* (Lafayette, LA), November 15, 1890, 7; Mary S. Lockwood, *Historic Homes in Washington: Its Noted Men and Women* (New York: Belford, 1889), 263; Homestead and Martin, "A Chronological Bibliography of E.D.E.N. Southworth's Works," 304–5.

14. "Mrs. Southworth: Talk with the Eminent Novelist," *National Republican* (Washington, DC), April 29, 1882, 1; "The Binder's Table: Silent Tale Told by Worn-Out Covers at the Pratt Library," *Baltimore Sun* (Baltimore, MD), May 19, 1893, 8; "Libraries at Atlanta," *Washington Post* (Washington, DC), October 13, 1893, 23; E.D.E.N. to Lottie, June 10, 1892.

15. E.D.E.N. to Lottie, September 24, 1892, LOC; "Entertaining the Indians," *Evening Star* (Washington, DC), April 23, 1880, 4; "Reception to Red Cloud," *Critic* (Washington, DC), March 23, 1885, 2; E.D.E.N. to Lottie, May 27, 1892, LOC.

16. Charles Warren Stoddard, "Mrs. Emma D.E.N. Southworth at Prospect Cottage, an Old Sweetheart of Mine," *National Magazine* 22 (1905): 180–86.

17. E.D.E.N. to Lottie, August 8, 1893, LOC.

18. Martha D. Lincoln, "Prospect Cottage," *Washington Post* (Washington, DC), October 1, 1893, 16.

19. E.D.E.N. to Lottie, August 19 and August 21, 1893, LOC.

20. E.D.E.N. to Lottie, July 10, 1896, LOC.

21. E.D.E.N. to Lottie, August 12, 1890; January 14, 1893, LOC.

22. E.D.E.N. to Lottie, December 23 and May 13, 1890; September 12, 1891, LOC.

23. E.D.E.N. to Lottie, September 17 and September 19, 1894; November 12, 1895, LOC; E.D.E.N. to Bonner, circa 1877, RL; "Robert Bonner Is Dead," *New York Times* (New York, NY), July 7, 1899, 1.

24. E.D.E.N. to Lottie, August 5, 1892, LOC; "Last Words of Mrs. E.D.E.N. Southworth, the Authoress," *Evening Star* (Washington, DC), July 15, 1899, 3; "Slowly Sinking: Condition of Mrs. E.D.E.N. Southworth Somewhat Worse," *Evening Star* (Washington, DC), July 29, 1899, 3; "Mrs. Southworth Sinking: Faint Hope That the Aged Novelist May Recover," *Washington Times* (Washington DC), June 29, 1899, 2; "Her Condition Such That Death Is Hourly Expected," *Evening Star* (Washington, DC), June 30, 1899, 3.

25. "A Peaceful End: Death of Mrs. E.D.E.N. Southworth, the Novelist," *Evening Star* (Washington, DC), July 1, 1899, 10; Sarah M. Huddleson, "Mrs. E.D.E.N. Southworth and Her Cottage," *Records of the District of Columbia Historical Society* 23 (1920): 79.

Chapter 13

1. Sarah M. Huddleson, "Mrs. E.D.E.N. Southworth and Her Cottage," *Records of the District of Columbia Historical Society* 23 (1920): 52.

2. "Connolly and Wallace," *Times Tribune* (Scranton, PA), October 3, 1902, 3; "American Home Classics Series," *Buffalo Jewish Review* (Buffalo, NY), November 21, 1924, 24; "Old-Fashioned Stories That Are Always New," *Evening News* (Harrisburg, PA), April 30, 1930, 13; "The Souvenir Bookstore," *Windsor Star* (Ontario, Canada), December 6, 1902, 3; "Tomorrow," *Post Star* (Glenn Falls, NY), 7; Weare Holbrook, "Any Old Sport in a Storm: We Seem in a Recrudescence of Parlor Games," *Baltimore Sun* (Baltimore, MD), October 26, 1930, 102.

3. "Mrs. Southworth's Old Home," *Evening Times* (Washington, DC), December 20, 1901, 3; "Affairs in Georgetown," *Evening Star* (Washington, DC), July 25, 1903, 2; Daisy Fitzhugh Ayers, "Memories of Mrs. Emma Dorothea Eliza Nevitte Southworth," *Times Democrat* (New Orleans, LA), August 6, 1905, 25.

4. "The Old Southworth Cottage: How Petty Graft Has Flourished There," *Washington Post* (Washington, DC), July 2, 1905, E8.

5. Huddleson, "Mrs. E.D.E.N. Southworth and Her Cottage," 77–78.

6. Sue McNamara, "Penwomen Plan House around the Library of Mrs. Southworth," *Star Press* (Muncie, IN), September 9, 1928, 20; John Leo Coontz, "Southworth Cottage to Be Preserved," *Washington Post* (Washington, DC), July 15, 1928, SM1; "New Bust of Mrs. Southworth," *Evening Star* (Washington, DC), April 12, 1929, 5 (the bust is still housed at the National League of American Penwomen in DC on the top shelf in the second-floor library); "Pen Women Plan National Building," *Sunday Star* (Washington, DC), July 15, 1928, 14.

7. "Home of Famous Storyteller May Be Made a Shrine," *Intelligencer Journal* (Lancaster, PA), August 3, 1928, 24; Elisabeth E. Poe, "Washington Is Redolent of Literary Memories," *Washington Post* (Washington, DC), July 16, 1933, 30; "Pen Women Sell Clubhouse Site Purchased in 1929," *Washington Post* (Washington, DC), April 4, 1939, 13.

8. John Clagett Proctor, "Washington Loses Another Famous Landmark," *Sunday Star* (Washington, DC), April 12, 1942, B4.

9. Willa Sibert Cather, "In Washington," *Nebraska State Journal* (Lincoln, NE), March 3, 1901, 12.

10. "'Give What You'd Like to Keep' Slogan of Victory Book Drive," *Lincoln Star* (Lincoln, NE), January 3, 1943, 22.

11. "One-Time Reporter Now Bowdoin Professor, Author of Literary Study," *Morning Call* (Allentown, PA), December 8, 1940, 5, 9.

12. Charles Honce, "Best and Super Best Sellers," *Daily News* (New York), November 2, 1947, 321; William McCann, "Forgotten Books Possess Sad Durability of Unloved," *Lansing State Journal* (Lansing, MI), July 31, 1966, 55.

13. "Questions and Answers," *Austin American* (Austin, TX), September 12, 1948, 34; "Ethics and Religion Still Score in Books," *Courier Journal* (Louisville, KY), March 20, 1955, 45; "Wanted to Buy," *Morning Call* (Allentown, PA), November 14, 1965, 56; "Wanted," *Lansing State Journal* (Lansing, MI), September 28, 1967, 73.

14. "Course at Dominguez Hills College Soap Operas Explored," *Press Telegram* (Long Beach, CA), April 9, 1975, 27.

Bibliography

Archive Collections

BPL Boston Public Library Special Collections. Ch. B. 5. 101. Boston, MA. Courtesy of the Trustees of the Boston Public Library/Rare Books.

BSFP Beecher-Stowe Family Papers. 1798–1956. A-102; M-45, Box 5, no. 246. Arthur and Elizabeth Schlesinger Library on the History of Women in America, Radcliffe Institute for Advanced Study, Harvard University, Cambridge, MA.

CBP Clara Barton Papers: General Correspondence, –1912; Spencer, Sara A., 1887 to 1902, undated. 1887. Manuscript/Mixed Material. Library of Congress, Washington, DC.

CRAL Charles Roberts Autograph Letters Collection. American Novelists, Roe-Sty. Box 8. Folder 9. Haverford College Library, Haverford, PA.

CWBL Emma Dorothy Eliza Nevitte Southworth Papers. 1852–1894. Accession 8315. Clifton Walter Barrett Library of American Literature, University of Virginia, Charlottesville, VA.

GM Gratz Manuscripts. Case 6. Box 35. Historical Society of Pennsylvania, Philadelphia, PA.

JHR John Hawkins Rountree Papers. 1826–1907. Platteville Mss G. Platteville Micro 7. Micro 560. Southwest Wisconsin Room, Karrmann Library, University of Wisconsin, Platteville, WI.

LOC Emma Dorothy Eliza Nevitte Southworth Papers. 1870–1918. MSS50849. Library of Congress, Washington, DC.

PW Pickard-Whittier Papers. MS Am 1844 (664). Box 11. Houghton Library, Cambridge, MA.

RL Emma Dorothy Eliza Nevitte Southworth Papers. 1849–1901. OCLC20188549. Rubenstein Library, Duke University, Durham, NC.

Books

Abate, Michelle Ann. *Tomboys: A Literary and Cultural History*. Philadelphia, PA: Temple University Press, 2008.

Blackwell, Elizabeth. *Pioneer Work in Opening the Medical Profession to Women: Autobiographical Sketches*. London: Longmans, Green, 1895.

Blanton, DeAnne, and Lauren Cook. *They Fought Like Demons: Women Soldiers in the American Civil War*. Baton Rouge: Louisiana State University Press, 2002.

Boyle, Regis Louise. *Mrs. E.D.E.N. Southworth, Novelist*. Washington, DC: Catholic University of America Press, 1939.

Briggs, Emily Edson. *The Olivia Letters*. Washington, DC: Neale, 1906.

Brockett, F. L., and George W. Rock. *A Concise History of the City of Alexandria, VA., from 1669–1883 with a Directory of Reliable Business Hours in the City*. Alexandria, VA: Gazette Book and Job Office, 1883.

Brown, Allston. *A History of the New York Stage: From the First Performance in 1732 to 1901*. Vol. 1. New York: Dodd, Mead, 1903.

Butterfield, Consul Wilshire. *History of Grant County*. Chicago, IL: Western Historical Company, 1881.

Campbell, Henry C. *Wisconsin in Three Centuries*. Vol. 4. New York: Century History, 1906.

Chapin, Mrs. E. N. *American Court Gossip; or, Life at the National Capitol*. Marshalltown, IA: Chapin & Hartwell, 1887.

Cheney, Ednah Dow, ed. *Louisa May Alcott: Her Life, Letters, and Journals*. Boston, MA: Roberts Brothers, 1892.

Crew, Harvey W., William B. Webb, and John Wooldridge. *Centennial History of the City of Washington DC*. Dayton, OH: United Brethren, 1892.

Denning, Michael. *Mechanic Accents: Dime Novels and Working-Class Culture in America*. New York: Verso, 1987.

Dobson, Joanne. Introduction to *The Hidden Hand; or, Capitola the Madcap*, by E.D.E.N. Southworth, xl. Edited by Joanne Dobson. New Brunswick, NJ: Rutgers University Press, 2009.

Earls, Michael, S. J. *Manuscripts and Memories: Chapters in Our Literary Tradition*. Freeport, NY: Books for Libraries Press, 1935.

Franklin, Caroline. *The Female Romantics: Nineteenth-Century Women Novelists and Byronism*. New York: Routledge, 2013.

Freibert, Lucy M., and Barbara A. White, eds. *Hidden Hands: An Anthology of American Women Writers, 1790–1870*. New Brunswick, NJ: Rutgers University Press, 1994.

Fuller, Margaret S. *Woman in the Nineteenth Century*. New York: Greeley & McElrath, 1845.

Gernes, Todd Stevens. "Recasting the Culture of Ephemera: Young Women's Literary Culture in Nineteenth-Century America." PhD diss., Brown University, 1992.

Gjerde, Jon. *Catholicism and the Shaping of Nineteenth-Century America*. Edited by S. Deborah Kang. New York: Cambridge University Press, 2012.

Glasson, William G. *Federal Military Pensions in the United States*. New York: Oxford University Press, 1918.

Greve, Charles Theodore. *Centennial History of Cincinnati and Representative Citizens*. Vol 1. Chicago, IL: Biographical Publishing Company, 1904.

Hale, Sarah Josepha. "Southworth, Emma D.E. Nevitte." In *Woman's Record; or, Sketches of All Distinguished Women, from the Beginning til A.D. 1850*, 793–94. New York: Harper, 1853.

Harris, Susan K. *Nineteenth-Century American Women's Novels: Interpretative Strategies.* New York: Cambridge University Press, 1990.

Hart, John. "Emma D.E.N. Southworth." In *Female Prose Writers of America: With Portraits, Biographical Notices and Specimens of Their Writings*, 211–15. Philadelphia, PA: Butler, 1855.

Heatwole, Cornelius J. *A History of Education in Virginia.* New York: Macmillan, 1916.

Hibbert, Christopher. *The* Illustrated London News' *Social History of Victorian Britain.* Sydney: Angus & Robertson, 1975.

Hickey, Donald R. *The War of 1812: A Forgotten Conflict.* Champaign: University of Illinois Press, 2012.

Holford, Castello N. *History of Grant County Wisconsin Including Its Civil, Political, Geological, Mineralogical Archaeological and Military History and a History of the Several Towns.* Lancaster: Teller Print, 1900.

Homestead, Melissa J. *American Women Authors and Literary Property, 1822–1869.* New York: Cambridge University Press, 2005.

Homestead, Melissa J., and Pamela T. Washington, eds. *E.D.E.N. Southworth: Recovering a Nineteenth-Century Popular Novelist.* Knoxville: University of Tennessee Press, 2012.

Howe, J. B. *A Cosmopolitan Actor: His Adventures All over the World.* London: Bedford, 1888.

Hudock, Amy E. "No Mere Mercenary: The Early Life and Fiction of E.D.E.N. Southworth." PhD diss., University of South Carolina, 1993. Ann Arbor, MI: University Microfilms (ON9400225).

Hughes, Amy E., and Naomi J. Stubbs, eds. Introduction to *A Player and a Gentleman: The Diary of Harry Watkins, Nineteenth-Century US American Actor*, by Harry Watkins. Ann Arbor: University of Michigan Press, 2018.

King, Andrew. *The London Journal, 1845–1883: Periodicals, Production and Gender.* New York: Routledge, 2004.

Krone, Joe. *Land of the Free: Wartime Rules for North America 1754–1815.* New York: Osprey, 2014.

Leech, Margaret. *Reveille in Washington, 1860–1865.* New York: Harper, 1941.

Lockwood, Mary S. *Historic Homes in Washington: Its Noted Men and Women.* New York: Belford, 1889.

Macdonald, George. *Annals of a Quiet Neighbourhood.* New York: Routledge, 1872.

Malone, Dumas, ed. *Dictionary of American Biography.* Vol. 17. New York: Scribner, 1935.

Maynard, Nettie Colburn. *Was Abraham Lincoln a Spiritualist?; or, Curious Revelations from the Life of a Trance Medium.* Philadelphia, PA: Hartranft, 1891.

Mott, Frank Luther. *Golden Multitudes: The Story of Best Sellers in the United States.* New York: Macmillan, 1947.

Pease, Verne S. *The Life Story of Major John H. Rountree: The Public Career of a Colonial Gentleman on the Frontier in Wisconsin.* Baraboo, WI: Sauk County, 1928.

Pryor, Elizabeth Brown. *Clara Barton: Professional Angel.* Philadelphia: University of Pennsylvania Press, 1987.

Schultz, Jane E. *Women at the Front: Hospital Workers in Civil War America.* Chapel Hill: University of North Carolina Press, 2004.

Shields, Chris. *The Beulah Spa, 1831–1856: A New History.* Morrisville, NC: Lulu Press, 2019.

Skinner, Maud, and Otis Skinner. *One Man in His Time: The Adventures of H. Watkins, Strolling Player 1845–1863 from His Journal.* Philadelphia: University of Pennsylvania Press, 1938.

Smart, Charles. *The Medical and Surgical History of the War of the Rebellion.* Part 3. Vol. 3, *Medical History.* Washington, DC: Government Printing Office, 1888.

Smith, Matthew Hale. "Robert Bonner and the *New York Ledger.*" In *Sunshine and Shadow in New York,* 604–21. Hartford, CT: Burr, 1868.

Southworth, E.D.E.N. *The Bridal Eve.* Philadelphia, PA: Peterson, 1864.

———. *The Bride of Llewellyn.* Philadelphia, PA: Peterson, 1866.

———. *The Bride's Fate: A Sequel to "The Changed Brides."* Philadelphia, PA: Peterson, 1869.

———. *The Changed Brides.* Philadelphia, PA: Peterson, 1869.

———. *The Deserted Wife.* Philadelphia, PA: Peterson, 1886.

———. *The Discarded Daughter; or, The Children of the Isle.* New York: Lupton, 1876.

———. *Em: A Novel.* N.p.: Bonner, 1892. Reprint, N.p.: Burt, 1904.

———. *Em's Husband: A Novel.* N.p.: Bonner, 1892. Reprint, N.p.: Burt, 1904.

———. *Fair Play; or, The Test of the Lone Isle.* Philadelphia, PA: Peterson, 1868.

———. *The Fortune Seeker.* Philadelphia, PA: Peterson, 1866.

———. *The Haunted Homestead, and Other Nouvellettes.* Philadelphia, PA: Peterson, 1860.

———. *Her Love or Her Life: A Sequel to "The Bride's Ordeal."* New York: Street & Smith, 1904.

———. *The Hidden Hand; or, Capitola the Madcap.* Edited by Joanne Dobson. New Brunswick, NJ: Rutgers University Press, 2009.

———. *How He Won Her: A Sequel to "Fair Play."* Philadelphia, PA: Peterson, 1869.

———. *India: The Pearl of Pearl River.* Philadelphia, PA: Peterson, 1875.

———. *Ishmael; or, In the Depths.* Philadelphia, PA: Peterson, 1876.

———. *The Lady of the Isle; or, The Island Princess.* Philadelphia, PA: Peterson, 1886.

———. *The Lost Heir of Linlithgow.* Philadelphia, PA: Peterson, 1872.

———. *The Missing Bride; or, Miriam, the Avenger.* Philadelphia, PA: Peterson, 1874.

———. *Retribution: A Tale of Passion.* Philadelphia, PA: Peterson, 1856.

———. *The Three Beauties; or, Shannondale.* Philadelphia, PA: Peterson, 1878.

———. *Vivia; or, The Secret of Power.* Philadelphia, PA: Peterson, 1857.

———. *The Wife's Victory, and Other Nouvellettes.* Philadelphia, PA: Peterson, 1854.

Spooner, Walter W. "Lawrence, James Valentine." In *Westchester County, New York: Biographical,* 153–56. New York: New York History, 1900.

Stanton, Elizabeth Cady, Susan Brownell Anthony, and Matilda Joslyn Gage, eds. *History of Woman Suffrage.* Vol. 3, *1876–1885.* Rochester, NY: Anthony, 1886.

Swisshelm, Jane. *Crusader and Feminist: Letters of Jane Grey Swisshelm*. Edited by Arthur J. Larsen. St. Paul: Minnesota Historical Society, 1934.

———. *Half a Century*. Chicago, IL: Jansen, McClurg, 1880.

Thiel, Richard P. *The Timberwolf in Wisconsin: The Death and Life of a Majestic Predator*. Madison: University of Wisconsin Press, 1993.

Tucker, Spencer C., ed. *The Encyclopedia of the War of 1812*. New York: ABC-CLIO, 2012.

Tuke, Margaret. *A History of Bedford College for Women, 1849–1937*. New York: Oxford University Press, 1939.

Woody, Thomas. *A History of Women's Education in the United States*. 2 vols. New York: Science Press, 1929.

Articles

Ayers, Daisy Fitzhugh. "Memories of Mrs. Emma Dorothea Eliza Nevitte Southworth." *Times Democrat* (New Orleans, LA), August 6, 1905, 25.

Baden, Frances Henshaw. "Willful Lottie; or, What Will She Do Next." *New York Ledger* 24, no. 22 (July 25, 1868): 3.

Cather, Willa Sibert. "In Washington." *Nebraska State Journal* (Lincoln, NE), March 3, 1901, 12.

Coontz, John Leo. "Southworth Cottage to Be Preserved." *Washington Post* (Washington, DC), July 15, 1928, SM1.

Cowell, Henry Clayton Blackwood. "A Noted Novel-Writer: Produced One Book for Nearly Every Year of Her Life." *Washington Post* (Washington, DC), December 2, 1894, 17. (Before being known as an author, Henry Clayton Blackwood Cowell was a newspaper reporter, but, not wanting to be labeled as such, he used his initials H. B. C. as his byline.)

Evans, Jonathan Henry. "Some Reminiscences of Early Grant County." *Wisconsin Historical Society Proceedings*, 1909, 232–72. https://genealogytrails.com/wis/grant/history_reminiscences.html.

French, John C. "Poe and the Baltimore *Saturday Visiter*." *Modern Language Notes* 33, no. 5 (May 1918): 257–67.

Gallup, Robert. "More Letters of American Writers." *Yale University Library Gazette* 37, no. 1 (1962): 32.

Gilfoyle, Timothy. "The Hearts of Nineteenth-Century Men: Bigamy and Working-Class Marriage in New York City, 1800–1890." *Prospects* 19 (October 1994): 135–60.

Greenwood, Grace. "An American Salon." *Cosmopolitan: A Monthly Illustrated Magazine*, February 1890, 438.

Hale, Sarah. "Novels, Serials, Pamphlets, Etc." *Godey's Lady's Book* 49, no. 26 (December 1854): 555.

Hasegawa, Guy. "The Civil War's Medical Cadets: Medical Students Serving the Union." *Journal of the American College of Surgeons* 193, no. 1 (July 2001): 81–89.

Homestead, Melissa J., and Vicki L. Martin. "A Chronological Bibliography of E.D.E.N. Southworth's Works Privileging Periodical Publication." In *E.D.E.N. Southworth: Recovering a Nineteenth-Century Popular Novelist*, edited by

Melissa J. Homestead and Pamela T. Washington, 285–306. Knoxville: University of Tennessee Press, 2012.

Honce, Charles. "Best and Super Best Sellers." *Daily News* (New York), November 2, 1947, 321.

Huddleson, Sarah M. "Mrs. E.D.E.N. Southworth and Her Cottage." *Records of the District of Columbia Historical Society* 23 (1920): 52–79.

Lincoln, Martha D. "Prospect Cottage." *Washington Post* (Washington, DC), October 1, 1893, 16.

McCann, William. "Forgotten Books Possess Sad Durability of Unloved." *Lansing State Journal* (Lansing, MI), July 31, 1966, 55.

McNamara, Sue. "Penwomen Plan House around the Library of Mrs. Southworth." *Star Press* (Muncie, IN), September 9, 1928, 20.

Nelson, Jessica. "The Gilded Page: How International Copyright Law Helped Create Mark Twain's International Success." *Journal of Publishing Culture* 17 (May 2017): 1–12.

Page, Thomas W. "The Transportation of Immigrants and Reception Arrangements in the Nineteenth Century." *Journal of Political Economy* 19, no. 9 (November 1911): 732–49.

Poe, Elisabeth E. "Washington Is Redolent of Literary Memories." *Washington Post* (Washington, DC), July 16, 1933, 30.

Proctor, John Clagett. "Washington Loses Another Famous Landmark." *Sunday Star* (Washington, DC), April 12, 1942, B4.

Rayne, M. L. "The Cottage Where Mrs. E.D.E.N. Southworth Wrote Her Numerous Novels." *Detroit Free Press* (Detroit, MI), March 2, 1890, 8.

Ricker, Lisa Reid. "(De)Constructing the Praxis of Memory-Keeping: Late Nineteenth-Century Autograph Albums as Sites of Rhetorical Invention." *Rhetoric Review* 29, no. 3 (2010): 239–56.

Schwartzberg, Beverly. "'Lots of Them Did That': Desertion, Bigamy, and Marital Fluidity in Late Nineteenth-Century America." *Journal of Social History* 3737, no. 1 (Spring 2004): 573–600.

Scott, Alison, and Amy Thomas. "The Hidden Agenda of *The Hidden Hand*: Periodical Publication and the Literary Marketplace in Late-Nineteenth-Century America." In *E.D.E.N. Southworth: Recovering a Nineteenth-Century Popular Novelist*, edited by Melissa J. Homestead and Pamela T. Washington, 49–73. Knoxville: University of Tennessee Press, 2012.

Smith, Laura Rountree. "When Platteville 'First' Began to Appear on the Map." *Platteville Journal and Grant County News* (Platteville, WI), July 26, 1922, 2.

Smith, Stephen, and George F. Shrady. *The American Medical Times: Being a Weekly Series of the* New York Journal of Medicine. Vol. 3, *July–December 1861*. New York: Baillière, 1861.

Snodgrass, J. E. "A Pioneer Editor." *Atlantic Monthly* 17 (June 1866): 749.

Southworth, E.D.E.N. "Ch. IX: Shipwreck." In *The Island Princess: A Romance of the Old and New World*. *New York Ledger* 13, no. 16 (June 27, 1857): 1–2.

———. "Ch. XV: The Girl Captain." In *The Island Princess: A Romance of the Old and New World. New York Ledger* 13, no. 19 (July 18, 1857): 5–6.

———. "From Washington. Mrs. Southworth's Letter, Washington City, Jan. 24, 1850." *Pittsburgh Saturday Visiter* (Pittsburgh, PA), February 2, 1850.

———. "Leaves from Shannondale, Number II." *Saturday Evening Post* (Philadelphia, PA), July 26, 1851, 1.

———. "Leaves from Shannondale, Number III." *Saturday Evening Post* (Philadelphia, PA), August 2, 1851, 1.

———. "Leaves from Shannondale, Number IV." *Saturday Evening Post* (Philadelphia, PA), August 16, 1851, 1.

———. "Leaves from Shannondale, Number V." *Saturday Evening Post* (Philadelphia, PA), August 23, 1851, 1.

———. "Leaves from Shannondale: Stage Coaches—Monroe's Residence—Braddock's Road—Gen. Morgan—Young Washington—Celebrities—Shannondale." *Saturday Evening Post* (Philadelphia, PA), July 19, 1851, 1.

———. "Leaves from Shannondale, 'The Tourney.'" *Saturday Evening Post* (Philadelphia, PA), September 27, 1851, 1.

———. "Letters from Shannondale Springs." *Virginia Free Press* (Charleston, VA), August 23, 1850, 2.

———. "Mrs. Southworth's Letter, Washington City, Jan. 24, 1850." *Pittsburgh Saturday Visiter* (Pittsburgh, PA), February 9, 1850.

———. "Washington Letters—#1, Washington City, Thursday, January [*sic*] 7, 1850." *Pittsburgh Saturday Visiter* (Pittsburgh, PA), February 16, 1850.

———. "With Lady Byron: Mrs. Southworth's Memorable Visit to the Poet's Widow." *Evening Star* (Washington, DC), October 25, 1890, 13.

Stoddard, Charles Warren. "Mrs. Emma D.E.N. Southworth at Prospect Cottage, an Old Sweetheart of Mine." *National Magazine* 22 (1905): 179–91.

T. H. Y. "Biographical Sketch of the Author." In *The Haunted Homestead, and Other Novelettes, with an Autobiography of the Author*, by E.D.E.N. Southworth, 29–42. Philadelphia, PA: Peterson, 1860.

Welter, Barbara. "The Cult of True Womanhood: 1820–1860." *American Quarterly* 18 (Summer 1966): 151–75.

Whittier, John Greenleaf. "Barbara Frietchie." *Atlantic Monthly: A Magazine of Literature, Art, and Politics* 12, no. 72 (October 1863): 495–97.

Whittle, Gilberta S. "Mrs. Southworth and Her Novels: How Her Famous Literary Career Was Begun." *Times* (Philadelphia, PA), October 28, 1894, 12.

———. "Traits of Two Authors: Richard Malcolm Johnston and Mrs. E.D.E.N. Southworth." *Times* (Philadelphia, PA), June 4, 1893, 22.

Wilson, J. Ormond. "Eighty Years of the Public Schools of Washington—1805 to 1885." *Records of the Columbia Historical Society* 1 (October 30, 1896): 119–70.

Windle, Mary J. "Summer Sketches—No. 1." *Southern Press* (Washington, DC), July 19, 1851, 4.

———. "Summer Sketches—No. 2." *Southern Press* (Washington, DC), July 23, 1851, 4.

———. "Summer Sketches—No. 6." *Southern Press* (Washington, DC), August 5, 1851, 2.

———. "Summer Sketches—No. 8." *Southern Press* (Washington, DC), August 14, 1851, 2.

Periodicals

Alexandria Gazette (VA)
American Telegraph (DC)
Anti-Slavery Bugle (OH)
Baltimore Sun (MD)
Biblical Recorder (NC)
Boston Courier
Boston Traveller
Chicago Tribune
Daily Madison (DC)
Daily National Intelligencer (DC)
Daily News (NY)
Era (London)
Evening Star (DC)
Evening Post (NY)
Grant County Witness (WI)
Green Mountain Freeman (VT)
Guardian (London)
International Monthly Magazine of Literature
Kansas City Times (MO)
Lancaster Intelligencer (PA)
Literary World
Liverpool Mercury (UK)
Lloyd's Weekly (London)
London Journal and Weekly Record of Literature, Science, and Art
Louisville Daily Courier (KY)
Morning Post (London)
Natchez Weekly Courier (MS)
National Era (DC)
National Intelligencer (DC)
National Intelligencer and Washington Advertiser (DC)
National Republican (DC)
Native American (DC)
New York Ledger
New York Times
New York Herald
New York Tribune
Northern Badger (WI)
Peru Miami County Sentinel (IN)
Pittsburgh Saturday Visiter (PA)
Platteville Witness (WI)
Representative (WI)
Richmond Dispatch (VA)
Sandusky Register (OH)
Saturday Evening Post (PA)
Sonoma County Journal (CA)
Southern Literary Messenger
Southern Quarterly Review
Star of Freedom (UK)
Sun (NY)
Sunday Star (DC)
Telegraph and Daily Advertiser (MD)
Times (PA)
Times Picayune (LA)
Times Union (NY)
Vermont Journal
Vicksburg Daily Whig (MS)
Virginia Free Press
Washington Globe
Washington Post
Washington Times (DC)
Washington Union (DC)
Winfield Courier (KS)
Wisconsin State Journal
Yonkers Gazette (NY)
Yonkers Statesman (NY)

Index

About the Author

Courtesy of Kimber Brown Photography

After more than twelve years of researching American author E.D.E.N. Southworth, **Rose Neal, PhD**, is one of the preeminent scholars on the author's work and life. In 2012, she finished her master's thesis on Southworth before embarking on a doctorate in literature from Swansea University in Wales, where she successfully defended her dissertation on Southworth's impact on female education. Dr. Neal has also presented numerous academic papers about the author at professional conferences and libraries. While researching and writing about Southworth's fifty-plus novels, Dr. Neal also discovered that the novelist lived a fascinating life that spanned most of the nineteenth century—a story that Dr. Neal believed needed to be told. After more than twenty years teaching at both the high school and the university levels, Dr. Neal retired and is now devoting herself full time to a second career as a writer. In addition to her love of research and storytelling, she enjoys traveling with her husband, Chris, and spending time in her garden. She lives in Oklahoma City, Oklahoma.

husmor. Så langt foreldrenes midler tillot, fikk jeg alt fra leker til sykler og lignende. Om sommeren dro jeg til et gjestehus i det sørlige Niederösterreich hvert år sammen med min bror og min mor i to til tre uker. Min far, siden han av økonomiske årsaker måtte jobbe i uken, kom til oss på fredag med moped og ble til søndag. Det skal bemerkes at min far først tok førerkortet i 1972. På den tiden ble jeg også kjent med en familie som bodde i nærheten av pensjonatet. Det var to døtre i denne, den ene fem år yngre og den andre ett år eldre. Betyr at den eldre allerede har møtt meg med bleier.

September 1966 skole

Starten på min skolekarriere. På barneskolen gikk jeg i en gutteklasse. En utdannet ved daværende Pädag presenterte seg som lærer. Hun var rundt 25 år gammel og en vakker kvinne så vidt jeg kunne se på den alderen. Jeg kan fortsatt huske en anekdote som sjokkerte meg ganske mye på den tiden. I begynnelsen av skoletiden kom jeg til mamma og fortalte henne følgende: Du, mor, læreren malte fingrene hennes knallrøde. Hvordan kan du gjøre noe sånt? Bakgrunnen var at lærer Ulrike kun hadde malt neglene, noe som ennå ikke var vanlig for meg på den tiden. Jeg tror moren min snudde seg til siden den gangen og sannsynligvis måtte smile, for så å forklarte meg hva det dreide seg om. Vel, jeg gikk ut av barneskolen med veldig gode karakterer, bortsett fra å male og tegne. Men jeg hadde også respekt for «lærerinnen», som straffet lovbrudd med å «stå i hjørnet». Skoleveien, den gang var alt fortsatt til fots, var alltid en utfordring, for det var alltid en, to eller tre skolekolleger som man kunne sjonglere med på fortauet.

September 1970 videregående skole

Etter at jeg fortsatte å drømme om drømmejobben "lege" i denne alderen og grunnskolebeviset mitt var tilsvarende, registrerte foreldrene mine meg i nabodistriktet på videregående skole. I 1969 hadde faren min returnert handelsbevillingen for reparasjon av brusflasker fordi det ikke lenger var lønnsomt, og han vendte seg deretter til en ny jobb, nemlig å selge dagsaviser. Det betyr at han solgte den største avisen i landet vårt som kolportør på kveldstid til ca kl 23 på stand. Siden dette var halvveis lønnsomt begynte også mamma å selge aviser. Med dette kunne de spare seg for mye penger i årenes løp, vi begge, altså min bror og jeg, trivselen ble ikke forsømt. Vel, nå gikk jeg i første klasse på den humanistiske videregående skolen. På mandager var det alltid matte og engelsk etter hverandre. Vel, det gikk halvveis en stund, men etter en stund ble jeg syk og foreldrene mine skrev en bekreftelse til meg på at jeg var syk. Men siden lærerstaben ikke tok denne oppgaven fra meg, beholdt jeg den. Nå ble mandag med engelsk og matte mer og mer motbydelig for meg, så jeg fikk ideen om å gå "blå" på en eller annen mandag og ikke gå på skolen. Jeg fremla deretter bekreftelsen på at jeg var syk selv med foreldrenes underskrift. Siden det stort sett var de samme sykdommene og signaturen ikke lenger var den beste, ble det som det måtte. Plutselig fikk foreldrene mine en innkalling om å komme til skolen. Selvfølgelig ble de spurt om mine manglende dager og de resulterende karakterene, og de ble følgelig overrasket eller skuffet over meg. Konsekvensen av dette var at skolen dømte meg til en "katastrofe" (4 timers skrivestraff alene på skolen). Så vidt jeg vet, eksisterer ikke denne typen straff lenger i dag. Til slutt ble skoleåret avsluttet med to femmere. Så det betyr at jeg måtte gjenta 1. klasse, da det da fortsatt var påkrevd.

September 1971 internatskole

Etter denne avgjørende hendelsen for meg møttes familierådet i form av foreldrene mine og min sytten år gamle bror. Det måtte sendes på forhånd at min far var på en tysktalende internatskole noen år i skoletiden i Serbia. Dermed ble det gitt råd om hvilken skole jeg skulle fortsette å gå på. Siden jeg selvfølgelig i en alder av 11 ikke ante eller bare begrenset hva som ventet meg, måtte jeg godta avgjørelsen fra familierådet. Siden jeg ble døpt protestantisk fra fødselen av, ble min registrering ved katolske internatskoler, for eksempel skolebrødre i Strebersdorf, ikke akseptert. Denne avgjørelsen innebar at jeg gikk på internat i 13. krets, som også omfattet en humanistisk grammatikkskole. Jeg kranglet lenge med denne avgjørelsen fra mine foreldres side, fordi jeg var mer eller mindre innelåst der fra søndag kveld til lørdag middag. Hvis jeg hadde "knust" noe i løpet av uken, ble det selvfølgelig ikke noe utfall i helgen heller. Heldigvis var det sjelden slik i 13. distrikt. En ting var interessant i dette huset, fordi lederen av denne institusjonen var barnebarnet til Adalbert Stifter (navnet hans var det samme). Denne regissøren var en ivrig piperøyker, hvor røyken kunne luktes over hele bygningen, og med økende intensitet visste vi at faren var overhengende. Jeg var 3 år på Himmelhof, det var slik internatet der het. Så flyttet jeg til internatet med samme navn i 2. distrikt med samme lærer Franz. Men skikken der var den samme som i 13. distrikt. Det betyr at dersom det var uredelighet fra min side i løpet av uken, fikk jeg ufrivillig tilbringe helgen med straff på internatet. Siden tilsynet der ikke var særlig stort og jeg selvfølgelig også har blitt eldre, ble det ofte helger på internatet. På den tiden, 13 år gammel, ble jeg kjent med sigaretter, noe som også resulterte i at jeg ble tvunget til å bli i hjemmet. Dette vennskapet med nikotin har fulgt meg til i dag. Det hele gikk rimelig greit opp til 4. klasse og så fikk vi en Kärntenlærer i biologi som nettopp var ferdig med studiene. For oss elever mellom 14 og 15 år var hun selvfølgelig en utfordring i forhold til puberteten, for hun var en pen kvinne med tilsvarende figur. Så jeg lot meg rive med til ett utsagn i løpet av leksjonen som ga meg den dårligste oppførselskarakteren. I tillegg samlet jeg også de dårligste karakterene i ulike objekter, slik at jeg måtte gjenta 4. klasse. Dette hadde lykkes og siden dette ikke lenger ble undervist i huset, måtte jeg gå i 5. klasse på den humanistiske grammatikkskolen i nabodistriktet. Siden jeg fortsatt ønsket å bli lege, antok jeg at jeg ville bruke gammelgresk, da jeg også likte det latinske språket veldig godt. Det var interessant på den tiden at jeg havnet i en blandingsklasse for første gang, men det var bare 6 jenter og resten av guttene. Det første semesteret var jeg fortsatt litt ivrig etter å lære, men siden jeg ikke likte gammelgresk i det hele tatt, så karakterene deretter ut. Det stoppet ikke med dette faget alene, så jeg ville ha måttet gjenta timen, bare det var ikke lenger mulig på den tiden. Så foreldrene mine bestemte, siden jeg nå var 17 år gammel, at jeg skulle begynne i lære. Da jeg var rundt 16, da jeg fortsatt gikk på internat, ble jeg oppsøkt av Ernst, som var sønn av en venninne av min mor, om jeg kanskje ikke ville gå på folkedans hver fredagskveld. Det var selvfølgelig en vanskelig oppgave på internatet, da det ikke alltid var slik at man skulle ut derfra. Til slutt fikk jeg lov til å gå ut på fredag fra 18.00 til 22.00. Folkedansen fant sted i Donau-schwabernes hjem i 3. distrikt. Da jeg først kom dit, fant jeg rundt 30 unge menn og kvinner, hvorav jeg var en av de yngste. En innfødt Donau-schwaber presenterte seg for meg som lederen, som øvde på folkedansene med oss. Men siden jeg var et desidert anti-talent når det kom til dans, hadde denne mannen også vanskeligheter med å lære meg det. Jeg kan fortsatt huske en episode der veilederen tok låret mitt i hånden fordi jeg ikke forsto rekkefølgen av et vekslende trinn. Sannsynligvis har ingenting endret seg på det til i dag. På disse kveldene studerte vi folkedanser med 8 til 10 par, som vi så fremførte i ballsesongen i januar og februar. I løpet av tiden utviklet det seg en gruppe mennesker på samme alder som gikk på bowling to ganger i uken i Wien Prater. Det betyr trening en gang i uken og mesterskap på fredag. Siden vi hadde en sponsor, et rederi, kostet det oss ikke så mye. Rundt 1982 seilte 7 menn og kvinner med dette selskapet på et 10-manns seilskip fra Split til Dubrovnik om sommeren. Hver dag den uken dro vi til en øy, tok en pause og kjørte så videre. Det var en fantastisk opplevelse

<u>August 1972 helgehus</u>

Etter at min fars karriereskifte i 1969 var vellykket i form av sparing, klarte de å spare seg selv for en del penger. Nå gikk foreldrene mine på jakt etter et lite helgehus i Niederösterreich. De fant det de lette etter i det sørlige Wien-bassenget i en kommune med rundt 10 000 innbyggere. Det første synet slo foreldrene mine som et røverkjøp, men de kunne ikke forestille seg hva som kom etterpå. For meg som 12-åring var det selvfølgelig en fornøyelse, for det var masse frukttrær og busker på eiendommen som jeg fikk brenne etter å ha saget av, slik at bygningen fra 1930 også kunne sees. Jeg kan huske at brenningen etter en stund plaget naboene litt, på den tiden var dette fortsatt lov. Men ja, vi var «wiener» som kom til Niederösterreich for å utvide. Vel, trærne og buskene ble eliminert, og du kunne se huset. Den hadde den ulempen at den ikke hadde vært brukt på årevis og sto derfor i en øde tilstand med gulv og loft. Da jeg hadde brent alt tok jeg sykkelen og utforsket området med fjellene som hørte til og måtte kjøre forbi en arbeiderboplass gang på gang. En dag spurte en fyr som nettopp var der meg om jeg kunne gå av sykkelen og sette meg ned med ham. Jeg gjorde som han hadde bedt om og satte meg ned med ham. Så kom flere gutter og en interessant samtale utviklet seg. Fra dette møtet utviklet det seg et vennskap i minst ti år, og vi gjorde noe annerledes hver helg. Først i løpet av årene ble partnerne med, hver av disse vennene flyttet et annet sted i Niederösterreich og vennskapene ble oppløst.

Hus etter oppussing

1972 første kyss

Siden foreldrene mine alltid ønsket å reise på ferie om sommeren, spurte de den evangeliske kirken i Wien om at hele familien hadde samme tro. Dette resulterte i ferier med hele familien i Steiermark. Vi var ikke den eneste familien der, det var rundt 50 personer. Vi gjorde hver dag med alle utflukter og fotturer som alltid var hyggelig.

En dag, vi kom tilbake fra en utflukt litt tidligere, snakket Angela med meg, hun var omtrent ett år yngre enn meg. Hun sa at hun hadde oppdaget et hornet-rede på loftet i huset der vi bodde og at hun var redd for å se på den igjen alene, om jeg skulle bli med deg. Vel, hvorfor ikke, ingenting kan skje. Da vi sto foran dette redet snudde hun seg plutselig og kysset meg på leppene. Jeg ble forskrekket, det var bare mamma som fikk gjøre det og ingen andre fikk gjøre det. Men jeg holdt det for meg selv likevel.

Vintersalg 1975

Siden broren min ville tjene noe i tillegg til lønnen som bankfunksjonær, kjørte han fra en restaurant til en annen i 10. distrikt og solgte den største dagsavisen der. Men siden vi var ett hjerte og en sjel til han var rundt 20, sa han at jeg kunne selge aviser og kjøpe lommepengene mine. For å gjøre dette sto jeg i en gågate i 10. distrikt iført gul jakke og roste avisene mine. Vi gjorde så opp regnskapet for de 10 til 15 avisene om kvelden. Var ikke særlig lønnsomt, men lommepengene mine ble som sagt økt.

September 1977 læretid

Min far kjente HR-sjefen til en stor dagligvaregrossist og produsent i 16. distrikt, som var velkjent på den tiden, og derfor begynte jeg i lære som kontormedarbeider. Det første jeg gjorde var å jobbe med engrosregnskap. Jeg fant fire menn der på 50 år og der borte. Avdelingsleder for dette var underskriver. Men siden jeg nettopp hadde kommet ut av internatet før, nøt jeg min gjenvunne frihet. Dette viste seg ved at jeg ikke var så streng med å få en natts søvn på fritiden. Det betyr at nå som jeg hadde en venn i Wien ved navn Ernst, dro vi nesten hver kveld om kvelden. Det var selvfølgelig sent å reise hjem. Så min arbeidsprestasjon den påfølgende dagen var tilsvarende. Daglig leder, som jeg satt med ryggen til, banket på bordet gang på gang med kulepennen slik at jeg kunne jobbe videre. I løpet av tiden ble imidlertid arbeidet med å bare legge til 100 til 200 følgesedler på en hel dag for kjedelig for meg, og derfor bestemte jeg meg for å snakke med sjefen min om hvorvidt jeg kunne overføres til en annen avdeling i gruppen. Min forespørsel ble innvilget og jeg ble overført til teavdelingen. Der møtte jeg en ung ekspeditør og sjefen hans var autorisert underskriver. Her lærte jeg ikke så mye om kontoristen, men den gamle sjefen lærte meg mye om te. Så jeg måtte sette opp tesmakingen hver morgen, som gikk gjennom et helt spesielt ritual: Så jeg startet med å sette opp minst 10 boller med varmt vann og lot så bare tilsette nøyaktig 2 gram te. Så gikk herren gjennom og tok en slurk av hver bolle, holdt den i munnen og lot den renne over smaksløkene. Med denne håndteringen var han i stand til å bestemme kvaliteten på denne teen og deretter ble den tilsvarende kvantiteten bestilt. I løpet av arbeidet mitt på denne avdelingen ble det lagt til et automatisk system for produksjon av teposer, noe som fascinerte meg veldig, for på den ene siden var teen som ble levert i store bokser og til slutt de ferdige 20-25 teposene kom pakket ut. Men siden det var begrenset hva jeg kunne lære, ville jeg tilbake til en ny avdeling og derfor kom jeg til ferskvareavdelingen da jeg var rundt 18 år. Derfra ble frukt- og grønnsaksleveransene til de 250 filialene forberedt daglig. For å gjøre dette måtte de enkelte butikkene selvfølgelig ta imot bestillinger på telefon hver dag. Siden jeg allerede hadde nådd alderen hvor jeg fikk jobbe overtid etter ungdomsvernloven meldte jeg meg på søndagsgudstjenester som ble belønnet deretter. Kollegene mine var ganske mye på min alder, så det ble snart vennskap. Så nå og da dro vi for å ta en drink etter søndagsarbeidet, helt til noen sa han hadde med seg noe som bare kunne inntas i lukkede rom. Naiv som jeg var den gang, gikk vi inn i en leilighet og satte oss på gulvet i mangel av seter. Plutselig tok nevnte kollega en sigarett opp av lommen, tente den og ga den videre. Intetanende trakk jeg, som de andre, til seg denne antatte sigaretten. Da den så røk ut fikk jeg beskjed om at dette var en joint. Min oppsummering av det var bra, min godtroenhet og fremfor alt, jeg hadde ikke følt noe, så saken var avgjort for meg og jeg rørte aldri noe sånt igjen.

September 1978 Første leilighet

Etter at broren min i en alder av rundt 21 år hadde sagt at han ikke lenger ville ha kone og at han allerede hadde sin egen leilighet, fikk jeg den lille leiligheten på rundt 35 kvadratmeter i samme hus der foreldrene mine bodde i Wien. På denne tiden begynte imidlertid også hvor jeg måtte slite i ca 30 år. På den ene siden hadde jeg engangsvenner i helgen i Niederösterreich og en venn i Wien. Med sistnevnte gikk jeg ut nesten hver dag i uken, og slik ble det til at vi ikke gjorde så mye forskjellig. Vi gikk da mest på barer hvor man kunne spille kort. Men siden dette ble litt kjedelig over tid, bestemte vi oss for å spille for penger. Men det var heller ikke tilfredsstillende, og derfor så vi maskiner i lokale automater hvor du kunne sette inn penger og vinne. På den tiden ble de kalt enarmede banditter som man kunne finne over hele Østerrike. Ja, i begynnelsen var det alltid mindre eller større overskudd, men i tidens løp ble det selvsagt underskudd. Fremfor alt oppdaget jeg at slike enheter også var tilgjengelige i Niederösterreich. Og så begynte avhengigheten min, absolutt ikke med en gang, men i løpet av tiden hadde jeg krysset en grense som jeg ikke var klar over.

Mai 1978 fargeblindhet

På den tiden måtte jeg gå til de østerrikske væpnede styrker for utkast. På den tiden hadde jeg ingen helseplager, men så ble det presentert et kort med forskjellige fargede prikker og jeg ble bedt om å lese et tall og en bokstav fra det. Men jeg klarte ikke dette, selv om jeg så på kartene fra forskjellige vinkler. Det ble med andre ord funnet ut at jeg er fargeblind, nemlig rød-grønn-blind. Kommisjonen har imidlertid bestemt at jeg ville være fullt ut kvalifisert. Et halvt år senere ønsket jeg å ta motorsykkel- og bilførerkortet sammen med faren min. For å gjøre dette måtte jeg også tåle en test. Jeg fikk blant annet presentert et annet fargekort som jeg ikke kunne lese noe fra igjen. Da sa de at jeg måtte gjennom ytterligere undersøkelser, inkludert reaksjonsprøve hos respektive forstanderskap og psykologisk prøve i 3. distrikt Denne psykologiske prøven var på ca 20 sider og den var kjedelig å fylle ut fordi jeg ikke lagde følelse av det. Argumentet mitt, som jeg også ga uttrykk for, var at jeg er fullt kvalifisert og jeg har ikke lov til å ha førerkort, ja da skyter jeg deg bare fordi jeg ikke klarer å velge mellom rødt og grønt. Så vidt jeg vet er det bare det røde ved lyskrysset som alltid er på samme sted. Jeg har endelig fått førerkort for minst en bil, jeg ga fra meg den for motorsykkel, selv om jeg hadde 2 mopeder da jeg var 16 og 17, og jeg har aldri hatt noen ulykker med dem.

Oktober 1980 føderale hær

I begynnelsen av oktober avtjente jeg min militærtjeneste hos det østerrikske forsvaret i Martinek-kasernen (pensjon?). De første seks ukene var grunnleggende trening og også utmattende. Da jeg hadde bursdag i begynnelsen av desember, var jeg på vakt, av alle ting, og det på en helligdag. Det betyr at rundt 15 personer hadde fått utdelt 20 skudd med skarp ammunisjon for hver av vakten på vakt. Nå måtte jeg sitte ved bordet og vente på at det skulle komme en ordre, si å gå rundt i brakkene. Jeg vet ikke hvordan, men plutselig sto det en 2 liters flaske med hvitvin på bordet og kameratene mine heiet meg til bursdagen min. Ja, men det var dessverre ikke den eneste flasken vi spiste. Det betyr at under neste runde med kontroller i brakkeområdet ble stien smalere og smalere og på slutten måtte jeg losse rifla med 20 skudd skarp ammunisjon i smutthullene. Jeg hadde ikke klart dette selv, en kamerat hjalp meg. Det hele forble ustraffet bortsett fra en tvangsrapport med følgende formaning. Etter de første seks ukene ble jeg tildelt pressevaktens kontor. Denne majoren var der om morgenen, men forlot så kontoret og kom tilbake en time før arbeidsslutt. Min jobb der var å lete etter reportasjer om suverenen i de ulike dagsavisene. Det var ikke en tidkrevende oppgave, den ble fullført ganske raskt. Så jeg klarte å ta igjen det jeg hadde veldig lite i løpet av natten, nemlig søvn. Da jeg flyttet inn i oktober var jeg 65 kilo fordelt på lengden min. I området rundt brakken ble jeg kjent med Baden-vin fordi jeg ikke hadde kjent det før. Da jeg avvæpnet etter 8 måneder veide jeg ikke 65, men 72 kilo, som jeg ikke hadde overskredet før i dag.

<u>September 1980 yrke</u>

Jeg hadde fullført læretiden min som kontorist, militærtjenesten mindre vellykket, og så tenkte jeg med meg selv hvordan jeg skulle gå videre. Nå ble jeg interessert i kveldskurs og begynte på regnskapsførerkurs, noe som snart viste seg å være feil for meg. Så jeg fant ut at datamaskiner hadde en fremtid, og fra 1980 til 1981 tok jeg programmeringskurs på WIFI Wien, som gikk hver kveld fra 18.00 til 22.00. Jeg fullførte dette med eksamen i hvert fall i Pascal, i Cobol besto jeg ikke. Med sertifikatene mente jeg at jeg hadde bedre sjanser på arbeidsmarkedet og i slutten av august 1981 sa jeg opp jobben hos dagligvaregrossisten. Jeg fikk straks jobb igjen som kontorist i en bedrift som produserte rør og koblingsbokser, som lå i 5. distrikt. Etter omtrent et år flyttet vi til 11. distrikt, hvor fabrikken til dette selskapet også lå. Der hadde jeg en sympatisk eldre bedriftsutdannet som hadde prøvd igjen og igjen å inspirere meg. Men da han ble pensjonist, kom en kvinnelig sivilingeniør som hans etterfølger. Dette hadde som mål å gjøre innsparinger og slik kom det til at jeg fikk sparken etter to år og ni måneder. Den gang var det fortsatt sluttvederlag med minst to lønninger, men først etter tre år i selskapet. Så jeg måtte se meg om etter en ny jobb og fant ut om det i dagsavisene. Så fant jeg en jobb der forhåndsutvalget ble gjort i et testpsykologisk institutt. Så jeg kom til dette instituttet i begynnelsen av mai 1984 og ble presentert med en bunt på 20 sider med tester å fylle ut. Etter å ha skrevet et par oppføringer i denne avisen, tenkte jeg for meg selv at jeg allerede hadde holdt disse arkene i hånden. Og akkurat sånn var det, år tidligere måtte jeg ta samme prøve for å få førerkort og den dagen for å søke jobb. Høres litt rart ut. Etter å ha vurdert informasjonen min, ble jeg bedt om et intervju i 8. distrikt. Forutsetningen for denne stillingen var at det kun var en ettårig foreldrepermisjonsvikar. Der måtte jeg redegjøre for stipendiaterne som jobbet ved forskningssenteret i Niederösterreich og også passe på bankboken. Men siden det hele var litt for liten utfordring for meg, siktet jeg meg inn på videre oppgaver. Disse inkluderte økonomi, budsjett og aktivaregnskap. Dataspråkene jeg hadde lært, som jeg hadde tilegnet meg mange år før, ble ikke brukt fordi dette ble forhindret av den eksisterende "programmereren". Så det første året med svangerskapspermisjon gikk mot slutten og min daværende sjef, som jeg nå hadde en stein i styret med, forlenget kontrakten uten å nøle. Men siden kontoret i 8. distrikt ble stengt rundt et år etter at vi begynte i dette selskapet (halvoffentlige), måtte vi flytte til Niederösterreich. Vi hadde muligheten til å bruke firmabussen fra Wien. Men arbeidet startet ikke før klokken 08.30, og det var for sent for meg. Så jeg snakket med en kollega om at vi skulle kjøre til jobb sammen med min andre bil. Derved bidro hun til reiseutgiftene. Det betyr å stå opp av sengen hver arbeidsdag kl. 06.00, kjøre 35 km ut og 35 km tilbake om kvelden, uansett vær. Men siden jeg i det hele tatt verdsatte dette arbeidet i Niederösterreich, aksepterte jeg det. Tiden jeg tilbrakte der var ikke bare profesjonelt, men også personlig det erfaringsrike arbeidet jeg hadde i livet mitt, spesielt siden jeg hadde lært mye av det. Innen regnskap var det navnet på avdelingen der jeg jobbet, det var rundt 15 kvinner og kun 2 menn, noe som i utgangspunktet påvirket meg mindre. Gjennom årene ble jeg imidlertid venner med en kollega som jobbet to rom unna. Hun var omtrent 2 år yngre og ganske smart, bodde i nærheten av arbeidet sitt sammen med foreldrene i et to-familiehus. Etter hvert som det måtte komme, ble det mer vennskap. Mesteparten av tiden bodde jeg hjemme hos henne, men fortsatte å gå tilbake til leiligheten min i Wien. Så en dag fortalte hun meg at hun var gravid med meg. Jeg var da rundt 26 år gammel og han så det som min plikt å fri til henne fordi hun takket ja. Vi var allerede på utkikk etter en kirke eller et registerkontor og satte mer eller mindre en dato for bryllupet. I selskapet ryktes det selvfølgelig i det skjulte at det var noe på gang som jeg egentlig ikke likte. Men siden det fra hennes side kun var erklæringen om graviditet og jeg ikke kunne se eller høre noe annet i løpet av månedene, ble jeg skeptisk til om dette ville være sant. Nå ble i tillegg «presset» fra kollegene større og større. Så på slutten av 1987 bestemte jeg meg for å si opp stillingen min etter tre og et halvt år og la henne ta forrang i selskapet fordi hennes kvalifikasjoner var mindre enn mine. Det ble selvfølgelig heller ikke oppgjør på to lønninger, siden jeg selv hadde sagt opp. Jeg sjekket den påståtte graviditeten til kjæresten min den gangen en tid senere, men hun var nok aldri gravid. Jeg var lei meg for denne stillingen fordi jeg hadde lært mye, selv om forholdene ikke alltid var de beste.

Januar 1988 ansatt hos far

Siden faren min var 58 år i år, bestemte jeg meg for å begynne å jobbe for ham som kontorist, noe som betyr at jeg var mer eller mindre selvstendig næringsdrivende på dette tidspunktet, fordi en far ikke kan gjøre for mye for sønnen sin. Siden jeg hadde bokføring på fagskolen, bestemte vi at vi skulle gjøre bokføringen selv. Vår skatterådgiver hadde kun i oppgave å utarbeide respektive selvangivelse eller balanse og levere den til skattekontoret. I 1989 sa denne skatterådgiveren at et beløp på 0,25 S på balansen bare var et Mikke Mus-beløp og derfor var irrelevant. Så vi sa opp kontrakten vår med ham og for de neste årene utarbeidet jeg selvangivelsen og den resulterende balansen. Den eneste ulempen med dette var selvfølgelig at jeg ikke hadde noen erfaring med dette. Så året etter fikk jeg et brev fra ansvarlig skattekontor. Da jeg åpnet den, leste jeg et krav på 1,5 millioner schilling på etterskudd. Heldigvis satt jeg da jeg åpnet dette brevet. Jeg gjorde en kommafeil mens jeg fylte ut det relevante skjemaet. Etter ca 4 til 5 avtaler, rettet jeg det. I løpet av denne tiden hadde jeg rundt 100 kolportører (kunder) som jeg måtte levere hver dag, svært få hadde tid til å komme til våre forretningslokaler i 20. distrikt. For å forklare en kolportør var en person som solgte dagsaviser om kvelden eller om morgenen med fargede jakker på torg, togstasjoner og gater. For meg ble de alltid ansett for å være uavhengige kjøpmenn. Det betyr at de kjøpte blader av meg, det vil si periodiske trykksaker, til en viss rabatt og deretter solgte dem til en fast sluttpris som er spesifisert på hvert produkt. Ulempen med denne bransjen er at det er 100 prosent returrett. Hvis en kunde kjøpte 10 stykker av et magasin av meg og bare solgte 5 av dem, kunne han returnere de resterende 5 stykkene til meg når magasinet var nytt og disse ble deretter motregnet. Jeg hadde selvfølgelig også rett til mine leverandører, som grossister og forlag. Det hele var selvsagt forbundet med enorm tid og fremfor alt med en presis kontroll av de respektive fakturaene. En 50 til 60 timers uke var altså ikke unntaket, men snarere regelen.

september 1992 selvstendig næringsdrivende Faren min var allerede 62 år i år, og jeg måtte argumentere for ham mange ganger om at han endelig hadde begynt å pensjonere seg etter 47 års innsats. Det ville ikke gitt ham særlig mye økonomisk. Så jeg overtok denne bladgrossisten med to handelslisenser, det var ingen annen vei den gang. Betyr to medlemskap i kammerdivisjonen og, som et resultat, to avgifter for det. Så to til tre år senere dukket det opp en konkurrent. Denne herr Robin fikk muligheten til å sette opp sin egen kolportasje fra en mindre dagsavis. Han forsynte med andre ord flere utenlandske personer med jakker og dagsaviser og distribuerte disse menneskene over hele Wien. I tidens løp erfarte jeg imidlertid at denne mannen ikke ga plassene fri til folket, men krevde innskudd i 5 til 6-sifrede skillingsbeløp fra hver enkelt og det allerede før en plass ble tildelt ham. Siden dette, så vidt jeg vet, kun var skrevet svært sparsomt skriftlig, mistenkte jeg allerede på dette tidspunktet at dette ville gå galt på et tidspunkt. Siden dette ikke bekymret meg så mye, lot jeg ham styre. Så en dag kom han bort til meg og sa at vi kunne gjøre motforretninger, noe jeg ikke hadde noe imot. Jeg fikk blader fra noen wienske forlag på gode vilkår, og det var ikke veldig annerledes med ham. Dette gikk bra en stund, han leverte til meg, jeg til han og det ble utlignet. Men en dag, det var ikke så mye å få tak i, telefonen ringte og Robin var på linjen. Han sa at jeg fortsatt skyldte ham noe og at han ville kreve det. Det gjorde meg så rasende at jeg sa at jeg takket nei til forespørselen min og ikke ønsket å høre fra ham mer. Ja, det var bare mitt ønske. Han ansatte flere og flere arabere, pakistanere og indere og dro til slutt til mine to hovedleverandører. Bakgrunnen for dette er at da jeg begynte å jobbe i magasingrossist, snakket jeg med disse to leverandørene for å få den 4,9 % høyere rabatten. Det betyr i stedet for 28,2 % den høyeste med 33,1 % brutto. Min forespørsel om det forble ubesvart selv da jeg kjørte til hovedkontoret til en leverandør i Salzburg, da hadde jeg oppnådd rabattøkningen omtrent 10 år senere. Mr Robin gikk til disse to leverandørene med hva som helst og hadde umiddelbart den høyere rabatten, hvilken sammenheng var tydelig for meg, men jeg vil ikke gi denne fra meg.

Næringslokaler i 20. krets med far

November 1988

Jeg var nå 28 år gammel, vennene mine i Niederösterreich hadde delt seg over hele forbundsstaten, dels av faglige grunner og dels av hensyn til partnerskap, så jeg var alene. Nok en gang var det en så kjedelig lørdag, og da gikk tanken opp for meg at det bodde to jenter der 30 kilometer unna, som jeg allerede kjente fra barndommen min da jeg tilbrakte sommeren med min bror og mor i Niederösterreich. Så jeg satte meg i bilen og kjørte til denne byen med 800 mennesker. Jeg fant ikke bare to jenter, men tre. Venninnen til den eldre kvinnen var på besøk. Etter kort tid kom jeg med forslaget om at vi kunne danse. Venninnen sa at hun var sliten og måtte reise hjem til mannen sin. Så jeg hadde de to igjen og etter litt tid med sminke og styling var tiden kommet. Vi kjørte bilen min ca 60 kilometer til nabodistriktet, det var veldig lite i området i denne forbindelse. Vel, nå satt jeg der på diskoteket med to jenter, den ene fem år yngre og ikke nødvendigvis pen, og den andre, ett år eldre og ganske "oppkledd". Nå hadde jeg ikke noe annet valg enn å veksle mellom å danse med den ene og så med den andre, og det for meg, da jeg var en så dyktig danser. I løpet av kvelden, det var allerede etter midnatt, den 13. november, da jeg satt ved bordet, la jeg merke til at det ene kneet stadig støtet inn i mitt og deretter ble liggende. Jeg tror de neste dansene fullførte tilnærmingen til de eldre og det kom som det måtte komme. Det var fantastisk. Dette varte da i godt 20 år.

Høsten 1995

Siden konkurrenten min ble mer og mer aggressiv med hensyn til salg av aviser og magasiner, og han tydde til høyere rabatter for sine kolportører, måtte jeg også reagere. Heldigvis hadde jeg noen østerrikske forlag på den tiden som jeg kunne leve av, for på det tidspunktet var det i hvert fall ingenting å gjøre med de nevnte grossistene. Dette kom til uttrykk i at jeg kun kunne selge varene mine i hemmelighet, for hver gang jeg kom til kundene mine – og det har de vært i årevis – var det alltid en araber som kunne bli tildelt Robin-selskapet, med min kjøper og dermed forhindret mitt salg. Så jeg måtte få magasinene mine for salg i en rundkjøring, fordi kjøperen av varene mine ville ha lidd økonomiske ulemper hvis de ble sett å kjøpe fra meg. Men siden intellektet til disse tilsynsorganene ikke nødvendigvis var det høyeste, fortsatte jeg å bringe varene mine opp, selv med vanskeligheter. På den tiden kunne jeg øke salget (ca. 600.000 Schilling balansetotal) og antall blader enormt, slik at hovedleverandøren min kom til meg i en stor lastebil i 20. distrikt, hvor jeg hadde overtatt min fars forretningslokale. Ofte var det 2 paller med varer med 10 000 magasiner. På den tiden hadde jeg klatret så langt, sannsynligvis av konkurransemessige årsaker, at uken gikk fra mandag til søndag. Samboeren min Britta, siden 1988, hadde med rette klaget på det og det måtte jeg endre på, og derfor tok jeg i det minste helgen fri. Men siden jeg er litt tykk i hodet og skal gjøre det jeg har satt meg fore. Så det ble som det skulle.I februar 1998 så jeg ved en tilfeldighet at en av de to hovedleverandørene hadde sluttet å levere til Robin-bedriften. Noen dager senere kunne jeg offisielt fastslå at Robins selskap var konkurs. Konkurssummen var ATS 35 millioner. Dette beløpet inkluderte absolutt bare en liten del av innskuddene som Mr. Robin og hans ansatte tok fra kolportørene. Det gikk rykter om at han hadde stjålet rundt 15 millioner schilling fra sine 100 til 200 kolportører. Jeg fikk også vite at denne mannen etter konkursen bare turte å gå ut på gaten med livvakter, sannsynligvis på grunn av tilbakeholdte depositum. På grunn av konkursen var de plutselig klare til å gi meg den høyere rabatten på 33,1 brutto. Ja, men da var det allerede for sent.

<u>Juli 1998 ferie</u>

Etter at jeg aldri var noen fan av å reise på ferie, hadde jeg fortsatt en 2-ukers ferie på Kreta, som den dag i dag nok var den vakreste i mitt liv så langt. Det var også noen opplevelser som satt fast i hukommelsen: Vi, samboeren min Britta og jeg, hadde fått låne moped. Det eneste dumme var at det var en halvautomat. Med andre ord, vi satt begge på dette kjøretøyet, og jeg lot tilsynelatende clutchen komme for raskt, og så satt partneren min på gulvet. Vel, ja, halvveis gjennom det første hinderet. Huseieren fortalte oss at vi bare fikk kjøre innenfor 50 kilometer. Vi hørte det og startet reisen. Men siden denne øya har den ulempen at man i motsetning til oss måtte kjøre opp og ned hvert fjell, så gjorde vi det også og de 50 kilometerne ble glemt. På toppen av fjellet tok vi en pause og satte oss på gresset. Da sa Britta plutselig at hun hadde sett noe oransje i lunden i nærheten. På et øyeblikk klatret vi under gjerdet og fant en appelsin som tilsynelatende ble oversett under innhøstingen. Vi plukket dem selvfølgelig med en gang. Da vi skrellet den kom det en utrolig sterk lukt inn i nesen og fremfor alt var nytelsen av denne frukten ubeskrivelig. Så kjørte vi videre, for vi hadde veldig lyst til å gå til nabofjellet til et kloster. Nå var det middag og sola slo ned ganske hardt. Veien var ikke asfaltert, det var en grusvei. Likevel fortsatte vi reisen. Plutselig merket jeg at mopeden ikke lenger reagerte slik jeg ville. Vi hadde en "leilighet". Det var ingenting langt og vidt. Så vi måtte skyve kjøretøyet i den største varme til neste bensinstasjon, som var trygt 5 kilometer unna. Vi hadde ikke fortalt utleier noe om hva som skjedde med oss, men det var en opplevelse for oss begge. Noen dager senere holdt hotellet vi bodde på en jeep-safari. Så vidt jeg kan huske var det minst 10 jeeper fullpakket med mat og vi kjørte over øya fra nord til sør og øst til vest til vi kom til Elafonisi (Maldivene på Kreta). Ja, vi hadde nok mat, fra kjøtt til salat, men det som manglet var bestikket. Så kvinnene gikk til havet, vasket hendene og laget salatene med hendene. Det smakte i alle fall godt. Et år senere, igjen i juli, dro vi på ferie til Lanzarote. Vi likte det ikke så mye der, da hele området virket veldig sterilt for oss, vi kunne heller ikke bade i sjøen, vannet var veldig kaldt (Atlanterhavet). Og igjen et år senere enn juli 2000 bodde vi på et gjestehus i Steiermark i noen dager, hvorfra vi gikk noen turer. Siden den gang har jeg nesten ikke hatt noen ferier, bortsett fra i 2017 til Italia om noen dager med buss, som selvfølgelig var mer utmattende enn å ta flyet.

August 2000

Da vi kom tilbake fra vår østerrikske ferie (3 dager - Østerrike-tur) i juli 2000 fortalte Britta at hun hadde magesmerter og at hun allerede hadde fått time hos gynekologen om dette. Etter denne avtalen ringte hun meg umiddelbart: Jeg var selvfølgelig bekymret og hun sa: For en god ting. Hva skulle det være? Hun sa jeg skal bli pappa. Jeg ble overrasket, men vi tok det begge for gitt at vi ville være der for dette barnet. Abortemnet ble aldri tatt opp, og det var bra, i hvert fall da jeg fikk vite om det. Forfallsdatoen ble satt til begynnelsen av mars 2001. Den 24. februar 2001, en lørdag, vekket Britta meg om morgenen og sa at tiden var inne. Til jobben min hadde jeg en varebil som var i ferd med å starte på flere år. Det snødde også en del dagen før. Så vi kjørte rundt 50 kilometer til sykehuset uten varmeapparat i bilen, for det fungerte ikke. Da de kom til sykehuset skjønte de at det ville ta en stund. Så vi gikk bare en tur i snøen i komplekset. Om kvelden forlot jeg henne med forespørsel om at jeg skulle bli informert, uansett tid på døgnet, om han kom. Ingen telefon kom, så jeg kjørte til sykehuset klokken 08.00 på Mardi Gras. Da jeg åpnet døren til rommet hennes, hilste hun meg med ordet: Overraskelse! Et øyeblikk senere åpnet døren seg igjen og en sykepleier brakte sønnen min til meg. Det jeg vil huske for alltid var øyeblikket da jeg holdt den i hendene for første gang. Ubeskrivelig.

Sønnen min på 10 måneder

1990 - 1991 leilighet

Frem til da bodde jeg i den lille leiligheten som jeg hadde da jeg var 18 år. Men siden eiendomsdriften og eieren av bygården ønsket en generell oppussing av huset, måtte jeg flytte en etasje ned til en litt større leilighet. Leiligheten min ble slått sammen med naboleiligheten med løfte om at jeg kunne flytte inn i den 70 kvadratmeter store leiligheten igjen etter at arbeidet var ferdig. Dette ble også observert og i 1991 flyttet jeg inn i denne leiligheten. Men siden avhengigheten min ble verre med årene, noe jeg ikke var klar over på den tiden, falt jeg på etterskudd med husleiebetalingene. Så det ble, som det måtte komme, til en utkastelsessak. Britta og jeg lette etter leilighet. Hun fant det hun lette etter i en annonse i en avis. En maisonette i 2. distrikt med en leie på rundt 10.000 schilling. Jeg påpekte at jeg ikke hadde råd, men det ble ikke nødvendigvis akseptert. Derfor leverte jeg tilbake leiligheten i 20. krets uten fraflyttingsvarsel og flyttet til 2. krets. Men siden lidenskapen min for spill ikke hadde blitt bedre, men heller blitt dårligere, ble jeg snart møtt med samme resultat som i 20. distrikt.

Så jeg lette etter en Garcionerre selv i det 20. distriktet som jeg kanskje kunne ha råd til.

1980 – avhengighet

Det hele startet i det små, kastet noen schilling i en maskin og kanskje vant noe en gang, men kastet det rett tilbake i denne bøtta, fordi det store overskuddet kommer. Det tok meg rundt 15 år å innse at jeg var avhengig av gambling. Samboeren min Britta oppfordret meg til å gå i terapi, men jeg måtte også innrømme at jeg var avhengig av dette. Så jeg så etter hjelp fra Gamblers Anonymous. Det var gruppebehandlinger en gang i uken og individuelle behandlinger etter avtale. Individuell terapi forårsaket et nervøst sammenbrudd i meg fordi jeg aldri hadde opplevd lignende før, spesielt siden terapeuten hadde gått veldig dypt. Gruppeterapien var ikke nødvendigvis vellykket fordi jeg satte meg i bilen etter økten og havnet i en arkade igjen. Så jeg så ingen vits i denne terapien. Jeg måtte tydeligvis gjøre mer i denne forbindelse. Britta spurte meg om fremgang med denne terapien, eller om jeg hadde sluttet å spille. Jeg svarer dette med "ja", at jeg ville ha sluttet å spille. Så vidt jeg vet, var det den eneste gangen i 20 år med partnerskap hvor jeg hadde løyet for henne. Men jeg hadde også for vane å dyktig unngå sensitive spørsmål, spesielt de av økonomisk art. Så på den tiden så jeg ingen vei utenom og selvmordstankene kom nærmere og nærmere.

Juni 2001 konkurs

15. februar 2001, ti dager før sønnen min ble født, hadde jeg en konkursforhandling. Dette ble innledet med å sende inn mitt eget initiativ eller min kommersielle forståelse. Jeg snakket med dommeren om dette og vi klarte å oppnå en kompensasjonsgrad på rundt 13,84 % som vi kunne tilby kreditorene. Ved denne høringen i handelsretten i Wien var to kreditorrepresentanter fra rundt 20 kreditorer til stede. Den tilbudte kvoten ble ikke akseptert av både kredittbeskyttelsesforeningens advokater og AKV. I midten av juni 2001 ba kommunene i 20. distrikt meg om å levere tilbake de to handelsbevillingene jeg hadde i snart 9 år. Grunnen til dette var at jeg hadde akkumulert en del gjeld over tid. Jeg gjorde dette og ble da registrert arbeidsledig. Min far, som var pensjonist på det tidspunktet, kjøpte igjen handelsbevillingen for magasingrossisten.

Og slik fortsatte virksomheten, men det stoppet meg ikke fra å spille og fremfor alt fra å gjøre noe med det.

2000 sorenskriver / finans

Rundt årtusenskiftet kom kundene mine stadig til meg og spurte om bekreftelse på inntekten. De respektive kontorene krever med andre ord tilsvarende inntektsbevis ved forlengelse eller ny innlevering av oppholdstillatelse. Det var offisielt forventet at en person som bor i Østerrike skulle ha en minimumsinntekt på € 700. For meg var det lett å fastslå fordi det var en fast rabatt og utsalgspris. Så jeg skrev dem til deg hvis beløpet var tilstrekkelig og du mottok det tilsvarende papiret ditt fra sorenskriveren. På ingen dag hadde jeg mottatt penger for å utstede dette papiret, i hvert fall ikke før i 2006. For meg var disse menneskene også uavhengige kjøpmenn og måtte også overføre beløpet jeg hadde skrevet til vurderingskanalen. Om de faktisk praktiserte det er utenfor min kunnskap. Men jeg definerte også dette på de utstilte papirene.

mars 2006 min fars død 25. februar 2006 kom foreldrene mine til oss, Britta, min sønn Gregor og meg til Niederösterreich.

Samboeren min inviterte henne til sønnens 5-årsdag. Etter at han gikk av med pensjon i 1992, gikk faren min opp rundt ti pund. Han var ikke feit, men nøt måltidet til fulle. Sønnen min hadde selvfølgelig funnet ut av dette allerede da han var 5 år, så han bombarderte faren min med bakverk ved snacksen. Bestefar ta kaken, jeg vet at du liker å bite også. Et kvarter senere kom han med en smultring og bestefar tok den og spiste. Neste morgen i butikken rundt klokka 7 var far allerede der, som vanlig. Vi satte oss i bilen og kjørte til en kunde. På kjøreturen fortalte han meg at han hadde sovet så dårlig den natten. I tillegg sto han opp hver halvtime for å gå på toalettet med tilsvarende brystsmerter. Da vi var i gang igjen en time senere, ba jeg ham innstendig om å gå til legen vår i samme gate for å ta en titt. Vel, ja, det var vinter 26. februar 2006 og min far gikk til legen med stor motvilje kun i genseren. Etter en time ringte telefonen min og det var hans tur. Jeg burde tatt med en jakke til internlegen nede i gaten, for fastlegen ville ha sendt ham til internlegen umiddelbart med mistanke om hjerteinfarkt. Denne legen lot seg ikke kjøre dit for en diagnose og ringte umiddelbart ambulansen for å frakte dem til sykehus. Vel fremme på sykehuset ble mistanken som de to legene mistenkte bekreftet. Der ble han sjekket gjennom i 11 dager og løslatt 10. mars, en fredag. Den 13. mars om morgenen, som alltid, kom jeg inn i butikken rundt klokken 07.00 og faren min var der allerede. Siden det første jeg lagde om morgenen var å sette ned en kaffe, gjorde jeg det den dagen også. I mellomtiden la jeg merke til at faren min gikk inn på toalettet i gangen. Som vanlig satte jeg opp en kaffe til mamma i første etasje i samme hus og gikk bakerst i butikken i trappeoppgangen. Jeg la merke til at lyset var på i korridortoalettet vårt (ugjennomsiktig glass) og jeg visste at det bare kunne være faren min, men det hadde gått 10 til 15 minutter sist jeg så ham. Jeg dro deretter til foreldrene mine og snakket med henne en stund. Da jeg gikk forbi toalettet igjen var lyset fortsatt på og gikk inn i butikken, men ingen var der. Så jeg gikk på toalettet igjen og banket på vinduet, men det kom ingen reaksjon. I mellomtiden hadde naboen som bodde ved siden av kommet ut av leiligheten hennes. Men siden det ikke var noen reaksjon på toalettet, hadde jeg ikke noe annet valg enn å knuse dørvinduet med albuen. Da så han ham allerede sitte lent mot veggen og med blod fra nesen. Naboen ringte umiddelbart ambulansen og tok også med meg klær til ganggulvet så jeg kunne ta det på meg. Redningen var der ganske raskt og de forsøkte å bringe ham tilbake med hjertestarter, men forgjeves. Ambulansen ga legen beskjed om at han skulle fastslå dødsfallet. I mellomtiden kom også politiet, hvor en mann sto ved den døde til legen kom. Dette kom etter ca 3 timer. Det første av spørsmålene hans var om det var noen nylige funn som jeg selvfølgelig kunne svare på. Da han hadde sett gjennom den, sa han: Med cocktailen var dette ikke noe overraskende og å dø i Wien på mandag var ugunstig, for vi har en trafikkork. Hvis jeg ikke hadde vært i sorg, hadde jeg ikke klart å beherske meg over slike uttalelser. Men det som likevel rørte meg var at jeg måtte fortelle det til mamma, som var i leiligheten hennes. Og neste problem var å informere broren min, som hadde vært uten kontakt i rundt 20 år, at faren vår var død. Han hadde kranglet med foreldrene om arven han hadde krav på. Men han var der innen en time uten noen stygge ord. Den 24. mars 2006 fikk vi ham gravlagt på Wien sentralkirkegård. Så da kisten ble senket, hadde jeg en avgjørende hendelse. Jeg arvet mye fra faren min, blant annet det at vi ikke kan snakke om problemer og at vi hele tiden unngikk dem, nå var det for sent.

Mars 2006 utpressing

Den 14. mars returnerte jeg farens to handelsbevillinger til den ansvarlige sorenskriveren i 20. distrikt. Jeg kjente allerede til håndteringen i denne forbindelse. 20. mars ringte telefonen min og nummeret ble holdt tilbake. I den andre enden var en mann som ikke sa noe navn, selv om jeg spurte flere ganger i løpet av samtalen. Han sa at jeg skulle fortsette å skrive bekreftelsene som jeg har skrevet siden årtusenskiftet. Da jeg spurte hvorfor jeg skulle gjøre det, fortalte han meg om omstendighetene på stedet der sønnen min vokste opp som du bare kunne vite hvis du var der. F.eks da han gikk i barnehagen i dag og lignende. Det gjorde meg selvfølgelig forbanna og jeg truet ham. Svaret hans var bare at etter forrige samtale ville han sende meg en utlending og jeg måtte utstede en bekreftelse. Jeg måtte belaste € 10 for én måned og € 15 for flere måneder, som disse personene deretter ville betale. I begynnelsen nektet jeg selvfølgelig og argumenterte for at jeg ikke lenger kunne skrive det fordi jeg ikke hadde rett til handelen, men over tid ble informasjonen om sønnen min, hva han gjorde, mer og mer reell og jeg måtte anta at han oppholdt seg i nærheten av Gregor, noe som ble bevist et år senere. I landsbyen med rundt 800 innbyggere og et areal på 34 kvadratkilometer, vekker ukjente naturlig nok oppmerksomhet, spesielt når de kjører foran offentlige bygninger, som en skole eller barnehage. Nå hadde jeg valget mellom å gå til politiet og anmelde, hvis det blir akseptert, og det blir tildelt beskyttelse for sønnen min i en uke eller to, og så må jeg skjelve om mannen kan finne på noe. Det andre alternativet var for meg å gjøre det på min måte, som jeg leste meg til å gjøre uavhengig av konsekvensene. Så samtalene kom flere ganger i uken med undertrykte numre og utlendingene, som jeg bare kjente delvis, fikk bekreftelsene sine mot betaling. Da jeg spurte personene hvor de hadde kontakt fra, fikk jeg ingen informasjon. Så jeg bestemte meg for å følge disse menneskene, men i det minste i begynnelsen var dette håpløst. I mellomtiden var det allerede høsten 2007, sønnen min gikk på barneskolen. I landsbyen ble en mann observert forskjellige steder der det ble antatt at han var pedofil, da han ble sett gjentatte ganger på skole eller barnehage. Men dette var en feil, det hele var ment for meg. En fredag etter skolen, som alle skoledager, tok sønnen min skolebussen hjem. Siden veien ca 500 meter fra utgangspunktet til bostedet ikke var helt synlig, kom det plutselig en bil fra sidegaten, stoppet hos sønnen min og passasjerdøra åpnet seg. En mann snakket til ham og ville gi ham godteri. Sønnen min reagerte en gang og løp umiddelbart mot huset hvor samboeren min hadde ventet på ham. Hun så kjøretøyet og ringte også politiet, bare inntil de kom var sjåføren over fjellet til tross for blindveien. Da sønnen min fortalte meg om dette samme dag, fredag kveld, snakket jeg med samboeren min om det og fortalte henne at dette ikke var en pedofil, det ville ha gjeldt meg, men hun holdt seg til pedofilens versjon.

13. desember 2006

Det var en fredag og igjen en 13. Jeg satt i butikken som hadde to utganger, en til gårdsplassen til huset og en til gaten. Jeg skrev på programmene mine, som jeg har gjort i lang tid, og ble absorbert deretter. Plutselig banket det på gårdsdøren, jeg hadde låst den andre døren. Det var rundt middagstid og antok at det var en hjemmefest. Da jeg åpnet døren var det en mann på ca 190 cm høy med et velstelt utseende. Han identifiserte seg med sitt navn og ID som «offisiell direktør» for skattekontoret i Wien. Nå sa han, med et A4-papir i hånden, at han holdt en bekreftelse i hånden hvor firmastempelet mitt og min signatur var å finne på. Han hevdet også at det var trykt på begge sider. Han spurte også om han kunne komme inn, noe jeg ikke takket nei til. Men da måtte jeg umiddelbart tilbakevise påstandene hans. På den ene siden hadde jeg aldri gitt papirer som var trykket på begge sider, og på den andre siden hadde jeg heller ikke satt stempel på slike brev, som allerede var med i programmet som jeg selv hadde skrevet for dem. Jeg hadde aldri brevet som denne påstanden var basert på. Nå sa han om han kunne se på stand-PC-en min, noe jeg ikke nektet. Han ville også se på og ta bilder av kontoutskriftene mine, som jeg hadde i hyllen bak meg, noe jeg ikke takket nei til, fordi jeg ikke var klar over noen skyld. Nå begynte han å ta minutter. Da han spurte hvordan slike inntektsbekreftelser kom til, fra når og hvorfor, avsluttet han besøket med spørsmålet om hva jeg ville ha fått for det, og han mente ikke bare penger, men også naturprodukter. Hva skal jeg svare ham nå, for i mellomtiden skjønte jeg at han trengte følelsen av prestasjon, og på den annen side hadde jeg fortsatt utpresseren min på dette tidspunktet, som satte meg under ganske mye press. Så jeg svarte på spørsmålet hans med svaret: Jeg har ikke fått noe tilbake. Hans reaksjon var at han ikke trodde på dette. Året etter kom han til butikken min to ganger til uten forvarsel og fortsatte å lete. Forrige gang spurte han om han kunne ta med seg stand-pc'en til skattekontoret, noe jeg svarte bekreftende på etter litt tid for å tenke meg om. På tide å tenke på at det ikke nødvendigvis hadde vært gunstig for datamaskinen, men jeg hadde selvfølgelig ingenting å skjule. Jeg hadde den i stand igjen innen to dager, men han fortalte meg ikke om noe ulovlig ble funnet eller ikke. Så langt så bra eller ikke. Høsten 2007 kom det så «invitasjon» til skattekontoret i 22. distrikt. Der tilbød han meg resultatet av skatterevisjonen sin, som det heter på finanstysk. Han hadde allerede antydet for meg at han måtte sette pris på meg hvis jeg ikke fortalte ham hva jeg ville gjøre for å utstede resultatregnskap, og derfor ble vi enige om dette navnet. Hans estimat var at han trodde jeg ville ha mottatt € 100 for hver bekreftelse, fra 1998 til 2008. Med andre ord en inntekt på € 40 000 og en "imøtekommende" utgift minus 50 %. Så i hans øyne hadde jeg tjent € 20 000 år etter år med dette arbeidet, noe som også gjenspeiles i den tilsvarende beskjedne inntektsskatten. I ett slag hadde jeg to krav fra skattekontoret og helseforsikringsselskapet på et 6-sifret beløp, som jeg umiddelbart svarte på klagen til det daværende finanssenatet som overordnet organ for skattekontorene. , i dag, så vidt jeg vet, er det den økonomiske prokuratoren. Alle ansettelser, og det var 9 år på det tidspunktet, ble avvist eller avslått av de enkelte embetene. Staten eller dens embetsmenn har stort sett rett, innbyggeren neppe. Det jeg imidlertid ikke hadde forventet på det tidspunktet, var det faktum at denne offisielle direktøren ikke bare så på det som et økonomisk lovbrudd, men også som et lovbrudd. Etter å ha fullført sin eksamen i 2008, videreformidlet han dataene han hadde konstruert, som han aldri kunne fremlegge bevis for, til statsadvokaten i Wien med det formål å kontrollere ulovligheten. I tillegg til mine ansettelser i 2008, for årene 2006 til 2008, da jeg endelig fikk tak i utpresseren min, utarbeidet jeg selvangivelser for disse 3 årene på til sammen € 2.500 i inntekt fra utarbeidelse av resultatregnskap, som har ikke tatt i betraktning den dag i dag. I årene 1998 til og med 2005 hadde jeg ikke noe inntak på grunn av denne omstendigheten. Dette statsadvokatembetet reagerte også i form av de respektive tingrettene, hvor jeg mellom 2009 og 2011 ble «bedt» om å møte som vitne til rundt 100 stevninger. Prosessen der var alltid den samme. Grunntanken i mine avhør ved den respektive domstolen var alltid den samme. Jeg ble spurt om jeg hadde gitt ut dette papiret og selvfølgelig hvorfor. Det satt alltid en utlending overfor meg som blant annet ble anklaget av Kommuneavdeling 35 for å ha fått eller kjøpt oppholdstillatelse med en slik bekreftelse. Papiret som denne prosessen var basert på ble presentert for meg, og jeg måtte finne ut om jeg hadde utstedt det eller ikke. 90 % av dem var mine papirer, men det var også forfalskninger, som er hva administrerende direktør hevder. De tiltalte utlendingene, som jeg kjente i det minste av utseende, fikk, hvis de virkelig ble funnet skyldige, 2 måneder til tre år, betinget, ikke mer. Som jeg allerede har nevnt, i mai 2008 fikk jeg endelig tak i utpresseren ved å følge en antatt kolportør nok en gang etter at han mottok en bekreftelse fra meg. Med "kraftige" argumenter bønnfalt jeg denne mannen om å slette nummeret mitt umiddelbart og aldri ringe meg igjen. Jeg hadde ikke så mye håp, men han holdt seg til det uansett grunn, og jeg så eller hørte aldri fra ham igjen, men hadde også endret mobilnummeret mitt. Jeg hadde aldri klart å finne ut hva han fikk ut av det eller ikke. Våren 2010 mottok jeg plutselig et rekommandert brev fra statsadvokaten i Wien - Kriminaldomstolen i Wien. I den ble jeg bedt om å møte som mistenkt ved statsadvokaten til avhør. Det fulgte jeg opp og satte meg overfor statsadvokaten. Jeg ble beskyldt for å ha utstedt resultatregnskap som ikke var i samsvar med loven. Siden denne middelaldrende mannen hadde noen mapper foran seg, bladde han i dem og spurte meg om han kjente til navnet han leste der og fremfor alt hvordan slike papirer ble til. Jeg bekreftet da spørsmålene hans, men ba ham vise meg bekreftelsene, hvor jeg igjen kunne gjenkjenne ca 10% forfalskninger, som han også så. Så vidt jeg kan huske var han med for andre gang i år. Det hele var kun avhør av en siktet fra statsadvokatens side. Våren 2011 fikk jeg nok et rekommandert brev, men denne gangen fra Kriminaldomstolen i Wien, hvor jeg skulle gå som tiltalt. Jeg møtte en dommer der, statsadvokaten, som jeg kjente nå, og min offentlige forsvarer, som på mitt første møte med ham hadde klaget over at han måtte lese gjennom 6000 sider med rettsdokumenter for rettssaken. Nå kom det til denne forhandlingen, der naturligvis alle sider stilte spørsmål. Spørsmålet om jeg hadde fått penger for denne utgaven av papirene var av underordnet betydning, akkurat som det var under avhøret hos statsadvokaten. Jeg klarte å overbevise dommeren best mulig med mine svar og argumenter. Advokaten min var mer motvillig, bare gravde en presedens som hadde veldig lite med tiltalen min å gjøre. Aktor var litt mer pågående og stilte ganske raske spørsmål. Resultatet av denne rettssaken, kunngjorde dommeren dommen, 24 måneders fengsel betyr ingen fengsel. Etter at dommen var avsagt, instruerte han meg om min beslutning om det; For å godta dommen umiddelbart, 3 dager til å vurdere eller anke umiddelbart. Det hadde jeg egentlig ikke forventet, for jeg antok at jeg kunne forlate retten som en fri mann og uskyldig. Så jeg så på forsvareren min og viste ham 3 fingre i 3 dager for å tenke på det. Men da han så at aktor så min nøling, sa han at han ville anke eller ta rettslige skritt. I februar 2012 fant den andre høringen for

Wien Higher Regional Court sted, hvor jeg antok at dommen ville være i min favør. Så jeg gikk inn i rettssalen til det foreskrevne tidspunktet og fant et dommersenat. Da dataene mine ble sjekket, snakket en av dommerne til meg: Dommen fra Kriminaldomstolen i Wien vil bli endret til 16 måneder betinget og 8 måneder ubetinget. Min reaksjon på det: Det kan ikke være det! Dommeren sa: Hvis du ikke forsto dommen, må du sitte i varetekt i 8 måneder. For meg kollapset en verden. På den ene siden hadde jeg gitt ut disse papirene i god tro til jeg ble utpresset, på den andre siden ville jeg beskytte sønnen min, som gikk dårlig i buksene. Jeg hadde nesten aldri en økonomisk fordel og ble straffet for det. Jeg spurte selvfølgelig advokaten min om hva annet som kunne gjøres i denne forbindelse, men måtte innse at det ikke var noen anke til denne dommen, kun en begjæring. Men han ga meg umiddelbart ikke noe håp om at noe i denne avgjørelsen fra Høyere Regional Court ville endre seg som følge av en slik begjæring. Men jeg ba ham gjøre det. Men det var også mislykket. Så jeg fikk da et brev fra retten, der jeg måtte være i Simmering fengsel senest 10. april 2012, for å begynne min 8 måneders fengselsstraff.

2006 til 2011 handler om omsorg

Da faren min døde i mars 2006, sto jeg som allerede nevnt nok en gang overfor en utkastelse fra min Garcionerre i det 20. distriktet. Nå, etter ektemannens død, var min mor helt alene, og etter nesten 53 års ekteskap ble taket over hodet fjernet, så det gjensto annet enn å flytte inn i en 75 kvadratmeter stor leilighet med argumentet på min del å gi henne gjensidig tilsyn, fordi hun var ganske deprimert etter døden. På det tidspunktet kunne jeg ikke si om avgjørelsen min var riktig eller ikke, og hun hadde allerede hatt 2 slag bak seg. Da mannen hennes gikk bort, veide hun rundt 80 kilo, var ikke feit, men tykk. Det første året med henne i leilighet var ganske bra, vi var på shopping, til legen og til undersøkelser. På dette tidspunktet måtte hun ta omtrent 10 tabletter om dagen på grunn av hennes tidligere sykdommer. Blant dem var et psykofarmaka, hvor jeg måtte gå til en nevrolog fremfor en fastlege hver gang for å få resepten. Jeg tror det ble skrevet ut fordi hun var blitt stadig mer deprimert. Det skal også sies at jeg gjorde arbeidet mitt i samme hus, bare atskilt av en gårdsplass. Betyr at jeg var i første etasje og hun var i leiligheten i første etasje. I det andre året begynte tilstanden hennes å forverres raskt, hun spiste mindre og mindre og ville ikke gå ut. Jeg kan huske en episode hvor vi to handlet i matbutikken ca 300 meter og hun ikke kunne gå lenger etter at hun betalte for kjøpet. Så jeg satte henne ned i butikken, løp de 300 meterne tilbake til butikken og hentet kjelken min, som jeg hadde hatt i årevis, kjørte den til butikken, satte den på kjelken med stor motvilje og kjørte den med henne hjem. Jeg brydde meg ikke om hvordan det så ut. Du ikke nødvendigvis. Det hele så ut som jeg tilbrakte i leiligheten med henne fra mandag til fredag og dro for å se familien min i Niederösterreich fredag kveld, Gregor og Britta. Men siden hun ikke nødvendigvis skulle være alene i helgen, kom broren min innom i to-tre timer på lørdag og det ble til en farse nesten hver gang. En gang ringte han meg fordi han ikke fant medisinen, en annen gang på grunn av noe trivialitet. Det vil si at han var ikke til stor hjelp for meg i denne forbindelse heller. Men siden den økende depresjonen, paranoiaen og demensen kom i tillegg, ble omsorgen for hennes person vanskeligere og vanskeligere, det vil si at døgnomsorgen ble utnyttet fullt ut. På dagtid, siden hun ikke lenger hadde et tidsbegrep, sov hun og om natten når jeg ville sove på naborommet, hjemsøkte hun leiligheten. Trengte ikke engang å hente henne i stua ved midnatt eller senere og legge henne tilbake. I tillegg hadde hun ikke lenger oversikt over hvilke husholdningsartikler hun hadde. Det hendte at hun ved 11-tiden om morgenen sto på balkongen og ropte navnet mitt høyt fordi hun sto, Peter, trengte minst to tuber med tannkrem. Så kom jeg inn på gårdsplassen, så henne gestikulere vilt på balkongen og sa hun skulle se i boksen, så vidt jeg vet var det minst 10 tuber med tannkrem der. Alt hun sa var at hun ville vite hva hun trengte og ikke jeg. Så jeg måtte kjøpe 11 og 12 rørene til henne umiddelbart og umiddelbart. Det har jeg aldri gjort, at jeg gikk på shopping. Den eneste gangen jeg måtte puste var de gangene hun kom fra det ene sykehuset til det andre, så jeg måtte bare besøke henne i ca en time, for det var ikke noe mer der inne. Det ble vanskeligere og vanskeligere for meg å snakke med henne fordi hun ikke så noe perspektiv. På de enkelte sykehusene tror jeg hun "besøkte" nesten alle sykehusene i Wien, men de holdt dem i maks 10 dager, fordi fysisk de ikke fant noe og hva psyken angår var det ingen som kunne hjelpe henne. Nå kom min kjære bror, som jeg som sagt ikke hadde kontakt med på rundt 20 år, til den strålende ideen om å uføre moren sin. For å gjøre dette gikk han til ansvarlig tingrett og sendte inn søknaden. Min mening om dette var at hun absolutt fortsatt var tilregnelig, selv om hun allerede var på god vei til å bli sinnssyk. Så en kveld, etter forhåndsvarsel, kom en advokat fra tingretten til leiligheten vår. Min mor og vi to sønner var tilstede. I begynnelsen stilte han spørsmålene til min mor, som svarte riktig på dem, men så fikk broren min, som hadde stilt søknaden, en ganske solid instruks fra denne advokaten. Han sa at kvinnen var fullt tilregnelig og hvorfor han hadde stilt søknaden, noe han selvfølgelig ikke kunne svare på. Denne anmodningen ble derfor avvist. Frem til dette tidspunktet var forholdet mitt til broren min fortsatt rimelig veloppdragen og saklig. Etter det ble det verre og verre, til og med fysiske angrep fra hans side i nærvær av vår mor. I september 2010 gikk hun rundt i leiligheten igjen på dagtid og falt i stua. Jeg var bare ute og gikk på den tiden. På den tiden hadde hun hjemmehjelp tre ganger daglig i ca 4 år, for jeg var ikke alltid der og resultatet ble nøkkelsafe ved inngangen til leiligheten, for selvfølgelig ble også hjemmehjelp og redningstjeneste brukt. I tillegg hadde hun et armbånd med nødknapp som hun kunne bruke ved behov. Så den dagen kom redningen, som også informerte meg om at noe hadde skjedd med min mor, og de kom også inn med nøkkelsafen. De tok henne deretter med til sykehuset, hvor det ble funnet at hun fikk boret et ribbein ned i lungene da hun falt i leiligheten. Kjørte nå til nærmeste sykehus igjen og snakket med overlegen på avdelingen. Hun spurte meg om moren min ville få omsorg 24 timer i døgnet etter at hun ble løslatt. Men jeg måtte svare nei på dette spørsmålet, fordi jeg var fysisk og mentalt utslitt ikke bare på grunn av det, men også på grunn av min avhengighet. Det måtte sendes på forhånd at min bror umiddelbart etter min fars død i mars 2006 hadde søkt om plass på aldershjem for henne. Da hadde det vært lettere for ham å se henne i et hjem en måned senere. Da jeg etter ca 2 år fikk et løfte om hjemmet i 20. distrikt kjente jeg dette huset ut og inn, og hun torturerte meg med beslutningen om hva jeg skulle gjøre: til hjemmet eller ikke. I denne forbindelse bør det bemerkes at dette hjemmet var i et av deres kjente omgivelser, og siden det ikke har vært på plass på lenge, er det også veldig vakkert. Mitt argument var at det ville være hennes egen avgjørelse og at jeg verken ville fraråde eller fraråde det. Broren min overtalte henne selvfølgelig umiddelbart til å ta plassen. Etter noen uker og måneder nektet hun. Nå lå hun som sagt på sykehuset og Wien kommune søkte etter sykehjemsplass, som hun fikk i slutten av 2010 i et nyåpnet hjem i 22. distrikt. Der i 8. etasje med heis fikk hun et rom på rundt 20 kvadratmeter. Så vidt jeg kunne se, var hun en av de yngste på den tiden, 78 år gammel. Det var et fellesrom ved siden av rommene hvor de innsatte kom sammen for å sladre eller spille spill. Jeg husker jeg sa flere ganger at hun skulle gå ut av rommet sitt og snakke med de andre. Men hennes paranoia eller demens var så langt fremmet at hun ikke lenger ville være rundt mennesker, fordi de kunne gjøre noe med henne, som jeg måtte høre fra henne på forskjellige sykehus når hun så folk med hvite frakker og som ville gjøre noe. til henne. Hun tillot ikke min argumentasjon om at dette kun var medisinsk personell som ønsket å hjelpe henne. Den 2. mars 2011 dro jeg nesten hver dag hjem til henne for å besøke henne. Den dagen var hun knapt tilgjengelig, og jeg klarte heller ikke å snakke med henne. Da jeg kjørte hjem, hadde jeg mine forutanelser. I løpet av natten slo jeg som vanlig av mobilen. Om morgenen da jeg skrudde den på igjen, så jeg en tekstmelding fra hjemmet. Forutanelsen min ble bekreftet, hun sovnet fredelig inn i armene til en sykepleier den kvelden. Nå gravla vi moren vår i den samme graven der min far var. Jeg var nå alene i en 75 kvadratmeter stor leilighet med eiendelene mine og en husleie på i underkant av € 500.

Mai 2011 Neocathomenat

Forholdet mitt til min mor var ikke akkurat det jeg hadde på den tiden, men hun var der for meg selv i barndommen, om enn i begrenset grad. Så jeg var litt i et dilemma når det gjaldt henne. En vakker vårdag tidlig i mai gikk jeg Donaukanalen i mine gamle klær en søndag, og satte meg så på en benk og begynte å skrive på mobiltelefonen. Siden jeg allerede hadde svært begrenset syn på dette tidspunktet på grunn av voksende grå stær, så jeg ikke for mye. Plutselig ble solen som skinte i ansiktet mitt mørkere. Da jeg så opp, var det to personer foran meg som jeg knapt kunne se. En kvinne spurte meg om jeg trodde på Gud etter å ha presentert seg som Anna. Hun introduserte også den andre damen, men jeg husker ikke navnet hennes. Det måtte sendes på forhånd at jeg til enhver tid ville ha unngått en slik diskusjon. Dette spørsmålet, som jeg ikke ønsker å svare på her, resulterte i en halvtimes samtale og sa på slutten til meg: Jeg inviterer neste lørdag kveld kl 20.00. Jeg skal skrive ned Wolfgangs telefonnummer for deg, hvis det skulle dukke opp noe i mellomtiden. Hva var det? To kvinner som var godt 10 år eldre enn meg inviterer meg. De fortalte meg også at de var fra den nykatolske, en del av den katolske kirke og ikke en sekt. Ok, nå hadde jeg et telefonnummer fra en viss Wolfgang og en invitasjon. Hva skal det være? Nå lå jeg i senga hver kveld og grublet på denne invitasjonen. Så denne lørdagen kom og jeg trodde jeg hadde penger som ingen, og selvfølgelig var jeg nysgjerrig på hva det var. Så, som vanlig, dro jeg hjemmefra tidligere og kom dit i 20. distrikt klokken 19.30. Da jeg kom inn i gangen hvor det hele skulle foregå, så jeg en mann i den andre enden av rommet som satt opp klappstoler. Da han så meg i døren, kom han bort til meg, rakte ut hånden og sa at han var Wolfgang. Først da skjønte jeg at dette måtte være en prest, for han var kledd i svart fra topp til bunn. Da han spurte hva jeg het, ble jeg litt forvirret og jeg begynte å stamme og sa: Jeg heter Eduard. Dette navnet ble med meg en stund, helt til jeg kunne overtale ham til å kalle meg Edi. Han spurte også om jeg kunne hjelpe ham med å sette opp lenestolene, noe jeg selvfølgelig gjorde villig. Nå var klokken nesten 20 og jeg forventet at noen eldre ville dukke opp, de rundt 20 lenestolene var klare og så satte jeg meg på en av dem. Så åpnet den andre døren til rommet seg og en jente på rundt 16 år kom inn med en gitar på ryggen. Over tid ble rommet fylt opp og jeg oppdaget at jeg var en av de eldste. Da det hele startet litt etter klokken 20, måtte jeg selvfølgelig presentere meg selv, noe jeg aldri hadde likt å gjøre før. Det viste seg da at det var en nattverd med to lesninger og et evangelium fra Bibelen. Jeg hadde fortsatt i bakhodet at bestemoren min, som var katolikk, ofte hadde flyttet meg til messe i den katolske kirken i skoletiden, og jeg trodde allerede da at det ikke var noe for meg, alle de gamle, som ba. og kneler og ber igjen. Men det var litt annerledes og ikke bare deltakerne. De to lesningene fra Bibelen ble utarbeidet og lest av de enkelte deltakerne selv. Wolfgang, som fremstilte seg selv som en prest, presiderte bare og måtte lese evangeliet og deretter analysere alle lesningene i en preken. Vi, alle deltakere, kunne også kunngjøre hva den respektive lesningen ville ha fortalt oss og det frivillig. Jeg likte også at gitaren ikke bare var der for å se på, men at en sang alltid ble tonet mellom de individuelle lesningene, og vi sang alle sammen med den. Vel, dette ble fullført rundt 22.00 og jeg ble informert om at det ville være en ordliturgi påfølgende tirsdag kl. Etter at jeg hadde lovet meg en slik messe, dro jeg tilbake på tirsdag. Jeg ble deretter en bror til det som da var det 10. fellesskapet i Neokathomenat, som jeg også praktiserte i syv år og som personlig brakte meg mye. Prosessen i dette fellesskapet var alltid den samme, 3 til 4 personer fra denne gruppen måtte forberede den respektive liturgien eller eukaristien hos en av de 3 til 4 personene hjemme noen dager i forveien og deretter presentere den den dagen. Det var ikke alltid lett å finne nok folk til å delta. Vi hadde også en fellessøndag hver eller annenhver måned og omtrent to ganger i året en felleshelg på et hotell i Niederösterreich. Da jeg kom til dette fellesskapet i mai 2011, hadde det bare eksistert i et halvt år. Med andre ord, man kjente hverandre ikke så godt, men dette endret seg med årene, ettersom man fortsatte å forberede seg sammen med noen andre og dermed så miljøet han eller hun beveget seg i. På den tiden ble jeg venn med to søstre, Maria og Giada. Maria ble født i Polen og studerte i Østerrike, Giada var en ung utvekslingsstudent fra Capri/Italia, rundt 20 år gammel. Jeg hadde gjort mye med dem begge, men Giada måtte tilbake til Italia sommeren 2012 da hun allerede snakket perfekt tysk. Det som forbandt meg med Maria var at hun unnet meg avhengigheten min like mye som jeg gjorde, bare ikke så overdrevent.

<u>April 2012 fengselsstraff</u>

Så 10. april kjørte jeg med eiendelene mine til 11. distrikt for å begynne fengselsstraffen min, ettersom de ble færre og færre. Dette ble innledet av at jeg to måneder tidligere hadde en ny utkastelsessak med henrettelsesdatoen 10. mai 2012 på nakken. Så jeg hadde liten tid til å forlate leiligheten i 20. distrikt. Maria og min kollega, som jeg kommer til senere, var til stor hjelp for meg fordi jeg satt i varetekt på det tidspunktet. Da jeg kom til arresten ble jeg ransaket grundig og deretter satt på lukket avdeling i en celle på ca 10 kvadratmeter i par. I starten fikk jeg beskjed om hva jeg skulle og ikke skulle gjøre, samt informert om hvilken avdeling det var. Det ble bare en times tur på gårdsplassen på dagtid, dersom været tillot det. De første to månedene hadde jeg

selvfølgelig nok tid, det var ikke alltid lett å snakke med min medfange, så jeg tok Bibelen og leste den fra begynnelse til slutt, til tross for grå stær. Etter to måneder ble jeg overført til det avslappede fengselssystemet, hvor man kunne jobbe i arresten. Det var 6 til 10 personer i lokalet som hadde jobbet på ulike avdelinger. Men siden jeg er en person som nyter friheten hans, lot jeg meg forflytte meg igjen og havnet i friluft. Det betyr å stå opp klokken 04.30 og kjøre fra 11. distrikt til brakkene i 14. distrikt, hvor jeg ble satt til hagearbeid sammen med andre innsatte. Siden det ikke akkurat var behagelig å stå i sola hele dagen i juli august 2012, lengtet vi etter jobbslutt kl.16. Etter det måtte vi være tilbake i interneringssenteret ved 18-tiden. Fellesskapet jeg ble med i et år tidligere ga meg enorm støtte i løpet av den tiden. Dette kom til uttrykk i det faktum at for hver eneste dag jeg besøkte, kom tre av mine nåværende søsken på besøk og ga meg trøst. Siden jeg også hadde mulighet til å tilbringe helgen utenfor institusjonen med uteavdelingen, kunne jeg blant annet være med på en fellessøndag. Det som også måtte noteres her var at alle slektningene mine, inkludert noen i form av 4 kusiner og en tante og onkel, ikke dukket opp i besøkstiden, jeg vil ikke engang snakke om broren min, fordi han visste at jeg sitter. I tillegg la søsteren min Maria mye press på meg for å forsone meg med foreldrene mine, fordi jeg gjorde henne skyldig for der jeg var nå. Så det skjedde en søndag morgen da jeg fikk lov til å gå ut på denne samtalen i 8-tiden. Vel, ja, de var begge døde, hva skal jeg snakke om med steiner. Men siden kirkegården lå i nærheten av interneringssenteret, gikk jeg av trikken og gikk til graven. Først visste jeg ikke hva jeg skulle si, men så tror jeg at jeg snakket med dem i omtrent en halvtime og endte opp med at tårene rant nedover kinnene mine. Da jeg gikk tilbake til trikken, følte jeg meg 10 kilo lettere. Siden den gang har jeg sluttet fred med foreldrene mine, selv om de bare var steiner og et ondt ord om foreldrene mine vil komme fra leppene mine igjen, det har jeg ikke krav på, jeg burde gjøre det bedre, men det ser ut til at jeg ikke lyktes heller, i hvert fall til nå. En morgen da jeg kjørte tilbake til brakken for å jobbe, skjedde det en ulykke med meg. Vi hadde mulighet til å servere i brakkene. Det betyr at vi kunne spise frokost, lunsj og nå og da mat i form av bokser for kvelden. Vel, jeg gikk, som vanlig, for å spise frokost klokken 06:30 og spise en solid fersk rundstykke. Plutselig la jeg merke til at det øvre tannsettet mitt var ødelagt på midten. På kvelden i arresten ordnet jeg således at et besøk til tannlegen ble tillatt, fordi bittet mitt ikke ble gitt. Jeg fikk det også og måtte bli på institusjon den dagen. Det skal på forhånd sendes at jeg ikke hadde helseforsikring under varetektsfengslingen og at utgifter til eventuell behandling ble dekket over rettsvesenets budsjett. Så jeg kom til en tannlege som ikke nødvendigvis var den beste, men som hadde belastet rettsvesenet mye for å reparere tennene mine. På den tiden hadde jeg allerede registrert det, grå stæren ble så mye verre at jeg til slutt bare hadde 2 % syn. Det betyr at jeg måtte ta fortauskanten ved hjelp av føttene. Var den feilaktige antagelsen at denne operasjonen også kunne gjøres mens han var i varetekt, men hadde rett øye for operasjonen to dager etter løslatelse fra varetekt 12. desember og den andre en uke senere.

Avskjediget 10. desember 2012

Den dagen ble jeg løslatt og sto nå på gaten med ca € 700,- en visjon på 2 % og mine sølle eiendeler og uten tak over hodet. Men siden en bror ved navn Werner hadde tilbudt å flytte inn i kabinettet sitt i 8. distrikt mens jeg satt i varetekt, takket jeg gjerne ja. Han sa bare til jeg fant noe. Siden jeg nå hadde for mye penger på lomma klødde det naturlig nok, jeg hadde ikke et slikt utseende under forvaring, selv om det nok hadde vært basert på tiden. Så det ble som det måtte, jeg fortsatte å spille og etter en stund spurte bror Werner meg hvor langt leilighetssøket hadde kommet. Etter å ha sett at jeg ikke hadde lagt for mye iver i det, ga han meg med rette et ultimatum. Det lot jeg også passere, og derfor måtte jeg søke Wien kommune om et hjemløseasyl, som jeg også fikk i 16. distrikt sammen med en andre i et rom på 20 kvadratmeter. Etter min fantasi hadde jeg sett for meg at du ikke skulle betale noe for det, men det var en feil. Absolutt ikke beløpet for en husleie, men det var i det minste € 160 jeg var i stand til å betale i begynnelsen. Men i løpet av tiden var det ikke lenger mulig. Til tross for sosialrådgivere ble de tvunget til å fjerne meg fra huset. Hva nå? Så min arbeidsgiver og venn Kamal tilbød meg å innkvartere meg i kjelleren i virksomheten sin, uten toalett og vann, siden året allerede var fremme og vinteren var rett rundt hjørnet, måtte jeg godta det, selvfølgelig uten den andres viten. hjemmefester. Jeg var ikke alene der nede, jeg hadde også kjæledyr i form av mus som løp over ansiktet mitt til tider i løpet av natten når jeg sov. Det var nok tiden da jeg tenkte minst en gang i uken hva jeg levde for. Jeg hadde ikke oppnådd noe, tvert imot, jeg ødela alt, i en alder av 11 år måtte jeg lyve for sønnen min at jeg måtte jobbe i Berlin og ringte ham derfor bare en gang i uken fra fengselet. Selvmordstankene mine var allerede veldig ekstreme den gang. Mine brødre og søstre i samfunnet visste selvfølgelig også om hele elendigheten, men de kunne ikke hjelpe meg heller, selv om det gikk så langt som kateketen.

24. desember 2014 slutt

Nå var det jul, en slik den hadde vært tidligere år. Jeg sov i kjelleren, hadde med meg kjæledyr og 20 € i lommeboken. Det var fortsatt noen få dagligvarer, for over tid klarte jeg å leve på € 6 om dagen for mat og røyking. Vel, hva gjør du med disse pengene, du går til nærmeste spillehall og beløpet var borte. På dette tidspunktet ble det bestemt i Wien kommune at det lille sjansespillet skulle avvikles 1. januar 2015. Betyr at alle maskinene som jeg matet i over 30 år ble stengt, men bare i Wien og ikke i Niederösterreich. Vel, det nye året kom, det var ikke flere maskiner i Wien og pengene var tilbake i lommen min. Nå fikk jeg muligheten til å sette meg på toget, kjøre til en forstad til Wien og fortsette å spise disse bøttene. Men det var ikke tilfelle, hvorfor jeg fortsatt ikke kan forklare meg den dag i dag, men uansett vil jeg absolutt ikke stille spørsmål ved det. Med andre ord, etter godt 30 år og de påfølgende vanskelighetene, ble jeg kurert for denne avhengigheten 24. desember 2014. Fra den dagen av hadde jeg aldri rørt en maskin igjen. Jeg kunne selvfølgelig ikke svare på hva jeg hadde gamblet bort over tid, men jeg antar at det definitivt var et 7-sifret beløp. Jeg hadde med andre ord betalt min skatt på overskudd og omsetningsavgift med jobben min og det er ikke altfor lite, i hvert fall fra min side, men jeg kan ikke bedømme om dette havnet hos de respektive kontorene som skattekontor og kommune. Det som var interessant var at da jeg hadde mitt tvangsopphold i 2012, trengte jeg ikke å spille og knapt i frihet, fortsatte det igjen. Hvordan gikk det nå? I februar 2015 søkte jeg igjen plass på bostedshjem og fikk det umiddelbart i 16. distrikt. Nå skjedde alt i rask rekkefølge. Sosialarbeideren som passet meg la et stort press på meg for å få tildelt en fellesleilighet. Gebyret for plassen i € 160,- var ikke lenger et problem, så de ble betalt regelmessig. Siden jeg allerede i januar 2013 presenterte en fellesleilighet, håpet jeg egentlig ikke at det skulle gå denne gangen. I 2013 ba de meg om å bekrefte mine registrerings- og leiekontrakter for de siste tre årene. Jeg var i stand til å oppfylle registreringsbekreftelsen, men jeg kunne selvfølgelig ikke gi en leieavtale. Argumentet om at jeg var østerriksk statsborger og født i Wien hjalp heller ikke. Jeg var så rasende den gangen at jeg lot meg rive med av å si at dette negative varselet skulle sendes til meg, fordi jeg trenger dette papiret for et bestemt sted. Vel tilbake igjen. Sosionomen i dette hjemmet ba meg sette inn et visst beløp i huset måned etter måned slik at jeg skulle ha penger til leiligheten når jeg forlot hjemmet. 1. juli 2015 fikk jeg en liten leilighet på 36 kvadratmeter i 20. bydel, hvor jeg fortsatt bor i dag. Men siden jeg nesten ikke hadde møbler, måtte jeg kjøpe alt fra innbyggingskjøkken til skap. Siden leiligheten ligger i 5. etasje hjalp en samboer fra bostedshjemmet meg. Det som foregikk, spilleavhengigheten var borte, jeg hadde min egen leilighet, hvor det ikke er husleieetterslep den dag i dag og fremfor alt hadde jeg plutselig mer enn 10 euro i lommeboken. Det var en fantastisk følelse, og ingenting har endret seg så langt. Med andre ord, jeg vekket meg selv til live, hva det var da jeg var spiller, det ville jeg ikke nødvendigvis tilordnet det.

Februar 2016 normalt liv

I begynnelsen av 2016 flagret et postkort inn i postkassen min. Jeg leste dette og fant ut at det var en nettportal hvor du kunne registrere deg gratis. Etter at det var gratis, gjorde jeg det også. Det hele var en nettside med godt hundre forskjellige grupper, avhengig av deres interesser. Siden jeg alltid har vært en nysgjerrig person, så jeg på gruppene og fant omtrent 4 til 5 grupper som snakket til meg. For to av disse satte jeg aktiviteter på 50+ klubber og 60+ klubber, som også tilsvarte alderen på medlemmene. Nå organiserte Helmut, administratoren for gruppen 60+ Treff, restaurantbesøk annenhver uke klokken 18.00 på kvelden. Hver gang i en annen restaurant. Siden jeg ikke kjente noe sånt fra fortiden min, var det en glede for meg å alltid spise godt der og å sladre i omtrent 3 til 4 timer med de 8 til 10 personene som var der. Den andre gruppen, 50+, var en utfordring for meg fra starten av. Så skrev administratoren, jeg har glemt navnet mitt, igjen hver 2. uke fredag kveld kl. 18.00 et møte i en markedsbod i 3. distrikt. I denne gruppen var fokuset imidlertid ikke på mat, men mye mer på samfunnet. Men siden disse møtene ikke var optimalt organisert, kom det kun en håndfull til disse samlingene, men så mye mer var det ikke mulig, det var ikke plass til flere på denne standen. Administratoren Helmut fra gruppen 60+ Treff gjorde dette mye mer presist frem til han døde i 2019. Jeg tok alltid med meg vennen min Roman på begge møtene fordi han var singel på det tidspunktet, men jeg kommer tilbake til ham senere. Som sagt var det ikke så mye som skjedde i 50+-gruppen, og derfor tok jeg initiativet til å legge ut møter på nett annenhver uke gjennom denne gruppen. Gruppen hadde rundt 100 medlemmer på den tiden, og derfor annonserte jeg et møte på et spisested og ikke i en markedsbodbuffet i portalen. I starten var det kanskje 7 til 8 personer fra denne gruppen og hovedfokuset var selvfølgelig ikke på mat, men på samtaler og samtaler. Det var interessant at med hver og en av dem var det konsekvent flere kvinner enn menn til stede hver 2. uke. Det betyr at det til tider hendte at Roman og jeg var de eneste mennene. Men etter at jeg elsket å omgi meg med kvinner, noe som også var en ny opplevelse for meg, tok jeg imot kvinnene deretter. Det betyr kyssing til venstre og høyre, hvor jeg så innså at dette hadde innvirkning på den etterfølgende kvaliteten på samtalen. Det var litt tungvint i starten, men etter hvert kom det flere og flere til disse møtene. Medlemstallet i denne gruppen steg også jevnt og trutt, helt til slutten med vel 500 medlemmer. Siden jeg ikke var admin for denne gruppen, var det selvfølgelig fiendtlighet til andre medlemmer av denne gruppen, blant annet med argumentet om at dette var en partnerutveksling, som jeg la igjen på nettsiden med tilsvarende kommentarer. I 2018 og 2019 hadde jeg tanken om at man ikke nødvendigvis trenger å gå på pub, men at det også finnes kultur og lett idrett. Disse møtene ble ikke nødvendigvis akseptert av medlemmene. Det var kabaret, bowling, biljard eller minigolf, så ingen fancy ting. Bare rundt 5 til 6 personer kom på slike møter, så jeg gikk tilbake til de lokale møtene. Da pandemien kom i 2020, hadde vi vårt siste møte i 3. distrikt i februar. Noen måneder senere ble jeg informert av Pamela om at hun ikke lenger kunne finne gruppen 50+ Treff på nettsiden. Men siden slike møter ikke kunne finne sted med lockdown og andre restriksjoner, la jeg ikke merke til dette faktum. Jeg undersøkte det og fant ut at både gruppen 60+ Treff, som imidlertid ikke hadde noen aktiviteter etter administratorens død, og gruppen 50+ Treff og dens medlemmer var fjernet fra denne siden. Bakgrunnen var, og det viste seg en tid i forveien, at programvaren (angivelig Ubuntu) bak hadde krasjet og ny programvare ble installert via denne nettsiden. Siden jeg nå kaller meg programmerer, skrev jeg til dette selskapet, eierne av denne siden, omtrent to ganger for å finne ut hva som ville ha skjedd der. Svaret var at noen gamle grupper ikke lenger kunne gjenopprettes. Jeg kom selvfølgelig også med min kommentar om at dette godt kan gjøres, men også med et enormt tidsforbruk, fordi dataene må være tilgjengelige, det er bare å lese det opp og legge det til den nye portalen.

Dansearrangementer høsten 2015

Min venn Roman, som jeg hadde kjent i en årrekke, spurte meg en gang om vi kunne danse på pensjonistforeningen i Wien på en lørdag, noe vi gjorde da. Og så danset vi hver lørdag kveld enten i 2. distrikt eller i 20. distrikt til pandemien kom i 2020 og det var selvfølgelig ingen flere arrangementer. Jeg var ikke pensjonist på den tiden, men hva pokker, jeg likte det, selv om jeg ikke er en profesjonell danser (håpløst tilfelle).

Familie

Vel, ja, det hadde jeg sikkert i rundt 10 til 11 år, men da jeg gikk på internat, må forholdet ha blitt dårligere, for der, enten jeg ville eller ikke, måtte 90 % av avgjørelsene mine tas alene. Ved å gjøre det var det knapt noen ved min side med råd. Om jeg ville ha akseptert det eller ikke er også tvilsomt. I min barndom hadde jeg et godt forhold til mine 3 søskenbarn i helgene, som er litt yngre enn meg, med den fjerde hadde jeg kun kontakt to ganger, etter eget ønske. Det betyr at jeg så de 3 jentene i 11. distrikt nesten hver helg. Når det gjelder broren min, var vi ett hjerte og en sjel i omtrent 16 år. Det endret seg da han sa at han måtte ha en kone nå. Da han var rundt 30 til 35 år gammel, krevde han arven i kontanter fra foreldrene i mitt nærvær i Niederösterreich. Bakgrunnen var at han nå var gift og hadde to døtre og sa han måtte bygge en tilværelse her og nå i Tyskland. Siden denne forespørselen ble uttrykt med fysisk styrke, "sa han farvel" i godt 20 år. Vi hadde ingen kontakt med ham før kort tid før vår fars død. Selv i dag har jeg ingen kontakt med ham, og jeg vet ikke om han eller meg om hvor vi bor. Når det gjelder sønnen min, som nå er 20 år, skal det sies at jeg i 2012 ikke kunne fortelle ham at jeg var varetektsfengslet, men at jeg måtte jobbe i utlandet, han var da 11 år. Dette var jeg og samboeren min blitt enige om. Jeg hadde et godt forhold til han i hvert fall helt til jeg ble tvunget til å bli i 11. distrikt, selv om det bare var i helgen. Men siden han etter min mening ble informert av en kjær slektning til min ekspartner hvor jeg egentlig var i 2012, til tross for flere forsøk siden april 2018, har jeg ikke hatt noen kontakt, sist jeg så ham var 15. juli, 2017. Forholdet til min mor var egentlig bare godt de første årene av livet mitt, men siden vi var veldig forskjellige karakterer endret det seg senest med internatet, men det endret ikke det faktum at jeg stod på av henne de siste årene av hennes liv. Men det som slo meg veldig og som bekymrer meg fortsatt i dag, at jeg aldri kunne snakke med faren min og han kunne nok ikke snakke med meg heller.

Venner

Gjennom årene har jeg sikkert hatt flere venner som jeg prøver å klassifisere her, selv om jeg egentlig ikke har krav på det, men som sagt, det er slik jeg ser det. Blant mine beste venner var sikkert de fra Niederösterreich, som jeg visste allerede da jeg var 12 år gammel lært. Men siden de var spredt over hele forbundsstaten Nedre Østerrike, tok vennskapet slutt etter rundt 15 til 20 år. Når det gjelder min wienervenn, vet jeg fortsatt ikke hvorfor han aldri hindret meg i å bli avhengig av gambling. Men jeg vil gjerne gi ham æren for at han ikke ville vært i stand til det. I 2005 eller 2006 hadde jeg problemer med stand-PC-en min i butikken, og siden pengene vanligvis var knappe, lette jeg etter en datamaskinreparasjon, som jeg også fant i det 20. distriktet. Der kom jeg til en kjellerrestaurant to gater unna. Da jeg så personen som heter Kamal, skjønte jeg at det måtte være en araber og henvendte meg til ham på den måten, siden jeg hadde forholdt meg til disse menneskene i mange år før. Han svarte på mine arabiske ord og sa også at han ble født i Alexandria, men nå er østerriksk statsborger. Et år eller to senere flyttet han to gater ned til en restaurant i første etasje, hvor han ansatte meg en tid senere, han er ansvarlig for maskinvare og jeg for programvare. Det var han som tilbød meg husly i kjelleren det året jeg ikke hadde. Omtrent et år senere kom en litt eldre herre til butikken vår i 20. distrikt, som det viste seg, han var 20 år eldre enn meg. Han sa at han hadde problemer med sin egen nettside, siden programvaren var tilpasset, visste han ikke lenger hvordan han gikk og han ønsket å legge til et par ting. Jeg vil kanskje se hva jeg gjorde på stedet. Der fant jeg en ganske stor nettside som han selv hadde jobbet med i årevis, og jeg leste meg inn i det systemet. Til slutt klarte jeg endelig å fikse samtaleproblemene han hadde med det nye systemet. Et vennskap utviklet seg fra begge møtene, som fortsetter den dag i dag og som jeg heller ikke ville gå glipp av. Ja, det ble opprettet forbindelser fra gruppene 60+ klubber og 50+ klubber, men de slapp ut igjen med pandemien.

Partnerskap

Det første samarbeidet med kollegaen min ved forskningssenteret skuffet meg litt, da jeg ble litt snudd på at hun hadde tvunget meg og et barn til å flytte under samme tak som foreldrene hennes, hvorved faren hennes godtok meg veldig godt, men kona hans gjorde som måtte vite alt irriterte meg litt. Når det gjelder min andre kone i mitt liv, var hun ubestridt kvinnen i mitt liv, ellers ville ikke partnerskapet vart over 20 år. At det gikk i stykker, til tross for den 8 år gamle sønnen på den tiden, er vel 95% min feil. Jeg hadde bare i ettertid funnet ut at vi aldri snakket om oss selv og problemene våre, og så, som vi gjorde etter bruddet, var det alt for sent. Kanskje det ville endret noe hvis vi hadde uttalt oss tidligere. Jeg vet ikke. Siden gruppen 50+ Treff ble sagt å være en slags partnerportal helt fra starten av mitt arbeid for denne gruppen, ble det som det måtte. Det var en fredag før pinse i 2017, 8 år etter at Britta fra Niederösterreich hadde skilt seg fra meg. Vi hadde et møte der igjen i en bar og pubhagen. Jeg dro dit som vanlig med min venn Roman. Så kom Pamela, medlem av 50+ Treff-gruppen og et år yngre enn meg, og satt mellom Roman og meg. I løpet av kvelden utviklet det seg en engangssamtale mellom meg og Pamela og vi snakket og lo mye, slik at jeg egentlig ikke la merke til de andre deltakerne lenger. I prosessen la jeg merke til at hver gang vi hadde noe å le av, klappet hun meg på overarmen eller låret. Jeg registrerte meg bra, men hva nå, for jeg var ikke den modigste i denne forbindelse.

Men jeg tok motet til meg og spurte henne om vi ikke kunne møtes et sted pinselørdag for å gå en tur, noe vi også gjorde dagen etter. Jeg falt ut av skyene og dro til fellesskapet i samfunnet mitt på pinsesøndag. Men siden det alltid var vanlig på slike dager, etter en kort bønn, å snakke om stien og egne erfaringer med den, og det foran et 20-talls mennesker, selvfølgelig frivillig, begynte jeg etter hvert. Jeg var som sagt 57 år og hadde snakket med Pamela på telefon før jeg gikk inn i bygningen. Så jeg sa at jeg led av en uhelbredelig sykdom som kunne ramme hvem som helst og andre blomstrende utsagn fra min side. Jeg så meg rundt og bortsett fra fortvilte ansikter kunne jeg egentlig ikke skjønne noe. Hva snakket jeg om? Vel, selvfølgelig var det spørsmål og utsagn, som: du snakker som en 16-åring og en av de tilstedeværende, en 22 år gammel student, spurte meg: Edi er du forelsket, noe jeg selvfølgelig kunne ikke nekte. En måned senere, den 15. juli 2017, forestilte jeg meg at Pamela og jeg var et par, jeg dro for å se sønnen min i Niederösterreich for siste gang, noe jeg ikke visste på den tiden. Siden han snart skjønte at jeg var overspent, tilsto jeg for ham at det var en ny kvinne i livet mitt og viste ham også et bilde av henne, som jeg angret på etterpå. På den tiden var Pamela allerede på kur i Steiermark. Da hun kom tilbake, fant jeg ut at et annet medlem av 50+ Treff-gruppen hadde fulgt henne på dette kurstedet og Pamela hadde tatt meg bort. Siden denne mannen heller ikke nødvendigvis var omgjengelig, var dette partnerskapet mellom Georg og Pamela bare midlertidig. Vel, det var flere møter og i august 2018 fant et møte sted på en Heuriger i 19. distrikt. Noen personer i denne gruppen så vel som jeg hadde startet en gruppe i Whatsapp og sendt oss bilder frem og tilbake over alt. Så på denne fredagen kom en ny kvinne inn i gruppen, ved navn Anna, innfødt fra Polen og fin å se på. Hun kunne le veldig hjertelig, noe som imponerte meg veldig. Hun ble også med i gruppen vår i Whatsapp og kom så stadig med morsomme bidrag, som ga denne gruppen et løft. En dag i september 2017 la hun ut at druene i 22. distrikt var modne og at noen fra denne gruppen ikke kunne hjelpe henne med druehøsten. Hun hadde øremerket en dag til dette neste helg. Svaret på dette var null. Så jeg tenkte for meg selv, hvorfor ikke, gå og les druer og gjør en avtale i 22. distrikt. Jeg fant virkelig mange druer som vi plukket i løpet av dagen og så bearbeidet til sirup og juice om kvelden. Men siden ingenting «løp unna» en lørdagskveld, gikk tiden og vi ble et par den dagen. I midten av oktober, etter en måned med partnerskap, sa hun at hun ville føle seg mer komfortabel hvis hun ble alene, noe jeg måtte akseptere. Bra eller ikke, det brøt også opp, men det var alltid møter i gruppa og så i november 2017 i 3. krets. Der var vi rundt 20 personer, hvor vi hadde litt plassproblemer i denne restauranten. Da det hele var over rundt klokken 9, gikk vi, Roman og jeg, ut på gaten der to kvinner, Tine og Julia, sto. Plutselig spurte Tine: Hva gjør vi nå? Jeg ble litt forvirret fordi jeg ikke hadde forventet et slikt spørsmål fra en kvinne. Vel, så vi dro til en kafé i nærheten og ble der i omtrent en time. Så fant Tine ut at jeg var opptatt med datamaskiner, og hun fortalte meg om jeg kunne fikse problemet med datamaskinen hennes hjemme hos henne, som hun antok etter å ha oppgitt adressen sin i 14. distrikt. Kvinnen var omtrent to år eldre enn meg og ikke nødvendigvis slank. Denne reparasjonen av datamaskinen eller dette besøket ble til mer, selv om jeg ikke nødvendigvis likte det fra utseendet. Mesteparten av tiden tilbrakte jeg med henne og med henne. Hun hadde ny leilighet, men følte seg tydeligvis ikke helt hjemme der, så vidt jeg kunne skjønne, for hun måtte alltid ut for å kjøpe noe eller bare for å gå et sted, hun var en lidenskapelig sjåfør. I løpet av denne tiden overøste hun meg med klær og andre ting, og hadde alltid betalt på puben. Da jeg spurte henne at det ville jeg ikke, fordi jeg hadde nok klær i boksene mine i mellomtiden, var hun litt nervøs. Så en helg kjørte hun til søsteren i det dypeste Burgenland og ringte fra bilen på vei dit. For meg var det det som knuste fatet. Hun hadde bestemt alt uten å konsultere meg og sa at hun kunne kjøpe kjærligheten min med haugevis av gaver. Så denne episoden var også over. Sommeren 2018 dro jeg og Roman til dans i 1. distrikt, begge singel, vi hadde kjent arrangementet lenge og fremfor alt de to arrangørene. Da vi kom dit var det nesten ikke plass igjen, så vi måtte begge sette oss ned ved et bord der det allerede satt to kvinner. Den ene het Graziella (delvis italienske foreldre) og jeg husker dessverre ikke navnet på den andre. Nå som vi satt ved samme bord måtte jeg også be damene danse og så satt Graziella og jeg snart ved siden av hverandre og hun fortalte at hun hadde problemer med pc-en sin. Jeg kjente argumentet godt nå og Graziella var mye eldre enn meg, men bekreftet likevel at jeg ville se det hjemme hos henne i 16. distrikt. Også der ble det samme resultat som med Tine, vi kom sammen. Hun hadde en langtidsleie i 17. distrikt med et lite hus i den tilsvarende store hagen, hvor man ikke lett kunne bevege seg foran et enormt antall planter og trær. I tillegg hadde hun vinranker over takterrassen, hvor vi også høstet druene og deretter bearbeidet dem, igjen en aha-opplevelse. Siden det ikke bare var mulig å bevege seg i hagen, gjaldt dette også interiøret i huset og til slutt også leiligheten din. Samarbeidet var derfor tidsbegrenset. Selv er jeg ikke akkurat en dum for rengjøring, men jeg vil gjerne kunne bevege meg på et rom, jeg var trang nok i 2012. I begynnelsen av november 2018, en lørdag morgen etter frokost forlot jeg denne forbindelsen i en skynde deg. Jeg falt ned i et dypt hull på dette tidspunktet da jeg måtte lure på hva jeg gjorde galt. 4 kvinner og med alle gikk det ikke, var det min fortid, var det min "rikdom"? Vel, det var nok et dansearrangement i slutten av november en lørdag 24. november 2018 Min venn Roman overtalte meg til å gå på denne dansen i 2. distrikt. Men jeg hadde ikke lyst. Til slutt kom han meg så langt. Vi satt ved et bord med ca 8 personer. Overfor meg så jeg en blond kvinne som etter min mening var i selskap med en eldre herre. Jeg hadde ikke danset så mye den kvelden fra kl. 18.00 til 21.00 til levende musikk. Mot slutten kom den aktuelle damen tilbake til bordet og sa til Roman og meg om vi ikke ville danse der i det hele tatt. Jeg hadde bare dårlig forstått denne uttalelsen og reagerte derfor ikke. Roman spratt umiddelbart opp og danset med henne. Nå var dette arrangementet over og vi gikk til garderoben. Plutselig sto denne kvinnen, som het Ully, ved siden av meg og spurte: Går du med meg og da mener jeg Roman og meg. Etter at det var lørdag kveld og ikke sent heller, hadde jeg ikke noe imot å bli med meg, og det sa jeg til Roman også. Han takket også ja og så etter en lang leting havnet ca 8 personer på en bar i 1. distrikt. Før hun gikk til garderoben ga hun Roman mobilnummeret sitt, som jeg bare registrerte marginalt. Vel, nå satt vi Ully ved siden av meg i denne baren og Roman holdt et foredrag om sjamanisme og energi. I løpet av kvelden viste det seg at Ully ikke hadde kommet sammen med den eldre herren, men med venninnen Monika. Så fort jeg registrerte dette ble jeg litt flau, noe jeg likte med damen. Nå hadde Roman nummeret hennes, men jeg kunne umulig be om det. Så jeg tok et visittkort fra restauranten og skrev telefonnummeret mitt på baksiden. Da jeg forlot restauranten, ga jeg henne dette kortet, som Roman også la merke til, dessverre. Så jeg var på djevelens kjøkken og Ully hadde to mobiltelefonnumre fra Roman og meg. Dagen etter, søndag, ventet jeg for å se hva som foregikk. Det skjedde ingenting om morgenen, men klokken 2 var mobilen og Ully på linjen. Hun spurte meg om vi ikke engang kunne ta en kaffe. Mitt svar på dette: Umiddelbart og umiddelbart - du har en pause i overføringen. Ja, hun må fortsatt fikse noe og ringer meg tilbake om en time. Men det var ikke en time, bare en halvtime og vi møttes på en kaffebar i det 20. distriktet. Så dro vi på kino der og fordi det ikke var nok dro vi også på en lounge i 1. etasje. Jeg fortalte henne, ettersom jeg var vant til det, alt om mitt tidligere liv, som kanskje ikke nødvendigvis var produktivt. Plutselig snudde hun seg mot meg og kysset meg på kinnet. Vi har vært et par siden da, selv om det er noen års forskjell i alder. Hvorfor? Fordi jeg tror hun er best av de 4 kvinnene før.

Nykatolsk slutt

Da jeg ble med i fellesskapet eller stien i 2011, var det klart fra starten at det ville ta rundt 30 år å gå denne stien. Nå i 2017 i pinsehelgen måtte jeg gjøre mine erfaringer, hva tolkningen av partnerskap på denne måten betyr og derfor ble jeg litt grublende. Da min søster Maria fra samfunnet tok sitt eget liv i april 2018, etter 7 år med tilhørighet, bestemte jeg meg for å avslutte veien og gjorde det samme i mai 2018 på en Vesper for avdøde. Min tanke i denne forbindelse var at jeg ikke lenger kunne være enig i noen argumenter underveis. Det gjaldt selvfølgelig tolkningen av partnerskap, så vel som hvordan man kan bringe tro til live. Er jeg nå troende eller ikke: Dette spørsmålet kan ikke og vil jeg ikke svare her, fremfor alt kan det enkelte individ selv? For min del prøver jeg nå å leve etter troen etter å ha forlatt samfunnet. Siden har jeg fortsatt vært i kontakt med Gud, selv om dette bare kommer til uttrykk i stille bønner med ham.

Kunder

I løpet av livet har jeg absolutt hatt flere hundre kunder som jeg alltid behandler med respekt og høflighet, uansett om de er innenlandske eller utenlandske. Når det gjelder kundemassen på den tiden jeg solgte aviser og magasiner, har jeg hatt flere negative opplevelser. Siden 99 % av dem alltid var utlendinger, trengte jeg ikke engang å se på pengene mine, siden folket hadde dratt til hjemlandet og ignorert kravene mine. Kundene mine, som jeg allerede er helt annerledes i datasektoren, blir alltid glade når de ringer meg. Du vet at jeg ikke hviler før problemet er løst, og det kan ta tid. Men jeg husker ikke en kunde fra den tiden jeg laget programvare. Dette er bosatt i Tyskland, men av en annen opphav. Hans tre selskaper inkluderer en tannlegepraksis, et tannlaboratorium og et tanndepot. Høsten 2010 kom hans medarbeider fra tanndepotbutikken til butikken vår. Bakgrunnen var at regneprogrammet ikke fungerte lenger og han spurte om jeg kunne fikse det. Siden denne mannen ikke nødvendigvis hadde kommersiell kunnskap, fant jeg ut at dette programmet ikke lenger kunne lagres. Nå hadde jeg lagt merke til at det hele i bunn og grunn besto av tre selskaper med et bredt spekter av tilnærminger. Dermed har vi som en del av vår bedrift i 20. distrikt laget et tilbud til alle tre bedriftene med økonomi- og lagerregnskap, åpen varehåndtering. Kunde- og leverandøravropshåndtering og mye mer. Jeg presenterte dette for sjefen og han begynte å akseptere enkelte deler av dette tilbudet og avvise andre. Men siden jeg alltid har ambisjonen om å skape alt 100%, var det også tilfellet i denne saken, og selvfølgelig også med tanke på at det ble tatt beslutning om å akseptere en annen del av tilbudet vårt. Men siden programvare ikke er statisk, ble programmet ofte tilpasset. Så jeg dro til tanngrossisten hans opptil fire ganger i uken for å gjøre dette, hver gang for en takk i syv år. Siden de ansatte tilstede der ikke nødvendigvis var kjøpmenn, kunne de ikke gjennomføre den årlige inventeringen. Det vil si frem til inventaret i 2017, dette ble utført av meg med hjelp av de tilstedeværende der. Men siden jeg fra min kommersielle erfaring vet at noe slikt bør gjøres innen maksimalt to dager, hadde jeg mine vanskeligheter i denne forbindelse. Siste inventar ble gjennomført i etapper i løpet av to uker. Det var på forhånd avtalt at fakturaen vi sendte inn skulle betales tre ganger. Det første delbeløpet med et tresifret beløp i euro er betalt, resten er fortsatt åpent. Klientens argument var at programmet mitt ikke fungerer, noe som i bunn og grunn motsier seg selv. På den ene siden fungerte programvaren feilfritt i syv år, og på den andre siden bruker de den fortsatt i dag og har også brukt den i fire år. Så vi kom tilbake til en god 4-sifret. Til og med et brev fra en advokat som truet med betalingspålegg ble uaktsomt. Når det gjelder mine nåværende kunder, som jeg ivaretar som en del av vår virksomhet i dag, la meg si at de er helt entusiastiske for meg, fordi de vet hva de får fra meg. På den ene siden er dette ikke bare den raske avtalen, men også kundens kunnskap om at jeg ikke gir opp før jeg finner en løsning. Det kan godt være at det tar tid, men jeg blir også glad hver gang jeg ser at det fungerer.

Gjenoppta

Du som leser kan nå tenke at du har lest dette er ikke noe liv. Ja, det kan være det, men som allerede nevnt, det var utelukkende mine avgjørelser, om de var riktige eller gale, kan alltid bare bestemmes i ettertid. Så det neste spørsmålet dukker opp, om jeg er fornøyd. Men siden dette er en rent subjektiv vurdering, ville alle svart forskjellig på dette. Jeg er glad. Hvorfor? Når jeg tenker på avhengigheten min, var det egentlig ikke det som kalles livet, så jeg er glad jeg kom meg gjennom denne perioden. Hvordan jeg klarte det den gang er fortsatt ikke klart, men jeg er glad jeg kom meg gjennom den tiden. Hvorvidt jeg er fornøyd, slik jeg formulerte det i min 1. bok, forblir ubesvart. Grunnen til dette er at min nærmeste venn skilte seg fra meg etter eget ønske etter godt 10 år, noe jeg fortsatt ikke forstår den dag i dag. Jeg vet ikke hva annet livet har forberedt for meg, men ingenting mer kan faktisk komme som ville ryste meg.

Produksjon og publisering:
BoD - Books on Demand, Norderstedt
ISBN: 9783755760856